CRITICAL ACCLAIM FOR PIO NONO

"The career of the creator of the modern Papacy was full of color and dramatic episode. Mr. Hales has presented it sympathetically but conscientiously in a work of painstaking scholarship."

The Catholic World

"*Pio Nono* is far and away the best book of the last five decades on the central period of the nineteenth-century struggle between Church and State."

America

"*Pio Nono* is the first biography of Pius IX in English in this century, and the first which is written in a spirit of deep sympathy with the Pope and with the Papacy . . . Mr. Hales writes lucidly, with historical understanding and with considerable fairness, of the history of Italian unification and of the Catholic Church as seen through the eyes of Pius IX."

The New York Times Book Review

"*Pio Nono* makes fascinating reading . . . It is to be hoped that this scholarly, balanced study will receive a warm welcome in the United States."

Books on Trial

". . . a fascinating account of the politics and the personalities of the era in a style that is surprisingly easy for so complete a treatment. The book is a must for students of history and is highly recommended to readers in general."

The Record

"Mr. Hales has produced an excellent study in European politics and religion in the nineteenth century . . . He writes with scholarly conviction, citing authority as he works his way through the material, determined to be fair to a much maligned person."

Catholic Review

PIO NONO

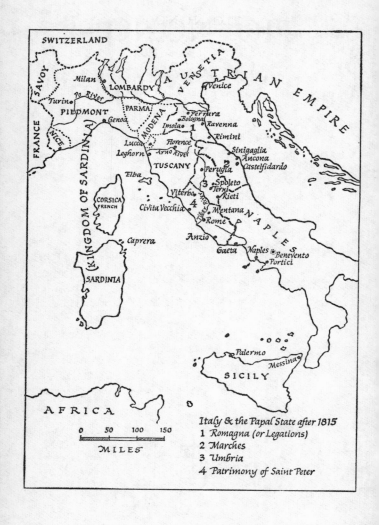

Italy & the Papal State after 1815
1 Romagna (or Legations)
2 Marches
3 Umbria
4 Patrimony of Saint Peter

PIO NONO

A STUDY IN EUROPEAN
POLITICS AND RELIGION
IN THE NINETEENTH CENTURY

E. E. Y. HALES

IMAGE BOOKS
A DIVISION OF DOUBLEDAY & COMPANY, INC.
GARDEN CITY, NEW YORK

TO MY WIFE

Image Books edition 1962
by special arrangement with P. J. Kenedy & Sons

Image Books edition published February 1962

282
H16

Nihil obstat: John M. A. Fearns, S.T.D.
                Censor Librorum
Imprimatur: ✠ Francis Cardinal Spellman
                Archbishop of New York
                New York, April 14, 1954

38401

Contents

Preface

Why, since his death in 1878, has no study appeared in England of Pio Nono?

Perhaps because he was a Pope. Yet this seems insufficient answer since he was also a leading character—at first *the* leading character—in that drama so dear to Englishmen, the Italian Risorgimento. And even as Pope he forced himself upon the attention of Englishmen in his day by his "Papal Aggression" in restoring the Catholic Hierarchy to England, by issuing the Syllabus of Errors, by defining Papal Infallibility, by enraging both Gladstone and Exeter Hall, by reigning longer than any Pope had ever reigned, by recruiting an international army, by losing the most ancient sovereignty of Europe—the Papal State.

In an important sense Pio Nono was the central figure of the mid-nineteenth century. But we name epochs after their political arbiters, we talk of Metternich's Europe, and Bismarck's Europe, so that the period between the flight of Metternich in 1848 and the foundation of the German Empire in 1870 becomes Napoleon III's Europe—or Palmerston's. If, with Shakespeare, we were to choose for our title the suffering tragic hero, the symbolic central character, then the middle of the century would be called the age of Pio Nono—for the same reasons as Shakespeare called his plays *King Lear* or *Othello*, rather than Goneril or Iago. Those who were working for change, or for power, assailed the Pope's claims, and brushed him aside; but they could not prevent the eyes of a world-wide audience being fastened upon the stage of his misfortunes. Nor could they stop him from rekindling, in his old age, flames of fervour that have burnt ever since around the world.

The recent appearance in Europe of two major publications concerned with Pio Nono is a reminder of our own neglect. One is R. Aubert's *Pontificat de Pie Neuf*,[1] which is a history of the Catholic Church in this pontificate. The other is the correspondence of Pio Nono with Victor Emmanuel and Napoleon III, and of Cardinal Antonelli with the Papal Nuncios, between the years 1847 and 1863. P. Pirri, who has edited this correspondence,[2] has performed a very important service—the more so since the papers at the Vatican belonging to the period of Pius IX remain inaccessible to the historian.

The writing of an adequate biography of Pio Nono must clearly await the opening of the Vatican archives; this study makes little attempt to portray the life of the Pope. What it attempts is to look at the major issues of the time as Pius looked at them, to see, from his standpoint, the aspirations of Garibaldi, Mazzini, and Cavour; of Victor Emmanuel and Napoleon; of the Liberal-Catholics and the Ultramontanes. Thus far, in England, the Italian Risorgimento has been considered almost exclusively from the standpoint of its leaders. It has been assumed that, though they quarrelled with each other and differed widely in their aspirations for Italy, yet they all contributed to a result that was glorious. Their opponents were blind or ignoble or villainous, men whose only object was to keep Italians "enslaved". Equally black and equally white have appeared the protagonists in the wider struggle between Rome and the progressive liberalism of the time throughout Europe. On the one side were the "obscurantists" and "fanatics"— the intransigent Ultramontanes. On the other were the liberals, fighting for freedom and truth, whether as professors, as Protestants, or as Liberal-Catholics. Here and there a heretical scholar has appeared, even in England, who has doubted this liberal orthodoxy. G.F.-H. and Mrs. Berkeley, in their fundamental volumes on the *Making of Italy*,[3] have thrown the early part of the story—before 1848—into a new light, and have written much that is valuable about the first two years of Pio Nono's reign. And Dom. Cuthbert Butler, in his book on the Vatican Council,[4] has shown that that unique assembly was something quite other than a vast conspiracy to "subvert the conscience and enslave the mind". But the orthodox liberal tradition, especially in the period between 1849 and 1870 (the period of Mazzini's Republic at Rome, of Cavour's closure of the convents, of the overrunning of the Papal State, of the Syllabus of Errors, of Montalembert, Acton, and Döllinger), still holds English attention almost undistracted by any glimmer of light thrown upon the matter from the opposite viewpoint. It is still slightly shocking to suggest that aught but obstinacy and ill-will towards his fellow human beings dictated the Pope's retention of his sovereignty at Rome and Bologna, his issue of the Syllabus of Errors, his support for Ultramontanism.

It is the argument of this study that there was a case for Pio Nono in his policies as Italian Prince, at the time of the Risorgimento, and that there was a case for him as Pope at the time of the Syllabus and the Vatican Council. But the most important point is that they were two aspects of the same case. English scholarship has tended to separate the two because we have come to distinguish sharply between the temporal and the spiritual power and to relegate the latter to the "foro interno", to conscience alone. But Pio Nono conceived of a much closer interdependence of politics and religion. To him his sovereignty over the Papal State was an aspect of his spiritual sovereignty; and he was profoundly concerned with the policies of governments all over the world—not merely with their attitude towards clerical appointments, or church property, but with their legislation concerning education, or compulsory military service, or matrimony.

His enemies took a like view. Mazzini saw the political problem as primarily religious; his political dreams were only the reflections of his religious visions. And Napoleon III, or Cavour, or Bismarck might talk about separating Church and State, but what they meant was subordinating Church to State. They knew well enough that the two were interdependent, and they meant to put the State in control. The theories that flitted fitfully through Napoleon's imaginative mind, the utilitarian aspirations of Cavour, the Erastian ambitions of Bismarck had as their starting-point a "settlement" with the Church, and by this they meant control over clerical appointments and clerical pronouncements, or closure of convents, or launching of *Kulturkampf*. Shall we call their aspirations political or religious? No doubt we shall call them political, and rightly so, as we shall rightly call the Pope's religious; but they could not advance their purposes without fighting in the field of religion, and the Pope could not defend the Church without fighting on the front of politics.

That is why the study of Pio Nono's eventful reign has to be undertaken as a study in politics and religion. Every move made by the Pope or by his enemies demonstrates this. The defeat of Mazzini's Roman Republic in 1849 was a check to the political aspirations of Mazzini and Garibaldi, but it was also a (temporary) victory for the Papacy over Mazzini's Religion of the People. Cavour's victory in closing the Piedmontese monasteries was the prelude to his assuming political sovereignty over the Papal State. Napoleon's planned withdrawal from defending Rome in 1864 provided the occasion for the issue of that notorious religious-political document, the Syllabus of Errors. The Errors of that Syllabus were largely Cavour's, Mazzini's and Napoleon's. The Vatican Council was in constant danger of political intervention from abroad. It was Bismarck's political success that led him to invade the religious field with his *Kulturkampf*.

To understand the Roman viewpoint in these struggles it is no doubt advantageous to be in communion with the See of Rome; but it is not necessary. The man who best understood Pio Nono's purposes, in his later years, was the Protestant Premier of France, Émile Ollivier. And the most effective critic of Papal policy, in the same period, was the Catholic Lord Acton, to whom communion with Rome always remained "dearer than life itself". Nor, to appreciate Pio Nono's policies, is it necessary to be conservative in outlook. He started as a political liberal and became a political conservative; but he fought, always and everywhere, for the Church, and for freedom for the Catholic life, and that meant utilizing whatever political assistance lay to hand, in fact it meant political opportunism. His real and permanent achievement was to give victory to the Ultramontanes, but Ultramontanism by its very cosmopolitan nature was often compelled to be anti-conservative, and even politically rebellious, since it was necessarily hostile to the Gallican claims of legitimist princes. In the 'thirties and 'forties, and even in the 'fifties, Ultramontanism was very generally in alliance with political liberalism. By the 'sixties it was generally anti-liberal, and so was Pio Nono, but even in that decade the most persuasive of all the Ultramontanes was Montalembert, and he remained passionately liberal till his death in 1870. Pio Nono never ceased to protest his own indifference as to "forms of government". States might be absolute monarchies or popular republics so long as they allowed the Church her rights and liberties—a Papal view which the Neapolitan Bourbons found distressing.

The victory of the mob at Rome, in October 1848, and the peculiar character of the Papal State turned Pio Nono into an absolutist prince. But he had toyed—rather rashly—with liberalism and, to the end, he retained an open mind as to the extent to which, given peaceful conditions, the enlightened propertied classes might properly be given some share in his government. It was an open question in the later eighteen-fifties whether he would broaden the basis of his government; that he did not do so was due partly to the irksome (and far from disinterested) pressure brought to bear upon him from Piedmont and from France, and partly to the absence of a class of man in the Papal State to whom political power could possibly be safely entrusted. But all this is of small consequence. It is not as a petty Italian prince that Pio Nono will stand to be judged by history. He will have to be considered in his role as the most important opponent of the extravagant claims, political and ideological, of the nineteenth-century progressives, as the most obstinate and influential of those who denied the infallibility of progress, the moral authority of majorities, and the omnipotence of the State. By refusing, in the name of eternal truths, to accept the passionate enthusiasms of the men of Progress he earned for the Papacy much hatred in his own day. But he restored to it an authority within the Church and an influence without such as it had not enjoyed since the time of the Council of Trent.

He was, in short, the creator of the Modern Papacy.

For their generous help I would like to express my thanks to those distinguished scholars in the history of the Risorgimento, Mr. and Mrs. G. F.-H. Berkeley; to Professor A. M. Ghisalberti, Director of the *Instituto per la storia del Risorgimento Italiano*, at Rome; and to Mr. D. Mack Smith, Tutor of Peterhouse, Cambridge, whose important study of Cavour's diplomacy in the critical year 1860, shortly to be published by the Cambridge University Press, I have been privileged to see in proof. My book must not, of course, be taken as reflecting the views of these historians, nor those of the English historian of the Catholic Church, Fr. Philip Hughes, whose wide knowledge has enlightened me on various problems. For much help with the text I am indebted to Lady Helen Asquith.

Chapter One

THE LIBERAL POPE
AND HIS INHERITANCE

1. *Mastai Ferretti, Bishop,*
in Pope Gregory XVI's Dominion

There have not been many occasions which have caused a Europe suffering from ennui to cry out with the poet:

> "Bliss was it in that dawn to be alive
> But to be young was very heaven",

but there have been just a few. And if one was occasioned by the fall of the Bastille another was caused by the election, at the psychological moment, in 1846, of a liberal Pope.

To give the peculiar quality to such occasions there is necessary an illusion of rebirth, not merely a sweeping away of cobwebs, but a sense of cleansing such as suggests that cobwebs, dust, and dirt are something done with for ever. At such times men seem to be able to delude themselves that crime, oppression and wrong really are a bad dream from which they have now awakened, their human nature regenerated. So that when the excitement leads to excesses, and disappointments lead to murder, and tyranny arises, it is only those who have not forgotten what experience has taught them about original sin who are spared a bitter disillusionment.

Possibly such moments of pristine ecstasy have a value in making man's pilgrimage supportable; but it is certain that when reality reasserts her necessary claims then the actors who have been cast by the crowd for the central parts in their exaggerated drama must suffer. So Pio Nono, adored by the Roman crowds, hymned throughout Europe, welcomed even by the Master of Balliol as a "capital fellow" (an unique honour, this, for a successor of St. Peter), was to suffer, until he died cursed by the Trasteverian mob, with the mud of the Tiber thrown at his passing coffin.

The causes of the outburst of great joy, in that happy summer of 1846 when Pio Nono was elected, are well known. His predecessor, Gregory XVI, had been austere, recluse, and firm in his handling of revolution. Since his accession in 1831 he had pursued conservative policies, in harmony with those of Metternich, the Austrian Chancellor and arbiter of Europe; and the princes then ruling the different Italian states had mostly followed the lead of Chancellor and Pope. Moreover visionary programmes of political and social change put forward by democratic priests in France, in Germany, and in Italy had been denounced by Gregory.

Exiles from the Papal States were living penuriously in Paris, in Brussels, in Bloomsbury, along with their neighbours from Naples or Lombardy, from Modena, Parma, or Piedmont. Less fortunate victims were languishing in the Spielberg at Vienna or in the Sant' Angelo at Rome. Then, within a month of his election, Pio Nono, on July 17th, 1846, had amnestied more than a thousand of these unfortunates. And soon, smiling, handsome, and affable, he was planning weekly parties (for both sexes) in the gardens of the Quirinal, and talking of lighting the streets of Rome with gas. He was said to be interested in railways and scientific improvements in agriculture. He was a progressive. He was no friend of the Austrians. He would take the lead in liberating Italy! Racing ahead of the facts, the Italian imagination was casting him for the role of Julius II; he would drive the Austrians from Milan and Venice, where they had ruled since 1815, he would redeem and unite Italy and himself be her first President! In vast crowds the Romans congregated, almost nightly in the piazza at the Quirinal, to receive, on their knees, his benediction; in Piedmont and Sicily, in Tuscany and Naples, his name was painted on the plaster walls, carried on banners in procession, invoked as patron of every enterprise. *Viva Pio Nono!*

The new occupant of the Chair of St. Peter, who was expected to reconcile the ways of God and man, was a comparatively unknown Cardinal-Bishop from Imola in the Romagna, just south of Bologna, by name Mastai Ferretti, who had sprung from a family of some small position at Sinigaglia. He went up to the conclave with his head full of liberal ideas, which he had just been reading in some daring new books, but certainly not with any expec-

tation that he was going to be Pope—not even though, at
Fossombrone, a dove persisted in alighting upon the roof
of his coach, to the delight of the people who were sure it
was an augury, and were duly to be confirmed in their faith.

At the Quirinal the serious business of the election had
started on June 15th. Mastai was chosen as one of the three
scrutineers of the voting slips, and as he was the third of
them it fell to him to read aloud, each time, the name
on the paper. There were 52 cardinals present. The candidate most likely to succeed seemed to be the Secretary
of State, Lambruschini, conservative and close collaborator
with Metternich. The favourite of the liberals was Gizzi,
the Papal Legate at Forli. At the first count Mastai read
out Lambruschini's name fifteen times, his own thirteen;
less known as a liberal than Gizzi, he seems to have been
accorded more of the "moderate" votes than were won by
his colleague of Forli. No quorum having been won by any
candidate the voting slips were then burnt, thereby making the thin white smoke that showed the waiting populace
outside that no Pope had been elected. The next morning
the score was Lambruschini eleven, Mastai twenty, and the
poor Bishop of Imola, confused, and trembling with fear,
gave himself up to prayer until the afternoon scrutiny at
three. At that hour once more he had to act as spokesman
of the scrutineers. When he had read out his own name for
the eighteenth time he felt unable to continue; his hands
were trembling, and those who remembered his boyhood
epilepsy were frightened for him. He begged to be excused
further reading, but, as this would have nullified the election, he was persuaded instead to rest and recover himself. After a few minutes he resumed his task. When he
had read out his own name thirty-six times the quorum
number had been passed, and he fell upon his knees, once
more, in prayer.[1] He took the name of Pius, in memory
of Pius VII, the Pope Napoleon imprisoned, who had once,
like himself, been Bishop of Imola, and who had be-
friended the young Mastai in his student days at Rome.

At Vienna, Prince Metternich was soon to exclaim, in
exasperation, that he had allowed for everything except the
possibility of a liberal Pope. But he does not appear to

have been perturbed at first by the news of the election. It has often been said that he tried to prevent Mastai's election, but the evidence is against this. The Austrian Emperor preserved the habit, exercised also by other Catholic sovereigns in Europe, of occasionally presenting, through a friendly cardinal, his "non-placet", which would suffice to prevent the election of an uncongenial Pope. The tradition amongst Italian historians is that this veto was, in fact, in 1846, entrusted by Metternich to Cardinal Gaysruck of Milan, and that he had drawn it up so as to exclude both Mastai and the more renowned liberal candidate, Cardinal Gizzi. Gaysruck, however, delayed in starting from Milan, awaiting there the arrival of Metternich's instructions, and in the event he had only got as far as Florence when, at the third count, Mastai had secured the requisite two-thirds majority for election. On hearing the news Gaysruck, whose support had been expected for the defeated Secretary of State, Lambruschini, had nothing to do but have his heavy Berlin coach turned around and driven back across the Apennines to Milan. But there is no evidence that he was, in fact, in possession of Metternich's veto of Mastai,[2] though his considerable influence would almost certainly have been strongly exerted on the conservative side, and might have turned the scale in favour of Cardinal Lambruschini. The liberals were in a hurry to get the election achieved before Gaysruck arrived. It is rather surprising that the conservative forces, and Metternich in particular, were so dilatory, especially as the death of Pope Gregory XVI, at the age of 81, came as no surprise; but probably Metternich was not much concerned. A liberal Pope was, in his view, an impossibility; if one were elected he would be compelled, once he had assumed the triple tiara, to follow in the footsteps of his predecessor. And if there were disturbances in the Papal State it would only give the Austrian troops the better excuse to intervene. He seems to have been most anxious to avoid an extremist—*a zelante*.[3]

The Pope, who was so soon going to be greeted, all along the *Corso*, as far as the *piazza del popolo*, with triumphal arches of cardboard and coloured paper, with lanterns, flowers, and banners, was received rather coolly when

first announced to the people, early on June 17th. They
had been hoping for Gizzi. They had feared Lambruschini.
They were mystified by Mastai. Who was he? But he certainly began to win the heart of Rome on that morning
when he faced the crowd outside the Quirinal and three
times gave, with his strong and melodious voice, the apostolic benediction, his arms raised slowly to the sky to out-
line, with the full papal gesture, the sign of the cross.

Rome scarcely knew who he was. But in the provinces of
the Papal State he was well known. For almost sixteen years
he had been Bishop of Imola, having moved there in 1832.
For the five previous years he had been Archbishop of
Spoleto, further south in the state. His translation from an
archbishopric to a bishopric had, in reality, been promotion,
on account of the greater importance of the diocese of
Imola, and the fact that it had often conferred upon its
occupant a red hat. It had not done so, with Mastai, until
the year 1840, when he had been there nearly nine years—
a fact which is generally ascribed to the uneasiness felt at
Rome concerning the bishop's reputed liberalism.

Something of a reputation for mild liberalism had always
hung about Mastai. His parents, Jerome Mastai-Ferretti,
Gonfalonier of Sinigaglia, and the Countess Catherine
Solazzi were both regarded as "enlightened"—a term of
some reproach. At Sinigaglia, on May 13th, 1792, the future
Pope had been born; his brothers still lived there, and on
that same afternoon of the ordeal of his election as Pope
he wrote to them for their prayers. Further inland, at
Spoleto, his first diocese (1827–32), he had shown, in times
of disturbance and insurrection, a happy combination of
promptitude, firmness, and clemency. On one dramatic
occasion there he had persuaded a troop of insurrection-
aries, Carbonari who had taken part in the Romagnuol
revolt of 1831, to lay down their arms, and to disperse
peacefully. He seems to have procured the compliance of
these men with his wishes partly by his persuasiveness,
partly by more practical charity. One of the insurgents was
the adventurer Prince Louis Napoleon, the future Napoleon III, who came to the Archbishop's palace with his

mother, the Queen Hortense, and received from Mastai
passports which enabled them both to return through
Tuscany and Piedmont to their home at Arenenburg in
Switzerland. So began the strange relationship of the future Emperor and the future Pope upon which so much of
the destiny of France, of Italy and of the Church was going
to hang in the years to come.

Mastai was best known at Imola, whither he had been
removed soon after these excitements at the end of 1832.
The citizens of Spoleto had sent a delegation to Rome to
appeal to Pope Gregory to leave their much-loved Archbishop with them, but affairs in the Legations (the cities
of Ferrara, Bologna, Imola, Ravenna, Forli, and Rimini,
governed by Papal Legates and more often called the
Romagna) were so disturbed that the Pope needed to place
there men who could win some measure of popularity from
the populace. Much has been said about the tyranny of
Gregory's Papal Legates, but the fact is that two of them,
at least, were liberal-minded men, whom the kindly Mastai
Ferretti found personally congenial. One was Cardinal
Amat, the Legate at Ravenna, who became his intimate
friend; the future Pope carried on a correspondence with
him, recently published, which throws a clearer light upon
this period of his life than has previously appeared.[4] The
other was Cardinal Gizzi, Legate at Forli between 1844
and 1846, who was to be the popular candidate for the
Papacy in 1846; after the election Mastai made him his
Secretary of State.

The fact is that, after the dangerous Carbonari uprising
of 1831 at Bologna, Rome was anxious to see some tact
and even conciliation exercised by her "proconsuls" in the
Legations.

When Mastai became Bishop of Imola in 1832 the
situation in the Legations of the Romagna was at its worst.
Revolt had become endemic, the prisons were filled, and
hundreds were in exile; to some extent this was true further
south, in Umbria and the Marches; but it was much more
serious in the Romagna. Since the problem was to remain
with Mastai, first as Bishop and then as Pope, until he lost

these parts of the temporal dominion in 1859, it is worth
considering what the special difficulties were.

They may be traced to influences older than the nineteenth century and rooted deep in human nature. Thus it
was only in the fifteenth century that Bologna, as proud
as any of the proud medieval city states of northern Italy,
became incorporated in the Papal State. She never relished
her new status as a provincial town, satellite to Rome; she
felt as Pisa or Leghorn felt towards Florence, or as Genoa
felt towards Turin. Around Bologna, the country of the
Romagna has a singular record as the home of intractable
characters, the nursery of Caesar Borgia, of Benito Mussolini, and of the more determined of the Communists
whether in the days of Bakunin or today. In the opinion of
Rome, the Romagnuols were naturally ungovernable. The
government felt as the English government felt about the
Irish. Moreover they were a long way away. The Romagna
was accessible from the capital (some two hundred miles
distant) only by traverse of high ranges of the Apennines;
it was scarcely more easily reached, at least in winter, than
was Ireland from London.

During the period of the French revolution, the Romagna had been incorporated first in the Cisalpine Republic,
and then, with the Marches, in Napoleon's Kingdom of Italy. Thus had come about the break with old customs, and
the indoctrination of some with the "principles of '89" and
with the tenets of French Freemasonry, and then of
Carbonarism. The biggest revolt in this region was that
organized by the Carbonari in 1830–31. This secret society
of the "charcoal burners" had an interesting ideology, partly
derived from French Freemasonry, partly from more obscure Italian sources. Their motto was "despotism annihi-
lated"—an achievement symbolized on a medal by the
Goddess of Liberty slaying the Dragon of Tyranny. The
authority most particularly sought out for slaying was that
of the Church, though this was not disclosed, explicitly, to
any but those few who attained to the Seventh Grade of
initiation. Those initiated into the lower grades might, however, draw their own conclusions from the designation "The
Good Cousin" given to Christ, who was said to have

come on earth to preach liberty, equality, and "philosophy"; from the conversion of the Christian Trinity into salt (to symbolize earth), water, and fire; and from the avowed ultimate goal of a "free" Italy leading to a free fraternal humanity, without religion or papacy. It was all sufficiently pantheist and utopian to disclose to the observant that the Carbonari had inherited from the Freemasons principles which were certainly intended to combat Catholicism. They were to wage their war upon the Church subtly, indirectly. They were to persuade the priests that in subscribing to these principles and beliefs they were being truly Christian; they were to attempt no direct attack upon Catholicism, which was hopeless, but to corrupt her from within by subverting her beliefs; if possible, some day, they were to delude a Pope himself into furthering their aims without realizing that he was betraying the Catholic tradition.[5] In the case of those die-hards amongst the cardinals whom it was hopeless to subvert, propaganda should be put out, especially in the press, so to vilify their characters as to work up the most intense popular indignation against them.

The Carbonari spread the net of their organization most effectively in Sicily and in the Romagna, the two regions of Italy where the rulers were most distant, and the military and police power of the state least effectual. They enrolled persons of distinction or ability: the Bonaparte brothers, Napoleon and Louis, sons of Louis Bonaparte, ex-king of Holland, and their cousin the Prince of Canino; Ciro Menotti, Terenzio Mamiani, Guerrazzi, Gioberti, Garibaldi, and almost all of those who later became prominent in the story of the more radical side of the Italian Risorgimento. Most of these men broke away from the society, which, indeed, as an organized movement, was a spent force after the failure of the revolutions in the Romagna from 1830–32. Few of them were formally initiated into the higher grades. But the influence of Carbonari doctrines and ideas was certainly enormous because the society, for at least a generation in the earlier half of the century, was the main vehicle for spreading the rationalism, pantheism, and revolutionary utopianism of the French eight-

eenth century in Italy. Mazzini, although in founding his
own *Young Italy* he repudiated Carbonarism, was enor-
mously indebted to its teachings. And it even had some
success, at least indirectly, in sowing seeds which, when the
crisis came at Rome in 1848, seduced a few priests from
their allegiance to the Pope.

The seeds were sown by the Carbonari, and theirs was
the organization; but the immediate cause of the rebellion
in the Romagna of February, 1831, was the assertion by
Laffitte, and other ministers of the new régime of Louis
Philippe in France, that France would not tolerate intervention by other powers in the independent Italian states;
in other words she would not allow the Austrians to march
in to suppress revolutions. It was perfectly understood by
everybody that the governments of Parma, Modena, and
the Papal State counted upon the help of the Austrians,
who were just across the Po, at Milan and Venice, in case of
any revolutionary trouble; and it was also known to be the
policy of Metternich to discourage any liberal reforms in
the independent Italian states, because the same concessions would inevitably be demanded in those which Austria
herself ruled in Italy, namely Lombardy and Venetia. So
Laffitte's flamboyant pronouncement entirely upset the
equilibrium upon which everything rested, and the Romagnuol Carbonari moved rapidly. All the principal cities of
the Papal State, except Rome, Rieti, and Orvieto, were occupied within three weeks, and those three weeks were the
first three of the reign of a new Pope—Gregory XVI, Pio
Nono's predecessor.

Gregory was a saintly Camaldolese monk, with a reputation for learning, and at one time for liberalism. But these
first three weeks of his reign were not encouraging, although
Rome, including the rowdy populace of the Trastevere
quarter, remained staunchly loyal. He appealed for the intervention of Austria, and Metternich called the French
bluff by sending in his troops, who were quickly successful.
The French Government, however, in view of Laffitte's
high-sounding phrases, had to make some gesture; and so
it was that a conference of ambassadors was set up at Rome
with the intention of influencing the Pope to introduce lib-

eral reforms in his state. This was the first of several interventions on the part of France, with England in the background, designed, during the next thirty years, to persuade the Papal Government to introduce the latest approved principles of Anglo-French liberalism. Its outcome was a Memorandum, intended to guide the Pope in this matter of reform.

The Memorandum so produced became the rallying cry of revolutionaries and reformers during the pontificates of Gregory XVI (1831–46) and of Pio Nono. It stated that, in the view of the ambassadors, there should be elected local councils; there should be a central Junta, partly elected, to control finance; and laymen should be admitted to the higher as well as to the lower posts in the administrative and judicial system. These were the most important provisions, and the Pope, his Secretary of State Bernetti, and Metternich were all opposed to them. Though drawn up by the Prussian envoy, Bunsen, they really represented the liberal views of official France and England. Except in the recommendation that laymen be admitted to power, which concerned a special problem of the pontifical state, they represented ideas far beyond the practice of any Italian state, or indeed of the German states of the period. Coming, as they did, on top of a dangerous rebellion, engineered by revolutionaries whose headquarters were at Paris, it was hardly likely that the Pope would take kindly to them. In fact, however, he did allow Bernetti to introduce certain limited reforms: a committee of four laymen, to assist the Papal Legate in ruling the different provinces; nominated communal and provincial councils which might express "the wishes of the people"; some legal and financial reforms; and the Austrians to withdraw.

The Austrians did withdraw, but the Carbonari immediately rose again, as Bernetti and Metternich had foreseen they would. Bernetti, however, had begun work on the creation of a Papal army, and, for the most part, it was this army of 5,000 men which put down the renewed rising in the Romagna in January, 1832. Even so, Cardinal Albani, who was in charge, felt it necessary to call in the Austrians as well, and they occupied Bologna. Thereupon the French

acted, sending their fleet into the Adriatic, and occupying
the port of Ancona, against the wishes of the Pope.

This was the end of the uprising. Its permanent importance was that it made the condition of the Papal State
into a European question, magnifying it out of all relation
to its inherent importance, a magnification due to the fact
that the intense mutual jealousy between France and Austria (dating from the medieval rivalry of Hapsburg and
Valois in Italy) had now become centred upon the Papal
dominions. Austria was concerned to check liberal developments there lest they should spread to Lombardy-Venetia.
France was concerned to encourage liberal reform. But each
was most concerned to maintain its own influence in Italy
as against the other. This situation would last until 1859,
when France finally defeated Austria.

But the condition of the Papal State also became a European question because the revolutionary leaders who fled, or
were proscribed, were determined that it should do so. The
most distinguished of these were Louis Napoleon, the future Emperor, Count Terenzio Mamiani, later Pio Nono's
prime minister at Rome, and Antonio Panizzi, who had
been involved in an earlier uprising in the independent
neighbouring Duchy of Modena and who had fled to London, where in due course he became Librarian at the
British Museum and founded that great collection of Italian books and pamphlets, compiled for the most part by
revolutionaries, upon which English commentators on the
Italian Risorgimento have drawn ever since. There were altogether only thirty-eight (according to Farini, himself one
of the revolutionaries)[6] who did not receive the general
amnesty granted by Pope Gregory. Amongst the thirty-eight
was Count Ferretti, cousin of Bishop Mastai Ferretti, and
also General Zucchi (later a commander of Pio Nono's
army) who sailed from Ancona with a safe-conduct granted
by the Papal Legate but was intercepted by the Austrians,
who ignored the Papal safe-conduct and imprisoned him
at Venice.

Much the most unfortunate result of this uprising was
that Secretary of State Bernetti decided, as a result of it,
to introduce a voluntary part-time police force to help him

in maintaining order. He was moved to this because he found that the new army which he had created was expensive to maintain (Metternich had to help him to get a loan from the Rothschilds to pay for it), and at the same time he was anxious not to be dependent upon Austrian assistance. So he created the "Centurions", by voluntary enrolment, and they quickly attained to the proportions of a large force, estimated at some fifty thousand by the end of 1832. Though he had intended that they should, like the later Civic Guards, be officered by gentlemen of good reputation, it is clear from the bitter comments of friend and foe alike (e.g. Bishop Mastai Ferretti, or the historian and revolutionary Farini) that the rank and file, at least, were often despicable scoundrels. In effect he had armed one section of the population against another, and had given scope to the perennial Italian penchant for gang warfare.

All the same there was comparative quiet throughout the Papal State during the period 1832–43. Bernetti was succeeded, as Secretary of State, in 1836, by Cardinal Lambruschini, who did not share his predecessor's taste for mild reform, but did believe, very strongly, in maintaining both the Papal army and the Centurions. The Carbonari organization was broken and Mazzini and his *Young Italy* society were not as yet an effective force. A more important factor in maintaining peace was that the Papal Legate at Ravenna, who exercised rule in the Romagna, was the just and generous Cardinal Amat, close personal friend of Mastai Ferretti; and at Ravenna, also, reigned that humane scholar the Archbishop Falconieri.

The peace was disturbed, in 1843, by a rather curious conspiracy invented by an exile, Ribotti, to kidnap these two popular ecclesiastics, together with Mastai Ferretti, and hold them as hostages. This escapade, with one or two others of its kind (which finally disgusted Farini and turned him from a revolutionary into a reformer, or "Moderate"), was unfortunately taken too seriously by Lambruschini, and led to seven executions and more than fifty condemnations to the galleys. It led, also, to the setting up of military commissions, which moved about the state, and tended, in addition to their judicial function, to assume administrative

and governmental powers. It was these commissions, together with the Centurions (often called Sanfedists, a name
derived from the similar secret police who had emerged, on
the side of the Church, in the early days of the Carbonari
in Sicily), which gave so evil a name to the rule of Lambruschini, and made the last years of the reign of Pope
Gregory XVI (now an octogenarian) a by-word amongst
the progressive liberals of Europe for obscurantist tyranny.
Yet it is fair to note that a number of the better legates
and bishops opposed Lambruschini's policy resolutely, making no bones about thwarting the work of the commissions
by assisting revolutionary suspects to escape. Cardinal Amat
was recalled from Ravenna to Rome, in 1845, for doing
this, while Cardinal Gizzi absolutely refused to admit the
commissions into the area of his jurisdiction.

There was one more minor insurrection, at Rimini, in
1845, before the old Pope died. Not in itself of much importance, it issued in the "Manifesto of Rimini" an appeal,
in effect, to the powers of Europe that they should insist
upon the carrying out of the reforms proposed by the Memorandum of 1831. Thus was the question of the condition
of the Papal State kept on the European stage, though the
same thing was done more effectively, in the following year,
by the Piedmontese nobleman, Massimo d'Azeglio, in his
celebrated little book, *Degli ultimi casi di Romagna*. It was
printed at Florence, the city that so often proved itself to
be what d'Azeglio called it, the "Refugium Peccatorum"
from the Romagna.

D'Azeglio's book was the most effective and sweeping
criticism of the régime; it had a European audience. But
he was a Piedmontese liberal, with little experience of the
Romagna, and his information came mainly from the revolutionary exiles. His chief points are: there are too many
Papal Legates; the legal system is hopelessly confused; there
is no publication of financial returns or expenditure, and
no public control over them; the customs dues are too high
and their collection is farmed out. To these he added a
general criticism of the economic backwardness of the state,
especially its failure to promote railways, banks, agricultural and scientific associations. And he naturally includes

a sweeping condemnation of the Centurions and the military commissions. His main suggested remedy is agitation for popular representative institutions, including the admission of laymen to all offices of state.

D'Azeglio's criticisms were to be repeated by the historian of the state, Farini. Many of his views were shared by moderate-minded men, not revolutionaries, men like the legates and bishops already mentioned, or Mastai's friend Count Giuseppe Pasolini who was to have a large share in educating the future Pope in these matters. Most of his proposals (which amplified the Memorandum of 1831 and the Manifesto of Rimini of 1845) were to be implemented during the first two years of Pio Nono's reign. But what do they imply about the character of the Gregorian régime? They imply, essentially, that it did not embrace the latest political, constitutional and juridical notions of the progressive nations of the west, the principles, for example, implicit in the French constitution of 1830 or in the parliamentary and municipal reform bills of the eighteen-thirties in England. They also imply that it did not embrace up-to-date economic principles, deriving from the French physiocrats or from Adam Smith, and steadily, though slowly, winning favour in France and England at this time. More serious, they imply that a clear and recognised rule of criminal law, with swift and open procedure, and trial by jury, which in England, at least, had been established for 150 years, did not exist. The state was, in fact, old fashioned, in a sense it was patriarchal, with all the advantages and disadvantages of that form of society. It might be merciful, but it was inefficient, and undemocratic. To the western-liberal spirit of the times it seemed a small matter that capital punishment was very rare compared with the practice of contemporary England, that the lot of the peasantry was more tolerable, even in the Romagna, than was that of the Catholic peasantry of Ireland, or that slavery, still practised in the British colonies at the time of the Memorandum, was unknown and had been denounced by the Pope, for centuries, as a sin. It remained inexcusable that there was no published statement of accounts, and no public control of the purse. Misery and want might be much relieved by the very extensive private charity to which the faithful were exhorted (as Count Rayneval, a later French ambassador was going to point out)[7] and the hardship suffered might in fact be a good deal less than was endured by men, women, and children in the towns of Lancashire and Yorkshire. But the system, or lack of it, remained, in the western-liberal view, unpardonable. Even the harsh provisions of the English Poor Law of 1834 were considered preferable by enlightened liberals.

The valid criticism, then, of the Gregorian Papal State is that, by the most progressive western standards of the day, it was inefficient. That it was undemocratic is also true, but the dangers of democracy were more conspicuous in Gregory's time than were its merits. That it was a "clerical monopoly" is true, but the "clerks" were often only in minor orders, and they still comprised most of the educated population of the State. That the justice which it administered was arbitrary would be a very serious criticism were it altogether true. But it is necessary to distinguish between the justice dispensed by the roving legatine commissions, after the revolt of '43, and that dispensed by the ordinary courts. The commissions were dispensing martial law, which allowed the plaintiff little opportunity for self-defence. But the ordinary civil and criminal courts followed the traditional Roman procedure, with its formal depositions, and the main complaint was the delay occasioned by the congestion of business, not the arbitrary character of the proceedings.

In criminal justice the worst feature was the use of spies, a common practice of European governments both at that day and since, but none the less deplorable. The usual procedure adopted by Lambruschini was to send his secret police to the houses of suspects with the excuse that they were looking for smuggled contraband. From time to time one of these men, notably one Giuseppe Lucarelli, acquired so evil a reputation that he would be withdrawn; but Lambruschini was not prepared to dispense altogether with using spies. We meet with them in the notorious documents collected by Felice Orsini at the end of his memoirs. Lambruschini's instructions, printed amongst these documents,

show that it was the usual practice to secure information
by spying, using trumped-up excuses for entry into houses;
but nothing in the character of Orsini suggests that his own
commentaries and interpretation, which have been very
widely used by historians, are in the least trustworthy.
Orsini was a fanatical anti-clerical[8] who started his singularly irresponsible adult life by accidentally killing a cook,
and ended it by accidentally killing eight bystanders when
he threw a bomb at the Emperor Napoleon III. Nevertheless he made a great impression upon the audiences to
which he lectured in England during the 'fifties, and his
theme was usually his own past sufferings and the sufferings of the Romagna. Prominent among the latter was the
"torture" employed in convents. This is a theme upon
which he has something to say in his memoirs, but a careful
examination of the facts which he recounts discloses that
corporal punishment was employed occasionally in convent
schools, but only under the strictest safeguards, the nuns
not being allowed themselves to administer it. If Orsini's
English audiences contained those who were acquainted
with the disciplinary methods used in English schools at
that time it is difficult to believe that his examples of Italian torture made much impression.

A last question concerning Pio Nono's temporal heritage
calls for some answer—was it, as its enemies were fond of
asserting, "hopelessly corrupt"?

The part played by personal patronage in all the Italian
capitals at this time was, of course, enormous; at Rome, as
at Naples, Florence, Modena, Parma, and Turin it was the
very system itself. At Rome, it was important to know a
cardinal, and preferably an influential cardinal, in the same
sense that in eighteenth-century England it was important
to know the Duke of Newcastle. The receipt of bribes, and
the practice of private peculation, however, while easily indulged in an absolute government, appears not to have
been particularly characteristic of the Gregorian régime.
Farini recognises the high and even saintly quality of many
of the cardinals, while Gregory himself was an austere man.
The régime, indeed, of the Papal Secretaries of State between 1815 and 1846, the Secretaries Consalvi, Bernetti,

and Lambruschini, seems to have compared favorably in this respect with the subsequent régime of Cardinal Antonelli, under Pio Nono.

Mastai detested many features of the government which he was compelled, at Imola, to witness, and to some extent to share. Most of all he detested the violent and arbitrary activities of the Centurions, a dislike which was intensified by an unpleasant episode in the cathedral at Imola. He was kneeling there, in adoration of the Blessed Sacrament exposed, when some of these "police" pursued a fugitive right into the building and fatally wounded him. On another occasion he had to leave the cathedral to investigate the screams proceeding from the piazza outside the great open west doors, only to find that he was just in time to console the last moments of a victim of the crowd. The number of beggars whom he found on the steps of the churches at Imola was something greater than he had witnessed at Sinigaglia, his native city, at Volterra, in Tuscany, where he had been to school, or even at Rome, where he had studied for the priesthood. He was outspoken in his condemnations; far more outspoken than was likely to be good for his career. He implored the government at Rome to make provision, in time, to meet the chronic disasters brought by snow in the winter and by floods in the spring. He lamented the discredit brought upon the Church by the disorders, the comfort which they brought to her enemies, the scandal and even loss of faith which they brought to her friends. As for the behaviour of the Centurions, or Pontifical Volunteers, in his anger and distress about it he was prepared to brave even the displeasure of the Pope himself. He wrote:

"It grieves me most bitterly to lose the confidence of the Sovereign, an experience which I have had in recent days when the Colonel of the Pontifical Volunteers, the Cavalliere Della Noce, returned from Rome, passed through Imola and refrained from coming to see the Bishop making no secret of his reason: he sent the local Governor to me to tell me that it was the mind of His Holiness that I should give protection to the Pontifical Volunteers . . ."[9]

A little later on he was able to say that the Volunteers were "now behaving rather better", and the improvement seems to have been due to his having secured for himself the power of choosing the local commanders of these bands.

It was considered even by his friends at Rome that Mastai made his criticisms to the government somewhat freely and frequently and "perhaps not in sufficiently measured terms". It also seems that when Gregory XVI made him a Cardinal, in 1840, he took the opportunity to tell him that he hoped the favour which he had received would make his relations with the Holy See more devoted and more faithful in the future.[10] In some ways it did. He was more circumspect after that event. Being now so closely linked with the Holy See, as a member of the Sacred College, it was natural that he should weigh his words about the pontifical government more carefully. What is really more remarkable is that his attitude and behaviour at Imola remained that of a liberal, and not that to be expected of a friend of Pope Gregory or of Cardinal Lambruschini. Far from courting an easy popularity amongst the propertied classes, or the higher clergy, he continued to show, even after he had received the red hat, an independence and liberality of outlook which often cost him the friendship of the larger landholders in his diocese as well as that of the senior government officials. One of his opponents, in these later days, who thought him much too liberal, was the Gonfalonier of Imola. But the Gonfalonier's wife was an admirer of the Bishop, so, when their baby was born, she asked him to be godfather. The Gonfalonier refused categorically to allow it. A few weeks later the Bishop had been elected Pope. He then wrote to the Gonfalonier: "You refused, as godfather, the Bishop of Imola, would you accept the Bishop of Rome?" He did.

But Mastai's reputation at Imola did not rest upon any achievement in the spheres of administration, or of economic reform. He was not much interested in such things either at that time or later on at Rome. His popularity with the lesser people, the popolani, which was enormous, rested upon his many acts of charity, which constantly reduced him to penury, upon his simplicity, which yet never lacked style, and upon his sense of humour. And the deeper devotion which went out to him from all classes rested upon his piety. He never allowed the pursuit of material improvement—as so many allowed it—to loom larger than religion. His chief preoccupation was always the welfare of souls in his diocese. Twice he called in the Jesuits to hold a Mission throughout his territories. His own mornings were given up to the cares of his ministry, his afternoons usually to religious reading, or to visiting (generally on foot) the monasteries, convents, schools or hospitals. The low state of public morality, which tolerated concubinage and licentiousness, and which found expression in swearing and blasphemy, really grieved him. He was continually organising retreats, often giving them himself, praying, and exhorting others to pray before the Blessed Sacrament in the cathedral. His devotion to the Blessed Virgin was well known; throughout his life he would make no important decision, undertake no important act without first having recourse to her protection and assistance. He was constant, always, in prayer; later, he was very often called "The Pope of Prayer".

Though he lived simply, he was very careful about his appearance; and when he entertained he liked to do so in style, and with an ample generosity. He had no great reputation for learning, but he had considerable renown for his eloquence, which was aided by his sonorous voice; he was admired for the unaffected abandon of his devotions. The happiest occasions of his life at Imola were his frequent visits to the Convent of Fognano, ruled over by Mother Rosa Teresa Brenti, known as the "great Dominican reformer". To her and to her community of the Most Holy Sacrament, and to the ninety girls from all parts of Italy, as well as from France and Spain, who boarded at school there, he became protector and confessor. He took great pleasure in the growth, and in the spiritual excellence of the place, praying for the community continually, and demanding their prayers for him. He visited often, and the spiritual bond between him and them was very close. When he went to Rome, albeit to become their Holy Father, their sense of loss was acute. His relationship with the convent caused some comment, and even, from one quarter, some scandal. It was a price which he would have to pay, throughout his life, for a temperamental tenderness which brought his keenest sympathies into play when he was with women. He undoubtedly found them *simpatiche*.

A generosity of spirit, then, and sensitivity of temperament characterised Mastai. It was a quality that led him to regard reformers and progressives with more indulgence and less suspicion than they met with from "realists" like Bernetti, Lambruschini, or Metternich. But this humane quality might not have led him to embrace liberal principles had he not received a certain amount of specific education in the progressive notions of his day; and his first mentor in such matters was his own predecessor as Bishop of Imola, the Cardinal Chiaramonti, who later became Pope Pius VII.

As a young man, studying for the priesthood at Rome, Mastai had had two audiences with Pius VII; he revered that Pope who had stood up to Napoleon, and who, as Bishop of Imola, had issued a homily, in December, 1797, in which he demonstrated, most eloquently, that there was no necessary conflict between the principles of the Gospel and those of a true democracy, and that one could well be a good Catholic and a good Republican.[11] An Italian, it might be supposed, conversant with the often cordial relations between the medieval Church and the republics of Florence, Siena, or Venice, should have found nothing very startling about this. But 1789 had meant something different from the medieval republics. It had meant the Declaration of the Rights of Man. It had meant, in philosophy, Rousseau and the natural goodness of man, Voltaire and scorn for all that lay outside human reason. And, in practice, it had meant the spoliation of the Church—sometimes, when in Jacobin hands, the ridicule of the Church and the persecution of priests. With Bonaparte these ideas had crossed the Alps into Italy. The Cisalpine Republic, with a constitution modelled upon that of the French Directory,

had been created by the young general (still, at that time,
the servant of the Directory) in July, 1797, and the new
Republic had included the Romagna, included therefore
the diocese of the Bishop of Imola. So the future Pius VII,
as reigning Bishop, had had a practical problem to meet
when he issued his homily in December of '97. With vague
excitement, the Romagnuols, like the Milanese, had welcomed these French "emissaries of freedom". There had
been much talk of Liberty, Equality, and Fraternity, and
much stimulus to the growing Carbonari movement. It had
been necessary for the Bishop to meet the situation; and
he had sought, not without hope, to Christianise democracy
in his diocese. As Pope, however, Pius VII had been fated
to see the principles of '89 yielding the bitter fruit of un-
regenerate secular despotism, and to suffer, himself, as the
prisoner of Napoleon. He knew that as the fruits of faith
those liberal principles were good, but that as the fruits of
human pride and revolution they were bad, and could only
give rise to lawlessness or despotism. So, as Pope, and ruler
after 1815 of the restored Papal State, he was more conservative than he had been as Bishop of Imola. Nor were
his successors, Leo XII (1824), and Pius VIII (1829) inclined, in the circumstances in which they found themselves, to encourage political liberalism.

But the impressionable mind of Mastai, at the time of
the Conclave of 1846, had recently been receiving some
stimulating draughts, at Imola, from a liberal count, a
neighbour, Giuseppe Pasolini, of Ravenna, and his charming and intelligent wife Antonietta. These up-to-date people had been in Paris in 1844, and had heard the ardent
Lacordaire preaching in Notre Dame. Though residents of
Ravenna, they had a house at Montericco, near Imola,
which Mastai liked visiting, and where he enjoyed hearing
Antonietta read aloud the latest books. Pier Desiderio Pasolini, Giuseppe's son, has recorded on a marble tablet in
that house the memory of Mastai's conversations with his
father. It tells the significant facts with a useful simplicity:

"In August of 1845, *Giovanni Mastai*, Cardinal Bishop
of Imola, who in June of the following year was created

Pope with the name of Pius IX, often visited in this villa the count *Giuseppe* and the countess *Antonietta Pasolini*, born Bassi of Milan. Here he received from them the book on the hopes of Italy by Cesare Balbo and that on the primacy by Vincenzo Gioberti. Here in friendly conversations he was led to recognise the griefs and the shames of the present and the unavoidable necessities of the new age so that these walls heard him deplore the blindness of the governments, the secret sects, the foreign domination, and with tears implore from God a Church purified from worldly passions and an Italian fatherland free and well ordered . . ."[12]

"Dear Count," Mastai had written, as he was setting out for the conclave,

"the Pope will certainly not be myself, but tell your wife, be sure to tell her, from me, that I have put in my bag those books which she gave me at Montericco and that I shall make the new Pope read them."[13]

By far the most important of the books which Mastai is likely to have put into his bag was Gioberti's bulky "Primacy"—*Il primato morale e civile degli Italiani*—which had appeared in 1843. This was the book which enlightened people, people like the Pasolinis, were all reading, because in it there had appeared, for the first time, a reasonable and scholarly study of Italy's past greatness, her present dejection, and her future opportunity. For the first time normal moderate-minded educated men, who were also Christian, were shown, in this book, a path of reasonable reform and a programme of political action which did not require that they should become revolutionaries, or heretics, or subscribe to new sects in order to redeem Italy. That was the reason for the immense success of Gioberti's book, and although it could only circulate freely in Piedmont, and, for a time, in Tuscany, it was, in fact, being read in Naples, in Rome, in the Romagna, and in Austrian Milan and Venice as well.

Gioberti was a priest, who had been born at Turin. Although he resigned his chaplaincy to Charles Albert, the

Piedmontese king, in 1833, because his philosophical spec-
ulations had given rise to doubts about his orthodoxy, he
remained within the Church till his death, in 1851. He
was in trouble with the police, rather than with the Church,
because of the ardour of his enthusiasm for Italy, his liberalism, and his acquaintance with Mazzini and *Young Italy*,
the new society which was plotting revolution in Piedmont
and the Romagna. Accordingly, in the autumn of 1833 he
was exiled, and lived first at Paris and then at Brussels. It
was at Brussels that he published his *Primato*, in 1843.
Not until 1848 did the political situation enable him to
return to Italy, where, for a few months he seemed likely
to guide the destinies of the peninsula, especially during
his brief tenure of the premiership of Piedmont.

Gioberti argued that it was quite erroneous to suppose,
as did the revolutionaries, that the rebirth of Italy must
come through what Mazzini, or the Saint-Simonian sect
in France were already calling a "new religious synthesis",
which would soon supersede Catholicism, or through the
equally anti-Catholic fraternities of the Freemasons or the
Carbonari. On the contrary, the chief glory, almost the
raison d'être of Italy was the Church, and the Papacy, and
to them she must look for her regeneration. Through the
Church Italy had civilised the west; the Papacy was her
richest asset, the closest bond of union between all Italians.
If Italy was to become a political reality it was inevitable
that the Pope should take the lead. The princes must introduce some measure of popular representation into their
governments; each should set up a *Consulta* which should
give the people a voice in the government though not control over it. And the different states must federate, under
the presidency of the Pope, in such a way as to have a
common army, navy, colonies, commercial and foreign policy, while retaining their local life and customs, and indeed,
their local princes. There was no need for a merging of the
very different customs and institutions of Naples and Tuscany, of Rome, Piedmont, Milan, and Venice; the Italian
peninsula was the nursery of such very different, as well as
brilliant centres of civilisation that she was singularly un-
suited to a complete national fusion, such as was involved

in the republican unitary gospel of Mazzini. Let her rather be a federation of "consultative monarchies".

But Gioberti was a citizen of Turin, as well as a Catholic philosopher, and the role for which he casts the Piedmontese monarchy is only second to that which he assigns to the Pope. Charles Albert, King of Piedmont,[14] had the only effective Italian army, and by his strength for war he had "laid open the way to the long-desired union of Italy". Austria is not named, but everybody knew against whom the Piedmontese army would be needed.

The importance of Gioberti's teaching has received increasing recognition; for long it was obscured by the fact that, in the end, the Piedmontese monarchy and the Church were thrown into conflict, so that the Risorgimento of Italy was, ultimately, accomplished by Piedmont alone, to the immeasurable detriment both of Church and State. That Gioberti perceived the true character of the problem was recognised by all moderate men at the time; by d'Azeglio, by another Piedmontese, Cesare Balbo (who also wrote an influential book, *Delle speranze d'Italia,* which looked to Piedmont to take the initiative, but was profoundly Papal and Catholic in standpoint), by Farini, by Pasolini, by all except the men of the secret societies. He was later called a dreamer; yet his real merit lay precisely in his practical common sense, which saw that, Italy being innately Catholic, Risorgimento and Catholicism must necessarily be reconciled, or, more accurately, true Risorgimento could only flower from the Church.

Amongst those who were convinced by Gioberti was, then, Mastai himself, who read the *Primato* with the Pasolinis in 1845. In 1846, as Pope, he set to work to carry out Gioberti's programme, not only in its broader purposes, but in its particulars, by granting a *Consulta,* extending a wide measure of freedom to the Press, encouraging scientific and agricultural societies, and working towards some measure of federation in Italy. The years 1846 to 1848 at Rome witnessed, in fact, the rare spectacle of a prince consciously pursuing the programme of a political philosopher. The programme ultimately went awry for various reasons we shall have to notice later; but until that

happened Italy looked to Rome; and Rome was guided by
the concepts of Gioberti's book. It cannot be doubted that,
had Rome been in a position to retain the leadership, as
Gioberti hoped and intended, the miserable and bitter internal struggle which disfigured the Risorgimento, dis-
traught pious Italians, and fatally weakened the new Kingdom of Italy might have been avoided. There was no truer
word spoken, in the Italian Risorgimento, than that of
Gioberti in his *Primato* when he said that the fate of Italy
depended upon the alliance of Rome and Turin. Instead of
that alliance there was destined to be a generation of conflict; and when "Turin" became "The Quirinal", in 1870,
there was still to be nearly sixty years of strife before an
agreement was reached. The blame for so great a disaster
has been variously placed; in England it has been generally
put at the door of Pio Nono. Whether it belongs there,
or rather at Turin, is a question which for the moment we
must postpone.

Gioberti's insistence upon putting the Pope and the
Church in the forefront, when treating of the Italian question, was not original with him, although he first made a
philosophy and a programme of the matter. The idea was
in the air because Italian historians like Gino Capponi and
Carlo Troya had recalled the glorious history of the Papacy,
and particularly the great patriot-Popes, Alexander III, Innocent II, and Julius II, who had withstood the foreign
barbarians in the peninsula. The most popular writer of
the period, Alessandro Manzoni, in his *Promessi Sposi*,
made Italians feel, with shame, the misery of the foreign
oppression, and taught them to turn to the Church for their
regeneration. Articles which played upon the same theme
ran the gauntlet of the censorship in the Milanese *Concil-
iatore*, or the Florentine *Antologia*. And in 1836, a fellow
exile of Gioberti, Niccolò Tommaseo, from Tuscany, had
produced at Paris a little book, not widely read in Italy,
called *Le Nuove Speranze d'Italia* whose aim was to teach
Italians to look to a reforming Pope for their deliverance.

It is against the background of these aspirations that one
has to envisage the delirious excitement which throughout
Italy greeted Pio Nono's early reforms in his State. It was

not so much that the tyranny of the princes was intolerable
—d'Azeglio, Balbo and Gioberti are agreed in denying that
charge. It was rather that political and cultural life were
dead, that there was a longing for something new, an aspiration for power mingled with new emotions of Italian nationalism, and a realisation that the present policies of the
princes, and of Austria, their support, stood in the way.

2. *The Beginnings of Liberal-Catholicism*

Gioberti, wholly concerned with Italy, thought in terms
of enlightened reforming princes, who would be guided
by the Church. Outside Italy Liberal-Catholicism was
more radical. In the German and Austrian states and provinces, where political conditions resembled those in Italy,
similar ideas to Gioberti's about enlightened princes were
to be found; but in Poland, in Belgium, and in Ireland the
Church often openly sympathised with revolution. In fact,
with Mickiewicz in Poland, with the professors of Louvain
in Belgium, and with O'Connell in Ireland Catholic leadership was providing the inspiration of liberal and revolutionary movements aimed against alien rulers.

This alliance of Church and People against the state was
rather startling in the nineteenth century, though it had
been a commonplace of the Middle Ages; but in Poland,
Belgium, and Ireland the foreign ruler happened also to be
outside the Church, which helped to make the alliance
seem natural. In France, on the other hand, the struggle for
liberty was an internal struggle, with the Church traditionally on the side of legitimate authority; yet in these same
decades there was emerging in France a Catholic leadership
that based itself upon popular support.

What was happening in France still mattered very much
more to Europe than what was happening anywhere else.
Despite the fall of Napoleon, and despite the power of
Metternich, French ascendancy, so marked since the days
of Richelieu, was still paramount. Gioberti inveighed

against it, knowing that Italians would never achieve their
regeneration until they ceased to keep their eyes fixed upon
Paris. Mazzini inveighed against it, for precisely the same
reason as Gioberti. Cavour recognised it as a fact, and util-
ised it to his advantage. It was an evident truth, though
unpalatable to Italians, that neither their romantic literature, nor their political or religious philosophy was more
than a reflection of French literature and philosophy. Gioberti himself owed a heavy debt to the French Catholic
revival. Mazzini owed more to a French movement, that of
the Saint-Simonians, than to any other single source. The
ideas of the Carbonari and of the Freemasons were both
French in origin. It was a well-established European habit
to accept French leadership; and for the Papacy the habit
went right back to the days when the Eldest Daughter of
the Church earned her glorious title, back to Charlemagne
and to Pepin, those Most Christian Kings to whom the
Holy See owed the protection of the Patrimony of St. Peter.

It was the French who invented the theory of Liberal-
Catholicism, just as they had invented the theories of Gallicanism, Ultramontanism, and now, in the nineteenth century, were going to evolve a "Neo-ultramontanism" which
was to come to a head at the Vatican Council of 1870.

The traditional theory of Gallicanism had been defined
in the Four Articles[15] of the year 1682; and although these
articles had been declared null and void by the Pope they
had, in fact, been taught in all French theological schools
since the days of Louis XIV. The immediate effect of the
French Revolution and the rule of Napoleon had been only
to give a further impetus to Gallican tendencies; and the
restoration of the Bourbons had re-established the Church
in the same constitutional dependence upon the monarchy
as in Louis XIV's day. To Count Joseph de Maistre, who
was the real father of the French, and thus of the European,
Catholic revival of the nineteenth century, it appeared
painfully clear that to Gallicanism must be attributed the
withering of Catholicism in France, and all the evils which
had fallen upon that country, and through her upon Europe
(du Pape, 1819). Such were the rationalist and profane
errors of the eighteenth century, the ascendancy of Vol-

taire and Rousseau, the atheism of the French Revolution, the tyrannies of Robespierre and Napoleon, the alternate bullying and patronising indulged by Napoleon towards Popes Pius VI and Pius VII, the subordination of Church to State retained in the Concordat of 1815. The Church in France had been cut off from proper participation in the life-stream of the Church Universal because her free intercourse with Rome, her animation by the heart of the whole system, had been impeded. There was only one solution: to reassert the absolute supremacy of the Holy See in all that concerned the welfare of the Church. Thus, with de Maistre, was reborn Ultramontanism, a revival, in terms more sweeping than the traditional definition (that of Cardinal Bellarmine, in his *Controversies against the Heretics of our Times*, 1586) of the belief in Papal Supremacy.

De Maistre died in 1821. Already, by that date, a new star was rising in the religious firmament of France, the star of the tempestuous Breton priest, the Abbé de Lamennais. Lamennais had learnt from de Maistre to look to Rome for salvation for the Church from bondage to the State. In the eighteen-twenties his Ultramontanism was as fervent as his master's. But unlike de Maistre he combined his faith in Rome with a faith in the People as ardent and even as eloquent as Rousseau's, and he thus became the most powerful social prophet of his generation, with an influence extending far outside the ranks of those who could pretend to any Christianity at all. To Lamennais there was no inconsistency between Ultramontanism and Liberalism; the People inherited the Tradition; the Pope was their mouthpiece, he interpreted the Tradition just as Rousseau's Legislator interpreted the General Will. The cause of Pope and People was the same, being that of Truth and Freedom against all pretensions of temporal princes and aristocracies whatsoever. Thus Lamennais became the founder of Liberal-Catholicism, as well as the champion of Ultramontanism.

But the prophetic style which won for Lamennais an audience in the French reviews unsurpassed even by his illustrious contemporaries, Chateaubriand, Lamartine, and Victor Hugo, only helped to make him unpopular with the

French hierarchy, and notably with the Archbishop of
Rouen and the Archbishop of Paris. The French hierarchy
was Gallican, so were the ministers of the last of the Bourbon Kings, Charles X, soon to be driven into exile by the
revolution of 1830. Charles X may have been a royal mar-
tyr, and have lost his throne, like James II of England, for
intransigently following his faith, but it was a Gallican faith
and as such Lamennais attacked it freely, so that his writings were suppressed, and he found himself prosecuted.

The arrival of Louis Philippe, in July 1830, on the
French throne, changed the circumstances, because Catholicism was declared no longer the official religion of the
State. A wider liberty of the press gave Lamennais, and
his friends Montalembert and Lacordaire, the opportunity
to develop their liberal ideas in a paper of their own, the
Avenir. The victories of the Belgian Catholics in defying
the Dutch king and winning freedom for their religion,
for the press, for education, were what inspired Lamennais;
the similar victories of O'Connell were the inspiration of
Montalembert, who had been in Ireland. Rome, they said,
must not accept favours at the hands of princes, as Pope
Leo XII had accepted concessions for the Church in France
at the hands of Charles X; she must demand and fight
for what the Church needed.

So the *Avenir* stood for the separation of Church and
State, for freedom of education from state control (Montalembert and Lacordaire opened an independent Catholic
school, which was promptly suppressed), for liberty of the
press, for freedom of association, for an extension of the
suffrage, for an increase in the number of elections, and
for an extension of communal and provincial liberties. For
the brief year of its existence it was the leading liberal paper in France. Victor Hugo and Lamartine wrote for it.
The *Revue des deux mondes* praised it. At last a serious
attempt was being made to reconcile the Church with the
Revolution, to harmonise religion with the "Principles
of '89".

Yet in November 1831 Lamennais suspended publication. He was coming up against the growing hostility of the
dignitaries of the Church. Cardinal Lambruschini, the fu-

ture Secretary of State of Gregory XVI, and Mastai's conservative rival at the Conclave of 1846, was at this time
Papal Nuncio at Paris, and he had turned against Lamennais. In 1827 he had approved of him, liking his Ultramontanism, and swallowing his sociology, and Lamennais
had regarded Lambruschini as a "man of great sense".
Now Lambruschini reported on him to Rome as tending,
by his principles, "to put society into a state of revolution".
In February 1831 Gregory XVI had become Pope, and Fr.
Ventura, a friend whom Lamennais had made when he visited Rome in 1824, was reporting a change in the atmosphere there. Moreover, some of the ardent young bishops in
France, notably Bishop Dupanloup of Orleans, had come
out against Lamennais. Some bishops were refusing to allow their clergy to read the *Avenir*.

Certain of his theological orthodoxy Lamennais decided,
at the instance, it seems, of his pupil Lacordaire, to appeal
to Rome; and the last number of the *Avenir*, November
15th, 1831, announced the forthcoming departure of the
three "pilgrims of God and of liberty".

This decision was certainly a mistake. In their ardour
they had overlooked the well-established fact that to ask
from Rome a blessing for a revolutionary programme
which, if carried out, would turn upside down the entire
existing order of Church and State was to ask for the impossible and to put the Papacy into an embarrassing position. Often enough the founder of a new Religious Order
had found at Rome sympathy and support. But this was
quite different. To approve the programme of the *Avenir*
would have meant to disapprove agreements upon which
the whole outward structure of the Church at that time
depended.

On December 30th, 1831, the pilgrims arrived in Rome.
The moment was far from propitious. Gregory XVI had
just been engaged in calling in the Austrians to put down
the revolt in the Romagna—that Carbonari revolt which
Bishop Mastai had helped to disperse by his charity. The
French and Austrian ambassadors were urging, in the light
of all the disturbances of 1830–31 in Europe, the necessity
of supporting law and order, the danger of adding any fuel

to the flames of revolution. None of the ambassadors was willing to press for a Papal audience for the three pilgrims. But Gregory accepted a memorandum drawn up by Lacordaire, and informed the three, in reply, that he would examine it, although he was mistrustful of dangerous controversies; meanwhile they were free to return home. Eventually, however, the Secretary of State, Bernetti, arranged, before their departure, an audience, of a strictly non-controversial character, for the pilgrims. This they duly attended on March 13th, but it was quite uneventful. Immediately afterwards Lacordaire left Rome.

But Lamennais decided not to go. Fr. Ventura arranged for him to stay at a monastery at Frascati where, within sight, across the Campagna, of St. Peter's dome, he waited day after day, week after week, hoping to be summoned by the Vicar of Christ to expound his vision of the reconciliation of Freedom and the Church. But no word came. On July 9th, with Montalembert, he left Rome. He went to Munich, to seek the views of Schelling on his *Essay on a System of Catholic philosophy*. In August, while he was still at Munich, the Papal Encyclical *Mirari vos* reached him. It did not mention Lamennais by name, and it recognised implicitly the virtues of the Liberal-Catholic leader; but, amongst many other things, it reprobated freedom of conscience (in the sense of doctrinal indifference), freedom of the press, and doctrines likely to lead to disobedience to princes. It expressed opposition to the separation of Church and State and to alliances "for the common good" of men of all kinds of religion. The programme of the *Avenir* stood implicitly condemned in the eyes of Catholic Europe. Lamennais accepted the condemnation and was silent.

Such was the *affaire Lamennais*. It seized the imagination of Europe. It set the stage for the coming conflict between Pio Nono and his times. What was really decided, when Lamennais waited at Frascati for the word that came not from St. Peter's, was that the Church was not reconciled with the "Principles of '89", not reconciled with the suggested separation of Church and State, with popular freedom as it was then being advocated, with the ideas of the progressives about Liberty, Equality, Fraternity, or with revolution. Nor can we be surprised at her attitude. The essence of Mennaisianism, as Lamennais' doctrines were called, was the idea that in a free society the Church would prevail because Truth would always come to the top. But it didn't seem to Rome that it necessarily would. The Reign of Freedom had been ushered in by a prostitute on the altar of Notre Dame. It had despoiled the Church, closed the monasteries, persecuted priests, abducted two Popes, secularised education. Behind Lamennais the Pope saw Rousseau; and it is certainly true that, although Lamennais believed, to the end, in the Fall, and in Original Sin, he was nevertheless influenced (as what French writer since the revolution, except de Maistre, was not?) by the idea of the natural goodness of man, by the idea that Liberty, Equality, and Fraternity would somehow in the end make a brave new world.

After all that had happened, in France and in Europe, it was really quite impossible that the Church should regard the popular freedom demanded by the advanced liberals as anything other than the unleashing of popular passion; and it has been one of her perennial beliefs that the unleashing of passion is an evil and that the spiritual life, which it is her divine mission to foster, can normally best be lived in an orderly society. She had therefore welcomed the restoration, all over Europe, in 1815, of legitimate monarchs who, even in Protestant countries, were prepared to allow the Church to carry on her normal work of the salvation of souls. Such rulers naturally appeared, in 1815, not merely to the future Gregory XVI, but to the saintly reigning Pope, Pius VII, and to his far-seeing Secretary of State Consalvi, as a blessing from heaven. So thankful was Rome for an atmosphere in which the Church could at least carry on her work with only the normal everyday frictions inevitably arising from contact with the State, that she was not prepared to risk disaster by tackling afresh the old grievances of Gallicanism in France, and of its counterpart Josephism[16] in Austria. Whatever their defects, the legitimate princes seemed readier to allow the Church her liberties than did Danton, Robespierre, or Napoleon; nor did the Popes see any convincing reason for opening the field any wider to the Freemasons or the Carbonari.

The most striking example of the readiness of the Papacy to go to almost any lengths at this time for the sake of the preservation of law and order was to be found not in Gregory's condemnation of the *Avenir*, which probably caused him little hesitation, but in his *Brief to the Bishops of Poland*, issued in the same month (August, 1832). The Poles had risen in 1831 against the intolerable oppression of the Tsar, and the sufferings of the Catholic Church in Poland were a major cause of the revolt. Yet Gregory now counselled the Poles to be patient, and to acquiesce. No doubt it was the spectacle of so many recent revolts in Europe, mostly, like the Carbonari revolt in his own states, anti-Christian in inspiration, that determined Gregory's attitude towards the Poles. Yet the counsels of moderation which he sent them failed to appease the tyranny of the Tsar Nicholas.

Through Lamennais, this Polish uprising, and its cruel suppression, had repercussions in Europe and fed the growth of Liberal-Catholicism, and of liberalism more generally. In the year 1833, in May, there appeared in French a translation by Montalembert of an eloquent appeal by the Polish poet Miçkiewicz called *The Book of the Polish Pilgrims*. The tract was a religious appeal for liberty, romantic and poignant, born of the sufferings of the Polish patriotic and religious martyrs. Montalembert added a preface. The tract had a great effect amongst liberals and revolutionaries in Europe; Mazzini found in it inspiration for one of his most eloquent essays. Lamennais added a *Hymn to Poland* to the translation, and soon afterwards published his own *Paroles d'un Croyant*, part prayer, part polemic, part appeal, in the style of Miçkiewicz, but much more profoundly subversive, being indignantly hostile to all civil authority—in fact, anarchist. The publication of the Polish book in France, thus sponsored by Lamennais and Montalembert, met with hostility on the part of the hierarchy because it showed that the encyclical *Mirari vos* had not silenced the French pilgrims, a matter which had been in some doubt. But the *Paroles d'un Croyant* put Lamennais, personally, into a new position in regard to Rome, because the book was censured in the encyclical *Singulari nos*, issued in June, 1834, in terms far different from those adopted by *Mirari vos* towards the tenets of the *Avenir*. It was roundly condemned and its principles held to be worthy of eternal reprobation.

As a result, Lamennais lost his belief in Rome, and that was followed by the loss of his faith in the Christian revelation itself. Sad, embittered, and proud, he came to occupy an isolated position, estranged from the Faith, yet still too Catholic, with his convictions about Original Sin and the Fall, to satisfy his new progressivist friends like Mazzini and Georges Sand, or the early French socialists.

Yet his name remained a watchword, the hope of those who hungered to reconcile the Revolution and Religion. And Gregory, though he condemned the satanic pride evidenced by the *Paroles*, and by Lamennais' later works, never excommunicated him. In 1836 he told Montalembert that he was praying to the Father of Mercies for his friend.

Then, at last, in August, 1847, Lamennais' old friend, Fr. Ventura, now very close to the newly elected Pio Nono, wrote to the Breton priest from Rome:

> "I have an overture to make to you; it is on behalf of the angel whom heaven has sent us, from Pius IX whom I saw this morning. He has charged me to tell you that he blesses you and awaits you to embrace you."

But Lamennais was silent. The fact was that, in ceasing to perform his office as a priest, he had come to suspect and to denounce the priesthood itself. "The People" had become, for him, sole interpreter of God—a view which drew him very close to Mazzini. He watched Pio Nono's progress in the paths of liberalism with curiosity, even with fascination. But the arms which not only the new Pope but the Liberal-Catholics of Italy and France—who still regarded his early writings as their inspiration—were stretching out to him, he rejected. Five years later he was to die, unrepentant.

Lamennais' friends Montalembert and Lacordaire remained in the fold of the Church and won for her and for religious liberty considerable practical victories in France. Montalembert, as a layman, elected to the Chamber of Peers, applied himself to fighting for specific liberties and rights, about which Catholics were agreed, and about whose essential justice he was going to convince many who were indifferent. His most notable achievement came after Louis Napoleon had won power. As President of the Second Republic Napoleon made de Falloux Minister of Education and Cults, which enabled him and Montalembert between them to secure the passage, in 1849, of the Falloux law, giving the Church freedom to run schools.

Lacordaire's mission was different. As a priest he was making his appeal from the pulpit. From January, 1834, at the chapel of the Collège Stanislas, his conferences, or impromptu sermons, were attracting the cultural élite of Paris. Chateaubriand, Lamartine, Victor Hugo, Sainte-Beuve were all to be seen at the chapel. He remained a "Man of the Left" in the sense that he was no friend of princes, or of aristocracies, but he was absolutely obedient to his ecclesiastical superiors. When he spoke he kept strictly to the basic Catholic themes: God, Creation, the Origin of Evil, Original Sin, the Redemption, Human Nature, the Prophecies, the Incarnation. He lived down the suspicion that he was tainted with Mennaisianist errors,[17] and in 1836 he began his great series of conferences from the pulpit of Notre Dame.

In the words of his friend Ozanam, "our temples, so long forsaken, see their solitude re-peopled, the Abbé Lacordaire thunders forth the Word of God over an assembly of six thousand men, crowded into the mighty nave of Notre Dame". One of those who heard him was, as we have seen, Bishop Mastai's friend Count Pasolini. Early in 1839 Lacordaire left for Rome, to be received into the Dominican Order. It was to be one of his missions in life to reintroduce that Order into a France from which it had been banished since the days of the Revolution. It was another to remain always in contact with the liberals, and when the Second Republic arrived, with the revolution of 1848, to take his place, quite naturally, amongst the men of the Left; he might later regret doing so, on account of the materialist philosophy with which he found his associates imbued, but the interesting thing is that it seemed to him natural to sit with them in 1848. His own career, like those of his friends, showed that, although there might be little encouragement from authority, it was not necessary, even in the conservative days of the Gregorian Papacy, to enter the wilderness, like Lamennais, in order to work for liberal ideals.

The Liberal-Catholic movement had thus already become a reality in France before the advent of Pio Nono; it had not been killed by the encyclical *Mirari vos* which had checked Lamennais. *Mirari vos* had been a warning that the liberal ideas were dangerous, that freedom of conscience was widely interpreted at that time as meaning doctrinal indifference (i.e. that one belief was as good as another—it was all a matter of personal choice), and that freedom of the press, and encouragement towards disobedience to princes, were similarly dangerous. But the liberal propositions of the *Avenir* were not condemned as heretical, and Lacordaire, Montalembert and their friends found themselves quite able, with due caution, to continue their campaign and to increase their following, and their Italian friends and imitators did the same. To these men, naturally, the advent of the liberal Pope, in 1846, came like a draught of water in the desert; and a mighty hope coursed once more through their veins.

Frederic Ozanam, founder of the Societies of St. Vincent de Paul, who signally assisted Montalembert in his fight for Church schools in France, and who helped Lacordaire, in his early days as a preacher, became Professor of Foreign Literature at the Sorbonne in 1844, and the appointment, about which there was some hesitation, was another symptom of the extent to which Liberal-Catholicism had by that date softened the hostility of even a State university, dominated by the ideas of the positivist philosopher, Comte. In 1847 Ozanam was at Rome, in the first excitement of Pio Nono's early months. The professor and his wife called upon the Pope.

"We had the honour of being received in a private audience. His Holiness made my wife sit down, and caressed and blessed my little daughter of eighteen months. He spoke to us of France, of the youth of our schools, of the duties of professorship, with a nobility, an emotion, and a charm that are indescribable. When I said that the deserved popularity of his name would hasten the return of public feeling towards Catholicism, 'I know', he replied, 'that God has worked that miracle, and that prejudice against the Holy See has suddenly given way to respect and love; but what utterly confounds me is that He should have made use of a wretch like me to effect this change.' "[18]

Ozanam wanted, before he left Rome, to see one of the torchlight processions to the Quirinal, in honour of the liberal Pope, which were already famous. He was lucky enough, on April 22nd, 1847, just before his departure, to witness the one which greeted the news that the Pope would summon a representative *Consulta* from the provinces of his state.

"We were just coming into the house when we were informed that the people were getting ready to thank the Pope for his new edict, and that there would be a beautiful *fête aux flambeaux*. We swallowed our dinner as quickly as possible, and then, with the Abbé Gerbet and a few friends, who had come to say good-bye to us, we hurried to the Corso. The rendezvous was at the Piazza del Popolo. Torches were being distributed, and those who took them ranged themselves ten abreast, with a leader of the file. But the crowd was so great that we could only get a little above the Church of St. Charles. There we were able to see the outset of the triumphal march. It opened with lines of men with lighted torches; then came the circular of Cardinal Gizzi [announcing the *Consulta*] printed on white linen, and carried aloft like a large banner; then a band of military music; then a dense column of men holding torches, to the number, it is estimated, of about six thousand. Nothing is more striking than the order which reigned in the impromptu army, and nothing was more touching than to see walking side by side, in the same ranks, men of the highest classes, workmen in blouses, priests in their *soutane*, many of them with white hair, and all united in the same feeling, expressed in the same cry, *Viva Pio Nono! Viva Gizzi!* This is the first time I ever heard *vivats* addressed to a minister."[19]

He goes on, after describing the profound silence which descended upon them all when the Pope blessed them, outside the Quirinal, to note that, during the whole demonstration, it did not occur to anybody

"amidst so many other cries, to utter one against Austria, Cardinal Lambruschini, or against any of the partisans of the late Government; nothing that displayed hatred or animosity, nothing but respect alone."

Ozanam shared the respect for the Pope.

"He has resumed, one by one, all the active functions of the Episcopacy,—preaching, giving confirmation, visiting, *incognito*, schools and hospitals, and the poor in their garrets, going to say Mass in any obscure chapel, and distributing Communion to all who are present, as my wife and I had the happiness of receiving it from him. And, with all this, a purity of life that was the admiration of those who knew him as a young priest, and a charity so boundless that when he set out to come to the Conclave he was obliged to borrow six hundred crowns for his journey . . ."[20]

In Ozanam's view, the Liberal-Catholics of France had found their Pope.

If Liberal-Catholicism was the new enthusiasm of Europe, does this mean that a liberal policy had by now become the course of least resistance for a Pope?—and in as much as Pio Nono, like most benevolent men, enjoyed popularity, was he merely sailing with the wind when he played the Liberal?

The realities of his position were far different.

A liberal policy might be the course that would win applause from the populace in Rome, and in the Papal States —though even there, as Pius quickly saw, it was bound soon to lead to difficulties. It might win the enthusiastic approval of Liberal-Catholics in Europe and the world generally and even—as it did—the goodwill of Protestant liberals in England and in America. But none of these people were, or could be, in the nature of things, the Pope's chief concern. His chief concern was necessarily the interests of the Church and her mission for souls. As Head of the Church he was bound to consider her welfare in every country, and the fact was that her welfare still appeared much more likely to be served by maintaining the alliance with political conservatism. There were, for example, her relations with Austria, her most reliable supporter. So cordial had these grown, that discussions had already taken place for the removal of the serious disabilities under which she had suffered in the Austrian Empire since the days of Joseph II. That Emperor's "enlightenment" had led him to pursue Gallican policies—now called Josephist—and, in particular, even to interfere with communications between the Religious Orders, and the Bishops, under Hapsburg rule, and their superiors in Rome. Before three months of his reign were over Pius had, indeed, like his predecessors, felt obliged to raise these matters with Metternich. But his liberalism was such a serious obstacle to understanding that matters were not straightened out before the cataclysm descended. It was the same with Russia. Here the main trouble was the piteous plight of the Poles. Pope Gregory had been accused of deserting them; but in 1842, in his Allocution *Haerentem diu*, he had nevertheless denounced the persecution of the Church in the Russian Empire, both the fate of the Roman and of the Uniate Church. In 1845 the Tsar Nicholas had come to Rome. Negotiations were opened for a Concordat. But the advent of liberal Pio Nono was a stumbling-block; it was bound to encourage the Poles and to make Nicholas suspicious again.[21] Relations with Prussia had become excellent—but, again, Prussia was involved in the question of the Poles, so that Pio Nono's liberalism was suspect at Berlin. And nearer home, in the Italian States, every ruler was the natural ally of the ruler of the Papal States, and not one of these rulers was a liberal. Pius' liberalism could only embarrass them, perhaps lead to further revolts; and if there were disturbances the Papal States, and particularly the Romagna, would be in danger. It would, of course, be the greatest error to suppose that men like Farini, d'Azeglio or Pasolini represented anything but a very small liberal-intellectual minority. Neither they, nor the Mazzinian republicans represented a party upon which any Italian ruler could possibly hope safely to rest his power in 1846. And all around the Pope, at Rome, were the Gregorian cardinals. Particularly experienced and influential in affairs of state were Lambruschini and Bernetti, both sometime Secretaries of State, and both conservatives. Many who had voted for Mastai, of whom they knew little, had done so with the idea of keeping out Gizzi, of whose liberalism they knew too much. It is clear enough that neither they nor the bureaucracy throughout the Papal States were at all prepared for what was coming. How should they be? Mastai was known to be a kindly sort of bishop at Imola, but no worse. It was still only a year since Antonietta Pasolini had read Gioberti to him, and he had begun to dream about a *Papa Angelica* for Italy. Imola was a long way away; how were the cardinals to know with what ardour he had packed those books for the new Pope to read?

Pio Nono found that, amongst the cardinals, there were only his friend Amat, from the Romagna, and Gizzi, from Forli, who were strongly of his way of thinking. It was going to be very hard indeed to carry through reforms. It would be difficult to imagine anything more erroneous than the supposition that Pius was sailing with the wind in adopting liberal policies. He was not a great political thinker, and he was not averse to being applauded in the street—though he generally tried to avoid it. But he was certainly not so foolish as to suppose that a liberal policy was going to be easy. And even if he had been the experience of his first month, as Pope, in drawing up his amnesty for political offenders would have disabused him.

Chapter Two

THE REFORMING POPE
(1846–1848)

1. *Pio Nono, Political Reformer*

The amnesty it was that took the world by storm. Placarded on the walls of Rome, on the hot summer evening of July 17th, 1846, it spelt release for more than a thousand captives and return from exile for hundreds more.

Pio Nono had worked on it with a committee of six cardinals, Lambruschini and Bernetti (the ex-Secretaries of State), Macchi and Mattei (two more conservatives), and Amat and Gizzi, who were two liberal friends. But his right-hand man was the secretary, the very liberal Corboli-Bussi; and outside the committee he was encouraged by his sometime tutor in theology, the Abate Graziosi.

There was opposition to the project—and not without reason. It was bound to lead, as Metternich foresaw, to the return of incorrigible revolutionaries who would foment trouble; the promise of good behaviour required from them was of small value—Mazzini's agents, men like Galletti, who was soon to lead the revolution, returned now, with promises and tears of gratitude that were very soon forgotten. Mostly they were Romagnuols, or from Umbria or the Marches. Very few were Romans; the Romans, even under Gregory XVI, had remained, for the most part, enthusiastically loyal; almost all the later revolutionary leaders inside the city came from elsewhere, though some, like Ciceruacchio, belonged to the Trastevere slum across the Tiber.

If the Pope must make a gesture, thought Metternich, let him grant a pardon. An amnesty of this sort, liberating, or bringing home from exile hundreds of revolutionaries seemed to suggest a change of outlook, almost an acceptance of pernicious principles. "God never grants amnesties," Metternich observed, "God pardons." As usual, Metternich was right; the world did not take the amnesty as a sign of mercy, it took it as a sign of political change of heart. That was why it made so great an impression in Europe, and why it started off the whole movement of reforms in the states of Italy which led to the constitutions of 1848, and to revolution.[1]

The amnesty was no flash in the pan. Pio Nono, appointing the liberal Gizzi as his Secretary of State, went straight ahead in the path of reform, maintaining the lead in Italy until the spring of 1848.

The range of these reforms was wide. The first, which followed closely upon the amnesty, was the commission on railways. Pius had never been sympathetic with Gregory's mistrust of railways. He set up a commission as early as August 22nd, and received its report on November 7th. Four lines were projected, one from Rome to the Neapolitan frontier, one to Anzio, one up to Civita Vecchia, and one right across the Apennines into Umbria. A gold medal was offered as a prize to the person who could find the best route for this last line across the mountains. The work was to be undertaken by private companies. Unfortunately the revolution had occurred before it was seriously started.

While these plans were being laid, others were being prepared to provide gas lighting in the streets. There was to be established a distillery for gas outside the town, to contribute "not only to the beauty and splendour of the streets but also to the safety of the citizens". To some this was to symbolise, rather literally, the break with the obscurantism of the Gregorian régime.

Then there was to be an Agricultural Institute. Agricultural Institutes were all the rage at that time in Italy, stimulated by the visit of Cobden to Florence, and the enlightenment of the Georgofils society in that city. The Institute was not merely to study practical problems, like cattle breeding, in the light of new scientific knowledge, but to give advice to agriculturists, of the kind county agricultural committees have given more recently in England. It was also to educate the rural unemployed and even to start rural infant schools. It was to be a private affair, with the chance of earning a government grant later on. Pius was very keen about it, as he was about the holding of scientific congresses in the Papal States—another new enthusiasm, particularly in Piedmont. He was genuinely interested in his reforms, especially those that concerned education; he was always dropping in to inspect the convent schools and he was liable even to visit a night school.

It would be superfluous to list all his reforms of this kind. At the end of '46 he introduced a measure of tariff reform, mainly to tidy up the complicated customs dues; he eased the lot of the Jews, excusing them from the tiresome obligation of listening to a Christian sermon once a week and inviting them to share in the Papal charities. He simplified the complicated system of criminal courts, and even undertook a general reform of the criminal code. He ordered the regular inspection of prisons (which he visited himself) and endeavoured to establish a general system of *habeas corpus*. In all this he was playing the part of the benevolent despot, but playing it à la nineteenth-century. More was necessary if he was going to be an up-to-date liberal monarch, and he knew it. Some measure of freedom would have to be conceded. His first step in this direction was his press law of March 15th, 1847, which established a free press, subject to a council of five censors, four of whom were to be laymen. From this new freedom arose the plethora of newspapers, estimated at the beginning of 1848 at nearly a hundred in Rome alone, and destined in the new circumstances of that year to become, with the newly formed clubs, the chief agency in bringing about the Pope's own downfall.

But the big issue was a reform of the government. The main complaint was that it was exclusively in the hands of ecclesiastics. It is, perhaps, not altogether surprising that it should have been since "clerks" (a high proportion of the so-called clergy were only in minor orders) formed the larger part of the educated population. All the same, critics like d'Azeglio or Farini, who were educated men of advanced but constructive opinions, were always urging the introduction of the lay element into the government and it was a point which the French liked to make in the advice on governmental matters that they were never slow to proffer. The Roman populace had been taught to think that their grievances would be remedied if the government were no longer ecclesiastical; so that when the first of Pius' major governmental reforms, that by which he formed a Council of Ministers in June, 1847, made no provision for lay Ministers of State, there was a chilly silence on the part of the Romans, deliberately staged to contrast with the habitual demonstrations of enthusiasm. It need hardly be said that the idea of laymen in the government was not one which it was likely that the College of Cardinals or the Curia would welcome with much enthusiasm, and it is very natural that Pius decided to tackle first problems of administrative and economic reform of which the object was to do something practical and to do it as soon as might be.

A start was, however, made towards introducing laymen into the government as early as April, 1847, when the Pope invited lay representatives from the provinces to confer with him on the form which some sort of Consultative Assembly at Rome might take (this produced, on April 22nd, the popular demonstration of thanks which Ozanam witnessed). By October 14th his plans were ready, and, with the warmest demonstrations of enthusiasm yet witnessed, Rome greeted the news that there was to be a *Consulta* to assist in the work of government. It was to consist of twenty-four councillors, elected by indirect vote from the state as a whole, beginning in the communes. No member had to be a cleric, but the president was to be a Cardinal nominated by the Pope. There was a property qualification for members. As its name implies, it was only consultative. But it had the right to discuss all matters of state before they went to the Council of Ministers, and to make suggestions. When coupled with the new freedom of the press this right meant that the people had been put into the picture in the matter of government, even though they might have little legal power. And two other governmental changes, carried out at about the same time, should be considered with the *Consulta*. One was a municipal government for the city of Rome, with a deliberative council of 100 members; these members were nominated in the first instance by the Pope, but recruitment was to be by co-option and only four were to be clerics. To this body a very large part of what had hitherto been done by the Papal government was transferred. And the other was a reorganisation of the Council of Ministers, so that by *motu proprio* of December 29th, 1847, it became a committee of the nine heads of departments. The most important minister, the Secretary of State, who was responsible for foreign affairs, was to be a cardinal. Otherwise the ministers might be laymen.

Such were the constitutional reforms of the new liberal Pope. They represent what Pio Nono was prepared to concede as being reasonable, and even desirable, in order to bring his state into harmony with enlightened and moderate liberal opinion in his day, while at the same time ensuring that the last word rested with him and that he could not be pushed, against his will, into doing what he did not approve. The peculiar importance of this last point, in the case of the Papal State, arose from the dual role of the Pope as a temporal Prince and as Head of the Church. In theory these two functions might be distinguished, but in practice the distinction never proved to be possible. Later on, in 1848, when Pius had been driven by popular pressure and by the revolutionary hurricane in Europe into sanctioning a number of steps which gave him the greatest misgiving, an attempt was to be made by various men, notably Terenzio Mamiani, to separate the spiritual and the temporal power—to set up, for instance, two distinct ministries of foreign affairs, one for the temporal power and one for the spiritual power. But so long as the Pope remained in ultimate possession of both powers such a distinction could not work. He could not, for instance, bless his spiritual children in Catholic Austria, and at the same time declare war upon them as ruler of the Papal State. He could not denounce the civil marriage laws or the dissolution of the monasteries, in Piedmont or in Switzerland, and yet be obliged, at the instance of a lay minister or assembly, to agree to such measures in his own state. His dual role made it impossible for the Pope to become a constitutional monarch in the sense of possessing a limited sovereignty, a power which was subject to the will of an elective assembly. That was the position into which he was going later to be forced by the constitution which was imposed upon him in March, 1848. It proved to be an untenable position. He could, indeed, veto what he refused to approve, but that only brought government to a standstill and an angry crowd into the streets.

But we are here concerned with what was happening in 1847, not with the upheavals of 1848. Pio Nono knew that with the granting of his *Consulta*, in October 1847, he had gone as far as he could rightly go, and he made his position abundantly clear. When the new body met for the first time, on November 15th, under the presidency of Cardinal Antonelli (there was only one other cleric on it) he took the opportunity, in thanking them for their address of loyalty, to reiterate that their functions were purely consultative:

> "Greatly deceived is anyone who thinks that his duties are different from these; greatly deceived is anyone who sees in the Consulta thus set up some Utopia of his own, and the seeds of an institution incompatible with the pontifical supremacy."[2]

This, then, was Pio Nono's limit. It is worth noting that it seems to have been a further limit than any of the cardinals had contemplated. Even Gizzi, regarded as the liberal candidate for the Papacy in '46, and now Secretary of State, resigned his office rather than go on supporting such changes. But before he did this, he issued, on June 22nd, '47, a formal *Notificazione*—of course approved, and possibly written by Pius—in which he warned the people that the reforms must not be misunderstood, and in particular must not be interpreted as meaning that the Pope was hostile to Austria.

> "His Holiness has not been able to see without serious distress of mind that some restless spirits would take advantage of the present conditions to set forth and cause to prevail doctrines and thoughts entirely contrary to his maxims; and to push on or set up claims entirely opposed to the calm and peaceful disposition and the sublime character of one who is Vicar of Jesus Christ, Minister of the God of Peace, and Father of all Catholics alike— whatever be the part of the world to which they belong; or, similarly, to excite in the populations, by writing and

by speech, desires and hopes of reform beyond the limits above stated."[3]

2. *The Pope Becomes a Constitutional Monarch*

Gizzi had issued his warning in June, '47. In July he resigned.

The leading liberal amongst the cardinals was finding the new Pope's changes altogether too sweeping; the immediate cause of his resignation was the granting of a Civic Guard.

All over Italy there was an agitation going on for the formation of these "Home Guards". The idea was to form a volunteer force which could be used either to restore order (which was the purpose that the "moderates", alarmed by the revolutionaries, had in mind) or else to train men to fight the Austrians (which was what the revolutionaries had in mind). In June, '47, following some mild disturbances in Rome, the moderates were successful in persuading Pius to allow the formation of such a guard within the city. They were confident that they could officer it themselves, and keep it under their own control; but Gizzi saw the danger quite clearly. Putting arms into the hands of the people meant, in the long run, putting power into their hands, or into the hands of whatever revolutionary leaders might succeed in gaining their ear. Profoundly aware that this was the beginning of revolution, he held unofficial and highly confidential conversations with Metternich's ambassador at Rome, Count Lützow, to see whether, in the event of serious disturbance, Austrian help would be forthcoming. Lützow was evasive. Gizzi resigned, and Pius replaced him with Cardinal Gabriele Ferretti, who was then serving as Legate at Pesaro, on the border of the Romagna. Gizzi had probably been more realistic than Pius, but he had shown that the more liberal Cardinal had, in fact, been elected Pope.

What Pio Nono only came to realise—to his horror—during the winter of '47–'48 was that, to Italians, and to the revolutionary liberals everywhere, the significant thing about his régime at Rome was not the sensible reforms themselves but the fact that he was carrying them out. There was no middle party in Italy, anyhow as yet; there were only "the tradition" and "the revolution", and the Pope seemed to have sided with the latter. The result was that every demonstration, every insurrectionary outbreak put his name upon its banner, so that busts of him were being carried in honoured procession, in places as distant as Sicily or Milan, by crowds that were demonstrating against the Bourbons, or against the Austrians, or against any rulers whatsoever. And in the same way, those, like the Mazzinians or the Carbonari, who were interested in promoting general revolution, and whose headquarters were at Paris or at London, saw in what was happening at Rome merely the opportunity to grind their own axes. Their policy was to secure control of the newly formed political clubs there, and to turn men's minds towards gaining effective leadership in the whole peninsula and particularly towards driving the Austrians out of Lombardy-Venetia, because it was from Milan and Venice that Metternich was able to exert his decisive influence in maintaining the rulers in the other Italian capitals.

Lambruschini had few illusions about the true state of things, but Lambruschini no longer held power. There was, however, one man who was in a position to act, and who understood.

Metternich's experience and understanding of Europe were unique. There was now nobody else left, if we except the Duke of Wellington, who had had to grapple with the revolution, incarnate in Napoleon. As he had been the architect in chief of the 1815 settlement of Europe, so, of all men, he understood the menace to that settlement which lurked, implicit, in every liberal revolution. He was perfectly aware that a storm was being whipped up by the spiritual children of Rousseau, and especially by Mazzini, that was likely to engulf everything; and he was equally aware that the new Pope had an inadequate appreciation of the gravity of the danger. How, indeed, should Pio Nono have appreciated it when, apart from a one-year mission to Chile, as a very young man, he had not been outside Italy, and had scarcely been outside the Papal State?[4]

In these circumstances Metternich had felt it his duty to educate the new Pope. He had started as early as the first month after his election, writing to Lützow, at Rome: ". . . I think it my duty to submit to him some impressions which are the product of the advance of my mind and of my long experience of public affairs." He went on to recommend that there should only be one Secretary of State, in supreme charge, at home and abroad—Pio Nono agreed about this—then to discourage amnesties, in the terms already discussed, then to discourage concessions in general:

"A concession always presupposes, if it is concerned with a moral question, an act renouncing a *right*, and, if it is concerned with something material, renunciation of a *property* . . . Are such concessions at the free disposition of the reigning Sovereign?"[5]

Metternich's teaching had some success with the Secretary of State, Gizzi; in the Pope he roused little but resentment. But when Pius put arms into the hands of his citizens by granting them the Civic Guard, and Gizzi resigned, then it seemed to the Austrians that the time had come for more than good advice. Already, in November, '46, Metternich had nipped revolution in the bud in Poland, by occupying Cracow. The time had come to make a move in Italy.

The first step was not taken by Metternich personally, but on the initiative of the veteran Austrian commander in Lombardy, Radetzky, now eighty years of age, but destined, in the following two years, to achieve victory in two more campaigns. He decided to reinforce, with some ostentation, the garrison which Austria maintained, by the Vienna treaties, in the citadel of Ferrara, in the Romagna. His men were marched in on July 17th, 1847, the day when all Italian cities were celebrating the anniversary of the amnesty. Nor did he give any warning to the Papal Legate at the city, Cardinal Ciacchi, that he would be needing billets for his soldiers. All the same, he was acting within his rights.

But Pio Nono was thoroughly roused. Anticipating the move, he had instructed Cardinal Ciacchi not to find billets in the town for the Austrians, and to report any move on their part at once to Rome. Ciacchi had obeyed, and the new Secretary of State, Ferretti, had made a formal complaint to Lützow. What particularly impressed Lützow was the personal resentment of Pius over the matter; the Pope regarded it as a deliberate and insolent affront, and even as a hostile act.

On August 6th, the Austrian commander in charge of the operation, Count Auersperg, informed Cardinal Ciacchi that, on account of popular demonstrations against his troops, he would be obliged to extend his occupation to other strategic parts of the city, as well as the citadel; his aim seems chiefly to have been to protect his men from insult. The upshot of this was no less than an appeal by the Pope to Europe, addressed by the Secretary of State, but written by Pius. Lützow was astonished. He told Metternich the Pope was merely yielding to popular pressure. But there is no reason to suppose this. Pius knew the Romagna, knew the Austrian itch to interfere there, remembered his own conversations at Imola with Count Pasolini. There seems little doubt that he shared with his subjects a strong Italian amour-propre, and that he was genuinely angered by what he considered were clumsy and arrogant Germanic moves. But further, he was always, at every stage of his pontificate, insistent upon maintaining the independence of the Papal State, and the integrity of his sovereignty within it.

Nevertheless, on August 13th Auersperg proceeded to the full occupation; whereupon Pius' Secretary of State threatened first to break off diplomatic relations, then, if necessary, to excommunicate the Austrians; after that he might appeal to the Italians to drive them out.[6]

At this point in his career Pius IX stood poised between the Revolution and the Tradition. He was the idol of Italy, fantastically popular, the one man for whom, at a word, the country would have risen. Any crowd, in any town or village, shouted *viva Pio Nono*, whatever the object it had

in view. The "Hymn to Pius" was chanted through the
streets. He was the Patriot-Pope—the *Papa Angelica*. Even
Mazzini, who for years had ridiculed the "Effete Papacy"
and the "Moribund Church", yielded at last to the popular
passion, recognising in Pius the one man who might, at
that moment, save Italy. On September 8th, from London,
he addressed an Open Letter to him.

Mazzini's Open Letter to Pio Nono was clearly sincere
in the sense that he believed the Pope to be a good man,
believed him capable of achieving a great deal for Italy,
and would have been glad to see him initiate a national
revolution. That does not mean either that he accepted, for
himself, the Pope's religious faith, or that he did not in-
tend, after making use of Pius, to direct the revolution,
through his own party, into the channels he wanted; nor
does it protect him from theological absurdities, not to say
impertinencies.

"There is no man," he writes, "I will not say in Italy but
in Europe more powerful than you. You have, therefore,
most blessed father, immense duties; God measures
them in accordance with the means which he gives to his
creatures. Europe is in a tremendous crisis of doubts and
of desires. Through the passage of time, aggravated by
your predecessors and the exalted hierarchy of the
Church, beliefs are dead; catholicism is lost in despotism: protestantism is losing itself in anarchy. Look
around you: you will find superstitious men or hypocrites, but not believers. Intellect wanders in the void.
. . . Do not deceive yourself, most holy father: this is
the state of Europe. But humanity cannot live without
heaven. The social idea is none other than a consequence
of the religious idea. We shall therefore have, sooner or
later, religion and heaven.

"We shall have them not from the kings and from the
privileged classes whose very position shuts out love, the
spirit of all religions, but from the people. The spirit of
God descends upon the many, gathered together in His
name. The people has suffered for centuries upon the
cross; and God will bless it with a faith."

This is almost pure Lamennais. It is the *Paroles d'un Croyant* once again. But what is the Pope to do?

". . . To fulfil the mission which God entrusts to you two things are necessary: to believe, and to unify Italy. Without the first you will fall by the wayside, abandoned by God and by men; without the second you will not have that lever with which, alone, you can achieve great, holy, and enduring things."[7]

No doubt Mazzini, optimist as he was, hardly hoped to convert the Pope from Catholicism to his own religion of the Nation and Humanity; but whatever interpretation we put upon his publishing the letter it is immensely significant. Even if, as is often supposed, he wanted to show Pio Nono up as no true prophet of the New Italy, it is remarkable that he should have thought it necessary to point out the distinction between the Pope's faith and the peculiar brand of pantheism of which he himself was the leading prophet. It implied that others, too, were failing to make that distinction.

Pio Nono found that his bold stand against Metternich over the Ferrara affair had had the most lamentable results. Everywhere it had fanned the flames of Italian ardour, everywhere the cry was now "out with the barbarians!" and he was hailed throughout Italy as the national leader. It was appalling. He had no intention of merging the Papal State in a unified Italy controlled by Mazzini. Nor had he any idea of aggression against the Austrians, who were his faithful Catholic children. To turn them out of his own state, if they trespassed at Ferrara, was one thing; but to wage aggressive war against them in their legal dominions, or to encourage others to do so, was quite another, and altogether incompatible with his spiritual position.

The quarrel with Metternich over Ferrara was protracted, but in the end it was Metternich who gave way; the Austrians retired again into the citadel on December 16th, 1847. It was a diplomatic victory for the Pope, which meant that again he appeared in the light of the Champion of Italy.

Thus once more did he store up for himself inevitable future embarrassment.

One cannot be surprised that Metternich raised his eyebrows at the political naïveté of the new ruler of Rome. In October he had written sadly to the Austrian Ambassador Apponyi at Paris:

"Each day the Pope shows himself more lacking in any practical sense. Born and brought up in a *liberal* family, he has been formed in a bad school; a good priest, he has never turned his mind towards matters of government. Warm of heart and weak of intellect, he has allowed himself to be taken and ensnared, since assuming the tiara, in a net from which he no longer knows how to disentangle himself, and if matters follow their natural course, he will be driven out of Rome."[8]

This was accurate prophecy. So was his letter in December to his agent, Ficquelmont, at Milan. After lamenting the influence of Gioberti, Balbo, d'Azeglio, and their French prototypes, he says that, looking back over the past few years, he could:

". . . write the history of the conspiracy which has ended by giving birth to *Pio Nono*. The spectre has assumed a body in the visible Head of the Church . . ." but "A *liberal* Pope is not a possibility. A Gregory VII could become the master of the world, a Pius IX cannot become that. He can destroy, but he cannot build. What the Pope has already destroyed by his liberalism is his own temporal power; what he is unable to destroy is his spiritual power; it is that power which will cancel the harm done by his worthless counsellors. But to what dangerous conflicts have not these men exposed the man and the cause they wanted to serve!"[9]

As the fateful year 1848 opened Metternich foretold what would happen:

". . . many realities will have lifted from them the veils with which they are still covered . . . The veil is liberalism; it will disappear in Italy, as in every other country, before radicalism in action."

And a final warning—the radicals would not stop at upsetting the State:

> ". . . the starting-point, to seize upon, of the social
> movement which today covers the world, is to be found
> in the reformation of the sixteenth century, in that im-
> mense catastrophe, religious, political, and moral which
> has divided Europe into governments and countries
> catholic and protestant. From the reformation in the six-
> teenth century to the social upheaval it was only a step,
> and it is the same to-day from reform of the government
> to reform of the catholic church."[10]

But by the end of 1847 Pio Nono, too, was beginning to
see a little more clearly what lay behind the dangerous elements that were being stirred up in Europe. At the end
of November '47 had come to Rome the news of the crushing of the seven Catholic cantons of Switzerland—the *Son-
derbund*—in a quick civil war, by the Protestant Federal
Diet, supported by the majority of the cantons. In Europe
this sharp struggle, long foreshadowed, was widely appreciated for what it was, namely the crushing, by the majority,
of the Catholic liberties of the minority; its result was
the expulsion of the Jesuits, the closing of other religious
houses, and interference with the free working of the
Church in Switzerland. Metternich had tried to prevent it,
in conjunction with France; but Guizot, though pressed by
Lacordaire, Montalembert, and their friends, had not felt
sure enough of French support to join with him, and the
Swiss liberals had therefore defied the Austrian chancellor.
The revolutionaries in Rome applauded the victory of the
anti-Catholics in Switzerland, and proceeded to demonstrate against the Jesuits, to the pain and grief of Pius.
They were making it very clear to him that liberal revolution
might not prove compatible with freedom for the Church.

There was another discovery that Pio Nono was making
about this time which compelled him to consider more
carefully what a big national disturbance, and particularly
any rising against the Austrians might bring: he had discovered that the Piedmontese government of King Charles
Albert was not interested in his own Giobertian idea of

linking the Italian states together into some sort of federation. This could only mean that the Turin government had plans for expanding the territories and influence of the House of Savoy in northern Italy, which must, inevitably, upset the balance of the Italian states and involve some sort of Piedmontese hegemony, which would be fatal to the Papal State. Pius had started, in August '47, by proposing a customs union, imitating the policy of the German states which had already formed the *zollverein*. He found the Grand-Duke of Tuscany enthusiastic, but Turin very awkward. By November '47 he had secured a basis for discussion, but nothing concrete. What the negotiations had shown was that, behind the matters under discussion, there lay a real difference of outlook: Pius was working for the peaceful evolution of an Italian federation, Charles Albert was biding his time for the moment when he could make war on the Austrians and unite northern Italy under himself. For this war he would evidently want, in due course, a Papal blessing and a military alliance; but Pius was not prepared to give either.

The new year, 1848, was only twelve days old when the first revolution of that year of revolutions broke out in Sicily. The grievances of the island were mainly local, and the revolutionaries were more concerned with freeing Sicily than with freeing Italy, but the extreme boldness of the Sicilians, and the surprising success of their movement when it spread to the Neapolitan mainland, where it foreshadowed Garibaldi's successes eleven years later, quickened the excitement and ambition which had ben whetted by the Austrian hesitation in face of Pio Nono at Ferrara. More and more widely Pio Nono found his name being used as the symbol of revolution and a war of liberation against Austria.

Filled with foreboding by the behaviour of the Mazzinians, by the revolution at Naples, by the designs of Piedmont, and convinced that the independence of the Papal State might soon be in danger, Pius put something of his own Italian political philosophy into words, in his *motu proprio* of February 10th, '48. It was really a last despairing attempt to arrest the course of events, though it was interpreted very differently. The argument which Pius sought to impress upon Italians was that their true security, in a turbulent world, consisted in the very existence, in their midst, of the Papal State.

"For Us especially—for Us as Head and Supreme Pontiff of the most holy Catholic religion—if We were unjustly assailed, is it possible that we should not find for our own defence innumerable sons who would support the centre of Catholic Unity as though it were their Father's house? A great gift from heaven is this: one of the many gifts which He has bestowed on Italy; that a bare three million of our subjects possess two hundred million brothers of every nation and every tongue. In times very different from these, when the whole Roman world was disordered, this fact remained the salvation of Rome. Owing to it, the ruin of Italy was never complete. And this will always be her protection so long as the Apostolic See stands in her midst.

"Therefore, O Lord God, bless Italy and preserve for her this most precious gift of all—the faith! . . ."[11]

His meaning was clear enough; yet such are the perversities of politics, such the delusions of enthusiasts (egged on, undoubtedly, by interested parties) that they took up the cry "O Lord God, bless Italy" as being the Papal blessing upon their dream of an Italy freed and united from the Alps to the Mediterranean, the dream of Mazzini, and the anti-Austrian war party. It was as though Pius had already launched a crusade. He could no longer exercise any control over opinion; he had been cast by the enthusiasts for the role of Peter the Hermit, and his words were interpreted to fit the part. All that remained for him, and he was not going to flinch from it, was to refuse, as sovereign, to take the expected actions.

When the crowd came, as usual, to the Quirinal, the day after the *motu proprio*, to congratulate him, and to thank him for blessing Italy, he was found, for the first time on such an occasion, to be very sad. He seemed to be ill.

It was the day after this that the news came of Ferdinand's granting a constitution at Naples; a week later it was reported that the Grand-Duke had granted one at Florence. On February 24th the Paris revolution broke out, and Louis Philippe was fleeing to England. On March 5th Charles Albert gave way and granted a constitution at Turin. Finally, on March 13th, there came the revolution at Vienna itself with Metternich, too, in flight. But before the arrival of that dramatic news even the College of Cardinals had become convinced that Europe's most progressive sovereign could hardly, overnight, become the most retrograde; the granting of a constitution by Pius, which occurred on March 15th, had, indeed, become inevitable.

The details of the Roman constitution of 1848 are not of very great interest.[12] There was a standard pattern of limited monarchy generally available to European liberals at this time, the prototype being that of 1830 in France, the constitution under which Louis Philippe had ruled and which, ironically enough, at this moment of its adoption in the Italian and German states, was being abandoned in France. The Roman version was drawn up by a commission of the Sacred College, which was careful to see that the rights of the Church and of the Cardinals were not endangered. The two Councils, a High Council and a Council of Deputies, which were created, were incompetent to discuss religious matters, which included education, and moral (not political) censorship, and all bills which they passed had to be submitted first to the Sacred College, to be pronounced upon, and then sent to the Pope, who either approved or vetoed. The Pope could thus be sure of not being constitutionally compelled to agree to measures of which he disapproved, but stalemate was made likely enough by the fact that any civil administrative or political law, including the imposition of taxes, had to be voted by the Councils. There was thus a real division of power, a situation entirely different from that which existed under the régime of the merely advisory *Consulta*, which the Pope had previously established. Ministers had to command a majority in the Councils. The Council of Deputies was elected, by indirect vote, on a property qualification; the Higher Council was nominated by the Pope, on the advice of his government and the Sacred College.

Of more constructive consequence than the new legislature thus set up were some of the "fundamental rights" acknowledged by the new constitution, and notably the independence of the courts, with irremovability of judges; equality before the law, with abolition of special tribunals and commissions extraordinary; freedom from arrest without cause shown; abolition of exemption of any corporate body from state taxation; state guarantee of the public debt; abolition of political press censorship. Some of these, and notably the legal reforms, had already been introduced by Pius, and were, indeed, dear to his heart.

The constitution was not going to last long because an absolute impasse between Pius and the Chambers on the issue of war or peace was to cause a revolution the following November. But a contributory cause of that revolution was the bourgeois character of the Councils themselves. The Mazzinians were working for "God and the People", not for God and the propertied classes, and by autumn of '48 the clubs in Rome had superseded the Councils as the real seat of power—a repetition of what happened in Paris in 1793, with the rise of the Jacobin club.

The Roman populace duly demonstrated in front of the Quirinal in gratitude for the constitution. But the news that came in from abroad continued to be even more exciting. The rejoicings for the constitution were still continuing when the much more heady news of the flight of Metternich arrived. This was, of course, the most important news of all. If there were revolution at Vienna it was obvious that Italy's opportunity had come. Moreover the maintenance of the established order in the Italian states was personally identified with Metternich and his policy. A new and presumably liberal government in Vienna was expected to be sympathetic with the liberals in Italy. But first Radetzky and his troops must be driven from Lombardy.

3. *The War Against Austria*

The immediate effect of the Viennese revolution was the
uprising of Venice under Manin (March 17th) and the
famous "Five Days" (March 18th–22nd) when the Milanese populace rose and threw the Austrians out of their city.
Charles Albert's declaration of war came on March 24th;
and on the same day General Giovanni Durando led out
of Rome the advance guard of a Papal army officially intended to defend the northern frontier of the Papal State
against any possible Austrian incursion.

Giovanni Durando was a Piedmontese professional soldier. He was one of the influential Piedmontese clique
at Rome, of whom much the most important was Massimo
d'Azeglio, now rather a friend of Pio Nono's; their aim was
to try to influence the Papal Government in a direction
consistent with Piedmontese policy. But, as we have seen,
Pius' ideas for Italy were not those of the Piedmontese Government, and it was to prove very rash to entrust the Papal
army to a Piedmontese general.

Durando, then, with the Papal army, left Rome on
March 24th; he was closely followed by another army of
Roman volunteers under Colonel Andrea Ferrari. Durando
was still on the march when, on April 5th, he published a
proclamation written by d'Azeglio, who had just been visiting Charles Albert. In it he said:

"We are blessed by the right hand of a great Pontiff just
as were our ancestors of the days gone by. He is a Saint.
He is just . . . His saint-like heart could not but be
saddened at the thought of the evils that come with war
. . . and on his august lips there remained suspended
the words which were to make those lips the instruments
of divine vengeance.

"But the moment arrived when kindness would have
become mere blameworthy connivance at iniquity."

Radetzky, it went on, had waged war on the Cross of Christ.
Pius had seen this and had blessed their swords which were
to exterminate the enemies of God and of Italy. The war
was not merely national but highly Christian. The soldiers
were therefore to be adorned with the Cross of Christ, and
the war-cry was to be "God wills it".[13]

Farini and Minghetti are agreed that Pius explicitly ordered his generals to do no more than proceed to his frontiers and defend them. But it is clear enough that they
always intended to join in the war with the Piedmontese,
and that Durando was, in fact, imbued with the Piedmontese idea of using the Pope's enormous influence and prestige to rouse Italians in support of the Piedmontese war.
Pius, not unnaturally, was furious. What they wanted from
him was an excommunication of the Austrians. So far
from being willing to consider this he was, as Minghetti
records, with great difficulty dissuaded from publicly denouncing his general. He contented himself with an official announcement explaining drily that the Order of the
Day had expressed ideas and sentiments as though they
were dictated by His Holiness, "whereas the Pope, when
He desires to make known His sentiments, speaks *ex se*
and never through the mouth of any subordinate person".[14]

It is clear from the attitude of d'Azeglio that the idea
was to push ahead, assuming the Papal benediction, until
the troops were fairly committed in Lombardy. On the
one hand the Piedmontese party regarded Pius as a good-
natured man who was "easy to push"; on the other they
recognised that he was in a genuine dilemma and felt they
could help him out of his difficulty by taking the bit between their teeth, and pretending they had his support.

Either way they quite misunderstood the situation. It
was impossible that he should throw his army into an aggressive war, still more impossible that he should invoke
the spiritual arm against the Austrians. Despite the warlike propensities of Pope Julius II, in the days of the turbulent condottiere-ridden Italy of the early sixteenth century, it was not the practice of the Papacy to make any
but defensive war. The predecessor whom Pio Nono so
much revered, Pius VII, had, in 1810, steadily refused to

place his ships at Napoleon's disposal against "Protestant England", insisting that England had done him no harm, and it would be quite wrong for him, as Vicar of the Prince of Peace, to make war against her. Pio Nono maintained the same attitude, and it is easy to overstress the importance of the fact that the Austrians were Catholics. For the Pope to promote any war—save in defence of the Temporal Power—clearly appeared to Pius highly improper, and he grieved exceedingly, in this spring of '48, that he seemed to have helped, albeit unwittingly, to bring about the general cataclysm. It horrified him that his name was on the lips of violent men. He saw himself as the Father-in-God of all men, whether they chose to recognise the fact or not; he could not promote wars between them. This attitude will seem natural enough to the modern English reader, who is more inclined to be surprised that the Pope should have felt it necessary to have had an army at all, and been willing to defend his own state, than that he should have declined to promote war generally. But Pius was as ardent in the defence of his state as he was opposed to war and revolution. It never occurred to him that he did not have a duty to defend it. Here again Pius VII had stated the theory, as a warning to Napoleon, in an Allocution of July, 1808:

"In order that none of them [the secular princes of the earth] should feel justified in hampering the full exercise of his spiritual primacy by the head of our religion on the ground that he [The Pope] was subject to some temporal power, God has willed that the Sovereign Pontiff should possess a temporal sovereignty independent of any Power."

The Papacy has normally regarded the duty of promoting peace as primary. To this duty, in 1848, was added the special consideration that any semblance of encouragement, on the part of the Pope, for an Italian uprising against the Austrians, meant running the risk of schism amongst the Germans. Count Lützow, still Austrian ambassador at Rome, was not slow to point out this danger to Pius. And the Dutch minister, Liedekerke, unimpressed by Durando's proclamation, drily observed: "I doubt whether this likening them to the Turks will afford much pleasure in Germany: it might even cause serious trouble for the interests of religion . . ."[15]

In a report to the Grand-Duke of Tuscany of an interview he had with Pio Nono on April 20th (just nine days before the Allocution which was finally to separate the Pope from the war) the Tuscan ambassador, Bargagli, throws some interesting light on the Pope's mind.[16] He shows that the Pope was, by now, very much distressed by the demagogic ideas which were pouring into Italy from Paris (Mazzini was now in Paris) but that he thought the Piedmontese would act as a check upon any wild ideas of a Mazzinian republic for Italy. It reassures the Grand-Duke that the Pope had never countenanced the ideas contained in Mazzini's Open Letter. He had been:

"the first to perceive the poison concealed beneath the veil of religion in such schemes; no one was more certain than himself that, once the agitators of this type had obtained their desire, the sovereignty of the Tiara would be thrown to the earth even sooner than that of any other monarchy, and banished from the scene."

The Pope also told the ambassador that he was very much saddened by the efforts that were being made in Germany to turn the present quarrel into the occasion of a schism. There were those in Austria, "Josephist" in outlook, who were showing signs of trying to set up a state church. Finally, the blame for the cataclysm which seemed to impend could not fairly be laid at his door. His reforms had been merely those which France and Austria had themselves proposed to Gregory after the revolt of 1831 in the Romagna, in the celebrated "Memorandum of the Powers". What had forced the pace in Italy, and brought about the present situation was, the Pope insisted, on the one hand the revolutionary movement in Sicily and Naples, and on the other the obstinacy of Austria.

So the Allocution, which censured the extremists of 1848, was published on April 29th, 1848, and the Pope and the Risorgimento parted company.

The Berkeleys have shown that this Allocution probably did not come as such a surprise, anyhow to official circles at Rome, as used to be supposed. But it is very certain that neither the Italian people nor the world generally had wind of it and the Italians, at least, who had reason to appreciate its importance, were thunderstruck. For in it Pio Nono made it clear not only that he was not, as was popularly supposed, the leader of the Risorgimento, but that he was not even in sympathy with it—and this at the very moment when excitement about national liberation was at its highest pitch and when the Pope's blessing was assumed. It was, in fact, an act of the highest courage, a deliberate thrust of the rudder turning the bows of the barque of Peter right against the current of the tide at the very moment when hopeful enterprises had brought it to the flood. It was a decisive act of policy. It handed over the leadership of the Risorgimento to Piedmont, or to Mazzini, whichever could wrest it from the other. And it marked the beginning of the end of the Pope's attempt to lead European liberalism, to baptise the "Principles of '89".

The Allocution was divided into three parts.[17] The first goes right back to the days of Pius VII and traces the history of the reform movement, rubbing it in that Pio Nono's own reforms, and particularly his *Consulta,* were entirely in harmony with the Memorandum of the Powers of 1831. Significantly it says nothing about the constitution wrested from him in March 1848. That was not part of his reforms; that was part of the European cataclysm, for which he now disclaimed responsibility. The second part is concerned with the war. Pius states that, while he cannot prevent his subjects from volunteering to fight with Charles Albert against the Austrians, as volunteers from all the Italian states were doing, nevertheless he cannot declare war because, though unworthy, he represents on earth "Him who is the author of peace and the lover of concord" and he "seeks after and embraces all races, peoples and nations, with an equal devotion of paternal love". And the third part tackles directly the myth about his being infected with Mazzinian republicanism. He denies any share in the scheme for making Italy a united republic under his presidency and he urges all Italians to eschew such ideas and to remain loyal to their princes.

In short, the Allocution was a necessary and overdue statement of the policy of the Church, and it infuriated almost everybody. From fantastic popularity Pio Nono sank, overnight, to what Farini describes as the same position in the public estimation as that previously held by Gregory XVI.

Such was the action, at the first great crisis of his pontificate, of the Pope whose critics have been fond of saying that he courted popularity.

The Florentine and Piedmontese ambassadors stress that Pius was very calm at this time, as always in his life when he reached a clear decision as to what he must do. But the revolution at Rome nearly came now. The man who averted it was Terenzio Mamiani, a revolutionary exile who had returned to Rome after the amnesty, and who was grateful to Pius because the Pope had allowed him to come home without having to make the formal "promise of good behaviour" required by the amnesty. (Mamiani had previously taken an oath never to make any such act of submission!) The Civic Guard had mustered and had taken possession of the key points in the city, including the Sant' Angelo. Deputation after deputation, including the Piedmontese and Tuscan ambassadors, called at the Quirinal to try to persuade Pius to give way about the war. To the envoys of the new revolutionary governments of Milan, Venice, and Sicily, he cried: "I am more Italian than you are, but you *will* not make the distinction in me between the Italian and the Pontiff." At the same time the popular clubs and the Civic Guard were demanding a new provisional government—to grant which would be to treat the Pope as deposed. Mamiani, however, parried their demands and reasoned with them very skilfully; violence was, in the event, averted by Pius asking Mamiani to form a ministry, which meant accepting his terms. These were that Cardinal Antonelli must cease to be Secretary of State, that there should be two foreign ministries, one for ecclesiastical and one for lay affairs, and that, while there should be no declaration of war, unless the Pope wished, the armies of Durando and Ferrari, which had crossed the frontier of the Romagna and were now fighting the Austrians in Austrian-ruled Lombardy, should not be recalled, and in the meantime should be taken under the protection of Charles Albert.

If the Italians felt they had a grievance against Pius it was because they had misinterpreted him; but the Austrians had a genuine grievance. In their hour of danger (the Italian provinces were not the only part of the Austrian Empire that had seized the opportunity afforded by the Viennese revolution) they found themselves confronted, in Lombardy, not merely by volunteers, and by the Piedmontese regulars, but by the Pope's army, although they were the traditional defenders of the Papal State, and had saved the situation for Pio Nono's predecessor in 1831. It was certainly surprising, nor can the Pope be said to have quite regularised his behaviour, even by his audacious Allocution, because the policy which he accepted when he accepted Mamiani as premier was this ambiguous one that Durando's army should now take its instructions from Charles Albert, the Austrians' principal enemy in Italy. The other Roman army of 9,000 volunteers under Ferrari was another matter; Pio Nono could reasonably take the line that he was in no position to prevent them from going. Similar bands of volunteers—they were much smaller than the revolutionaries had hoped to see—were going to the war from every Italian state.

The Pope followed up his Allocution by a personal appeal, on May 2nd, to the Austrian Emperor to withdraw his troops from Italy. In view of the grave dangers besetting Vienna it seemed not impossible that his mediation would be accepted. He reminded the Emperor:

"... in Our Allocution of the 29th of last month, We asserted that to declare war would revolt Our paternal heart; and announced Our ardent desire to contribute towards the restoration of peace. Let it not therefore be displeasing to your Majesty that we should address an appeal to your piety and religion, and exhort you with paternal affection to withdraw your arms from a war which can never reconquer for your empire the minds of the Lombards and Venetians; and can only bring with it the fatal series of calamities that always accompany war, and are certainly both repulsive and detestable to yourself.

". . . We are confident that the German nation itself, being honestly proud of its own nationality, will not engage its honour in an attempt to shed the blood of this Italian nation; but will rather engage it in nobly recognising her as a sister—for both are Our daughters and very dear to Us; let each of them be content to live within her own borders by honourable agreement and beneath the blessing of the Lord."[18]

This appeal, which had no effect, is interesting as showing that Pius, too, was thinking about an "Italian nation". His idea, the Giobertian idea, was that it should be a federation which would grow out of a league between the states. During all this critical time he had been redoubling his efforts to secure such a league. He seems to have thought that, once established, it would inevitably have drawn the Austrian-controlled provinces Lombardy and Venetia into it, on account of natural economic and linguistic ties. And just before the outbreak of war he seemed to be succeeding in his policy, for, by March 19th, '48, Piedmont had agreed in principle, and even the canny Antonelli thought that the league was as good as made. But on March 24th Charles Albert had declared war and ceased to be interested in concluding such a league, which the Pope was insisting must be defensive only. What Charles Albert naturally now wanted was soldiers—and as few political commitments as possible. But to the Pope and the Grand-Duke, and to the lesser princes as well, it became clear that what would emerge, in the case of Piedmontese success, was a Kingdom of North Italy (such as did, in fact, appear for a month in the summer) which would be a threat to the independence of their states perhaps more serious than the Austrian threat, and one which would in any case upset the balance of power in Italy. The Piedmontese policy was, in fact, fatal to the federal policy for Italy. Moreover, from the Pope's point of view it was far better to depend upon the guarantee of the great Catholic powers of Europe than upon a political neighbour who was clearly looking towards the assumption of some sort of leadership in the peninsula. It was always Papal policy to try to avoid being at the mercy of any one power, and that was what seemed likely to happen if Piedmont were successful—what, of course, did happen later on, in 1859.

However, in 1848 Piedmont failed; Charles Albert was defeated by the Austrians at Custozza on July 25th, and signed an armistice on August 19th. And the immediate effect of his defeat was to cause a swing of opinion in Italy away from the Piedmontese king, now called "the traitor", and to strengthen the extremists, the Mazzinian republicans. The reaction of sentiment was especially strong in Rome. The armies of Durando and Ferrari had accomplished little; Ferrari had been defeated at Cornuda, while operating on the flank of the Austrians, trying to cut their communications, and Durando, who had occupied Vicenza, lost that city on June 10th in an engagement which had a direct bearing upon the Austrian victory at Custozza in the following month. It was a sorry business; the volunteers blamed the Papal regulars, the regulars blamed the volunteers, and everybody felt that the Pope's refusal to declare war had taken the heart out of the matter. They poured back into Rome, disillusioned men who had tasted violence, the material of which revolutions are made. And was not all this what Mazzini had predicted when, for so many years, he had urged Italians not to put their trust in princes but to work for a rising of The People and the founding of a Republic? So it seemed to the disillusioned volunteers, frustrated and furious, hanging about in the public places of Rome, under the hot August sun of 1848.

On July 14th the Austrians were back in Ferrara and what could the Pope do about it this time? On July 19th Mamiani resigned. Although his skill had saved Pius after the Allocution he had not been a success as Prime Minister. His policy was to try to separate entirely the temporal and the spiritual power in the Papal government, but in prac-

tice the setting up of parallel foreign ministries proved quite
unworkable—the great Catholic powers, in particular, were
not disposed to deal with the lay minister at Rome; their
ambassadors had always dealt with the Pope's Cardinal
Secretary of State. This was something which Palmerston's
special envoy, Lord Minto, who had been roaming around
Italy a few months earlier, giving good advice to everybody
along sound Whig lines, entirely failed to understand. He
appears to have supposed that it was just as easy for the
Pope to separate his spiritual from his temporal functions
as for Queen Victoria to do so; in this he ignored first the
primacy of the Pope's spiritual function, to which his temporal function was ancillary, and second the cosmopolitan
character of his rule.[19] Mamiani, of course, was not so
naïve as this. His immediate aim was to secure enough
authority for himself and for his government to enable it
to declare war; that was probably what he hoped to get out
of separating the foreign ministries. But this amounted to
pushing the Pope right out of the picture so far as the
Papal State was concerned, and confining him to ecclesiastical affairs—in effect the end of the Papal State as such.

Mamiani was one of those who wanted to limit the
Pope's spiritual as well as his temporal power. He made
some indiscreet remarks about its being the function of the
Pope "to pray, to bless and to pardon", which called forth
Pius' retort that it was also his duty "to bind and to loose".
Mamiani's resignation on July 19th was a relief to the Pope;
its chief cause was that he was identified with the policy
of active prosecution of the war, and since the defeat of
Piedmont it was no longer practical politics for any Italian
state to prosecute war against the Austrians.

4. The Murder of Rossi and Flight of the Pope

There was an unreality about the parliamentary and min-
isterial proceedings, in Rome, under the new constitution
of 1848. As in Paris, in the days of the Legislative Assembly

and the Convention, we have to look elsewhere than in the elected chambers for the reality of power. In any case, the Chamber of Deputies had only been elected by about one-third of the electorate, whether in Rome or in the provinces, and the electorate itself was a very restricted body. When the great day of the opening of Parliament came, less than a quorum (49 out of 100 deputies) turned up, an astonishing fact considering the Italian zest for an occasion. The whole situation in Mamiani's time was artificial; neither the Pope nor his ministers nor the deputies had any notion how this newfangled machinery (evolved over centuries in foreign countries) should be worked; they showed, not unnaturally, little sense of mutual responsibility. The effective power now rested on the one hand with the Pope, on the other with the political clubs, and which would win depended upon which could control the populace, and in particular which had the support of the new Civic Guard.

When Mamiani, on July 19th, resigned his impossible task, Pio Nono sought the help of another layman and sometime revolutionary, Count Fabbri. Like Mamiani, Fabbri enjoyed the support of the liberals and even of the republicans. He had been imprisoned and also exiled under Gregory; nevertheless his experience amongst the liberals disillusioned him. "The Chamber, the philosophers, the extremists, the obscurantists, the job-hunters and the high-command-hunters are the heroes of Italian liberty." He described himself as "a useless part of an entirely useless ministry", and he was thankful to go when Pius at last came to the conclusion that the only thing to do was to appoint as premier the one strong and able man in Rome. That man was Count Pellegrino Rossi. Pius called him to power on September 16th. He would have called him sooner if he had been more acceptable to the Chamber.

Rossi was yet another revolutionary—the fourth whom Pius had called to power since granting the Constitution in March. His career was one of the most extraordinary in nineteenth-century Europe. A Tuscan by birth, in 1815 he had been exiled for supporting Murat's attempt, in that year, to revive the Napoleonic Kingdom of Italy. He had fled to Switzerland, become a professor, taken a leading part in Swiss politics, and then, after losing his money, taken a Chair at Paris. There he had quickly become prominent in politics; he was soon a member of the Chamber of Peers and a close friend of Guizot. In 1846 Guizot sent him to Rome, as French ambassador, and at Rome, despite his reputation as a free-thinker, and his marriage to a Protestant wife, he became an intimate friend of Pio Nono. When the revolution occurred in Paris in February, 1848, Rossi ceased to be French ambassador. But he had remained in Rome as the friend of the Pope and he was the most astute political observer in Italy.

Rossi was a realist. Contemptuous alike of the demagogues in the clubs and of the politicians in the chambers he determined to take the necessary practical measures to save the Papal State, which was falling into chaos. The most urgent need was to enforce order. To secure order Rossi placed the disorganised and defeated Papal army under a veteran of the Napoleonic wars, Zucchi. Zucchi had taken part in the 1831 uprisings in the Romagna against Pius' predecessor, but in his new job he was efficient, loyal and firm, and he had no hesitation in ordering Garibaldi and his volunteers out of Bologna, whither they had wandered after their participation in Charles Albert's defeat by the Austrians. By disarming all who were not members of the Civic Guard Zucchi did something to restore order; but this move was not calculated to make him popular. Nor was the Napoleonic discipline which he insisted upon in the army.

Something, too, had to be done immediately about finance. The unofficial war, though it had only kept 9,000 Papal regulars under arms, had been a serious burden upon the state, and inflation was developing. Rossi persuaded the Pope to raise a "forced loan" of twenty-one million francs from the Church, and used it to pay interest upon a larger loan raised on Rothschild in Paris; the incidence of this levy was assessed in proportion to the value of Church properties, and it anticipated the method employed a few months later by Mazzini in raising money for his Roman Republic.

Confusion was not confined to Rome; the future of all
the Italian states was in the melting-pot, and so was the
future of Italy. But Rossi had a policy for Italy as well as
for Rome—Pio Nono's and Gioberti's policy of a league as
a step towards a form of federation; and he wanted the
Pope to be president. The Piedmontese government, however, never enthusiastic about the idea, had become still
cooler when the central Italian states had sent little support
for the war, and when Charles Albert had been able, for a
brief month, in the summer, to create a Kingdom of North
Italy of his own. Then had come the defeat of Custozza in
July, and the armistice in August, and with Gioberti now
in the government, Turin turned once more towards Rome,
seeing more clearly the advantages of some form of political association amongst the Italian states. The liberal-
minded religious philosopher, Antonio Rosmini, was sent
to Rome to explore possibilities, and he took with him his
own scheme, which was Giobertian; he wanted a permanent Italian confederation, based upon Rome. There was
much hope on all sides; but unfortunately, at the critical
moment (October) the war party once more won power at
Turin and the difficulties became insuperable because the
new government was determined not upon federation but
upon an offensive alliance against Austria,[20] with which the
Pope would have nothing to do; she also demanded a
guarantee from the other Italian states of another "Kingdom of North Italy" under the House of Savoy. Rome and
Florence were equally irritated by this; it was, indeed, a
little absurd, because they were being asked to guarantee a
hypothetical new state against Austria, although, militarily
speaking, they would have been powerless to defend it. In
return the Papal State and Tuscany were to be guaranteed
by Turin; but Rome preferred the protection of the great
powers of Europe to that of a close neighbour with a keen
appetite for aggrandisement. Rosmini resigned his mission
rather than pursue the policies of Turin, and he remained
at Rome. Rossi denounced the attitude of the Piedmontese
Government; history, he said, would blame them for their
avidity and their failure to form an Italian federation.[21]
It was at this moment that the "neo-Guelf"[22] answer to

the Italian problem lost its best chance of becoming the working programme. There were many, including Napoleon III, who were going to try to revive the idea as late as the 'sixties; but the best opportunity to create a federal Italy under the Pope disappeared in October, 1848. It had been lost partly because the Pope steadily refused to be put into a position in which he would have to take the initiative in driving out the Austrians (he thought that Lombardy-Venetia might either be left out for the time being, or else admitted while still under Austrian rule—in the same way that Austria lay within the Germanic confederation, yet at the same time was the centre of a distinct empire). It had been lost also because Turin demanded a kingdom in the north which could never be part of a federation, but must dominate the whole peninsula. Every other Italian state felt apprehensive about these claims, and this apprehension must be accounted the principal reason why no practical steps were taken at this time to implement a programme which answered to the highest aspirations of intelligent Italians. Had Rossi been able, as he and the Pope both hoped and intended, to proclaim from Rome the summoning of a Constituent Assembly, comprising official representatives of the Italian states, to draw up the constitution of the new Italian Confederation, it is possible that the ground would have been cut from under the feet of the revolutionary republican "fusionist" party of Mazzini, and that Pio Nono would never have been forced to flee from Rome. And it is probable that at this juncture such a solution to Italy's problem would have met with a wider measure of political support than any other, because neither Mazzini's extremist programme nor the hegemony of Piedmont was widely popular in the country as a whole. At all events, it was Rossi's failure to secure a viable Italian policy that was the real cause first of his murder in November, next of Pio Nono's flight, with the temporary triumph of Mazzini, and ultimately of the swallowing up of the whole peninsula by Turin and the House of Savoy.

Rossi was proud, and aloof, and he was inclined to be sarcastic. These attributes earned him enemies in all parties, but they have not been uncommon amongst successful statesmen, and they need not have led to his dramatic death. He was killed because his very presence thwarted the aims of the democratic extremists who by now were working to gain complete control in Rome. If he had been allowed to remain in power it would have meant the end of the ambitions of the popular leaders in the Roman clubs, and of the Mazzinian republicans throughout Italy with their goal of total fusion of the whole peninsula into a unitary state under the banner of "God and the People"—or sometimes just the People. It is to these extremists, whom we may now conveniently call the democrats, that we must turn to understand the next phase at Rome.

They had grown greatly in strength as a result of the failure of the war against Austria and the decline in Pio Nono's popularity. The brains of the party, in Rome, belonged to Dr. Pietro Sterbini, a medical student turned revolutionary. Exiled after the uprising of 1831, Sterbini had fled to Marseilles, where he became an agent of Mazzini in the *Young Italy* society. In 1846 he availed himself of Pio Nono's amnesty and returned to Rome; once there he worked first in the support of the Pope then in apparent support but actual antagonism to accomplish his revolutionary purposes. His influence would appear to have been greater than that of any other of the democrats in Rome and it was generally considered, in his own party, that it was he who organised the murder of Rossi. He was editor of the *Contemporaneo*, the most powerful of the popular newspapers. He was a member, in 1847, of the most important of the political clubs, the *Circolo Romano*; and in 1848 he was the leading figure in the yet more radical and powerful Club, the *Circolo Popolare*. But perhaps his chief means of influence was his ascendancy over the rotund mob-leader, Angelo Brunetti, who was always known as Ciceruacchio—a popular uneducated wine-carter of the Trastevere quarter of Rome. Ciceruacchio, like Sterbini, was a member of Mazzini's *Young Italy*, and had been since 1833. And it was Ciceruacchio's son, recently back from the Austrian wars, who struck the blow that killed Rossi.

There were other colourful democrats—for example Carlo

Bonaparte, son of Napoleon's brother Lucien, who had been given a villa at Frascati by Pope Pius VII, and created Prince of Canino; he was a revolutionary of the type of Philippe Égalité, embracing atheism and republicanism, and dabbling in most of the current fads, while retaining a social position in Rome. Like his cousin, Prince Jerome, he specialised in the ridicule of the Church. And there was Mazzini's personal friend, Galletti, whom Pio Nono was forced to accept as premier after Rossi was murdered. But the real leaders were Sterbini and Ciceruacchio, and the revolution was their work. How did they accomplish it?

Chiefly by the intriguing device, well-known to school-boys in the classroom, of caricaturing demonstrations of gratitude and overdoing occasions of festivity. The sponta-neous enthusiasm which greeted the amnesty, at the outset of the reign, and which was followed by so many pilgrimages of thanks to the Quirinal was genuine enough at first but it was soon seen that these occasions afforded a magnificent opportunity for demonstrating the desires of the populace. Thus advantage was taken, as early as the Pope's Press Law of March 15th, '47 (which was considered insufficiently generous) to insert requests into the popular cries; "Viva Pio Nono *solo*", they sang, under cheer-leaders organised by Ciceruacchio; and by *solo* they meant without the reaction-ary Gregorian cardinals who were supposed to be keeping the brake on the Pope. By the end of April, '47, "banquets", like those which were used to bring pressure upon Louis Philippe in Paris, were being organised by Ciceruacchio and Sterbini to give the opportunity for inflammatory speech making—not, of course, attacking the Pope, but extolling the glories of ancient Rome, of freedom, of civic virtue, of Dante, of the French Revolution, of Italy.

By the end of June, '47, the tone of the public demon-strations had become ominous; the mob leaders were determined at that time to win the Civic Guard, and Pio Nono was already beginning to be disillusioned and de-pressed. It was just a year after his accession. His great popularity in Rome was beginning to fail (in Italy and Europe this did not happen till after his veto upon the war in April, '48). Lützow, the Austrian ambassador, noted that he was looking ill: "People who had not seen him for some time thought him ten years older. He is growing very grey now, though he had no grey hairs at the time of his election."

A crisis was reached at the end of the year '47 in the matter of these demonstrations. On Pio Nono's birthday, December 27th, Ciceruacchio took advantage of the occasion to present thirty-five miscellaneous demands. They included some liberties which had already been granted, like liberty of the Press, and others which had already been recently referred by Pius to commissions of his newly formed *Consulta*. Others, like "the imposing on the priests and religious corporations of what is due to Pius IX and to the Church, namely love and respect" were merely insolent and quite out of place. As a birthday present, at the end of a year of ceaseless reforming activity unparalleled in the history of the Papacy, Pius found the document disappointing. He therefore decided that the giant demonstrations which the clubs were organising for New Year's Day should be called off. Troops were confined to barracks, the officers of the Civic Guard were kept at their quarters, and the *Carabinieri* were free peacefully to invite the groups that formed to disperse, while passing the word through the cafés that the Pope was not well enough to receive demonstrations. All this worked out smoothly enough; but, characteristically, Pio Nono was upset to discover that hundreds of people, who were still fanatically devoted to him, had been hurt by the implication that they had intended something more than a demonstration of gratitude and goodwill. So, though he was far from well, he decided to drive out through the streets the next afternoon. By the time he reached the Corso, from the Quirinal, his carriage was stopped and he was surrounded by a vast cheering throng. Overcome by the demonstrations the Pope began to feel faint, and when the word went round that he was unwell there was dead silence. When he was back in the Quirinal the crowd stood in pouring rain in the piazza, waiting for the benediction that never came; Pio Nono was, indeed, overcome. He had detected the note of menace

behind the enthusiasm—Ciceruacchio following his carriage
with a large banner, "Justice, Holy Father, for your people
which is on your side"; cries of "Down with the Police" and
"Death to the Jesuits" mingling with the Vivas; fanatical
faces, in the poor Trastevere quarter, staring into his carriage, staring their fear that he, the hero of the populace,
was weakening.

This dangerous mob pressure (to give it its true name)
increased monthly during the year 1848. Disappointment
because the Pope would not lead the war, frustration and
job-hunting in the Assembly, volunteers and regulars re-
turning from their dismal failure, the inevitable notion that
the "people" had been "tricked"—cheated of an utopian
social transformation by the Jesuits—combined to make the
clubs all powerful and opened the way to Mazzini. Only
Rossi remained in the way, but Rossi was formidable. As a
realistic statesman he might have proved that he had no
rival in the Italian Risorgimento save Cavour. It is true
that, when he went to confront the Chamber on the day
of his murder, November 15th, he had scarcely a friend
there; but how many times, a little later, did not Cavour
find himself in nearly the same position confronting the
Chamber at Turin, and get away with it? It was the opinion
of shrewd judges in Rome that Rossi would win through.
Ability and knowledge, coupled with rhetoric, could achieve
in the artificial democratic governments of '48 and '49, in
Italy as in France and Germany, successes unimaginable
in the traditional party system of England. Sterbini and
Ciceruacchio appreciated the danger; so they planned his
murder and they carried it through.[23]

To understand the situation one has to remember that
Mazzinian schemes for the summoning of popular constituent assemblies to unite Italy on a democratic basis were
being implemented elsewhere in the autumn of '48. This
was the result of disillusionment with "Charles Albert's
war" and the existence everywhere of resentful disbanded
volunteers. Florence, under the guidance of Montanelli,
was taking the lead, and when the extremist Guerrazzi won
power there, at the end of October, it meant that the democratic programme for Italian unification had acquired

official backing in Tuscany. If Rossi's plans for preserving the princes and federating the existing constitutional governments were allowed to prevail at Rome the popular uprising everywhere would be checked.

Rossi was a brave man, and though he knew very well that plots were afoot against him, and though he was particularly warned, from two different sources, not to attend the opening of the Chamber at the Palace of the Cancellaria on November 15th, it does not seem to have occurred to him to take very careful precautions. In the piazza outside the palace he had placed a few Carabinieri; the Civic Guard was present in fairly large numbers in the piazza, and in smaller numbers within the palace courtyard. At the request of the President of the Chamber no Carabinieri were brought inside the courtyard; probably Rossi had complied with the President's wishes in this matter in order to avoid any impression that he was trying to overawe the Assembly. As Rossi's coach clattered into the courtyard and stood still, the crowd became silent. Two lines were then formed flanking the way to the steps up to the Council Chamber; the men who thus formed a "guard of honour" were some fifty *reduci*, returned volunteers from Lombardy, armed with daggers. As he walked forward there were cries of *Abbasso Rossi! Morte a Rossi!* and as he set foot on the steps one man struck him, and then, as he turned, another, Luigi Brunetti, Ciceruacchio's son, drove his blade into his throat, while the rest shielded him with their cloaks. Within half an hour Rossi was dead. No attempt seems to have been made to try to make an arrest. No resolution was passed by the assembled Chamber which, indeed, dissolved soon afterwards because there wasn't a quorum. Later, Garibaldi, in his autobiography, was prepared to justify the crime.[24] The populace began to fraternise with the Carabinieri; it was clear that this was the beginning of a revolution that had been carefully planned. A gang of *Reduci*, members of the *Circolo Popolare*, and Carabinieri marched about shouting "Blessed be the hand that stabbed Rossi" and finally ended up under the windows of his widow, where they mockingly intoned the psalm *Miserere*.

Such was the triumph of the democrats. From now on all decent moderate reformers, men like Pasolini, whom we have met, and the historian Farini were estranged from the leaders of the movement.[25]

Pio Nono, though stunned by Rossi's murder, reacted quickly. He conferred the office of premier upon a young minister, Montanari; then he summoned his two friends, Pasolini and Minghetti, and after that the whole cabinet. But by midnight he was without a government; his cabinet had all resigned on discovering that the Carabinieri and the soldiers were both siding with the revolution. Not for the first time Pio Nono pointed out to his ministers—"you are always all right, you can always resign; but I have to carry on the government".

Rome that night was without a government, but Sterbini was taking over control. The Clubs were planning a giant demonstration for the next morning, when they were to demand the summoning of a Constituent Assembly to Rome, the proclamation of Italian nationality, authority for the Chamber to declare war, separation of the spiritual and temporal powers—i.e. the end of the Papal State and the adoption of Mazzini's programme.

The Pope had no intention of agreeing. Anticipating the demonstrations, he summoned representatives from the Chamber and the High Council to be with him by 7.45 in the morning; amongst them were Pasolini and Sterbini. When they were assembled the proceedings were almost disrupted by the Pope's indignation at their attitude towards Rossi's murder; Mgr. Muzzarelli horrified him by saying it was of little consequence. All refused to serve in a new ministry. Once the Pope said he would "give up the whole thing and go away"; later, reminded of the ruin he would bring on many, he said, "We will stay, and await the thunders from Heaven." Only two cardinals were with him that day; one was Antonelli who then, and on the following days, showed such great loyalty as the Pope never forgot. But the ambassadors of the Catholic powers called; the Spanish ambassador took the lead in bringing to the Pope the support, at this terrible time, of the Catholic world.

The representatives returned to the Chambers where
Galletti, who had been Chief of Police under Mamiani,
was chosen as premier. Galletti, we have seen, was an old
rebel, who had been exiled, and had returned with Pio
Nono's amnesty. He was a member of Mazzini's *Young
Italy*, and of all the democrats at Rome was the one who
was most closely in touch with and personally congenial to
the Chief of the Society. But he was also not entirely unacceptable to Pius who had granted him an interview, after
his amnesty, when he wanted to express his gratitude. The
Pope agreed now to send for him; but in the meantime a
vast crowd was on its way up to the Quirinal, the Civic
Guard and the Carabinieri had thrown in their lot with
the crowd, the Papal troops were fraternising. Inside the
palace there were only a hundred Swiss Guards, and Pio
Nono was walking up and down, calm, even serene, but
entirely deserted except by the foreign ambassadors and a
few servants.

The crowd brought the four demands already mentioned,
and Galletti was compelled to act as their mouthpiece. The
Pope was obdurate. To yield would be to be reduced to
impotence, to be allowed only "to pray and to bless", the
status, as he saw it, of the Patriarch of Constantinople. He
preferred martyrdom.

It looked as though he would get it. When Galletti,
standing on the platform used by Pius to bless the crowd,
tried to persuade them that the Pope could not yield to
force they rushed off to arm themselves. In an hour there
were some six thousand armed men in the piazza. Within
the palace were the hundred Swiss, and the ambassadors
of France, Spain, Bavaria, Portugal, Russia, Holland,
Brazil, Belgium and Prussia, Cardinal Antonelli, and a few
priests and courtiers. Soon bullets were penetrating into
Pius' ante-room, and a bishop, Palma, was shot dead at his
window. Then the Civic Guard brought up a field gun.
By eight o'clock Pius had made his formal protest to the
ambassadors: "I protest before you all against the force
which is being used towards me; and I wish to say that
do what they will, I do not consent." When they had
formally accepted the protest and departed he received

Galletti. In the end he accepted a cabinet which included Mamiani, Galletti, and Sterbini; but as regards the four demands he would only consent that they should be discussed in the Chamber, thus postponing the matter. The crowd regarded their victory as complete and departed. The next day they secured the disbanding of the Swiss Guards and installed the Civic Guard in the Quirinal. Pio Nono was now a prisoner, the only question left was whether he could escape. For the next few days Rome was ruled by a "Committee of Public Safety" comprising Sterbini and two others.

The Pope had remained calm and even decided in his behaviour on November 15th and 16th. After that he was watched over all the time by the Civic Guards; Pasolini, whose offer to stay at the Quirinal he declined, reported him as profoundly discouraged. Antonelli, though he was likely to get short shrift from the mob, always comforted him and counselled firmness. But it had become useless and indeed harmful for the Pope to stay at Rome. He could no longer protect his friends and supporters, which had been his main reason for staying, and he would soon be compelled to put his signature to the four-point programme, which his conscience would not allow.

The plot for his escape, an enterprise as hazardous as that undertaken by Louis XVI, was planned with care and executed with skill. The organiser was the Bavarian ambassador, Charles de Spaur, and the confidant within the Quirinal was Pius' valet, Filippani. Spaur was to take the Pope to Gaeta, whence a Spanish ship would take him to the Balearic Isles if he wished. On November 24th, the French ambassador, the duc d'Harcourt, who was in the plot, visited the Pope and spent some time reading out news, in a loud voice, behind closed doors in the library of audience, while the Pope in reality was being dressed by Filippani in the clothes of a simple priest. Filippani then conducted Pius down a secret passage but encountered a locked door and took some time going to find the key while the Pope remained alone, on his knees, in prayer. When they reached the courtyard they stepped into a waiting carriage and drove to the Church of SS. Pietro e Mar-

cellino, where Spaur replaced Filippani. Thence they drove
out past St. John Lateran and through the Lateran gate—
where Spaur had to answer a challenge—and made for the
Alban hills where the Countess Spaur and her son and a
monk, Liebel, were waiting. At Aricia the Countess Spaur
and her son, in a large Berlin coach, joined the Count and
the Pope, whom they found chatting with an unsuspecting
group of Carabinieri. So the journey was completed in the
Berlin, with the Count and a servant up beside the driver,
and inside the Pope and the Countess, with opposite them
the monk and the boy. The Pope first disclosed that he
carried on his person the Blessed Sacrament in the very
ciborium which Pius VI used when carried captive by
Napoleon into France; he had to restrain the others from
immediately falling on their knees. Later he entertained
them with an account of his flight from the Vatican, and
of how the good ambassador of France, d'Harcourt, after
reading loudly for a long time to an empty room, had left
saying that the Pope was feeling tired and did not wish to
be disturbed.

Arrived at Gaeta, Pio Nono and his friends—he had now
been joined by Cardinal Antonelli—had to find accommodation at a second-class hotel, the *Giardinetto*, where only
the Pope had a room to himself; Count Spaur had already
left them, to take word to King Ferdinand at Naples.
Antonelli—disguised—went off with his companion, Arnau,
to see the governor of the castle, a soldier of German origin
called Gross; when they announced to him the arrival of
the Bavarian ambassador, with family and suite, Gross
spoke to them in German and neither of them could reply!
—nor was Gross disposed to accept Arnau's explanation that
it was so long since he had lived in Germany that he had
forgotten the language. (This was, perhaps, the only occasion when Antonelli was nonplussed in diplomatic conversation!) The *Giardinetto*, with its occupants, was put under
police observation; but the next day King Ferdinand and
his suite arrived in three boats from Naples. The King was
a magnificent host, and he was determined to surpass himself for the Pope. In the end, rejecting offers of asylum
which had already come in from Spain, from France, from

Malta, even from England, Pio Nono decided to remain at the royal palace at Gaeta, so as to be as closely in touch as possible with Rome, and to avoid the political embarrassments which might arise from his accepting the hospitality of one of the great Catholic powers—or of a Protestant Queen. With the arrival at Gaeta of d'Harcourt, a few hours after Ferdinand, in a boat from Civita Vecchia, bringing with him some of Pius' faithful companions, together with his luggage, it was possible to proceed with the temporary arrangements for the Pope's sojourn.

The secret flight of the Pope, discovered next morning, left Rome dazed and bewildered. He had left a note; but it only instructed the minister Sacchetti to tell Galletti to arrange for the safeguarding of the Quirinal and the Vatican, and especially the staffs employed there, and to keep order in the city. It stressed that his personal household were ignorant of his plan to escape. A few days later a further instruction came from Pius and was duly posted on the walls. It explained that the Pope had been compelled, by the excesses of the revolutionaries, to withdraw himself, for the time being, from Rome, in order to be able freely to perform the duties of his pontificate; it placed the Government in the hands of Cardinal Castracane and six others, five of them laymen, and one of them the ex-revolutionary General Zucchi. But unfortunately Zucchi, and two of the others, were not at Rome, and decided, on receiving the instruction, to go to Gaeta to discuss matters. Cardinal Castracane was powerless, and, in fact, did nothing. The premier whom the Pope had been compelled to accept, Galletti, remained in office with his ministry, refused to recognise the legality of Castracane's position, and sent a deputation to Gaeta to persuade the Pope to return; this deputation was not received. In the increasing confusion, and with the departure of many of the more moderate men from Rome, disgusted by the antics of Ciceruacchio, Sterbini, and the Bonaparte Prince of Canino, a Junta was set up on December 12th, which consisted of Galletti and two others. On December 29th this Junta published a decree calling a Roman Constituent Assembly, to be elected by direct and universal suffrage, comprising two hundred members, to meet at Rome on February 5th. This was the end of the attempt to compromise with the Pope about the Temporal Power. The Junta explained that:

"the Supreme Law of the public good requires the Nation to be assembled, in order that by means of a correct and universal representation, armed with absolute power, it may declare its will, and take all needful measures . . . for settling the form in which to give a regular, complete, and stable organisation to the commonwealth, in conformity with the sentiments and tendencies of the entire population, or of its major part."[26]

Thus was put into effect the doctrine of popular sovereignty, the sovereignty of the will of the people, taught by Rousseau, and practised first by the French revolution in 1792. It was part of the dogma of Mazzini, whose party, with other sects, was now gaining control, through the clubs, in Rome. It offended the better of the moderates, Mamiani, Pasolini, Farini, who were convinced anti-democrats, even though they were equally convinced constitutionalists.[27] All except one of the governors of the provinces of the Papal State resigned; they were men who were moderates and constitutionalists like ex-premier Fabbri. Finally, any hope that the new Constituent Assembly would include others than the advanced democrats, the *esaltati*, was dispelled by the Pope. His reply to the proclamation was swift and sweeping. It was issued on January 1st.

"Within this peaceful retreat, whither it has pleased Divine Providence to lead Us, that We might be able to utter our sentiments and our decisions with freedom, We dwelt on the anticipation that our erring children would testify their remorse for the sacrileges and crimes committed against persons in our service, of whom some have been slain, others subjected to the most barbarous outrages; to say nothing of those perpetrated in our own Palace, and against our very Person. We have, however, received nothing but a bare invitation to return to our capital, without a word in condemnation of the above-

mentioned crimes, and without the smallest guarantee
to secure Us from the fraud or the violence of that same
gang of madmen which is still tyrannising, with a barbarous despotism, over Rome and the States of the
Church . . ." But now ". . . a new and more monstrous
act of undissembled treason and of sheer rebellion . . .
has filled up the measure of our affliction, and, as it will
sadden the Church at large, so likewise has kindled our
own just indignation. We herein allude to that proceeding, in every sense detestable, by which it has been pretended to proclaim the meeting of a self-styled General
National Assembly of the Roman States by a decree of
the 29th of December last, in order to establish a new
form of Government for the Pontifical dominions . . ."

". . . We are persuaded that, on receiving this shame-
less invitation, you will have been roused to an holy indignation, and you will have spurned away from you a
suggestion so criminal and scandalous. Nevertheless, in
order that no one of you may be able to plead that
he was misled by deceitful blandishments, and by the
preachers of revolutionary theories, or unaware of the
contrivances of all order, all law, all right, all true liberty,
and of your own welfare, We think fit this day once more
to raise and send abroad our Voice in such wise as to
certify you beyond all doubt of the strict inhibition We
lay upon you, of whatever class or condition, against taking any part in any meetings which may audaciously be
held for the nomination of persons to be sent to the
Assembly We have condemned. We simultaneously remind you, that this our absolute prohibition is sustained
by the Decrees of our Predecessors and of the Councils,
especially of the sacrosanct Council of Trent (Sess.
XXII. C. XI. de Reform.), wherein the Church has over
and over again fulminated her censures, and chiefly the
Greater Excommunication, to attach *ipso facto* to any
who shall dare to incur the guilt of any attack whatsoever
upon the temporal Sovereignty of the Chief Pontiffs of
Rome . . ."

But finally, ". . . while We once more aver our readiness, with the help of His almighty grace, to drain the cup of persecution even to the dregs for the defence and glory of the Catholic Church, which He for her salvation willed to be the first to drink, We will not desist from supplicating and conjuring Him to deign mercifully to hearken to the fervent prayers which, day and night, We never cease to put up to Him for the conversion and salvation of the wanderers . . ."[28]

The braver priests ran the risk of reading this Monitory from their pulpits. In places it was posted on the walls. How many it kept from the polls set up to elect the Constituent Assembly cannot be known; but obviously the earthly centre of the Catholic Church did not throw over its Catholic obedience overnight. Some amusing results were recorded; thus a very large proportion of the votes were cast for Pio Nono. The Bishop of Rieti defied the Papal ban in order to record his vote "for the return of the immortal Pius IX, our legitimate monarch, Vicar of Jesus Christ and head of the Catholic Church". Some voted for the General of the Jesuits. Some even voted for Saint Peter. But most did not vote at all. At Rome 23,000 out of 60,000 voted, but far fewer did so in the provinces. At Sinigaglia, Pio Nono's birthplace, only 200 voted, out of 27,000. That many who did not wish to vote were afraid not to visit the polls, or were bribed to do so, is suggested by the 52 blank papers found amongst the 90 votes recorded at Frascati.[29] But if the Monitory meant a considerable Catholic boycott of the Assembly it also meant that the Assembly, when it met, was bound to be hostile to the Church. Loyal Catholics as well as political moderates were going to be estranged from the new government. The way was being left open to the Mazzinians, who were already flocking into the city. It was now that the two or three priests who had espoused the democratic cause had finally to make their decision. Lamennais' friend, Fr. Ventura, submitted at once to the voice of the Church. But Mgr. Muzzarelli, who had so offended the Pope by belittling the importance of Rossi's murder, and who was a member of Galletti's government, had further burnt his boats by signing the proclamation announcing the Assembly; he stayed with his new political friends. So did Gavazzi, who later turned Protestant. The two of them exulted together publicly in the streets.

The Assembly duly met on February 5th, in the palace of the Cancellaria; 140 of the 200 members had turned up in time. Garibaldi, as well as other republicans from outside the Papal State, had been elected. The first sessions were stormy, with the Prince of Canino, Sterbini, and the republican poet Masi much in evidence, while Garibaldi was all for carrying the Republic by acclamation. It was with difficulty that Mamiani secured a hearing for his speech in favour of moderation. All this was too much for Count Pasolini; he took one look at the opening of the Assembly and then left Rome.

At two o'clock in the morning on February 9th, 1849, the Assembly voted, by 120 votes to 10, with 12 abstentions, the end of the Temporal Power of the Pope, and the establishment of a "pure democracy" to be called the Republic of Rome. On the 18th Cardinal Antonelli issued from Gaeta, on behalf of the Pope, a formal appeal to France, Austria, Spain and Naples, to intervene to restore the rule of the Supreme Pontiff. The stage for the struggle was set.

The contestants might appear to be very unevenly matched. But the Catholic powers were going to be slow and reluctant to move, and the two which effectively counted, France and Austria, were, as ever, at enmity with each other. France would never allow Austria to occupy Rome. Austria would not want to see France there. For the Pope, all would depend upon whether France were sufficiently Catholic to undertake the crusade. If not, if the Republic, newly proclaimed at Paris, proved to be anti-Catholic, like the Republic of 1793, or like this Roman Republic, what then? All, in fact, for the Pope, depended upon the Catholic revival which Montalembert, Lacordaire, and their friends in France had brought about. Would their influence force the hand of the new President, Louis Napoleon, sometime Carbonaro and revolutionary in the Papal States? Or would Napoleon choose to fight Austria, in support of the "Principles of '89", newly proclaimed at

Rome?—if so, Pio Nono's chances of restoration were slender.

And on the other side? Seemingly only a handful of second-rate demagogic politicians. What sort of a fight would Sterbini, Canino, Galletti, or Mgr. Muzzarelli show? Might not even the Neapolitan army be enough to chase them out?

But the issue was not going to be left to these men. Republicans from all over Italy were pouring in. Garibaldi was going to fetch his legion from Rieti, where, by April he had a thousand men under arms. The Polish legion of revolutionaries, which had served in Lombardy, was on its way. So was Luciano Manara, with his Lombard *Bersaglieri*. Rome was now the rallying-place of those who had volunteered to fight in the north, against the Austrians, before Charles Albert had been defeated. It was assuming the aspect later displayed by the Madrid of 1937; there were already in being the elements of an "International Brigade".

But, even when reinforced by Garibaldi, the politicans at Rome in February of '49 could never have put up the epic of resistance which has made the memory of the Roman Republic glorious. As yet Garibaldi's men were mistrusted and feared; they looked too much like soldiers of fortune. And Garibaldi himself was quite without political sense, animated only by a fanatical hatred of what he conceived to be tyranny, and of the Church. To elevate the democrats, the clubs, the sects, and the libertine mob of the Trastevere quarter into the realm of devotion and self-sacrifice a leader who lived in that loftier realm was needed, a leader who could supply a positive faith. And, as though they realised their need, the Assembly, on February 12th, conferred upon Mazzini Roman citizenship, and determined that all their laws and proclamations should be issued "in the name of God and the People" —Mazzini's motto.

Chapter Three

THE REVOLUTION
(1848–1849)

1. *Mazzini and the Dogma of the People*
2. *The Roman Republic*

1. *Mazzini and the Dogma of the People*

It was inevitable, now, that the Chief of the Democrats, who had first preached the republican faith in Italy, and had consistently maintained it, for twenty years, both in Italy and in Europe, should come to Republican Rome. The only surprising thing is that he was not there already, instead of lingering at Florence, trying to influence the Tuscan revolutionary leaders. Rome, he had always taught, would initiate the "new era": there would be a Third Rome. Now it had happened. The Pope had fled, and here was the Rome of the People. Since Pio Nono's flight to Gaeta Mazzini had waited, impatiently, for the Republic to be proclaimed. On December 5th he had written from Switzerland to a friend at Rome:

"... You can, if you will, create a well-ordered world. You have in your hands the fate of Italy, and the fate of Italy is that of the world. You do not know, oh ye forgetful people, the power exercised by the conjunction of the four letters which form the name of your city; you do not know that that which is merely a word elsewhere, when coming from Rome is a *fact*, an imperious decree—*urbi et orbe. Perdio!* Do not your monuments, your historical memories, put a single inspiration into the minds of the men who direct your affairs? ... Providence makes of a Pope a voluntary fugitive—takes every obstacle out of your path, like a mother for her child—and you, in ingratitude, remain doubtful, as if you had neither mind nor heart, nor history and sufficient experience behind you, nor a future before you—as if Italy were not in a ferment all around you, and Europe in a ferment round Italy—republican France at your side and republican Switzerland beckoning you on, and a dozen other reasons for decision—you still remain doubtful, and endeavour to govern with the help of the autograph letter about the palaces ..." [the letter left behind by Pio Nono, in which he had entrusted the protection of the Papal palaces and staff to the Minister Sacchetti.][1]

This was written in December; perhaps it helped to persuade the Junta to summon the National Constituent Assembly. There were Mazzinians at Rome, even though there was not yet Mazzini; Sterbini, Ciceruacchio, Galletti, and Masi had all been members of *Young Italy*—so had Garibaldi. And now, in February, others much more intimate with the Chief like La Cecilia, and his friend Aurelio Saffi, from Forli in the Romagna, were there and more were coming in daily. The Moderates having withdrawn, and faithful Catholics having ostracised the Assembly, it had screwed up its courage to proclaim the Republic from the Capitol, had adopted the banner God and the People, and had given Mazzini citizenship. Clearly he should delay no longer, watching and exhorting from afar. It was time for him to take the road to Rome; he entered the city on March 5th. On March 6th he was introduced by Galletti to the Assembly. He made a short speech which he concluded with these words:

". . . I trust that, please God, the stranger shall never again have to say that which to this day he oftentimes repeats in reference to our affairs, that this blaze from Rome is an *ignis fatuus*, a gleam that flits from tomb to tomb. No, the world shall see it as a star, everlasting, brilliant, pure, even as those which glow in our Italian sky."[2]

By March 29th he had been elected Triumvir, with Armellini and Aurelio Saffi. In the caustic words of the historian Farini, who had now withdrawn from the political arena, but was watching these events:

"Though the people, of course, continued Sovereign, and the Assembly was called Sovereign too, the Triumvirs were made Sovereigns over both, or rather in fact Mazzini became the Autocrat. In the end of March, then, began the absolute sway of Mazzini . . . the Roman revolution evolved a new form, or rather took on its preconceived and true form; it became incarnate in Mazzini."[3]

Strangely contrasted were the Absolute Pope, and the Absolute Democrat who replaced him. Pius, clothed in white, stoutish, benign, indulgent and reforming, careering along his liberal course regardless of Metternich's warnings, had conjured up Mazzini, clothed deliberately in black, in mourning for his country, thin, austere, with a sombre eye fixed upon his destiny, representing an opposite principle to that of the Pope, but a principle none the less.

Those who contend, as many historians have, that the issue fought out between Mazzini and Pio Nono at Rome, in 1849, was not a religious struggle, a struggle between the Church and her enemies, because it was concerned only with the political fate of the Papal State, ignore the attitude of the principal protagonists on either side in the drama. These were the Pope, with Antonelli; and Mazzini, with Garibaldi. All four men were quite clear what was at stake.

The Pope's view we have already seen. He had steadily refused to separate his spiritual from his temporal sovereignty. The States of the Church were the Patrimony of Saint Peter, the material means given to the Papacy by God to defend its spiritual independence. He never forgave Mamiani for trying, in 1848, to relegate him to the role of "praying and blessing". He was absolutely convinced of his religious duty to hand on the Patrimony, unweakened, to his successor. In his Allocution of April 20th, '49, *Quibus Quantisque*,[4] issued from Gaeta, he explicitly condemned those who made bold to pretend that the abrogation of the temporal power would serve the liberty and good of the Church—a condemnation which later became Proposition 76 of the famous Syllabus of Errors (1864).

But equally certainly Mazzini held no merely political view of the contest. The idea of the strict separation of religion from politics was always anathema to him—as though a political reawakening or revolution were not, for him, a religious manifestation governed by religious principles. He was never tired of criticising the "immorality"

of the English, in particular, for clinging to the concept of
such separation. But in any case he was quite explicit about
his purpose at Rome. Commissioned by the Roman Assembly, less than a month after he had entered it, to reply
to a message of congratulation from the new Republican
Assembly at Paris, he wrote to the French:

> "You, citizens, have understood all that is great, noble,
> and providential in this flag of regeneration floating
> above the city that encircles the Capitol and the Vatican
> —a new consecration of eternal right; a third world aris-
> ing upon the ruins of two worlds extinct . . ."[5]

The first of the two extinct worlds was the Roman Empire, the second, of course, was the Roman Church. On being chosen as First Triumvir he announced that the Roman
Republic was "to prove to Italy and to Europe that our
cry of *God and the People* is not a lie; that our work is
eminently religious, a work of education and morality
. . ."[6] A little later, when he was back in London, he made
his religious purposes at Rome very clear. It was at the end
of the following year, the year 1850, and Englishmen were
indulging in the hue and cry against the "Papal Aggression"
—the re-establishment in England, by Pio Nono, of the
Catholic hierarchy. Mazzini attended some of the protest
meetings, an ironical smile on his lips—if only some of these
prominent Englishmen, who declaimed so against the Pope,
had been willing to help him at Rome the year before!
There would have been no Papal Aggression against England if his Republic at Rome were still in being:

> "There exists great agitation at the present moment in
> Protestant England on account of the attempted en-
> croachments of Catholicism. Think you that these at-
> tempts would have taken place if the people's banner
> were still floating at Rome? Think you that the Pope
> would have sent his Catholic hierarchy from Gaeta?"
>
> ". . . Every so-called religious agitation against Papacy
> will be vain, which does not take in hand the Italian
> political question. While the Pope possesses Italy, he will

have a footing in every part of Europe. It is the Italian nation alone that can annihilate Papacy . . ."[7]

"Papacy excluded from Rome is, it is well known, Papacy excluded from Italy. Papacy excluded from Italy is Papacy excluded from Europe."

Without Mazzini's determination, which sprang from his faith, it is very doubtful whether there would have been a struggle at Rome at all, whether the French would not have brought the Pope back peacefully, as they expected to. Certainly the struggle could hardly have been protracted. Nor would the "Rome Myth" have been implanted. It was Mazzini who made the men of the risorgimento feel so mystically about Rome that they were ultimately impelled to seize Pio Nono's city for their capital in 1870.

It is necessary to understand Mazzini.

As a boy, he had extracted, from between the covers of his Missal, the text of the Mass, and had inserted in its place the *Tableau historique des progrès de l'esprit humain*, by the French *philosophe*, Condorcet. From that book, which he had read while others supposed he was following the Offertory, or the Canon, he claimed later to have acquired the notion of the inevitability of human progress. He may have done so, or he may have learnt about progress a little later, from the Saint-Simonian sect, in whom he was much interested, or from the lectures of Victor Cousin, which came to his home at Genoa. It doesn't much matter; progress, by 1830, was in the air. The peculiarity of Mazzini's conception of it was that he saw in it the evidence of God's working in Humanity. Humanity was the interpreter of God's Law, and God's Law was Progress.

His broad view of Progress was that the Greeks had introduced Liberty, Christianity had introduced Equality, and Catholic unity had introduced the idea of the oneness of humanity. The Mission of Catholicism had been accomplished by the time of the Reformation, that of Protestantism by the time of the French Revolution. The French Revolution had been the supreme affirmation of the free individual human spirit. Napoleon, Goethe, and Byron were the last and greatest exponents of the Religion of the Individual. The Faith of the Future was a collective

faith in the destiny of Peoples, freely united as Nations—
and, of course, of Italy in particular.

There was nothing original in all this, it was derived
from his reading—from Herder and Lessing, Cousin and
Guizot, Foscolo, Alfieri, Manzoni, and the romantic poets,
especially the French. What was important about it was
that it was a fair synthesis of the ideas of the post-
revolutionary Europe of his youth. But as faith generally
springs first from experience, rather than from reading, so
Mazzini's feeling for republicanism was born at his home
in Genoa. His mother was a Jansenist, and Jansenism in
northern Italy was more Calvinist than it was in France,
and thus, in spirit, if not always in policy, more republican.[8]
In 1821, when he was sixteen years old, he had witnessed,
in the street, the return of the defeated revolutionaries
of the Carbonari uprising of that year. Genoa, a free republic with a glorious history, was sullen at her forced unification, in 1815, with Piedmont, which placed her under
the kings of the House of Savoy. Hence Mazzini's life-long
mistrust of that Royal House, and of its dynastic ambitions.

Niccolò Tommaseo, the Liberal-Catholic friend of Gioberti, had visited Mazzini when he was in exile in Switzerland in 1834. Mazzini reports that:

". . . he talked religion to me, and politics—Christianity à la Manzoni. Christianity is dying for me: Catholicism is dead. I told him so straight . . . he asked me
what I wanted to put in its place. I told him it was not
my role, nor that of any individual to do that, but rather
of the first people which would or could constitute itself, in practice, the revealer of the moral law."[9]

And that new moral law—no less—was what he hoped
would emerge from the Roman Republic. He had been
nursing Italy for this supreme role of Prophet-People. He
believed, at Rome, in 1849, that the hour might have
struck. His supreme happiness would have been to have
carried down the Tablets of the New Law from the Capitol
to the Assembly, gathered in awe in the *Cancelleria*.

But meanwhile he had to recognise that there were other
possible Prophet-Peoples, besides the Italians. The heroic

Poles, for example, with their religious poet Mickiewicz, who had appealed to him strongly, as he had likewise appealed to Montalembert and to Lamennais. He read Montalembert's French translation of Mickiewicz's *Book of the Polish Pilgrim:*

"By the wounds, tears and sufferings of all the Polish
        prisoners, exiles and pilgrims,
            Deliver us, oh Lord.
For a universal war for the freedom of the nations,
        We beseech Thee, oh Lord."[10]

This he found magnificent—perhaps as good as Lamennais' *Paroles d'un Croyant,* which it inspired. "It is written," he says, "in the same style—less vigorous, but perhaps possessed of other qualities of equal value. Lamennais is inclined to imitate the prophets; the other rather the New Testament."[11] However, he turned from Mickiewicz to Lamennais. Mickiewicz is "a great poet and an excellent man, but exclusively Polish and does not concern himself, and would never concern himself except for his own country . . ." But he was wrong. In 1848 Mickiewicz founded his Legion, at Rome, to fight for oppressed peoples—the first twelve volunteers received from the poet crucifixes that had been given to him by Pio Nono. In the summer Mickiewicz led them to the war in Lombardy, and in the following year the Legion (though not its founder) was back at Rome fighting for Mazzini.

Mazzini always attributed to their innate Catholicism the failure of his revolutionary friends to embrace his full religious faith in "The People". He was right. There was an interesting gradation in the matter. If we place at the top the liberal Pio Nono of 1847, with his desire for a fuller and freer life for The People, but with naturally no tolerance of any departure from Catholic obedience, we may place next the ardent liberals of the type of Lacordaire in France, or Fr. Ventura in Italy, who were willing enough to sympathise and co-operate with revolutionaries but absolutely unwilling to consider disobedience to religious superiors. Thus Ventura, the close friend of Pio Nono, but also of the Roman revolutionaries, rejected the advances

which the Roman Constituent Assembly made to him.
With Lamennais we move a step further. The friend, always, of Ventura, as once of Lacordaire, he is prepared to
disobey, he ceases to say Mass, and he loses his faith; yet
the fundamentals of Catholic teaching on the nature of
man, and of God, do not leave him; he does not attack
these things, he knows what sin is, he cannot become a
disciple of Rousseau. Gioberti, likewise, is driven, in the
end, to virtual separation from the Church in his time, at
bottom because of his political programme; but his Catholic training and thought prevented his ever being in danger
of becoming a Mazzinian. It was a persistent delusion of
Mazzini's that he could win over the priests. When Lamennais had been censured in *Mirari vos* Mazzini made an appeal to the priests to join him, in his article *Sull Enciclica
di Gregory XVI*;[12] and a little later he did so more vehemently in his *patrioti e il clero*.[13] He was singularly unsuccessful. The hot-headed Barnabite, Fr. Gavazzi, who
turned "Protestant", and the crude Mgr. Muzzarelli, who
danced with him in the streets of Rome, and a handful
of others, were a slender and not an encouraging harvest.
It was not that the clergy were conservative by inclination;
in Naples, particularly, they were the soul of revolution and
perfectly prepared to help Garibaldi to throw out the Bourbons a little later on. It was simply that they were Catholic, that Mazzini's religion made no appeal, and that, so
far as Rome and the Papal State were concerned, they were
quite sure that those lands belonged inalienably to the
Church.

Mazzini had immense hopes of Lamennais. He called
him "Our Saint". He was to be the Luther of the Nineteenth Century. A young Mazzinian, Paolo Pallia, translated the *Paroles d'un Croyant* into Italian, and the Chief
of *Young Italy* kept in correspondence with the Breton
priest. But the Catholic concepts to which Lamennais clung
—Original Sin, the Fall, one Revelation and Redemption in
Christ—did not harmonise well with the Mazzinian dogmas
of Progress and Humanity. Nor did Lamennais approve of
Mazzini's attacks on the Papacy. The Italian was surprised
and shocked by this. He assured the Breton:

"The condemnation of the Papacy is decreed, not by us,
but by God; by God who now calls upon the People to
arise and found a new unity, embracing the two spheres
of temporal and spiritual power . . . In our epoch humanity will forsake the Pope, and have recourse to a
General Council of the Church—that is to say, of all believers—a council which will be alike Council of the
Church and Constituent Assembly . . ."[14]

Constituent Assembly. That was what a Constituent Assembly meant to Mazzini—no mere constitution-mongering
body, but a General Council, capable of giving birth to a
new faith, a Declaration, not this time only of the Rights
of Man, as in 1789, but of the Duties of Man as well.
How, he asked, could a Constituent Assembly, held at
Rome, mean less than this?

Mazzini had tried to interest Lamennais in calling an
"Oecumenical Council of Precursors of the New Religion".[15] Then, in 1846, they tried together to establish a
European Democratic Committee, which was intended to
give moral and political guidance to revolutionary movements throughout Europe. On this committee Lamennais
was the French delegate and Mazzini the Italian. After the
collapse of Mazzini's Roman Republic in 1849 Lamennais
organised a separate Franco-Italian-Iberian society to work
for the regeneration of France, Italy, and Spain under
the leadership of France. Mazzini was very offended. Lamennais was equally offended by Mazzini's association with
the French republican leader Ledru Rollin, upon whom the
Italian counted for support for his Roman Republic.

Mazzini was deeply disappointed in Lamennais. The in-
tensity of his interest in the abbé glows in his articles on
him for the English periodicals, in his letters to his mother,
in which he copied out nearly the whole of the Breton's
Affaires de Rome and his *Livre du Peuple*. He could not
recognise that, actually, Lamennais was watching the cult
of the liberal Papa Angelica, in '47 and '48, with a good
deal more interest and sympathy than he felt towards himself or his followers. Always Mazzini hoped that the priest's
dramatic apostasy would lead him to a New Revelation.

He had, however, to fall back in the end upon a judgment he had himself made earlier:

"Lamennais is a priest, and a priest who has been devoted during half his life to Catholicism, to the Papacy. It must have cost him much to destroy his idol. If his strength had not been exhausted by that effort Lamennais would have been led by the force of his logic and of his instincts to deny the divinity of Christ and thus to bring back Christ into Humanity, and not Humanity into Him; that is the first approach to the Faith of Humanity, in which I believe."[16]

Nowhere more clearly than in this letter did Mazzini define the heart of the difference between his own revolutionary faith, with its Saint-Simonian, Carbonari, and Masonic origins and allies, and the Christian revolutionary faith of the Liberal-Catholics of his generation. Is it important? It was of paramount importance to him, as it was of paramount importance to Pio Nono. Mazzini intended, himself, to expound some day the Faith of Humanity, but on one of his journeys across the Alps he lost the journal in which he had made his notes on the subject. Perhaps it may yet be found. In any case there is enough religion in the hundred and six volumes of his writings which have hitherto been published to enable the printing of a fairsized Testament. It would be found to correspond most closely with the teachings of the French prophet, Pierre Leroux, who, in his *Encyclopédie Nouvelle* (1836–43), accomplished the Mazzinian dream of interpreting life and history in accordance with the principles of progress and humanity.[17]

A last consideration, on the ideological plane, about Mazzini is important to our subject: his relations with Gioberti. Gioberti, foremost of Italian Liberal-Catholics, was having his practical chance, as premier of Piedmont, just after the Pope's flight to Gaeta; in December, that is, of 1848, and January and February of 1849. Mazzini was to have his, as Dictator of Rome, in the following spring and summer.

At one time Gioberti and Mazzini had worked together.

A letter from the one to the other had been published in *Young Italy*:

> "Compare the Pope [Gregory XVI] and Christ", Gioberti had written, "and when you have completed the comparison and have made clear the gulf which lies between them, between the sublime redeemer of the human race and that miserable oppressor of the peoples . . . then welcome warmly true and lively Christianity, enlighten it, explain it, . . . so that none may confuse it with that religion of servitude and barbarity which reigns today."[18]

Encouraged, Mazzini had appealed to Gioberti to "write a catechism for the people; a republican catechism, an Italian catechism, in which religion is united with risorgimento . . ." Gioberti promised to consider the matter. But what he produced was his great *Primato—The Primacy of the Italians in their Civilisation*—"The most beautiful subject that I know," commented Mazzini, only "he has filled it with ultra-Roman-Catholicism, eulogies of Charles Albert, and all possible stupidities."[19] Gioberti admitted that his ideas had changed, but retorted, in his *Rinnovamento civile d'Italia* (1851), that, "Since a man who has only one idea cannot vary, it is not to be wondered at that Mazzini is fixed in his thought and has that constancy concerning chimeras which simple people admire, but which wise people call *obstinacy*."

Gioberti had a venomous pen. His religious thought was a good deal closer to Lamennais than to Mazzini, but he hated in the Breton what he had come to hate in Mazzini, namely his exaggerated reverence for the Infallible People:

> "A weak reason, a predominating imagination . . . insolence towards Rome and the Church . . . incredible pride . . . no originality; repeats Maistre, Bonald, Rousseau . . . Profound ignorance of men, eras, and affairs: believes possible a theocracy as the role of the people, representation as the role of the Pope."

Gioberti believed in liberty, and he saw the Church as her surest guarantee. He was the true prophet of the Moderates, of those who wanted an Italian civilisation emancipated from the arbitrary tyranny of the princes, and of Austria; but an Italy free, too, from the Sovereignty of the People, that notion which Lamennais and Mazzini had both inherited from Rousseau.

With Gioberti we may return to the crisis in Italy, following Pio Nono's flight to Gaeta. For Gioberti was Premier, now, at Turin; but his great chance had come just one month too late. Had he been Premier when Rossi was still alive at Rome, and Pio Nono there, instead of winning power only on December 16th, exactly a month after Rossi's murder, the Liberal-Catholic dream might yet have been realised in Italy. As it was, at what was really the thirteenth hour, he made a desperate attempt to reconcile Pio Nono and the revolutionaries at Rome, and so to forestall Mazzini and lay the basis for an Italian Federation, the dream of his own *Primato*. He sent two envoys to Gaeta, to offer Pio Nono his services, and to invite him, meanwhile, to take up his residence at Nice—at that time still in Piedmontese territory. But Pius was not sympathetic. He had noted that the Piedmontese ambassador, the Marquis Pareto, had remained at Rome, and had not followed him to Gaeta, as had most of the ambassadorial Corps. He reminded the Piedmontese envoys of their government's opposition to his own recent plans for an Italian federation; he complained of the political instability at Turin, and the poor relations of Turin with Paris; he pointed out that he had already submitted the matter of the disorders at Rome to the governments of Europe.

But Gioberti persisted. He sent a new ambassador-extraordinary, Enrico Martini, to Gaeta. But he told him to go, en route, to Rome, and to try, quite unofficially, to prevent the Constituent Assembly, now announced, from ever meeting. Afterwards he was to go on to Gaeta and offer the help of Piedmont in restoring the Pope.

Enrico Martini met with an even chillier reception than his predecessors. Cardinal Antonelli, acting Secretary of State, pointed out that he could not receive him officially —he had treated with the Pope's enemies at Rome—that Turin was even at that moment accepting ambassadors

(Spini and Pinto) from the revolutionary government at Rome, and that the Piedmontese government had not bothered to follow the usual procedure of discovering in advance whether the new ambassador would be acceptable to the government to which he had been accredited. Only when Gioberti had agreed to break completely with the revolutionaries at Rome did Pio Nono, in fact, recognise Turin's new ambassador.

Farini criticises Antonelli and the Pope for their intransigence, and has been followed by later historians in his criticism. Intransigent, indeed, towards Turin, they now were; but the reasons are not far to seek; the painful impression made by the "Kingdom of North Italy", in the summer, not merely upon Rome, but upon her friends the rulers of Parma, Modena, and Tuscany, all of them overshadowed by the new kingdom; the rebuffs to Rossi, when he tried to form a Federation in October; the attempts of Gioberti to mediate between the Revolution at Rome and the Pope, instead of denouncing the former and refusing to have relations with it. To these must be added the beginnings of Papal indignation on account of secularist policies which the new constitutional governments were beginning to pursue at Turin.[20] All might, perhaps, have been different if Rossi had still been at Rome; but as it was, Gioberti, still desperately playing for an Italian Federation, under Piedmontese leadership, but estranged by now from the Pope, from the Mazzinians, and from the military party at Turin, overreached himself in February 1849. The Grand-Duke Leopold had fled before the revolutionaries at Florence to join the Pope at Gaeta, and Gioberti tried to persuade his king to intervene in Tuscany to restore him, and also to occupy Ancona, so as to compel attention to Piedmontese wishes at Rome, and at Gaeta. But Antonelli snubbed him by issuing, on February 18th, his public and urgent request to Austria, France, Spain and Naples to intervene to restore the Pope—omitting Piedmont from the invitation. And Charles Albert, his soul aflame to attack Austria once more, and to avenge Custozza, refused Gioberti's more sensible policy of a Piedmontese military intervention in central Italy.

There was nothing for Gioberti to do but resign; and with his resignation disappeared the last chance of a federal Italy, the last chance of a President-Pope, the last chance of solving the Italian problem in accordance with the tenets of Liberal-Catholicism, the last chance for the programme of the *Primato*.

Thus, for the moment, was the field left open for Mazzini.

2. *The Roman Republic*

Mazzini's Republic at Rome, and Garibaldi's defence of it, is a story very well known in this country. It is a story that lacks nothing, whether of drama or of true heroism, to create the perfect saga; and it found in Dr. Trevelyan a worthy narrator. The hero himself was mounted on a white horse, his red shirt was stained and tattered, and his sword became so bent, with much smiting, that it would no longer enter the scabbard. With his small band, d'Artagnan-like, he held at bay not only the armies of the leading military power on earth—France, once more ruled by a Napoleon— but defied the approach of the armies of Spain, of Naples, of the Austrian Empire. The soil which he defended was the soil of Rome, Rome a republic once again, Rome that had risen and shaken from her shoulders both the Empire and the Papacy. Yet even this was not all. For he strove not only with the despotic tyrants and the brutal professional soldiery of Europe, he strove with Principalities and Powers not of this world, with the priesthood, with the machinations of the Church, with what Dr. Trevelyan has called the "skirt", i.e. the cassock of the priesthood, symbol, we are told, of a sort of "third sex", which somehow exercised a sinister rule through the Confessional. And he was only defeated in the end by the monstrous treachery of France, the stab in the back of one Peoples' Republic murdering its twin brother.

There is another version of these events, more current on the Continent than in England. It is the saga of the "gang of atheistic revolutionary ruffians", ruled by the desperado with the dagger, Mazzini, and the "soldier of fortune", Garibaldi. These men had taken possession of the Eternal City, to despoil the Church, to murder the priests, to profane religion. The conscience of Europe had been aroused and a holy crusade, from all the lands, had risen and restored law and order in the home of the Head of the Church.

What are the facts?

So far as the diplomatic and military events are concerned there is little dispute now about them, and a brief reminder will serve.

Pio Nono's appeal for immediate military aid had been issued from the pen of Antonelli on February 18th, 1849. But in March there was small sign of any stirring in response to it. Not that there was any hesitation, on the question of principle, except in France. The Spaniards were ready, and sent two ships to Gaeta; but Piedmont and Austria were both opposed to a Spanish intervention in Italy. Naples was ready, and so, of course, was Austria; a joint move on the part of these two powers was projected, but France showed herself hostile. Austria had an anxious eye, at this time, upon the potential activities both of Hungary and of Piedmont. She would therefore only intervene at Rome in agreement with France, and she confined her activity for the moment to allowing her General Haynau to make the time-honoured move of emerging from the citadel of Ferrara and occupying the city.

Thus all, in fact, depended upon France. The Second French Republic had come into being in February 1848; General Cavaignac was temporarily in control. In November 1848, with the murder of Rossi at Rome, Cavaignac had assembled ships at Toulon, ready to go to the aid of the Pope in the threatening situation; but news of Pio Nono's flight to Gaeta came before they had sailed. The French Government then invited the Pope to take up his residence at the Papal palace at Avignon, but Pio Nono had no intention of suffering the fate of Pius VII, by putting himself into the power of France. In December and January, after Louis Napoleon had been elected President, the French policy was to support Gioberti, and to try to secure a restoration of the Pope through Piedmont. Palmerston, on behalf of England, proffered the same advice to the Pope. We have seen why this advice was unacceptable to Pius and to Antonelli.

In March, then, when Mazzini entered the Assembly at Rome, it was not at all clear what, in fact, would happen. Although offers came to the Pope from all over the world —even from the non-Catholic governments of Prussia and Russia—effective steps could clearly only be taken by France, Austria, Piedmont, or Naples; and political fears and jealousies appeared to paralyse their action. It was very generally expected that there would be a restoration by some sort of compromise, an expectation which persisted until the closing days of the drama in June. But no such expectation was entertained either by Pio Nono and Antonelli on the one side, or by Mazzini and Garibaldi on the other—at bottom because their religious positions were irreconcilable.

The impasse was broken by the sudden decision of Charles Albert to throw his Piedmontese army once more against the Austrians. This rash enterprise resulted in his total defeat at Novara (March 23rd), which left Austria once again in a dominating position in northern Italy. If Austria were to be prevented from now taking charge of the situation throughout Italy, and restoring the Pope on her own terms, France must act. So she called a Conference of Ambassadors at Gaeta. (Rayneval, the French ambassador at Naples, was there for France, Esterhazy for Austria, Martinez de la Rosa for Spain, Ludolfo for Naples. Cardinal Antonelli presided.) Antonelli, pursuing the policy of trying to prevent the Pope from falling into the power of any one great nation, favoured a combined intervention. But d'Harcourt, whom we last met assisting Pio Nono's escape from the Quirinal, was still French ambassador to the Pope; and he pressed the French Government's policy which had now become intervention by France, alone, at Rome. It was becoming very clear to Paris that if France

did not act Naples and Austria would; and on April 20th
Napoleon, having secured the agreement of his National
Assembly, despatched General Oudinot and a small force
to Civita Vecchia.

On the same date Pio Nono issued his allocution *Quibus
Quantisque*[21] in which he did not, as d'Harcourt (acting
on Napoleon's instructions) had requested him, promise
the Romans free institutions on his return, but chose rather
to recapitulate the outrages suffered by himself and his
ministers, in their attempts to carry out the popular will,
to denounce the spoliations and persecutions carried out by
the Republic against the Church, and to remind both the
Bishops and the princes of their duties in respect of her.
And it was in the same allocution that he openly condemned the proposition that the Church would benefit
from the loss of the Temporal Power. *Quibus Quantisque*
marks a new stage in the pontificate of Pio Nono. It is the
first considered and full statement in which he makes it
clear not only that he repudiates the revolution, but that
he will not have any strings attached to his return to Rome;
he will be master in his own State; nothing of his experience
as a constitutional monarch suggests to him that a liberal
régime is a suitable régime, at the present time, for Rome.
All the same, he will, of course, be generous and benevolent: *soyez tranquille* he replies to d'Harcourt, *Pie neuf
restera Pie neuf.*[22]

On April 25th, Oudinot and his troops landed at Civita
Vecchia—about nine thousand of them. The Governor,
after a protest, allowed them to land unimpeded—to Mazzini's furious indignation. But they only progressed in a
leisurely fashion towards Rome, some forty miles away,
hoping, in the meantime, to be accepted as umpires in the
situation without becoming involved in any fighting. But,
as it happened, the days between April 25th and April 30th
(when Oudinot eventually appeared outside the city) were
critical, because on April 27th Garibaldi brought in his
legionaries from the provinces, mostly from Rieti. Dr.
Trevelyan has described the impression which Garibaldi
made amongst the university students and the painters, of
all nationalities, when he opened his recruiting campaign

and they flocked to enlist under his banner; his face was so like the Christ of the renaissance pictures—they could not help but follow him! On the 30th, when Oudinot first attacked, Garibaldi beat him off and took some four hundred prisoners. First blood had been drawn by the Republic. Moreover another non-Roman regiment had entered the city on the 29th—Luciano Manara's *Bersaglieri*, from Lombardy, a regiment of fine spirit and discipline. Oudinot, and behind him the French Assembly, had, indeed, quite miscalculated the character of the opposition they would meet.[23]

During May and most of June the issue remained undecided. Meanwhile the Austrians slowly advanced down the east coast of Italy, occupying first Bologna (May 16th), where they re-established the Papal government under the shrewd and kindly Mgr. Bedini, then moving on to Ancona, where they occupied the fortress on June 15th. In the south, the Neapolitans made a half-hearted appearance at Velletri, were discouraged by the French who wanted a free hand at Rome, and withdrew, their rearguard harried by Garibaldi. Meanwhile the French Assembly, angered by Mazzini's unexpected rejection of the proffered mediation of its army, embarrassed at finding itself pushed into fighting a sister-republic, but most of all determined to safeguard the military reputation of France by bringing the crusade to a successful conclusion, determined to send reinforcements to Oudinot. Reinforcements were needed. The French general was, in fact, outnumbered, and had little prospect of taking Rome without more men and some siege artillery. But, at the same time, the French decided to send another negotiator, Ferdinand de Lesseps, to try to make terms with Mazzini. De Lesseps (who later won fame as the constructor of the Suez Canal) was a freemason, and had something in common with Mazzini; he fell, for a time, completely under the Italian's spell. By the end of May he had reached an understanding with the Triumvir which virtually placed the French army at the disposal, as an ally, of Mazzini's government, while keeping it outside the walls of the city. This agreement was promptly rejected both by the French Assembly and by Oudinot who, by now, had received his reinforcements. Oudinot began his assault on June 3rd—one day earlier than he had given Mazzini to understand that he would regard negotiations as ended. The fighting continued until June 30th, when Garibaldi declared further resistance hopeless, and the Assembly capitulated to the French, against the bitter opposition of Mazzini, who resigned rather than sign the capitulation.

Garibaldi withdrew with his legion before the entry of the French; Mazzini, after lingering for a week, unable to leave the Rome of his dreams, escaped to Civita Vecchia, and thence by boat. A large proportion of the revolutionaries managed, by one means and another, to get away before General Oudinot, accompanied by de Corcelles (who had replaced de Lesseps as French plentipotentiary) entered the city at the head of his army. After attending Mass at St. Peter's, Oudinot addressed the crowd in the great piazza:

"The re-establishment of the Papal authority is manifestly a work of Providence, and I am not a little proud that France should have been made its instrument. Upon the re-establishment of this authority rests the guarantee of the peace of the whole of Europe: it is a task which is equally both social and religious. I rejoice that the Romans express so loudly their feelings of goodwill for France, and for my part I can assure them of the most sincere reciprocation by our people. The war which I waged was not directed against the Romans, but rather against a crowd of strangers who were congregated at Rome from every part of Europe. Although this made the war inevitable, for this, at least, I rejoice, that Providence cut short the time of anxiety and of horror.

"The Romans have the honour to be children of the true religion and sincere Catholics; such are likewise the French. We are all members of one same religion, children of the same father, children of God. *Evviva Dio! Evviva la religione! Evviva il Papa!*"

And from Gaeta came a message from Pio Nono:

"to our most beloved subjects: from Heaven God lifted

high His arm, and to the tempestuous sea of anarchy and impiety He said: you shall go no further. He guided the Catholic arms to sustain the assaulted rights of humanity, of the belaboured faith, of the Holy See, and of Our Sovereign Authority. Eternal praise be to the Lord, who even in the midst of His wrath, forgets not His mercy."[24]

The Pope went on to nominate a commission to rule until his own return, which did not occur until April, 1850. The commission (yet another triumvirate, and known as the Red Triumvirate) consisted of the Cardinals Della Genga, Vannicelli, and Altieri[25] who arrived to take over from the French on July 31st.

Such, very briefly, were the diplomatic and military events. As regards what took place within Rome, during the period of Mazzini's rule, it is not, and presumably never will be possible to feel much certainty, because it is necessary to weave one's way amidst a plethora of "horror-stories" on the one hand and extravagant eulogies upon the other. The main issue is whether the revolutionary governments, and Mazzini's in particular, were murderous, sacrilegious and spoliative in their policy towards the Church; and the question is obviously of the first importance, not only for religious but for economic reasons, because so large a proportion both of the population and of the property of the city was, at that time, directly or indirectly Church property.

Some of the so-called "clerical" writers may fairly be charged with having spread a picture of Mazzini and Garibaldi as "atheistic plunderers" in a sense in which they certainly were not; the sense that they were deliberately plundering, and plundering for their own gain. Pio Nono knew that it was not so, and later in his life he said as much when he exclaimed, with his disarming smile, that he and Garibaldi seemed to be the only people who had not made anything out of the risorgimento! He might have added, as a third, Mazzini, who never in his life made any money for himself, and if any came into his hands gave it to some needy person or spent it on *Young Italy*. For personal sim-

plicity and personal generosity there was little to choose
between Pio Nono, Mazzini and Garibaldi. The difference
between them was a difference of faith, a different view of
truth and justice, not the difference between greed and generosity. Some of the other revolutionaries at Rome (notably
Sterbini, who enjoyed a profitable position as minister of
commerce and public works, before Mazzini came to
power) were not so scrupulous when they found themselves
in power; it would, indeed, have been very surprising if
they had been.

It was hardly practicable politics, whether in the earlier
weeks after Pio Nono's departure, or in the days of the
Triumvirate, for a serious attack to be made by the revolutionary governments at Rome upon the Church. In the
earlier weeks there was the constant expectation of the
Pope's return and the establishment once more of a constitutional régime; this was not only the expectation, it was
the general desire, even amongst the revolutionary politicians. Only Mazzini and Garibaldi (who were not yet at
Rome) and a handful of ardent Mazzinian republicans
really wanted to see the end of Papal Rome; and if the
Pope and the Cardinals were coming back it was wise to
play for safety. And later, when Mazzini was dictator, he
had the strongest motives for protecting the Church. He
wanted to stave off the intervention of the Powers, and
particularly of France; and the best way to secure this was
to demonstrate that Rome was not in the hands of a band
of hooligans. He also wanted to win the clergy to the cause
of republicanism, as Muzzarelli, Gavazzi, Dall 'Ongaro, and
Garibaldi's friend, Ugo Bassi, had already been won. He
still expected the priests to go, in the end, the way of
Lamennais, and, further than Lamennais, to become some
day the priests of the Religion of The People. Meanwhile
all religion was sacred, and the priests were indirectly aid-
ing the cause by comforting the wounded and the dying,
the mothers and the widows. So we find him ordering the
release even of French priests, who had been interned, and
restoring to their rightful places confessional boxes which
had been pulled out of the churches to make barricades.
And Garibaldi's attitude, though he was far more bitterly

opposed than was Mazzini to the priests, was the same, officially, as the attitude of the Triumvir. He would not condone the profaning of the churches by his motley troops (who, as Dr. Trevelyan admits, included convicts), even though he seems to have been often disobeyed by them. His attitude was that of the higher-minded Puritan commander in the English Civil War: the smashing of images might be all the vogue, and his instinctive sympathies might rest with the iconoclasts, but it was lawless behaviour, and lawlessness could not be tolerated. After all, if they were smashing images of the Virgin today, they might be smashing private property tomorrow.

Mazzini prided himself that his government was lenient, and always, in later days, he boasted of the few punishments imposed under his rule. He was, indeed, no Robespierre. His rule was lenient, and the cause of the serious disorders is to be found precisely in that fact. That priests were murdered, just because they were priests, and that the murderers got away with it, is admitted by both sides. The most notorious of the assassins were Callimacho Zambianchi, and his gang, the *Finanzieri*, who were responsible, amongst other crimes, for the murder of Dominican and other priests at the convent of San Calisto. The estimate of the number of their victims at that convent varies from the six admitted by Dr. Trevelyan to the ninety accepted by Pelczar, the latter being the number of corpses quoted at the subsequent trial as having been dug up in the convent grounds.[26] Zambianchi was not brought to trial by the Triumvirate, although they knew about and stopped his massacre at the convent. He later left Rome in company with Garibaldi, as part of his legion.

Rioting, and in particular attacks upon the clergy, were, however, more widespread in the provinces than in the city of Rome. Amongst the most notorious were the murders carried out by the *Congrega d'Inferno* at Sinigaglia, and the feud between the Republicans and the Centurions at Ancona. The latter reached such proportions that Mazzini sent Orsini (the one who later threw the bomb at Napoleon III in Paris) to restore order. That there were not more violence and disorder within Rome can probably be attributed

to the fact that the more ardent spirits were engaged, per-
force, in manning the ramparts against the French. All the
same, the important difference between the sporadic violence in Mazzini's Rome and the holocaust of the September Massacres of the French Revolution should be recognised. It was never the policy of the Roman Republic to
extirpate any class of people; at least five cardinals remained, throughout the revolution, unmolested in the city.
And although the motive force behind the leaders of the
Republic was strongly anti-Catholic, and although Mazzini
was never tired of haranguing the Assembly about God and
The People, and the Third Rome, he refrained from indulging in anything like Robespierre's fancy of inventing
new religious services such as the Feast of Reason. Once,
it is true, he allowed himself, on Easter Day, to attend
St. Peter's, with his fellow Triumvirs, carrying the flag of
the Republic, while an army chaplain called Spola, assisted
by Gavazzi, said Mass at the altar reserved to the Pope.
Spola followed the Pope's custom by blessing the people
afterwards, with the Blessed Sacrament, from the Papal
balcony, Mazzini following on to the same balcony and likewise addressing them. The whole thing was called the "New
Pasch", and the priest Dall 'Ongaro wrote in the *Monitore
Romano* afterwards: "There lacked the Vicar of Christ; but
by no fault of ours; and though he was away, we had the
people, and we had God." This looked like the beginning
of an attempt to turn Catholicism into Mazzinianism, but
in fact it was a desperate endeavour to have the Papal celebrations at Easter carried out in the Papal way, to satisfy
the people. It had been intended that they should be carried out by the Canons of the cathedral, but the Canons
refused to arrogate to themselves the Pope's function, and
incurred, in consequence, a fine of 120 crowns each, imposed by the Triumvirate.[27]

But Mazzini seems to have been working, half secretly,
towards religious changes, and it is difficult to believe that,
if he had been granted a little more time, he would not, in
attempting social reconstruction, have given some practical
scope to his social-religious visions.[28] De Lesseps, during
his negotiations with Mazzini, was watching from the in-

side what was being done in Rome. He came to the conclusion that the Triumvir was trying to promote his new
religion. He went so far as himself to warn the Roman
Assembly of the danger. In his notebook he jotted down:

"I suspect Mazzini—a remarkable and very influential
man—of wishing to favour a religious schism: his writings
ought to make one fear it. He has frequent conferences
with English travellers; he sees Protestant Missionaries
of all nations."[29]

De Lesseps goes on to talk of this behaviour as "treason
to the cause of Italian liberty, which cannot exist apart from
Catholicism".

Farini, the most impartial critic, has some observations
on this matter which are very interesting. He had watched,
at St. Peter's, what he regarded as the "cursed hypocrisy" of
the "New Pasch", and he was ruminating upon the muddled
religious thinking which he found around him:

"In the midst of this chaos have arisen certain believers,
I know not how far in the truths of Christianity, but at
any rate in its civilising tendencies and in the reality of
the popular devotion, who consider Christianity, whether
an holy law from God or not, to be an excellent basis
for the law of man, but then it requires to be renovated
and disentangled from Roman Catholicism. They are political innovators, who would fain innovate in religion
too. They are not, or do not seem, or do not profess
themselves, Protestants of any of the known sects; yet
their language is a protest, and they take pleasure in
Protestant proselytism, and countenance it either un-
awares or for the advantage of their political sects . . .
look at Mazzini; he is not satisfied with the unity of Italy,
a scheme contested, an aim in my opinion not good, nor
grand, and at all events unattainable in these times; he
is not satisfied with the destruction of monarchy, a pes-
tilent idea, as I think, for the modern European society,
at any rate one yet more resisted than the former, and
an end little likely to be gained; nor yet with pure democracy, a phrase of equivocal meaning, a term itself inde-

terminate, if we construe it in the sense of certain persons: no, nor yet with the destruction of the Pope's temporal power, an undertaking, as is plain, vastly difficult; all this is too little; Mazzini thinks it a light matter to destroy in Italy Roman Catholicism to boot. It is an historical and political absurdity, it is the delirium of a schoolboy. Italy, I repeat, is Catholic; and there is no Catholicism but the Roman . . . when they come to assail the Catholic Religion, they will have against them the masses, who will brook, perhaps, any and every oppression except that which tramples on religious conscience."[30]

Farini, then, who shared Mamiani's belief in a Constitutional Papal Monarchy for the States of the Church, was satisfied that Mazzini was intending to make war upon Catholicism. No doubt he was right in supposing that the people would not follow; but the immediate effect of the Pope's departure was a spate of anti-Catholic demonstrations. There were blasphemous processions, dressed up in imitation of the cardinals and the Pope, but they seem to have been a sport mainly confined to the Trasteverian mob, who were liable to steal the Blessed Sacrament from the altars of the churches in order to ridicule it in the streets. These things were clearly the result of the sudden collapse of authority. When the anti-religious orgies of the French Revolution are borne in mind it is hardly to be wondered at that at Rome, a city in which the religious and the political powers were identified much more closely than in the Paris of the ancien régime, there should have been some licence after the Pope, the symbol of all authority, had been driven to flee. The Trasteverian mob drew the rather natural conclusion that all restraint was now over. The prostitutes were released from the San Michele prison; some were reported to have fought in the army, some to have found their way into the hospitals, replacing nuns who had been expelled. What the extent of the sexual immorality was can only be guessed at; certainly the reports of debauchery which were brought to the Pope at Gaeta caused him deeper distress than did the stories that reached him of the seizure of Church property.

There was no general seizure of Church property. Certain convents and other religious buildings were taken over for military purposes or as tenement houses; much of the land belonging to religious corporations was requisitioned to make allotments; certain "forced loans" were levied upon the higher clergy. On the whole, considering the economic crisis, which had been accentuated by the Austrian war, a more drastic confiscation might have been expected, but for the necessity for not outraging Catholic sentiment. The Triumvirate preferred to raise a new loan, and to repudiate the payment of interest upon the one recently raised by the Papal government.

It is interesting that there is not, really, much significant dispute between "clerical" and "Mazzinian" historians—or at least between the more responsible writers on either side —concerning all these happenings; and it is noteworthy that the two leading English historians of the period, Bolton King and Dr. Trevelyan, agree in accepting the account given by Giuseppe Spada (*Storia della rivoluzione di Roma*, 1869) as accurate, and fair, although Spada is "clerical" in his standpoint. The number of the murders and the extent of the robbery is disputed; but their existence is not. Nor are the official acts and policy of Mazzini's government, which, indeed, can readily be consulted.[31] The real dispute, which is sharp, concerns what can only be called the "merits" of the matter. The English historians, as well as "anti-clerical" writers in Italy, France, and elsewhere, have adopted the attitude that Mazzini and Garibaldi represented the popular will of the Romans, and that, on the other side, the Pope's sovereignty was merely an arbitrary tyranny, and the French intervention an act of foreign aggression, brought about by a "clerical plot". The other side, while often (though not always) ready to pay tribute to the heroism of Garibaldi and to the personal integrity of Mazzini, refuses to recognise the political right of the Republic to existence, and regards the French intervention as a natural and legitimate operation in the restoration of law and order. This latter view, though widely accepted on the Continent, can scarcely be said even to have been considered in England.

It was, of course, Pio Nono's view. To him, Rome was in the hands of a "group of unscrupulous men". Not for one moment did it occur to him to regard the mob stirred up by Ciceruacchio and Sterbini as representing the real will of his devoted subjects. Nor were the elections held for the Constituent Assembly anything more to him than a camouflage. The Eternal City was in the hands of "assassins" (the murderers of Rossi), "socialists" (Mazzinian believers in "The People"; the name had been earlier, and more exactly applied to the Saint-Simonians) and "Communists" (the name given to Louis Blanc's party in the French revolution of the previous year). They were also "foreigners"—by whom he meant non-Romans.

What justification had he for calling them foreigners? Obviously the question is crucial. We have become accustomed, since Pio Nono's day, to peaceful penetration, by ideological groups, into neighbouring countries, and their seizure of political power. Were the leaders of the Roman Republic really non-Romans?

Mazzini was a native of Genoa, Garibaldi of Nice. Both entered Rome for the first time with the revolution. The War Minister was Avezzana, from Genoa. Strictly speaking, then, the effective control was foreign, in the sense of extra-Papal State, though not in the sense of non-Italian. But, as regards the army, foreign and native elements were fairly evenly balanced. There is much dispute about the exact numbers, but Dr. Trevelyan analysed the different authorities.[32] Published lists of the wounded show that about a tenth were inhabitants of Rome, and about a half were inhabitants of the Papal States. Some of the regiments, like Garibaldi's own Legion, were mixed in origin; largely drawn from the Romagna, but also from farther afield—from as far as Monte Video, where the Legion was first founded. Others, like Manara's Lombards (the *Bersaglieri*) or Miçkiewicz' Poles, were more homogeneous national groups.

Most of the men in these fighting groups, though not all, were Italian; but it is very certain that only a small part of them, and that not the most effective, were natives of the city of Rome. That the people of Rome, confronting attack, behaved with heroism is attested by the witness of foreign residents, such as Arthur Clough and Margaret Fuller, as well as by Italian and French observers; but it is equally indisputable that the leadership, both political and military, was mainly non-Roman. The followers of Mazzini and Garibaldi were revolutionary zealots, and the régime was infused with two qualities: it was pan-Italian (anti-French and anti-Austrian), and it was anti-clerical. And both in its pan-Italianism and in its anti-clericalism it represented a small minority—an ardent minority, no doubt, but certainly a minority. It is universally agreed that very few, in any part of the peninsula, in the uprising of 1848 –49, were looking, as Mazzini was looking, to a United Italy; and as for anti-clericalism, there was, indeed, a strong desire for lay participation in the temporal government of the Papal State, even for lay control of it; but the general feeling of Romans, and of the rest of Italians about the Church, was, beyond question, that depicted in the passage already quoted from Farini.

Mazzini insisted, both at the time and afterwards, that his government rested upon the will of the people, the Constituent Assembly having been freely elected. The weakness of this argument consists in the fact that the Junta, under whose auspices the Constituent was planned, and the elections were held, in January '49, was itself quite without legal authority (being nominated by a small group of the old Assemblies elected under the Statute of March '48); and further that this Junta had, in fact, deposed the Papal government, and announced that the new Constituent would create a new régime, so that the Church, inevitably, had boycotted the elections, and (to judge from the number of voters) was followed by the large majority of the people in doing so. To vote for the Constituent was to vote for the Pope's declared enemies; and that was something which only the zealots, or those who could be bribed or frightened, appear to have been ready to do. It is necessary, also, to remember that, even when the Junta had been appointed, on December 12th, '48, the withdrawal of the moderates, on account of the disturbances ("from day to day someone either withdrew from Rome, or resigned his seat", says Farini) had reduced the Higher Council to 17 and the Chamber of Deputies to 56; that the month which followed was that which was known as the "Dictatorship of Sterbini", when "All the adepts in movements and insurrections, whom Italy had reared in her recent troubles, sped to Rome", and that these "adepts in insurrections", who were mostly, in name at least, Mazzinian republicans, spent the months of December and January "scouring the provinces, haranguing the Clubs, combining them in a league, affiliating them to a centre, and inflaming them with the notion of electing, by direct and universal suffrage, a popular assembly, to establish a pure democracy in the Papal States".[33] As was shown in the last chapter, their converts were clearly not very numerous, though they were certainly vociferous. In short, the importance of the Assembly was only that it gave a certain colour of democratic right with which to deck the sword of Garibaldi and the sceptre of Mazzini.[34]

The sympathies of Europe were with the Pope. Almost all governments, as we have seen, offered him help of some sort. Diplomatic recognition was not accorded by any of them to the revolutionary government at Rome. With this attitude both the government and public opinion in England for the time being concurred. Queen Victoria wrote a personal letter of sympathy to Pio Nono, the first addressed by any English sovereign to a Pope since the time of Queen Elizabeth the First. The *Times*, and the public at large (apart from Mazzini's personal friends, amongst whom should be accounted Carlyle) were agreed in deploring the outrages suffered by that "splendid fellow" the liberal Pope who had actually introduced into his state a constitution derived from that of England. Palmerston, receiving unofficially Mazzini's envoy Rusconi, strongly recommended that Mazzini should make terms with the French—advice which Mazzini deliberately concealed from the Romans, preferring to tell them that the English attitude was that of his own English friends.[35] Mazzini himself was at first widely regarded in England—unjustly—as a Robespierre. All this was very quickly going to change. The arrival, soon after the fall of the Republic, of large numbers of Mazzinian refugees in England, amongst them Orsini, Gavazzi, Spola, Saffi, and before long Mazzini himself, spread the saga in Brighton and Bristol, in London and Liverpool, and as far north as Edinburgh, where audiences listened spellbound to their tales.[36]

But much the most important, as well as the most acrimonious, dispute concerns the behaviour of France.

Inasmuch as the French revolution of February, 1848, had produced a republican Constituent Assembly at Paris, the appearance of a republic at Rome was not, of itself, calculated to disturb French political opinion, as it disturbed the English. But the treatment suffered by the Pope was shocking to all but a very small minority of Frenchmen. This is something which, though it was pointed out some time ago in England,[37] has been hardly recognised by English writers of histories, who have very generally continued to treat of the French intervention at Rome as the outcome of a "clerical plot", or of the machinations of the Jesuits acting upon a vacillating Napoleon, or merely as the pursuit of "la gloire"—even though Dr. Trevelyan, in his *Autobiography*, very handsomely admitted the anti-French bias of his own early work. Actually, on account of the Catholic revival fostered by Montalembert and Lacordaire, by Ozanam, by Foisset, by de Falloux, by Veuillot and by Dupanloup (all laymen except for Lacordaire and Dupanloup) it is no exaggeration to say that the Church had been reborn in the minds of Frenchmen, so that it was an outraged Catholic public opinion that forced the government to act at Rome. The close alliance with the monarchy which had rendered the Church so unpopular in the days of Charles X had become something far in the past by the year 1848. She had not been the ally of the throne of Louis Philippe; rather she had been struggling to win from his ostentatiously indifferentist governments the most elementary rights—and had often failed. As for the Jesuits, they had been withdrawn from France shortly before Pio Nono's accession, as a result, oddly enough, of negotiations which Rossi had undertaken when he was still French ambassador at Rome. Other Religious Orders were, indeed, beginning to appear once more in Paris, notably the Dominicans, who had been brought back by Lacordaire; but, politically speaking, if they belonged anywhere they belonged with the "People", on the Left, which was where, in fact, Lacordaire took his own seat when he was elected a member of the new French Republican Assembly in 1848.

It was no "plot" but popular, Catholic, "leftist" sympathy which first induced the Assembly, under the straightlaced republican Cavaignac, to issue those orders for the despatch of ships and troops to Civita Vecchia in November, '48, before the Pope's flight was even known in France, when all that was known was the murder of Rossi and all that was feared was that the Pope might be in some difficulty. And this same popular opinion continued to prevail, voiced effectively by de Falloux and Montalembert in the Assembly, until the striking occasion, in October, '49, when, by 469 votes against 180, M. Thiers carried his motion, against the will of Napoleon, that the restoration of Pio Nono should be effected without requiring any guarantees whatever from the Pope concerning the constitutional form which his restored government should take. There was, indeed, an opposition, whose spokesman was Jules Favre, which did not approve the intervention, or which wanted only French mediation between the Pope and Mazzini and a restoration as part of a guaranteed constitution for Rome. And there were others, like Mazzini's friends Georges Sand and Ledru Rollin,[38] or like Louis Blanc (whom Mazzini detested) who were absolutely anti-Papal. But by most of the Assembly, and by the public generally, the intervention was regarded as a crusade, a crusade not unmixed, certainly, with national pride, but a crusade in the traditional sense because it was an army going to the succour of the Church.

Napoleon's personal position in the matter was peculiar. When Cavaignac first issued the orders in November, '48, to prepare an expedition the future Emperor was only a plain deputy in the Assembly. He abstained from voting on the issue, and for that he was much criticised. His sympathies were, naturally enough, very much divided. He had once been a Carbonaro, and had fought, as we saw, against the Papal government, with his brother, in the Romagna, in the uprising of '31. His cousin, the Prince of Canino, was one of those in power at Rome. But Pio Nono, as we also saw earlier, had, as Bishop of Imola, been personally kind to him during the affair of '31, having helped him to escape when he had been in need of a passport and some ready cash. Napoleon never forgot that kindness, and the memory of it always tempered his personal relations with the Pope, even though he remained something of a Carbonaro at heart, and was obliged by his family name to reconcile a variety of theories such as the principles of '89 and the Legend of Saint Helena.

Napoleon found that he had not taken the popular line in refraining from supporting Cavaignac over intervention, and he put that matter right by championing the Pope in a speech he wisely made before offering himself for the Presidency. Successful, next month, (December, '48), in securing that office,[39] he tried, for a time, to get out of the Roman difficulty by securing a Piedmontese intervention; only after the Austrian victory at Novara in March did he decide that France must forestall Austria in restoring the Pope. After Oudinot had sailed he was sympathetic rather with those who wanted France to arbitrate than with those who wanted to restore the Pope unconditionally, and he was hopeful of de Lesseps' mission. But after Oudinot had entered Rome the President was defeated in his desire to impose conditions upon Pius by the large majority of the Assembly who thought it more fitting that the Pope should be restored unconditionally.

There is no need to glorify the motives of Napoleon, who was by no means a Saint-Louis, nor of the French or Austrian politicians, who were much concerned about prestige and power politics. But beneath the material motives evident amongst the Catholic powers, and also beneath the personal ambitions and destructive instincts that often disfigured the Republicans, there still remained a core of firm conviction, on both sides, which ennobled this struggle at Rome, and which gave to it its real significance. The Catholic faithful were convinced, and rightly convinced, that in reality it was the Church which was under attack. And the best of the Republicans were also imbued with a faith, a faith in the Idea of Italian Nationality, and in a religious notion of "The People". The Catholics came from France, as in later years they came from Ireland, Belgium, and other Catholic countries as well, because they recognised Rome as their city, and the position of the Pope as part of their religion. The Garibaldians came from Liguria or from the Romagna because they wanted a United Italy, and a Republic. Each side complained that the other side ought not to be there, and in a sense they were both right. On neither side was the fighting element native to Rome; yet for both sides Rome was the city of their dreams. For the one side the city was their eternal home on earth; for the other side it was the home of their new aspiration.

Chapter Four

PEACE AND RECONSTRUCTION
(1850–1859)

1. *The Restoration of Two Hierarchies and the Immaculate Conception*
2. *Peaceful Development in the Papal State (1850–1859)*

1. *The Restoration of Two Hierarchies and the Immaculate Conception*

The first three years of his pontificate had seen Pio Nono trying to ride, then trying to withstand the revolutionary storm. He was not well-equipped to do either. Metternich had been right about him; "chaud de cœur . . . faible d'intelligence", he had sown the wind and had reaped that whirlwind which the Chancellor had foreseen. Understanding little of politics, good natured, liking to give pleasure, hating cruelty, he had undermined his own political authority without fully realising what he was doing. But Metternich had also seen that his spiritual position would yet save him from his political ineptitude: "What the Pope has already destroyed by his liberalism is his own temporal power; what he is unable to destroy is his spiritual power; it is that power which will cancel the harm done by his worthless counsellors." And it had come to pass as Metternich had foretold. As soon as the spiritual power had been clearly threatened, which was when the democrats demanded he should bless, as Pope, a revolutionary nationalist war, he had drawn back, at once, even though everyone urged him on. From April 29th, 1848, he became the enemy of the Revolution; after the murder of Rossi he was openly at war with it. Acting in defence of the spiritual power, he saved, for the time being, his temporal power.

Without doubt the shock of the events of November, '48, and the subsequent spectacle of Mazzini and Garibaldi usurping the Quirinal, and scorning the teachings of the Church—defying at one and the same time the spiritual and the temporal power—made an indelible impression upon his sensitive mind, and convinced him till his death that the two powers were inevitably bound up together, that the Papal State was essential to the Church. Without doubt, too, the same events impressed upon him that liberalism, as Metternich had warned, was normally the forerunner of revolution, and was inimical to the Church as well as to the Papal State. Certainly, the seeds of the later Syllabus of Errors had, by these happenings, been planted in his mind. To hostile critics, such as Professor Sir Llewellyn Woodward, it has seemed that, in this way, the fortunes of the whole Catholic Church, and the immense opportunity which the Papacy had of leading opinion in a new and revolutionary era became sacrificed to a miserable obsession about a petty temporal principality.[1] But to Pio Nono it seemed that it was the Church that was at stake, that continental liberalism, of which Mazzini was both the heir and the supreme mid-nineteenth-century exponent, was full of error and presumption; it seemed that he must, in bearing witness to the truth, inveigh against this error and this presumption in allocution, in encyclical, and in brief; and he did so until he collected his denunciations together in the famous Syllabus of 1864. He was concerned with something much bigger than defending the Papal State; but he was indebted to Sterbini, Mazzini, and Garibaldi at Rome for demonstrating to him the real character of the revolutionary spirit towards which, both as Bishop of Imola and as Bishop of Rome, he had been unduly indulgent. He had now seen the marks of the beast in his own city; henceforth he would warn the world of those marks, not merely in order to save the Papal State, but in order to save the world.

It is odd that the Pope who is now, rightly, regarded by friend and foe alike as the founder of the "Modern Papacy", the Pope who recovered for the Holy See, throughout the Church Universal, an influence and prestige such as it had not enjoyed since the days of the Council of Trent, should also be regarded as having sacrificed the Church to the Papal State. The dramatic episode of Mazzini and Garibaldi in 1849 and the prolonged rearguard action by which Antonelli and Pio Nono tried to save their State from Piedmont, between 1859 and 1870, have helped to obscure the Pope's preoccupation with his unique spiritual office, to which, of course, his temporal sovereignty was wholly subordinate and ancillary. Much of this preoccupation cannot now be known. Thus he remained "the Pope of Prayer", but prayer is private; even so, his example in this may, for all we know, be his most important legacy. He granted an unprecedented number of audiences, he encouraged missionary activity in Africa, in Asia, and in America, which reached, during his pontificate, proportions never previously attained; but great as was the personal and practical help which he gave to the missionary movement the story of that movement is the story of the pioneer priests who were faithful in the midst of dangers and suffering in distant places; it is not the Pope's story.

But the important matter of the restoration of the Catholic hierarchies in England and in Holland is part of the Pope's story because he played a primary part in it, even though he played it at a distance; moreover the controversies aroused by those restorations had their bearing upon the central religious and political storms of the century which flashed and rumbled around Rome.

It is edifying to witness Pio Nono, in the summer of 1847, withdrawn from the Roman crowds, or from the problem of what to do with the Austrians at Ferrara, in order to discuss quietly with Nicholas Wiseman (who had been sent by the English Vicars Apostolic) whether the time had not come when the normal constitution of the Church might be restored to England. Wiseman could point to the increase to about a million in the numbers of the English Catholics, since the Emancipation Act of 1829, since the conversions arising from the Oxford Movement, and since the great influx of the Irish. The Pope pondered. Three times he said Mass, with the intention of invoking the guidance of the Holy Spirit; for three days he prayed before he was able to say "at last, I am assured".[2] And in the following year, just three weeks after the critical Allocution of April 29th, when the war against the Austrians still raged, and the popular pressure upon the Pope was strongest, we find him receiving the English clergy, Ullathorne and Grant, who had come to present their detailed scheme for twelve dioceses in England.

There was much to consider. By the English law of 1829 the new bishops must not bear the same titles as the Anglican bishops. And where were to be found in England priests of the necessary spiritual strength and administrative ability, who should be real leaders? It was a grave question. Newman thought they could not be found. Wiseman feared that "soft good persons" would be put in. And Fr. Luigi Gentili, a missionary in England of the new order of Rosminians (founded by the Piedmontese philosopher and envoy whom Pio Nono had kept by his side for some weeks at Gaeta) was sending confidential reports to Rome during 1847 and 1848 about the problems which must be confronted if the hierarchy was to be restored. He is not so much afraid of the opposition of Parliament, or of the Established Church, or of the existing Vicars Apostolic, as he is of the difficulty of finding the right occupants for the new bishoprics. In his anxiety that Rome shall tackle the problem along bold and constructive lines he writes to Pio Nono, personally, early in 1848, begging him to study the reports himself, since Cardinal Fransoni, to whom, as the Prefect of Propaganda, they were being sent, seemed to Gentili to be beyond making difficult new decisions.[3] The great popularity of Pio Nono in England at that date was an important factor in smoothing the way; the Prime Minister, Lord John Russell, had for some time made it clear that he was anxious to secure the renewal of diplomatic relations with the Holy See. Lord Minto had reported to Russell the project for a hierarchy, mentioned to him in Rome by Pio Nono; the Prime Minister had been indifferent. A smooth and rather unobtrusive transition from the old order of Vicars Apostolic to the new order of Bishops seemed assured.

The Bull of Restoration was already being drawn up at Rome in the autumn of 1848 and Ullathorne and Grant had left the city when there occurred the murder of Rossi and the flight to Gaeta. Everything was held up until after the Pope's return. Nor was it possible, in 1850, to follow quite the original plan. For one thing the Archbishop designated in 1848 for Westminster, Thomas Walsh, who was Vicar Apostolic of the Midlands District, had died in the meantime. Then Wiseman, the Vicar Apostolic in London, whose scholarship, ability, and initiative seemed to mark him out for the new Archbishopric, was suddenly called to Rome, in June, 1850, in order that he might receive a Cardinal's hat and take his place in the Curia. Wiseman

was well known at Rome, having lived there the greater part
of his life, and Pio Nono had great affection and respect
for him. From the experience which the new Cardinal had
recently gained at Oscott and at London the Pope hoped to
gain more understanding of what was possible in England.
He may also have sought to lessen friction amongst Catholics in England by withdrawing one whose foreward policies
were not everywhere looked upon with favour. But the appeals of the London Catholics, and especially of the converts, who saw in the removal of Wiseman to Rome a disastrous blow to the growing Catholic community in England, induced the Pope to send him back again. It was this
which necessitated a decision about the hierarchy, since
Wiseman was now to be a Cardinal and could therefore
scarcely return save as Archbishop. So, on September 30th,
the English hierarchy was announced in Consistory, and
Wiseman wrote:

"... this morning, the most memorable Consistory for
England, perhaps in history, has taken place. His Holiness has proclaimed the restoration of the Hierarchy, and
has conferred on me at once the two-fold dignity of Cardinal and Archbishop of Westminster ... Till to-day all
who have known what was proposed have been under
strict secrecy ..."

A few days later, on October 7th, still exultant, Wiseman issued his famous Pastoral Letter "from out the Fla-
minian gate" of Rome—and in England the storm broke.
No need to recount here that dramatic outbreak, the No
Popery cry in Parliament, Press, and Pulpit, the processions, the burnings in effigy of Pope and Cardinals which
can only be compared with those in the Trastevere quarter
of Mazzinian Rome eighteen months earlier. Wiseman yet
won a hearing, and Pio Nono proceeded calmly, and at
some leisure, to the institution of the new Bishops. The
Pope, like everybody else, had been taken by surprise by
the outburst. He pointed out that Lord Minto, when he had
been in Rome in the winter of '47–'48, had advised that
there would be no difficulty with the British Government.
In the circumstances he could only exhort the English faith-

ful to "pray insistently that the Lord may remove all the
obstacles and bring to the new Church a million, three million, indeed all your compatriots who at one time were torn
from that Church".[4] A million was, indeed, the number
which it was at that moment attaining, and three million
it would be when the centenary of these events came to
be celebrated. Yet by an act of August, 1851, the new titles
were, none the less, made illegal, while in the following
year public processions and even the wearing in public of
the ecclesiastical habit were prohibited for Catholics. These
acts remained, from the start, a dead letter; but the ministries which passed them were certainly bowing to popular
pressure in doing so, and the mild and patient Newman
could only sum up the situation by observing that:

> "late events have shown, that though I never have under-
> rated the intense prejudice which prevails against us, I
> did overrate that Anglo-Saxon love of justice and fair
> dealing which I thought would be its match".

Our concern here is with the Roman end of the strange
story. There is no reason to suppose that Lord Minto had
been misleading Pio Nono and there is good reason to believe that the project of 1848, had it gone through in that
year, would have passed almost unnoticed both in official
and in bourgeois England.[5] But the two years that followed
1848 were crucial, because during them the sentiments of
England changed on account of what occurred in Italy. In
1848 Pio Nono had been the popular liberal Pope, the
"most enlightened ruler in Europe". By the autumn of 1850
he was generally regarded in England as a tyrant. "Pio
Nono" had become, for Englishmen, "The Pope". The
change was due to popular sympathy with Garibaldi's and
Mazzini's stand at Rome, mightily fanned by the arrival
of the many exiles following the French and Austrian occupation. "Triumvir thou hast nobly done, Bravo Mazzini,"
sang Punch. The Carlyles, the Stansfelds, and Mazzini's
other English friends found themselves no longer a small
clique of personal sympathisers. The "Society of the Friends
of Italy" was formed to promote "Italian Independence and
political and religious liberty". Lecture-halls were crowded

to hear Fr. Gavazzi, or Aurelio Saffi, Mazzini's fellow Triumvir. Audiences would soon be sobbing as they listened to Orsini. Mazzini had returned to find himself, in the summer of 1850, a hero in London—a position very different from that which he had occupied in England when he left. But he found the presence of so many of his comrades a mixed blessing: "All exiles are concentrating here to a frightful extent," he reported in March, 1851.[6]

There emerged side by side in England, from 1850 onwards, an enthusiasm for the risorgimento and an indignation against the Papacy which nourished each other and which became confused in the minds of many in a general sentiment of angry contempt for "foreign tyranny"—a sentiment congenial at all times, and one which was mightily augmented not only by the Italian exiles but by all the other Europeans thrown out by the failure of the movements of '48–'49, men such as Ledru Rollin from France, or Kossuth from Hungary. A moment more unpropitious than the autumn of 1850 for the publication of Pius' Bull of Restoration, and the return of the new Cardinal could not have been found. The English liberals, who fêted the exiles, were not, indeed, drawn from the classes which felt pained by the Pope's challenge to the Established Episcopacy; but to the mob, whom the Establishment was only too willing to incite, it was all one in 1850 whether they were hustling the Austrian General, Haynau, at Southwark, in September, or burning the Pope in effigy in December. Foreign tyranny was foreign tyranny, and the distinction between the spiritual and the temporal was altogether too nice to be drawn. And if the skill and courage of Wiseman weathered the storm, and the hierarchy was able, after all, to carry on its work with little impediment, Pio Nono never recovered his popularity in Protestant England. Palmerston, hitherto so cautious in handling the affairs of the Papal State, but always sensitive to mass-sentiment, was soon to feel free to talk about Pio Nono's government as "the worst of governments", although in the meantime it had carried out a number of constructive reforms. Enthusiasm for the risorgimento, fanned by Gladstone's letters on the Neapolitan prisons, by respect for constitutional and scientific progress in Piedmont—even, somewhat perversely, by the bomb with which Orsini, outside the Paris opera, congruously concluded his eccentric career—had attained new heights in England by the time of Garibaldi's visit to London in 1864. The poets had adopted it, as Byron had adopted Greece; Browning, Tennyson, and Swinburne were in full song. And this risorgimento, of which Pio Nono had once been the adored symbol, was now violently anti-Papal, and for the most part anti-Catholic. Has sufficient allowance for English enthusiasm for the risorgimento ever been made in discussions of the reactions in this country to the Pope's Syllabus of Errors in 1864, or his proclamation of the Dogma of Infallibility in 1870?

His experience in restoring the hierarchy in England made the Pope cautious when he undertook, soon after, the work of restoring it in Holland. Yet in important respects that historic continental bulwark of Protestantism proved less resistant. On account of the traditional Catholicism of the peoples of the two southern provinces of Limbourg and Brabant, which accounted for more than half a million Catholics, there was a much stronger nucleus of Catholicism in Holland than in England. The Dutch total, like the English, was about a million, all told, but in a population of three million, as against the English population of some eighteen million. Increase in the number of Catholics in the northern provinces, and especially at Amsterdam, had been steady in the nineteenth century despite their continued disabilities. It was encouraged by the fact that, in the absence of any Church analogous to the Church of England, there was little alternative between Calvinism and Catholicism, apart from the small band of condemned Old Catholics, of Jansenist origin, who numbered at this time only some ten thousand.

Moreover the revolutions of 1848, whose backwash was inimical, in England, to the progress of Catholicism, had, by contrast, in the Protestant countries of Europe, including Holland, a marked effect in stimulating the Catholic revival. Most notably had this been the case in Prussia, where the constitution of December, 1848, had removed the heavy disabilities under which the Church had groaned, and replaced them with those principles of religious and educational freedom for all cults which the Belgian Catholics and Protestants, acting together, had already won from their government and for which the Catholics of France were still struggling against a suspicious and secularly minded State. The result of this new liberty, in Prussia, was the rapid growth of the Church in the Rhineland provinces, a growth so marked that the Prussian constitution, which had severed Church and State, became the ideal invoked even in Catholic states in Germany against "Gallican" or "Josephist" governments.[7] In Holland the constitution which had emerged, after much discussion, in 1849, had secured, if not full educational liberty as against the State (to which the Protestants were opposed) at least the vital principles of the equality of all religious groups before the law, freedom from State interference in clerical appointments, and free communication with Rome.

With these freedoms there were some, even amongst the Vicars Apostolic in Holland, who felt, as had certain of their brethren in England, that it would be wise to rest content. Was it sensible to challenge public opinion by parading the full panoply of the episcopal hierarchy? Pio Nono, remembering the independence of the Dutch Episcopal spirit, which had contributed to the Jansenist schism in Holland, had given no encouragement to a petition for a hierarchy for that country in 1847, although he was already encouraging the English movement by that date. Not until March 4th, 1853, following protracted negotiations with the Dutch government, and when it was clear that Wiseman was going to be able to maintain his position in England, was the Papal Bull of Restoration issued in Holland; the names of the new Bishops were published in the following month. The outcry which followed, known as the "April Agitation", was at least comparable in violence to that which greeted the hierarchy in England, and in as much as it led to the fall of the cabinet of Thorbecke, who had negotiated the settlement, it was more politically effective. The particular point of attack was that the city of Utrecht so illustrious in Protestant tradition, had been chosen as the seat of the new Archbishopric. The indignation which this aroused was analogous to that which the choice of Westminster had evoked in England; actually, in both cases the Pope was deliberately meeting the Catholic wish to revive an historic glory much older than the reformation. To ease the situation the Pope required the new Bishops to take an oath of loyalty to the king. The storm subsided, and progress, even more rapid than in England, soon followed. In Holland and in England was now to be seen, as in Belgium, what Montalembert had been invoking in France and Cavour was soon to give a name to in Italy, namely "a free Church in a free State". It was far from Pio Nono's notion of the ideal polity for a Christian society, as he was soon to make clear in his "Syllabus of Errors". Yet he had shown himself willing, in England and in Holland, to abandon all pretence to special relations with the State (such as had been embodied in the Dutch concordat of 1829, and Lord John Russell himself would have liked to secure in 1848), and, in doing so, though he had foregone all special privileges, and had placed the Catholic Church on the same footing as the Anabaptists in England or the Jansenists in Holland, he had nevertheless avoided state interference, and most notably those two bugbears, where Catholicism was established, namely the "placet" of governments to ecclesiastical appointments and the "exequatur", by which they liked to control the publication of Roman missives. It was a notable achievement and if, in later decades, the name of Pio Nono would most readily conjure up, in northern Europe, the controversies that raged around the Syllabus, Infallibility, and the Temporal Power, his settlement of the status of the Church in the traditional maritime strongholds of Protestantism should properly be reckoned as second to none of his practical accomplishments.

The labours at Rome in connection with the re-establishment of the hierarchies of England and Holland were, in the first instance, those of the Congregation of Propaganda, and in particular of its able secretary, Mgr. Barnabò. Only from time to time, in conversation with the English prelates

resident in Rome, Cardinal Acton, or Mgr. Talbot, or with
Wiseman, Ullathorne, or the future Archbishop of Utrecht,
Mgr. Zwijsen, on their visits to the Holy See, did the Pope
intervene personally in the details of these matters.

It was otherwise with another preoccupation of Pio Nono
at this time, the definition of the Dogma of the Immaculate Conception of the Blessed Virgin Mary. The initiative
here came, indeed, as almost always in the Church, from
below, and especially from abroad. But the Pope took this
matter very personally to his heart, and, in the event, he
carried through what was besought from him in a manner
all his own, a manner pregnant with consequences for the
future.

The demands for the definition of the dogma from
various countries, but most notably from France, were being received at Rome in increasing numbers from the seventeenth century; but the vision of the Blessed Virgin seen
by the novice, Catherine Labouré, in the rue du Bac, Paris,
in 1830, which included the inscription "O Marie, conçue
sans péché, priez pour nous qui avons recours à vous", gave
impetus to the popular movement. With the accession of
Pio Nono, who was known to have a special devotion towards the Mother of God, the demands were renewed; and
on June 1st, 1848 (at the most critical stage of the Papal
State's involvement in the Austrian war), he appointed a
commission of twenty theologians, of whom the leading
spirit was a Jesuit, Fr. Passaglia, to study the question
whether it were practicable to accede to the requests that
had by now been received.

So much misunderstanding was shown at the time, and
has been shown since, concerning this dogma and Pio
Nono's definition of it, that a few words on the problem
will not be out of place here although fuller statements are
readily accessible.[8] The belief in question, as it ultimately
came to be defined, was that the Virgin Mary, at the moment of her conception (which, in itself, was a normal, human, conception) was miraculously exempted from the
taint of original sin. There was, of course, no direct scriptural warrant for the belief, save that implicit in the saluta-
tion of the angel Gabriel, "Hail Mary, full of grace"; and

there was the difficulty, felt by St. Bernard, and by St. Thomas Aquinas, that if the Virgin were thus without sin she was in no need of the redemption, of which all mankind stood in need. The reply to this latter difficulty was that of Duns Scotus, that, in being freed from original sin, Mary was participating, in advance, and in a more perfect way, in the redemption won by her divine Son. And the answer to the absence of direct scriptural warrant was simply the tradition of the Church, and the deductions which it was logical to make from the great and peculiar privileges of Mary. The altogether exceptional nature of the sanctity of Mary was part of the belief of the early Fathers; her divine maternity was defined at the Council of Ephesus in 431; her freedom from actual sin seems never to have been doubted. As regards her conception, the Feast of the Conception of Mary, of eastern origin, was being celebrated in England in the eleventh century, and devotion to her Immaculate Conception was encouraged by St. Anselm, Archbishop of Canterbury. In 1439 the abortive Council of Bâle prepared a decree on the matter which remained unpublished; in 1476 Pope Sixtus IV approved the Feast of the Immaculate Conception, and explicitly encouraged the devotion. The Council of Trent carefully exempted the Virgin Mary from the taint of evil when defining the doctrine of original sin. It remained for Bossuet to voice the general attitude of the seventeenth century:

"If everything is singular about Mary, who can believe that there is nothing supernatural about the conception of that princess and that this was the only part of her life which was not marked by any miracle?"

From Gaeta, on February 2nd, '49, the Pope issued the Encyclical *Ubi Primum*, asking the Bishops for prayers and advice on the question. Of some six hundred replies, only that of the Archbishop of Paris, Sibour, with one or two others, took the line that the belief was not definable; a few more, mainly from Protestant countries, regarded it as inopportune. The overwhelming majority—nine-tenths of the whole—were enthusiastic. Drafts were then prepared by Fr. Perrone, the most noted theologian at Rome, and by

Fr. Passaglia, both Jesuits; hence the notion that the new dogma was "the invention of the Jesuits", a criticism which the Pope anticipated by allowing the Bishops whom he invited for the solemn proclamation, on December 8th, 1854, to introduce a number of modifications into the text at the last moment. "We must accept this humiliation," he is reported to have said, "so that it won't be said that everything depended on the Jesuits".[9]

Rejoicings followed throughout the Catholic world, and a great stimulus was given to devotion to the Blessed Virgin. Such dissatisfaction as existed, in certain circles in Germany, was only tacit, at least for the time being. For Pio Nono the proclamation of the dogma in St. Peter's was certainly one of the supreme moments of his life, and more than once he was overcome with emotion while reading it out. To commemorate the event he caused a very tall and graceful column to be erected in the piazza di Spagna, at Rome, surmounted by a statue of the Virgin as she had appeared to the novice, Catherine Labouré, at Paris. It is one of the more striking of the many monuments which he left in the city.

From the point of view of the future policy and procedure of the Holy See, however, the most significant thing about the occasion, as Mgr. Talbot observed at the time, was not the dogma itself but the manner in which it was proclaimed. A suggestion that the Bishops should be associated with the Pope in the proclamation was not taken up;[10] the dogma was pronounced upon the sole authority of the Pope, after he had fully consulted both the theologians and the episcopate. A precedent of the greatest importance was thus set, which had its influence upon the form in which the dogma of Papal Infallibility came later to be defined, in 1870. Encouragement was given to the ultramontane party in all countries, but notably in France, and the position of the Papacy, in relation to the Church, was strengthened.

And in one other respect the precedent set in this definition proved important. When, in 1950, Pope Pius XII came to define the analogous dogma of the Assumption of the Blessed Virgin into Heaven he followed a method of enquiry, and of consultation with the episcopate, which clearly derived from that employed by Pio Nono in 1854.

2. *Peaceful Development in the Papal State* (1850–1859)

At 4 p.m. on Friday, April 12th, 1850, Pio Nono rode in state back through the Lateran gate of Rome, from which he had made his escape, in disguise, on October 24th, 1848. French troops provided his escort, but the Roman crowd, as ever, was dense and enthusiastic. He rode, now, to the Vatican, henceforth to be his home in place of the Quirinal. According to the orthodox English tradition he emerged from Gaeta and Portici without a vestige of his earlier liberalism left, determined only to anathematise the new Italy, and with her the whole modern world. He had become the mouthpiece of obscurantist Cardinals (and Jesuits), the instrument of their dark designs.

Elements of truth have gone to make this picture, but the perspective is all wrong. We have seen what happened before the revolution at Rome, how the Pope consistently refused the leadership of a nationalist crusade, or any offensive war; how there was no change in his conviction about this during 1848, only a steady refusal to be swept into the leadership of a national revolution although the Italian popular imagination had cast him for that role. There was similarly no fundamental change in him after his return from Gaeta. He was merely more cautious. Experience had taught him to walk more warily in matters of state; it had taught him precisely that prudence which he would have been very wise to have learnt earlier from Metternich. He would go on reforming, as he had always reformed, the political, juridical, and administrative institutions of his state; he would promote economic progress; but he would not let the reality of his temporal power slip from his fingers, as he had begun to let it slip when he allowed a Civic Guard and when he reluctantly granted a

Constitution. And he would be more wary of offending friendly powers, and more chary of abetting either revolutionaries or potential aggressors like Piedmont. All this was merely common sense. After what had happened during the régime of Sterbini, Ciceruacchio, Mazzini, and Garibaldi no other choice was possible if he were to defend the Church at Rome and throughout Italy, which was his first duty.

Pio Nono returned from his Neapolitan exile a sadder and a wiser man, no doubt, but not a changed man, not the tool of the Jesuits, and not the tool of Antonelli. The Jesuits he allowed to found a new periodical at Rome, the *Civiltà Cattolica*, which grew in influence until by 1870 it was really important; but Fr. Curci and his friends, who edited this paper, went in constant danger of the Papal indignation, as we shall later have occasion to notice.[11] They were very far indeed from running either religious or political policy. No doubt their brethren of the Society, Frs. Perrone and Passaglia, the chief draftsmen of the definition of the Dogma of the Immaculate Conception, were influential; but even in the sphere of theology they were not allowed, as we have just seen, to have the last word. Certainly, they shared with Pio Nono a peculiarly strong devotion to the Blessed Virgin; but they did not inspire in Pio Nono this devotion, which we have seen was his inspiration long before he was elected Pope, nor did they inspire the definition of the dogma, which was petitioned by lay Catholics throughout the world.

It is altogether too easy to father upon the Jesuits conservative policies which experience had taught Pio Nono to adopt; and the process becomes all the easier if the man whose influence was really greatest at Rome, namely Cardinal Antonelli, is himself turned into a Jesuit—a surprising metamorphosis which occurred in a recent article.[12] In the sphere of politics, Antonelli, as Secretary of State, did exert great influence, after the restoration. He did so because one of the things the Pope had learnt was that, himself, he was a poor politician; he had come round to Metternich's view on that matter. He had learnt that, although religious and political policy were necessarily interwoven, and although he must always retain the last word in all matters pertaining to his sovereignty, yet it was common sense for him to have an efficient servant who would take responsibility, under himself, for the multifarious diplomatic business involved throughout the world in his headship of the Universal Church, and of the more limited diplomatic business occasioned by his headship of an Italian Principality. Antonelli himself perfectly understood the terms of his appointment; he must make no attempt to run counter to the Pope's wishes. When political interest (the humouring of Napoleon III, for example) conflicted with the Pope's convictions about Catholic religious interest the latter had always to be accepted. Time and again, but most notably at the Vatican Council in 1870, the Secretary had to accept policies which he knew must offend Paris and so endanger the very existence of the Temporal Power. Nobody who understood the relationship between the Pontiff and his faithful Secretary had any doubt about which was the master.[13]

It would doubtless be an exaggeration to say that the Prince delighted to honour Cardinal Antonelli, but he certainly found it convenient to do so. At Gaeta the Cardinal had only been pro-Secretary of State; after the return to Rome he was appointed to the full position, and he retained it until his death in 1876. His friendship with the Pope, such as it was, was certainly a friendship between opposites. Pio Nono, of good birth, personally fastidious, had always put the highest standard of purity in the forefront of his religious ideals; the Cardinal, a Neapolitan of peasant origin,[14] rather coarse in character, never admitted to the priesthood, was not above suspicion as to the purity of his life. When one remembers, too, the warm-hearted generosity of the Pope, and compares it with the acquisitive instincts of the Cardinal, whose brother ran the bank of Rome, and who himself died leaving a handsome fortune to his relatives, together with a notable collection of precious stones, one is almost driven to wonder at Pio Nono's choice. Yet it was natural enough. The Pope wanted somebody obedient, he wanted somebody courageous, and he wanted somebody able, and Antonelli was all three. His obedience

and courage had been proved to the hilt during that terrible
week in November, '48, at the Quirinal, when almost alone
he remained by the side of the Pope, although he would
have had little mercy from the mob if they had broken in.
His ability was proved at Gaeta, and most conspicuously in
his handling of the French government after their troops
had driven Garibaldi and Mazzini from Rome and had
come into sole possession of the city.

Napoleon, we have seen, had different views from Catholic France as to the terms upon which the Holy Father
should be restored to the Eternal City. For long he tried
to secure from Gaeta some specific undertakings as to the
liberties which the Pope would guarantee. But Antonelli,
who remained at Gaeta while the "Red Triumvirate" was
restoring order at Rome (removing on September 4th, '49,
with his master, to Portici, outside Naples), employed his
exceptional powers of prevarication to prevent Pio Nono
from becoming committed. He was in perfect agreement
with the Pope that it must never be allowed that the Papal
Government should become so dependent upon France as
to show itself obliged to rule in accordance with French
wishes. The limit to which they would go in the matter of
constitutional innovation was outlined in the Papal *motu
proprio* of September 12th, '49, issued from Portici. This
document, which formed the basis of the Pope's subsequent
reforms, extended an amnesty to all except the leaders in
the recent disturbances, and those previously amnestied
who had again supported revolution;[15] and it promised a
Consultative Assembly, similar to the *Consulta* of April,
'47, together with elective provincial and municipal councils, and an increase in the lay element in the administration. But it made no mention of restoring the Constitution
of March, 1848. And, while thanking the Catholic powers
in a general way for their intervention, it made no mention
of France by name. Napoleon was thoroughly annoyed. He
had been pressing, through de Corcelles, for an Elective
Assembly at Rome which should control the budget. To
Rostolan, who had succeeded Oudinot in command of the
French army at Rome, he had insisted that he must "allow
no act of violence or reaction which would dishonour our

intervention". In a letter to his personal envoy, Colonel Ney, which was published in the *Moniteur*, he wrote that he had been personally wounded to see no mention made of France, and he insisted upon an amnesty for all, a secular administration, the introduction of the legal principles of the Napoleonic Code, and a Constitution. Rostolan was so embarrassed that he resigned; and the French ambassadors, de Corcelles at Portici and Rayneval at Rome, were in a mood to do the same. Napoleon was, indeed, strangely out of touch with sentiment at Rome at this juncture, for in August, '49, he relieved Oudinot of his command, although Oudinot's popularity, in as difficult a situation as any commander could be asked to tackle, was such that the municipality received him in honour at the capitol, where they put up a bust to his memory, and the populace of the Trastevere offered him a sword of honour. One might suppose that Napoleon had an eye upon his political prospects in France, and was anxious to satisfy opinion in the Assembly that his army at Rome was really fighting for liberty; but if so he had miscalculated because not only Montalembert, who made one of his greatest orations in the French Assembly on this occasion, but the premier, Barrot, spoke in support of the independence of the Pope, and a resolution approving the restoration of Pio Nono without political guarantees was passed, as we saw earlier, by an overwhelming majority.[16] It was Thiers who (October 15th, 1849) summed up most exactly in this debate the state of affairs at Rome:

"France did not find the Pope less generous and liberal [after the fall of the Republic] than in 1847: unfortunately the circumstances were quite different. In any case the *motu proprio* [giving the Pope's programme of reform] represents, for anybody who judges without preconceptions, a really useful step. The Pope does not concede a liberty such as exists in England, whose destinies are committed to two chambers together with the executive authority; but it would be quite wrong to reprove him for having prudently profited by recent experiments and for having wanted to close the way to

new agitations amongst a people that has shown itself so
very unprepared for them. Municipal and provincial
liberty provides a first step in the education of a
people . . ."

Antonelli, then, in 1849, placing his confidence in the
strength of the Catholic revival in France, called Napoleon's bluff and won.

The Cardinal-Secretary had managed the restoration
prudently. During the eight months which intervened between the collapse of Mazzini's republic and the Pope's
return the three Cardinals of the "Red Triumvirate", together with the French army, were left to incur the un-
popularity inseparable from clearing up after a revolutionary régime. By the time Antonelli brought his master back
in April, '50, the unpopular measures had mostly been
taken,[17] and the welcome accorded to Pio Nono was genuine and warm.

With the return of the Pope there was no delay in carrying out the promises made in his *motu proprio* of September 12th, '49.[18] A Council of State (comprising the Heads
of the four main departments, Grace and Justice; Commerce, Agriculture, Industry, Fine Arts, and Public Works;
Finance; the Army) was set up forthwith. And in the same
year (1850) reappeared the elective provincial and municipal councils, whose members had to be small property
holders, and the *Consulta*, at Rome, half elected by the
provincial councils and half appointed by the Pope. As for
the introduction of laymen into the administration, by the
year 1856 it comprised only 289 ecclesiastics as against
6,836 laymen, and although ecclesiastics tended to hold a
rather larger proportion of the higher as compared with
the lower posts the total of the salaries paid to laymen
amounted to fifteen times the total paid to ecclesiastics.[19]
The Heads of the main Departments of State were as often
laymen as ecclesiastics. Only the Secretary of State had, by
long tradition, to be a cardinal—he might be, as Antonelli
was, in minor orders only.

Thus the main provisions of the Memorandum of 1831,
for so long urged by France and England upon the Pope,

had been put into effect by him. But although, by 1856, Napoleon had very seriously curtailed constitutional liberty in France, the reforms at Rome were now to be judged insufficient by the western powers, and more particularly by Clarendon and Palmerston. The "Papal Aggression" had recently occurred in England, and the British government found it both harmless and popular to humour Britain's Crimean war ally, Cavour, by denouncing the Papal government at the Paris Conference of 1856. No doubt Clarendon was sincere in the emotional outburst in which he denounced Rome as the "worst of governments"—more sincere than Palmerston who was now prepared to couple condemnation of the Pope with praise for Napoleon and respect for "that great reformer" the Turkish Sultan! But if Clarendon was sincere he was also misinformed, being worked upon by that interested party, Cavour, at Paris. By the time of the Paris Conference Cavour was already determined upon plans which would dismember the Papal State and include at least the Romagna in a kingdom to be ruled from Turin. As a witness to the condition of the Pope's domains he might, therefore, be suspected of some partiality. We may judge the sort of thing that was going on from the fact that during the Paris Conference Cavour employed Minghetti to draw up a memorial, for Clarendon's benefit, on the state of the Romagna; when this memorial proved insufficiently recriminatory for his purpose he persuaded him to produce, in two days, another document to prove that none of the reforms promised by the Pope since the memorandum of 1831 had ever been put into effect![20]

As sources of evidence about the condition of the Papal State the channels by which Palmerston and Clarendon were fed are unsatisfactory. There was, at this time, no British ambassador or minister at Rome.[21] The occasional English political visitors mostly liked the Pope, personally, disliked the Mazzinians, and supposed that all would be well if only Rome enjoyed the benefits of the British Constitution. The British ambassador in Italy who counted for something in London was Sir James Hudson, at Turin, who made no secret of his enthusiasm for the expansionist and anti-clerical policies of Cavour, and this enthusiasm involved him, necessarily, in anti-papalism. The Roman case then, as so often since, simply went by default in England.

The most interesting picture of the Papal State in the 'fifties was given by the French ambassador at Rome, Rayneval, in a report which he drew up in May, 1856, and despatched to the French foreign minister, Walewski. It was not to Rayneval's interest, at a time when Napoleon was looking for excuses to interfere in Italy on behalf of Piedmont, to send in a report which argued that the wisest course was to let well alone in the Papal State. Nor was it congenial to the ex-carbonaro French ruler to be advised to take with a pinch of salt what interested parties from the Romagna and Piedmont were disseminating to Rome's discredit. Yet that is what Rayneval did, and he paid the penalty for his honesty.[22]

His main point is to stress the progress that has been made with the laicisation of the Roman administration. He ridicules the notion that the Roman government is a bad government because it is a government of priests:

"Are we then to be told that the pontifical government is a model—that it has no weaknesses or imperfections? Certainly not; but its weaknesses and imperfections are of the same kind as are met with in all governments . . . the pontifical government is a government composed of Romans, acting after the Roman fashion . . . It likes alterations and accommodations. It is deficient in energy, in activity, in taking the initiative, in firmness, as is the case with the nation itself." But "when certain persons say to the pontifical government, 'Form an administration which may have for its aim the good of the people', the government might reply, 'Look at our acts, and condemn us if you dare'" . . . "There is, in truth, misery here as elsewhere, but it is infinitely less heavy than in less favoured climates. Mere necessities are obtained cheaply. Private charity is largely exercised. Establishments of public charity are numerous and effective . . . Important ameliorations have been introduced into the administration of hospitals and prisons. Some of these

prisons should be visited, that the visitor may admire—
the term is not too strong—the persevering charity of the
Holy Father."

After pointing to practical achievements—the expansion of
trade, the construction of railways, the building of houses;
and after demonstrating that the average Roman pays rather
less than half what the average Frenchman pays in taxation,
he concludes that "the pontifical administration bears the
marks of wisdom, reason, and progress".[23]

Reason and Progress were, however, the last words which
the progressives Minghetti, at Bologna, and Pasolini, at
Ravenna, were prepared to use to describe the state of affairs. Minghetti is the more critical.[24] He complains that
the Papal Legate at Bologna, Bedini, is getting "every day
more retrograde", that he chooses the wrong people as his
advisers (not Minghetti and his friends), that the French
are greatly to blame for not insisting upon reforms as the
price of the restoration. He and Pasolini can only take comfort in the new Bank of Rome, established in April, 1850
(Antonelli's brother was its director). The merit of that
institution was that it bore some resemblance, in its constitution, to the Bank of England. Always these gentlemen
of the Romagna—so temperamentally unlike even the lay
gentlemen at Rome—were looking to England, and thinking
about economics, and constitutional government. Pasolini
went to London in 1851 to see the great Exhibition. He
was armed with letters of introduction, from Minghetti, to
Cobden and Senior. He was delighted with the Exhibition;
he was thrilled to find Gladstone's translation of Farini's
history; Minghetti writes to urge him to buy Gladstone's
book on Church and State. The two friends exchange copies of the Illustrated London News, pore over pictures of
county agricultural shows, consider together Mill's "Political Economy". "England," writes Minghetti, "is most worthy
to be taken as an example," everything about England de-
lights him except the weather, but he appreciates most her
preoccupation with scientific and economic problems.

These men wanted to be the Gladstones, the Mills, the
Cobdens of the Papal State. But the difficulty, from Pio

Nono's point of view, was that there was only a handful of them, mostly in the Romagna. When they had tried to hold power, as at Rome under the Constitution of 1848, they had found themselves quite unable to retain it; the Sterbinis and Ciceruacchios were much more than a match for them. And so, Pio Nono saw, it would be again, if the Constitution were revived; Rome was not London, with her mighty middle class.

When Pio Nono was making his great tour of his state in the summer of 1857, he reached Imola, in early June, and there he received Pasolini, with whom, twelve years earlier, as Bishop Mastai Ferretti, he had discussed freedom and reform, in the hopeful days of Gioberti's *Primato*. And when he reached Bologna he received him again, more than once; but Minghetti he would not receive privately, only publicly—and rather coolly—having some knowledge of his collusion with Cavour. In his son's memoir Pasolini is reported as having this conversation with the Pope at Bologna:

PASOLINI: "The Constitution is a necessity of our times. There are no states governed nowadays without a Constitution, and your Holiness had granted it."

PIUS: "True, but you saw what bad use they made of it."

PASOLINI: "But all the demagogues of Italy had flocked to Rome in those days; there were then, and there still are now, many wise, upright men . . ."

PIUS: "Who are they? Except yourself, I know of none."

PASOLINI: "Here, at Bologna, is Minghetti, who remained faithful even in 1849."

PIUS: "Well, I don't object to Minghetti; but he is wholly Piedmontese in outlook, and Piedmont is dominated by anti-religious ideas and wants to take possession of the whole of Italy . . ."

PASOLINI: "Piedmont wants to expel the Austrians, and for this purpose the united strength of all the

	Italian states will be needed . . . What course does your Holiness propose to take?"
PIUS:	"Providence will direct us."
PASOLINI:	"Then we are to remain mere spectators of what the government may be pleased to enact?"
PIUS:	"I am very sorry, my dear Count, but there is a person waiting for me, and I have not time for further conversation."
PASOLINI:	"Oh yes! The other day, as well, when leaving here, I saw the Austrian general in the antechamber."

We are told how the Pope accompanied Pasolini to the door:

> "holding his hand, and saying many kindly words of that vague sort which rise to the lips in parting from a friend with whom one cannot agree. At the last moment he turned and said with tears, 'Then you also desert me, my dear Count?' 'No,' said Pasolini, deeply moved, 'we do not desert you but your Holiness has thrown us over.'"[25]

Whatever the accuracy of the report—and it can hardly be verbatim—it is clear from all we know of Minghetti's and Pasolini's views that it represents them. Pasolini, who was milder than Minghetti, yet feels free to stand his ground with the Pope, feels he has a right to advise him, and that if his advice is not taken he has been "thrown over". He claims the rights which, as a gentleman of independent means, he would at that date have enjoyed in England. And in particular he claims a Constitution, with an assembly where he could exercise his talents, as once, in 1848, the Pope had allowed him to exercise them, and as one day he was to exercise them again in the parliament of United Italy. But the Pope's mind was quite made up. "If these Liberal Governments are to imitate Piedmont," he told Pasolini at Imola, "they must be anti-Christian, and they cannot fail to disgust a great part of the population . . . I will not have fundamental changes, for in that case an army would be required."[26]

It was his pride that he needed no army. Other states all had standing armies, even small states like Piedmont and Naples. But he only had a token force, and that was a major reason why the taxation was so low. So long as the state was his state, the Pope's state, a sort of paternalistic demesne, it would not, he claimed, be attacked or disrupted, because that would be sacrilege, and the Catholic powers would always defend him. But if the power passed from him to the people then they would have to provide their own army for their own defence. It was a strong argument, and the Pope believed in it sincerely. To his mind it entirely justified the French and Austrian occupation; and indeed it does throw into a different perspective the situation which gave rise to the jibe that the administration of the Papal State stood condemned because it required two foreign armies of occupation to hold the people down.

The Pope was pleased with his tour. He had been acclaimed everywhere, triumphal arches had been erected, it had almost seemed reminiscent of 1847. From Bologna he wrote in July to his brother, Conte Gabriele Mastai, at Sinigaglia:

"At Ravenna and at Lugo all has gone not merely well, but very well. As at Bologna, so at Ravenna I have had long talks with the respective magistracies. None of them asked for anything it had not the right to ask . . . it is false what was printed in certain misguided papers that some of the magistracies would want to demand increased administrative powers and progressive concessions. Those are individual desires which have no counterpart amongst the majority; but it is true that those individuals are much heated and they cause the many to keep quiet, who only want to look after their own affairs."[27]

The Pope may have been a little naïve in supposing that nobody had fundamental reforms to suggest, for those who arranged the audiences did not encourage the bringing forward of embarrassing suggestions. But he was probably right in supposing that discontent was confined to the few, since the people were not interested in constitutional reforms, local or central, in which they would in any case have had no share; only men like Pasolini were interested in that sort of thing. The populace was interested in wages, and security, and the price of food, in the danger of famine, and in the charitable organisations which cared for its needy members. Was life getting harder, in these days, for the people of the Papal State?

Rayneval reports that "an appearance of prosperity strikes the eyes of the least observant. Gaiety of the most expansive kind is to be traced on the faces of all. It may be asked whether this can be the people whose miseries excite to such a degree the commiseration of Europe?"

But then, who ever saw an Italian crowd that did not look cheerful, that did not indulge in "gaiety of the most expansive kind"?

Prosperity is another matter. It is surprising to find Rayneval reporting prosperity, and of course one does not know just what he means. But there is reason to suppose that the people were better off in the 'fifties than they had been at the beginning of Pio Nono's pontificate. In an interesting study[28] Domenico Demarco has analysed some of the causes of the distress which certainly played its part in the revolution of 1848, prompting the wild-eyed men who jumped on the Pope's coach crying *"Corragio Santo Padre!"*, the men who were ready to follow Ciceruacchio and Sterbini. The most important cause was that they were hungry. There had been the shortage of grain, general in Europe after the failure of the harvests of '45 and '46, and again of '48, and the Roman merchants had found they could secure higher prices in Tuscany or at Marseilles than they could at home. The position had been aggravated by the fact that, ever since the occupation of the Papal State by the French in Napoleon I's day, the old *Corporazioni d'arti e Mestieri* —the traditional guild organisation—had been abolished, and uncontrolled hoarding and speculation had become far easier. Pius VII, in 1801, had similarly abolished the twenty-seven *Università* which had controlled the entire economic life of the State. He had done so on the grounds that their influence was restrictive. But Pio Nono, who had begun by restoring a few of the corporations, before the revolution, ended, in a *motu proprio* of May 14th, 1852, by restoring the entire organisation of the *Università*. This was not in accordance with the best laissez-faire principles of Adam Smith, and Cobden, and in a sense it was "unprogressive"; but it certainly appears to have checked speculation, lowered prices, diminished want, and been generally popular.

In many ways the burden on the State became much relieved in the 'fifties. The Civic Guard, whose arming had cost two million scudi (crowns), was mostly disbanded. The army, hurriedly raised in 1848, was also reduced; it was cheaper to let the French and Austrians protect the state. And now, once again, there was a big influx of visitors to Rome, who had been kept away by the disturbances of '48–'49. As a result of these factors, together with the much more systematic ordering of the state finances, introduced by Antonelli, the debt, which had stood at over two million scudi in 1850, was progressively reduced throughout the 'fifties, until by 1859 it had disappeared.[29]

As in the rest of Europe, so in the Papal State, the 'fifties were a period of economic development, but the development was slower there than in many lands because Central Italy is not naturally rich. Hemp (sent to England) and silk, produced in the eastern provinces, were exported, so were the *objets d'art* and furniture made at Rome which were to be seen in the Roman pavilion of the London Exhibition of 1851.

The industrial revolution was reaching the Papal State in the 'fifties. She was beginning to enjoy those improvements of the time which were common to most European countries—railways, ships, telegraphs, hydraulic and steam machinery; Pio Nono had a weakness for the latest mechanical wonders. In 1863 a steel railway drawbridge was constructed over the Tiber, near Porta Portese, which is still in use for road vehicles. It was a novelty, and the Pope went out, without previous warning, to witness the opening, to bless the bridge, and to congratulate the workmen. Three times the great structure was raised and lowered by a mere four men, in his presence, the crowd distracted between its excitement at seeing the bridge go up and down and the unexpected chance of getting close enough to the

Pope to catch something of his conversation. Foreign tourists who were crossing the Campagna stopped to watch; amongst them the British Chief Commissioner of Works, Lord John Manners. The Pope's friend, de Mérode, insisted upon introducing the Minister forthwith, despite his embarrassment at presenting himself to the Pope in his grey coat and straw hat, and carrying his umbrella. Pio Nono put him at his ease:

"I am very glad to see you, especially at this moment. You will be able to tell them, when you return to London, that the Roman Pontiff is not always in prayer, surrounded with incense, with monks, and with religious. You will be able to tell the Queen that Her Majesty's Minister of Public Works one day surprised the old Pope, in the midst of his workmen, attending the opening of a new bridge over the Tiber, and himself explaining pretty well the mechanism of the new invention."[30]

The railway lines between Rome and Frascati, and Rome and Civita Vecchia, were both completed by 1860; over the longer line from Rome to Ancona and Bologna there was some delay, though the flat section from Bologna to Ancona was opened in 1861. The Pope blessed the departure of the first train to Frascati. On its arrival, having completed the fourteen miles in twenty-eight minutes, there was a banquet at which the band played a march imitating the puffing of the engine, the grinding of the brakes, the noise of the train in motion, and the whistles. But the short tunnel had been the greatest attraction.[31] The line to Civita Vecchia the Pope was soon using personally, as he was interested in the developments being undertaken at the port; his train had three special coaches, painted in white and gold, a drawing-room, a dressing-room, and a "carozza-capella" (chapel-coach), a splendid affair on bogie-wheels, one of the first railway coaches ever to be mounted in that way.

There is a certain pathos about all these railway developments in as much as the lines Pio Nono was building were so soon to be lost to him through the Piedmontese invasion. Thus Cavour's occupation of Umbria and the

Marches, in 1860, left the Pope responsible for completing
and paying for the Bologna-Ancona line, the whole of which
then lay outside his territory. The centre of his interest,
however, was in Rome. He has left many monuments there,
of which the reconstructed *San Paolo Fuore le Mure* and
the column in honour of the Immaculate Conception are
only the most notable. He shared with his contemporaries
Louis Napoleon and the Prince Consort a strong interest
in the achievements of science and engineering; and not
unnaturally, at Rome, the science that was developing most
rapidly was archaeology. In de Rossi Rome produced an
archaeologist of genius; but his astonishing achievements at
the catacombs of Saint Calixtus and Saint Agnese, in the
Forum, the Colosseum, and the early churches would not
have been possible without the interest and backing of
the Pope, who was always striding forth, in the afternoon,
to look at the latest discoveries. Pio Nono loved a walk;
if he were not out seeing what de Rossi was doing he was
likely to be found with de Mérode, who was working effectively amongst the prisons, the hospitals, and the
schools, making them into a model to Europe. (Even when
the Piedmontese new broom was sweeping in the city, after
1870, de Mérode's institutions remained untouched.) That
energetic and fearless Belgian (brother-in-law of Montalembert) took the Pope right through the cholera ward of the
Sant Andrea hospital on one occasion; Antonelli, when he
heard, was much shocked, which added to Pio Nono's
pleasure in recounting the story when he returned home to
the Vatican.

The Papal State was a benevolent theocracy. There may
have been no longer a place, in the Europe of 1860, for
benevolent theocracies, and it may have been in the nature
of things that the rising tide of the risorgimento should
sweep this State away. But that is not a reason for stigmatis-
ing Pio Nono's government as oppressive, or corrupt, or
economically backward; nor was the revolt, whether of enlightened moderates or of revolutionaries, really a revolt
against oppression; it was rather a hankering after new
forms and the awakening of political ambitions.

At the Birmingham Oratory, in October 1866, Newman, in his best vein of truth-enfolding humour, preached a sermon about the Papal State:

" 'All the ancients of Israel, being assembled, came to Samuel . . . and they said to him . . . Make us a king to judge us, as all nations have.' Observe, my Brethren, this is just what the Roman people are saying now. They wish to throw off the authority of the Pope, on the plea of the disorders which they attribute to his government, and to join themselves to the rest of Italy, and to have the King of Italy for their king . . . [But Samuel warned them] 'He will take your sons and will put them in his chariots; and he will make them his horsemen, and his running footmen to go before his chariots. He will take the tenth of your corn and the revenues of your vineyards. Your flocks also he will take, and you shall be his servants.'

"Now here the parallel I am drawing is very exact. It is happier, I think, for the bulk of a people, to belong to a small state which makes little noise in the world, than to a large one. At least in this day we find small states, such as Holland, Belgium, and Switzerland, have special and singular temporal advantages. And the Roman people, too, under the sway of the Popes, at least have had a very easy time of it; but, alas, that people is not sensible of this, or does not allow itself to keep it in mind. The Romans have not had those civil inconveniences, which fall so heavy on the members of a first-class Power. The Pontifical Government has been very gentle with them; but, if once they were joined to the kingdom of Italy, they would at length find what it is to attain temporal greatness. The words of Samuel to the Israelites would be fulfilled in them to the letter. Heavy taxes would be laid on them; their children would be torn from them for the army; and they would incur the other penalties of an ambition which prefers to have a share in a political adventure to being at the head of Catholic citizenship . . ."[32]

Newman's prophecies were soon to be fulfilled, in the
new taxation and rise in the cost of living which followed
1870, in the costly disasters of Crispi's foreign policy, and
in the fearful sufferings of Italians in World War I; events
which were to be followed by the demands of Mussolini's
Fascism, and the "red-hot rake of war" scorching from Sa-
lerno, and Anzio, up to the Alpine passes.

It is easy to say that it was "in the nature of things" that
a new unitary state, Italy, should emerge, and that with
her emergence the old Papal State must necessarily disappear. But hardly anybody thought that, in Italy, in the
eighteen-fifties, and the view only properly belongs to those
who adhere to the historical school of thought that whatever happened was bound to happen. By the eighteen-fifties,
certainly, a lot of Italians were thinking in terms of Pope
Julius II's *"fuore gli barbari"*, and envisaged the peninsula
free from foreign occupation and from foreign interference.
But federalist views were still strong, so that in 1859, when
he had defeated the Austrians, it seemed natural to Napoleon III to propose a federalist solution. The great differences of history and outlook between Venice and Naples,
Milan and Rome, Turin and Florence, not to mention the
tenacious independence of the Sicilians, differences which
even Mussolini's steam-roller failed to flatten, were very
strong arguments for a federal Italy. And if there was going
to be a federal Italy, it was taken for granted, in 1859
as in 1848, that the Pope would be President, and the
Papal State would be a constituent member. Of all the
various solutions to the Italian problem, ranging from Mazzini's unitary republic to Turin's hegemony for the House
of Savoy, some form of Papal confederation still seemed
the most likely, even though the best opportunity had been
lost in 1848 and Piedmont would certainly now require
some position of precedence. The Germanic Confederation was still there as a model; if a state as militarily strong
as Prussia could exist within that federation, could not
Piedmont similarly exist within an Italian one? There were
plenty of Piedmontese patriots who thought so; but the
one who was ablest and most determined of them all had

further-reaching ambitions, and that fact decided the event. Cavour outwitted everybody—Napoleon, the Austrians, and Antonelli; and Cavour intended to secure the supremacy of his king.[33]

The diplomatic and military history of Pio Nono's principality, from 1850 to 1870, is, in reality, the story of a straight struggle between Rome and Turin; and although it was a struggle in which Antonelli, from the first, anticipated ultimate defeat, yet the cause of Pio Nono was maintained with such courage by himself, by the Pope, by de Mérode, by the soldier Lamoricière, and by the volunteers who flocked to Rome from all over the Catholic world, that they gave to the final dénouement the quality of high tragedy.

Chapter Five

TURIN VERSUS ROME
(1850–1860)

1. *The Religious Aggression in Piedmont* (1848–1856)

At the time of his flight to Gaeta, in November, '48, Pio Nono was already out of sympathy with Piedmontese political policy. He had been disillusioned by the obvious ambitions of Turin to build up an independent North Italian Kingdom under the House of Savoy, and by her rejection of Rossi's attempts to lay the necessary foundations for any future Italian federation. After his flight he was angered by Gioberti's attempts to mediate between the Revolution and the Pope at Rome, angered so that he left Piedmont out of the invitation to the Catholic Powers to reinstate the Holy Father.

In March, 1849, had come the defeat at Novara of the new Piedmontese attack upon Austria, the abdication of Charles Albert, the temporary eclipse of Piedmont as a leading political force in the peninsula, the accession of the young Victor Emmanuel.

Pio Nono had already conceived a strong, paternal affection for Victor Emmanuel. It was rather an odd affection because the Pope was under no illusion that the young Prince was a man of wisdom or capacity, and he had never met him. He had heard about him from his mother the Queen Maria Teresa, as well as from the Nuncio at Turin, and what he had heard made him doubtful whether so young a man, so little inclined towards thought or study, so ardently enamoured of the hunting field, and so acceptable to the liberals, were suited to the succession at that juncture. He had, indeed, advised Charles Albert against abdicating.[1] Yet his affection for the young King was so strong that it lasted until both rulers died, within a month of each other, twenty-nine years later; and it is one of the oddest friendships in history, surviving as it did, on both sides, the spoliation by the King of the Church in Piedmont and in the rest of Italy, and his seizure of the temporal domain of the Pope. Always, to Pio Nono, Victor Emmanuel was "led astray" by his counsellors, always he "understood nothing". Throughout, he wrote to him as though he were a naughty boy who needed to be reminded of his duties; and still stranger, in his letters, the King accepted that role. But he didn't stop doing what the Pope told him not to do, and for the Pope's patience it is hard to find a parallel, even in Papal history, unless it be in the attitude of Pio Nono's mentor, Pius VII, towards his persecutor, Napoleon.

Victor Emmanuel started, as he continued, anxious to do right in defence of the Church if circumstances permitted. But the current in Piedmont was now flowing very strongly in the secularist direction. Already, before Novara, before the Pope's flight to Gaeta, Charles Albert had warned Pio Nono of this, in a pathetic letter from Turin:

". . . we have reached a point so distressing for Religion that I can scarcely bring myself to speak of it. Our Country used to pass for a model of piety; Religion was triumphant there; daily she made immense progress; the Religious Orders were venerated there; they increased, bringing with them immense good; the education of youth pursued a course that was religious, edifying; when suddenly, two or three years ago, a fatal quarrel between two of our prelates gave birth to a great scandal in the Church; then to a terrible division amongst the clergy. An abbé of great renown [Gioberti] published several works setting forth opinions and judgments on the Religious Orders which were never publicly censured by the Church; these ultra-liberal principles were shortly afterwards encouraged and magnified by the declaration of the Republic in France . . . so great is the evil, Most Holy Father, that it is beyond human power to repair it . . ."[2]

Charles Albert thus laid most of the blame at the door of Gioberti's onslaught upon the Jesuits, dating from his virulent *Gesuito Moderno,* published in 1846. We may discern, too, a hint to the Holy Father (still at that date a constitutional monarch) of the consequences of indulging the liberals: "How many times have I longed to open my heart to Your Holiness, to confide my cruel sufferings; but I would have been increasing your own sufferings."

By the end of 1849 things were very much more serious. The popular Press in Piedmont was freely indulging in diatribes against the Church. There were demonstrations and disorders, particularly at Genoa. Strange sects emerged, like that which followed Grignaschi, the "Enthusiast" at Viarigi, in the diocese of Asti.[3] New sectarian churches were being built in Turin. The lifting of the censorship had admitted and disseminated anti-Catholic literature from Switzerland and socialist propaganda from France.

Victor Emmanuel was genuinely anxious to keep on good terms with the Pope. His mind did not run easily along the lines of religious and political principles, nor was he so noted as his father for personal piety, but he knew that his family had a good record of loyalty towards the Church—of which the Pope, the Queen, and the Queen Mother were at pains to remind him—and he had a general idea that the preservation of religion was important to the well-being of society. His difficulty consisted in the fact that he had sworn, at his accession, to be loyal to the Piedmontese Constitution of 1848 and he was persuaded by the liberals that if he challenged the will of the Chamber of Deputies he would assuredly lose his throne. French influences were uppermost in Piedmont, and the fate of Charles X and of Louis Philippe provided compelling testimony to the terrible power of the new liberalism. The King was by no means imbued with that affection for the Constitution which Cavour sought later to give him, and he told Antonucci, the Papal Nuncio at Turin, that he would like to control more firmly the destinies of his kingdom, but that it would be very dangerous to go to extremes, even though he "held the constitutional system to be the worst possible" and awaited "the opportunity to bring about its downfall".[4]

The Chamber, therefore, had the upper hand from the first, and within the Chamber the "Democratic" party, though not as yet in power, exerted much pressure, through Rattazzi and Brofferio, and was violently anti-clerical in temper. In the period before November, 1852, during which d'Azeglio was in power, the pressure from the Left was strong; when Cavour came to power, in that month, he was soon working with these men, and a year later he gave an important office—the Ministry of Justice—to their leader, Rattazzi, and this made inevitable the more extreme of the measures against the Church.

The difficulty in settling the points at issue, in 1849, had not seemed insurmountable. There was a quarrel about certain of the higher clergy in Piedmont, and notably about the Archbishop of Turin, Fransoni, and about Mgr. Artici, the Bishop of Asti, both of whom had been compelled to withdraw from their dioceses, and were being subjected to an investigation on the part of a committee of the Chamber. They were accused, with some justice, of insufficient hatred of Austria and insufficient enthusiasm for the Constitution. There was also a desire on the part of Turin for a revision of the Concordat with Rome, particularly in respect of Church Courts, the judicial privileges of the clergy, and the tenure of Church lands in mortmain. Political and business leaders wanted to reduce the number of Feast Days, and to restrict or abolish the right of Sanctuary.

On the Pope's side there was antagonism to the law already passed in October, 1848, restricting ecclesiastical control over education and giving effective control over both curriculum and the appointment of teachers to the State.

These were the points which first Balbo and then Siccardi were sent to discuss with Pio Nono and Antonelli, first at Gaeta and then at Portici. They both came back to Turin empty-handed, and it has been customary to say that they had encountered the intransigent hostility of Antonelli, who had set his face against allowing Piedmont to introduce those necessary reforms in her relations with the Church which "all modern states", including some Catholic states, had already introduced.

Yet what are the facts? The Pope showed a willingness to discuss the revision of the Concordat, even though the existing one had been agreed as recently as 1841 explicitly to safeguard the position of the Church Courts. He made no difficulty about the Feast Days. But the discussion of these and the further points was prevented by the fact that the envoys put in the forefront of their demands the

removal of the two unpopular Bishops; and Pio Nono was
inexorably opposed to throwing them to the wolves of the
Chamber, a betrayal which could only have had disastrous
effects upon the clergy suffering pressure from the State in
various other countries. The revision of the Concordat was
therefore never discussed; and although it was put about in
Piedmont that cold hostility had been encountered at Gaeta
and Portici the fact was that Balbo found Antonelli "one
of the most courteous men with whom I have ever conducted affairs",[5] while Siccardi found Pio Nono very ami-
able, ready to discuss the judicial question, but firm about
the Bishops,[6] and considered Antonelli even more courteous than the Pope, so that the Secretary of State seemed
to have been allotted the "dolce e conciliante" part to play,
while the Pope seemed the more "severe e imponente".[7]

But Pio Nono was very anxious not to increase the
difficulties confronting the bewildered young Victor Emmanuel, and he knew that when Siccardi departed from
Portici, at the end of November, '49, without concluding
any agreement, there was likely to be resentment in the
Chamber at Turin, and the King might well be confronted
with new anti-clerical demands.

It was essential, in some way, to lead the young ruler
to understand what was vital to the Church, and could not
be surrendered without injury to the faith, and what was
subject to negotiation and agreement. An admirable envoy
was found for this purpose in Mgr. Charvaz, who had been
tutor to the young Victor Emmanuel, and who enjoyed, till
his death in 1870, the King's respect and affection. Charvaz
was in Rome in November, '49, and it was judged important
that he should, if possible, reach Victor Emmanuel ahead
of Siccardi, who was still with the Pope at Portici. But a
series of misfortunes prevented this. He had, first, to go
to Portici to get his instructions from the Pope and Antonelli, and was delayed by a quarantine regulation from
entering the Kingdom of Naples. Then, when he got to
Turin, which he achieved ahead of Siccardi, he was confined to bed for a week with a fever. When he recovered,
the King was away in the country, hunting. So Siccardi got
his word in first, and Charvaz found the King in a fury.

Even so, he gradually brought him round. There was some hard arguing about Archbishop Fransoni, but in the end Charvaz got the King to agree that he should return to Turin, on the understanding that if his presence created such disorder that he could not effectively fulfil his duties the Pope should withdraw him. In his letter to Pio Nono Charvaz suggested that it would be a good thing if the Archbishop received from the Pope "quelques avertissements fraternels, pour se régler avec toute prudence, patience et charité". For the Bishop of Asti Charvaz could only secure that he be left unmolested in his country house. It was agreed to postpone but not to abandon the negotiation of a new Concordat concerning Church Courts and the judicial privileges of the clergy. Finally the King reaffirmed his belief in the right of the Bishops to exercise supervision and direction over education, which he would see embodied in a new law, and told him he had already drawn up a law to impose some measure of control over the sacrilegious excesses of the Press. If this law should fail to pass the Chamber he was ready to suspend the statute conferring the Constitution in order that he might take the necessary measures.[8]

The King's observation to Charvaz about the Constitution is a further indication of his want of enthusiasm for it; but it is not evidence that the Pope was trying to get him to suspend or withdraw it. There is no hint, whether in the instructions given to Charvaz by Antonelli, or in Charvaz' report of his conversations, that the Pope had such an object in view. Without doubt Pio Nono's recent experience had made him look with some suspicion upon Constitutions, and he was not proposing to restore that which he had granted to his own State. But he was very careful to avoid making recommendations to Victor Emmanuel on this matter, and when it seemed that the King thought this was what the Pope was getting at Antonelli sent a further letter to Charvaz, on January 29th, 1850, to explain that the Holy See was not concerned in any way to tender such advice, but solely to urge that "a Catholic Government make every effort to ensure that Catholicism is not thus attacked with impunity".[9]

Victor Emmanuel was so pleased with Charvaz that he offered him the post of Chief Almoner, at his court. This Charvaz declined; but a little later he reluctantly accepted the Archbishopric of Genoa, the most difficult position in the Piedmontese Church, and from that See he exercised a restraining influence upon everybody as the religious and political quarrel deepened and widened. With a breezy contempt for the Pope and Antonelli, d'Azeglio and his government went ahead with their plans, and Siccardi introduced the laws that bear his name abolishing the Church Courts, and the right of Sanctuary, and reducing the number of Feast Days. On all these points, which were covered by the Concordat of 1841, Pio Nono had been ready to negotiate a new agreement, offering the new Concordat with Tuscany as a model.[10] There was, in fact, no need at all for a major quarrel about them. But d'Azeglio was determined upon a popular victory on the issue; and what was really significant about the Siccardi laws, which were the outcome, was the deliberate gesture of defiance of Rome, the attitude that the "sovereign people" would settle Church affairs in its own way, even when their resolutions involved unilateral denunciation of a recently agreed Concordat. The King, who seems not to have appreciated, when the bill was first introduced, how far-reaching the effects of such a gesture on the part of his government must be, subsequently tried to withdraw it from discussion in the Chamber; but the Ministers went to him in a body to tender their resignation if he should do so, and he capitulated. By repeating the same tactics they also defeated an attempt by the King and Charvaz to secure a conference between Ministers and representatives of the Church, in the presence of the King. Yet they nearly overplayed their hand; some of the best men in the Chamber, including Balbo, pleaded for postponement, pointing out that the possibilities of negotiation with Rome had not yet been exhausted. It was Cavour, in the first of his great speeches in the Chamber, who won the day for the government.

By the end of 1852 Cavour was in power, and destined to be the controlling influence in Piedmontese policy till his death in 1861. With him the quarrel, which was still predominantly religious, was to become predominantly political, till it became open warfare. But before it did that it was going to be much exacerbated on its religious side. For having established, with the Siccardi laws, the principle that the State could do what it liked with the Church, irrespective of agreements with Rome, the ministers were bent upon a much more serious measure, the "Law of the Convents", by which they intended to dissolve most of the Religious Orders. The pattern, in fact, of the Henrician Reformation in England was being followed, which was one of the arguments put forward in favour of the programme. It was hardly, however, an argument calculated to reassure the Pope as well as it reassured Sir James Hudson; nor was Rome much more impressed by being reminded that France had done the same thing at the time of her great revolution and Austria something similar under Joseph II. France was now making amends; Austria was already negotiating a Concordat which would replace "Josephism"; even in England there were now Religious Orders flourishing. It was untimely that the State which sought to control the whole of North Italy should be setting such an example to Italians; she might conceive that she was being up to date and enlightened, but it was only the enlightenment of the eighteenth century that she was reflecting.

The onslaught upon the Religious Orders in Piedmont, an onslaught which was extended, in due course, to the entire Kingdom of Italy, confirmed Rome in the conviction that the whole movement which was now coming to be called the *Risorgimento* was essentially anti-Catholic. The Moderates, as well as the Mazzinians, seemed evidently hostile to the Church. These developments contributed powerfully towards making the Pope hostile to the "so-called party of Progress", to the mood which prompted him to sponsor the issue of the Syllabus of Errors, much of which was composed of his published denunciations of Piedmontese persecution. And they affected, too, his attitude to the preservation of the Temporal Power; how should he listen to suggestions that the Romagna might be handed over to some Piedmontese-controlled North Italian Kingdom if it meant that there, too, the conventual life of the Church would be suppressed?

In November, 1854, just before the introduction of the proposed "Law of the Convents", Charvaz, now Archbishop of Genoa, together with the Bishops of Maurienne and Annecy, was engaged at Rome, on behalf of Victor Emmanuel, in trying to reach an understanding with Pio Nono and Antonelli for the basis of a new Concordat. Despite all that had happened there was the strongest desire, on both sides, for this understanding; and the Bishops found "the most benevolent attitude both amongst the cardinals with whom we have been conferring and on the part of the Supreme Pontiff". But, at this hopeful moment, Rattazzi, Minister of Justice in Cavour's Cabinet, and Leader of the Left, introduced the Bill on the Convents into the Chamber. Its first clause stated its purpose succinctly:

"All the Religious Orders are declared abolished, with the exception of the Sisters of Charity and those of St. Joseph, and those Orders and Communities dedicated to public instruction, preaching, or the care of the sick, which are mentioned by name in the list . . ."[11]

Further provisions of the bill prohibited the constitution of any further congregation except by legislation, suppressed most of the ecclesiastical colleges, including one large priests' seminary, and abolished a number of benefices. The money thus acquired by the State was to be used for pensions for those dispossessed and for an increase in the payment of the poorer priests. The income of Archbishops was reduced by about four-fifths, and that of Bishops by more than half.

As always in measures of this kind there were two motives. One was economic, deriving from a widespread feeling, which was not unjustified, that the Church in Piedmont had acquired considerable wealth, and that it should not, therefore, be necessary for the national budget to provide, annually, a subsidy of about a million lire towards the stipends of the clergy. The other argument was religious, and derived from the opinion that monks and nuns were "useless", "medieval", "anomalous in modern society"

and should only be allowed to survive where it could clearly
be shown that they were performing a practical service of
real value to the community.

Cavour, who was never anxious to raise religious quarrels
if he could avoid them, relied upon the economic argument,
and the bill was therefore introduced as a finance bill designed to relieve the budget. But he very nearly involved
himself in defeat by taking this line because the Church
in Piedmont promptly offered, with the approval of Rome,
to produce the necessary million lire to relieve the State
budget of the burden of supporting the poorer clergy. She
thus rendered the bill, economically speaking, unnecessary. Cavour's bluff was called, and the poor King was profoundly relieved; a timely relief for he had had a most miserable winter. Within six weeks, first his mother, the Queen
Maria Teresa, widow of Charles Albert, then his Queen,
Marie-Adelaide, and finally his brother, the Duke of Genoa,
had died—each death occurring shortly after the Chamber
had resumed discussion of the bill. Both Queens had been
in the habit of corresponding with Pio Nono, from whom
they did not conceal their complete devotion nor their desperate anxiety to see amicable relations re-established between Turin and Rome. Their deaths were very bitter to
the Pope as well as to the King; with the disappearance of
their pious influence the chances of religious accord were
certainly much lessened.

Delighted with the Bishops' gesture in offering to pay
the million lire, which seemed to meet all the difficulties,
the King sent at once for Cavour to give him the "very
gratifying" news. This was on April 24th (1855), just one
day after the bill had appeared in the Senate. There was
nothing Cavour could do but agree that the offer should
be made known to the Senate; but he managed to secure
that that should not be done until two days later, which
gave him the chance, the next day, to make a long speech
in the Senate, himself, in which he took the opportunity
to shift his ground by portraying the quarrel as concerned
with something more than mere finance. He depicted it
now as "reaction" versus "progress". All the same, when,
the day after, the Bishop of Casale introduced the Bish-

ops' offer, it was accorded a great welcome, and Cavour found it necessary to suspend the sitting forthwith and to follow that gesture with his own resignation and that of his ministry. A remarkable campaign followed. The liberal press put it about that the Bishops' offer was a plot, hatched in Rome, to buy control of the government and to undermine the Constitution; actually, the offer owed most to the initiative of the liberal-minded Archbishop of Chambéry, Mgr. Billet, and was approved by the whole Piedmontese Episcopate except Fransoni of Turin. So far from being prompted by Rome, as part of a plot, it was only agreed to with extreme reluctance by Antonelli, in a letter which he sent on April 4th.[12]

However, Cavour and his followers were determined men. To prevent the King from being able to form another government they put it about that the British and French governments would never tolerate any premier but Cavour (the Crimean war was in progress, and Cavour had sent a contingent to help the allies). This rumour held sway until the Ambassadors of both the powers concerned denied it.[13] Then crowds of university students were encouraged to demonstrate noisily in the streets; silent crowds were organised to impress the royal palace, as a few years earlier they had been marshalled at the Quirinal. D'Azeglio reminded the King of the fate of James II of England and of Charles X of France. Cavour was recalled. By eleven votes the bill was squeezed through the Senate on May 22nd, and on May 29th the reluctant royal signature was given to the decree dissolving the congregations. When, in the following year, the deputy Oytana rendered his account to the Chamber of the financial proceeds from the closure members were shocked at the small return; no doubt, as the *Civiltà Cattolica* reported, exaggerated expectations had been encouraged at the time of the quarrel to give an edge to the agitation.

To the Pope, the economic aspects of the matter were without consequence in comparison with the frontal assault which had been carried against the very citadel of Catholic piety, namely the ideal of the contemplative life. The Bishops' offer had unmasked Cavour's purpose and compelled him to argue his case as a matter of moral principle, which, indeed, was how he really conceived it. To him, as he now told the Chamber, it was a question of social reform.[14] Monastic orders might have been useful in the Middle Ages, but they had no place in the century of progress. The Protestant countries, where, for a time at least, the Orders had been abolished, had made better economic progress than the Catholic—he drew his examples from the Protestant cantons of Switzerland, from Prussia, from England. "The claustral habit of abstention from work exercises a very bad effect upon industry, it renders labour less respectable and less respected . . ." Monks had become "not only useless, but actually harmful". In accordance with this theory the act of dissolution was drawn up, in the manner described, so as to exclude from its provisions certain Orders which were held to be performing useful functions. It was only concerned with what Cavour's biographer calls "the useless Orders". Yet, looking at the matter from the Pope's standpoint, those useless Orders happened to be pursuing what the whole tradition of the Church had always regarded as the most perfect way of life for those few who have the vocation to pursue it; and at that time the proportion endeavouring to pursue it in Piedmont was one-thousandth of the population,[15] the majority of them nuns. As the veteran statesman della Margherita drily observed in the Chamber: "The ancient Romans, though Gentiles, respected the virtue of the Vestals; but now, in a Catholic country, there is no respect for virgins consecrated to the service of God."

What answer could Pio Nono, as interpreter of the tradition of the Church, be expected to give? Cavour, a layman much influenced by rationalist and anti-clerical influences from abroad, was claiming to decide which Catholic religious rules were valuable and which were not. It is not altogether easy to accept the argument that Pio Nono should have allowed himself to be reassured by Cavour's protestations that he was doing all this "in the best interests of religion". It is scarcely wonderful that the Pope was as much impressed by the hypocrisy as by the spoliation. As he watched, in the years that followed, the spread of the Piedmontese rule over the whole peninsula it was the extinction of the conventual life, which always followed in its wake, that angered him most.

This struggle over the Law of the Convents, at Turin, in 1855, is central to the consideration of Pio Nono's pontificate. He had been early alive to the gravity of what was impending, and on January 22nd had pronounced an Allocution in Consistory condemning utterly the proposed law.[16] But while he left no doubt whatever of the Church's official standpoint, and threatened those responsible with the gravest ecclesiastical punishments and censures, in accordance with the canons of the Councils, if the law should be approved, his personal charity and his solicitude for the King were never more movingly evident. On January 26th he had just heard of the death of the Queen immediately following that of the Queen Mother, and in writing to the King it occurs to him that perhaps his monitory allocution will have reached Turin just after these tragic events—actually, Antonelli had had the publication of the allocution in Piedmont delayed out of respect for the royal sorrow.

"My heart," writes the Pope, "has been deeply moved by the news of these tragic events which have befallen you in the midst of the Royal family and they have moved me to turn to You and to assure You of the prayers which, especially at this present time, I have offered and offer for Your Majesty, that the Lord may be generous to You with help and comfort and may strengthen You more than ever with His holy counsel . . . For my part I can assure You that while charity has inspired me to offer up special prayers to God, and to write to Your Majesty, justice, claiming its rights, has compelled me to speak, as perhaps you will have seen by now. Conscience allowed me to remain silent no longer. But if I have spoken, my words have not been spoken from base or human motives, but to fulfil the sacred duties of the Supreme Pastor of the Catholic Church which compelled me to recall to a good attitude all those whom I saw going astray from the way of truth and uprightness."[17]

"Blessed Father," replies the King, "in the great sorrow which I am undergoing, which shatters my whole being, the tender words of charity which You, Most Blessed Father, have wished to send me bring the greatest relief to my saddened heart. If I have not written more, of late, to Your Holiness, I would like you to know that it is not out of indifference, on my part, for the affairs of the Church, but rather because I believed that on my side all means were exhausted, whether private or public, by which to achieve that desired purpose . . ."

He goes on to regret, in very frank terms, the publication in Piedmont of the Pope's allocution, which by now had taken place. He says that it has only inflamed anti-clerical passions and made it more difficult to prevent the passage of the law, which he thinks he could otherwise have managed; and in a really pathetic and highly confidential postscript, inserted into the letter on a separate slip of paper, he opens his mind to Pio Nono more fully:

"Your Holiness should know that it is I who prevented the Senate from passing the Matrimony law,[18] that it is I who will now do what is possible to prevent the passage of that on the convents. Perhaps within a few days this Ministry of Cavour's will collapse, and I shall nominate one from the right, and make it a condition, *sine qua non*, that it brings me as soon as possible to a complete adjustment with Rome. (Do me the kindness of helping me.) I for my part have always done what I could. (Those words to Piedmont[19] have not helped us in this, I fear lest they have ruined everything for me.) I shall try to prevent the law from passing, but help me, as well, Holy Father.

"Please burn this piece of paper."

On the 10th February came the death of the King's brother, the Duke of Genoa. Certainly, the Papal allocution had descended upon Piedmont at an unfortunate moment! But certainly, too, the whole idea of a Papal intrigue to change the Ministry, or to upset the Constitution, is wildly wide of the mark. There is still no hint of it in Antonelli's correspondence with the Nunciature at Turin;

it was the King who wanted to get rid of Cavour, and of the Constitution.

Meanwhile Cavour, the real victor, exhausted by his effort, had retired to his farm at Leri.

"After a bitter struggle, a struggle carried on in Parliament, in the salons, in both Court and street alike, rendered more painful by a series of tragic events, I felt myself at the end of my intellectual powers and have been obliged to come here and try to retemper my forces by some days of rest. Thanks to the elasticity of my fibre, I shall soon be able to take up business again. . . ."[20]

2. *The War of* 1859

The business to which the genius of Cavour was now to address itself was no less than to give his King the effective hegemony over the whole peninsula of Italy; the range of his vision may not yet have extended to cover Naples and Sicily, but it extended as far as the Patrimony of St. Peter, and if his rule reached thus far he would certainly control the whole.

It was an audacious conception, guessed at by few even within Piedmont, and supported outside only by La Farina's National Association and individual liberals, such as Minghetti. But those, abroad and at home, who were opposed to it were irreconcilably divided. Neither France nor Austria wanted to see the emergence of such a kingdom; but each was even more opposed to seeing the other gain ascendancy in the peninsula. Mazzini's followers, and those who were loyal to Pio Nono and the other princes, disliked it; but they disliked each other still more. Thus patience, tenacity, diplomacy, and a small professional army enabled Cavour to carry the day.

His first step was his notorious participation in the Crimean war, as the ally of France and England, in the hope of gaining their favours.[21] He was negotiating this in January, 1855, while the Law on the Convents was being debated at Turin; and even at this very early date he was plotting the dismemberment of the Papal State. On January 3rd, the Papal Nuncio at Paris sent a confidential letter to Antonelli:

"The adhesion [of Piedmont to the allies] is decided. An auxiliary corps of 15,000 men, General de la Marmora, Minister of War, commanding. Rapprochement with Austria, very distant plans for amalgamations of territory to the detriment of the States of the Pope. It is necessary to use this information with the very greatest caution . . ."

And a week later:

"I have been shown by a worthy person, who is a friend of mine, a letter written on the 3rd at Turin by a person I know well, a relative and intimate confidant of the Count Cavour, in which there is mention of plans, albeit distant ones, for territorial changes to the prejudice of the Pontifical States . . . I recommend . . . the greatest secrecy, because if it were known that this had been communicated to the Holy See either the person who wrote the letter or the one who gave it to me might find himself compromised. The plans in question on the one hand show the desires of Piedmont and on the other hand what would be the attitude towards us of those who give us protection and show concern and friendship for us."[22]

As yet all was not only secret, it was also only hearsay. Neither Cavour nor Napoleon had committed himself on paper; Cavour, after a struggle, had even failed to secure from Napoleon a secret clause about Italy in the treaty of alliance, a clause which he had already drafted to read: "The high contracting parties will, upon the establishment of peace, take into consideration the state of Italy." Neither France nor England could agree to that, because they were anxious to retain the benevolent neutrality of Austria. So Piedmont went into the Crimean war with no other material expectations than to gain prestige in the eyes of

France and England, and in support of the Government
of the Sultan, which then stood in somewhat greater need
of reform than did any government in Italy. And having
thus committed his country, against the will of the political
leaders of Right and Left alike, Cavour proceeded to insist
that the Piedmontese troops should be sent, direct, to the
fighting front at Sevastapol, not, as Napoleon wanted, to
the reserve at Constantinople. It was also part of his policy
that this extraordinary war should continue for as long as
possible: "He did not want it to end too soon," explains his
biographer. "It would be disastrous if peace came before
the Piedmontese troops had won their spurs."23 Fortu-
nately, on August 17th, 1855, news at last came to Turin
from the front that the Piedmontese had been in action,
that 200 men had been lost, and that General Montevec-
chio was dying of wounds. Cavour was able to write off
to the Commander, La Marmora, "The news has raised
the spirit of the nation and reconciled everyone to the policy
of the alliance. The King is enchanted . . ."24

The next task was to take the King on a goodwill visit
to Paris and London, a task not difficult in itself but very
difficult to carry off with good effect owing to the extraordinary gaucheness of the royal manners. Cavour's well-known
remark that at Windsor the King behaved "like a perfect
gentleman" provides a sidelight upon his behaviour in Paris.
His success with the crowd, in London, and especially with
Exeter Hall, was due to the supposition that he was initiating a Protestant Reformation in Piedmont; so that his
attendance at Mass came as something of a shock.

Napoleon asked Cavour in Paris what he could do for
Italy. Cavour answered in a memorandum which included
the surprising suggestion that the Romagna might be
handed over to the Duke of Modena—a ruler whose aversion
to liberalism was such as to make Pio Nono appear, even
in 1855, an advanced progressive, and which could only possibly be intended to pave the way for the absorption of the
Romagna by Piedmont.25 But Cavour's essential aim, the
inclusion of the "Italian Question" on the agenda for the
Peace Conference, had not been achieved when the devas-
tating news arrrived that Russia had agreed to peace pro-

posals put forward by Austria on behalf of the allies. The
Crimean war was at an end. Cavour was appalled:

> "Peace is deplorable for us, I am in despair about it, but
> not being able to stop it one must accept it, and try and
> draw all possible advantage from the bad position in
> which this crafty trickster Austria has placed us . . ."[26]

When the Conference opened at Paris in February,
1856, he had not succeeded in getting the Italian question
onto the agenda, and his difficulties were increased by the
birth of a son, the Prince Imperial, to Napoleon, and the
Emperor's determination to have Pio Nono for the boy's
godfather. It was not easy for Napoleon to beg the Pope
to stand as godfather while at the same time abusing his
government and opening the way for the Piedmontese; so
Cavour got less than he hoped out of Napoleon at the Congress and the most spectacular achievement was an outburst from Clarendon about the Papal government, the result of "warming him up" with reports from Sir James
Hudson and from Minghetti. But the Conference once
over, and the baby doing well, the Emperor returned to
those dreams of "doing something for Italy" and to the
time-honoured policy of humiliating the traditional enemy,
Austria.

If Napoleon were to use Piedmont and her minister's
ambitions as his ally against Austria it was necessary for
him to allow some scope to Turin's Italian aspirations, and
this meant discrediting the Papal government of the Romagna. So, despite the improvements Pio Nono had introduced, and his adoption of those suggestions put forward in
the Memorandum of 1831, the old cry of "Reform in the
Papal State" was raised again. Ambassador de Rayneval
(whose objective report on the Papal State had been so
embarrassing) was sent to Saint Petersburg, and the French
ambassador at Turin, the Duc de Gramont, who was
strongly Piedmontese in sympathy, was sent as ambassador
to Rome (August, 1857). Well might Antonelli point out
that to raise again, at this juncture, the question of reforms
(it was during the Pope's tour of his state, when he was
receiving ovations at least comparable to those Napoleon

was enjoying in France) could only undermine the authority of the government and the preservation of order. It had been one of the objects of the Papal tour to discover what further reforms were practicable and advisable, and the time of the Pope's return to Rome would have been the obvious time for further concessions. But, as Antonelli pointed out, with France bringing pressure to bear, for her own political and diplomatic reasons, "any concession which it was now felt desirable to make would be interpreted as the effect either of fear or of external pressure".[27]

But the aim of the "reformers" was, in reality, quite other than the securing of any specific reforms. Montalembert saw and expressed this clearly:

"I will not say that there are not reforms called for at Rome, as elsewhere. I do not see, however, nor does anyone in France clearly comprehend what reforms are necessary. We know not what reforms have been granted, or what are in contemplation. No one specifies them, or discusses them, and, in reality, no one is interested in them.

"Have not the organs of the Venetian population solemnly declared that no reform, concession, or boon whatsoever, emanating from Austria, would be capable of calming and harmonising the national mind? Their platform is *No Austria*; and the only platform of the revolutionists, in the Romagna as elsewhere, is *No Pope*. It is idle to talk of legislative and administrative reforms; they are no more wanted now than in 1848. In 1848, Pius IX conceded everything, or prepared the way for doing so; but what concession could satisfy Mazzini, or disarm Garibaldi?"[28]

To this challenge to Napoleon's motives it is fitting to add the dry question asked by Antonelli of the French ambassador, who was pressing the Cardinal for reforms: "Le peuple français jouit donc de tant de libertés qu'il éprouve le besoin d'enexporter?"[29]

The events of the next two years are very well known, though the mind of the Emperor still remains something of a mystery to historians and was no doubt not too clear to himself. He meant to "do something for Italy" but the

question is what, and how much? Cavour was in serious
doubt about this after the Paris Congress; and before re-
turning to Turin he went over to London to see whether
some bold words from Clarendon[30] meant that Palmerston
would extend some practical help. But he was much disillusioned in London—there were plenty of expressions of
sympathy, but he found that the only people who were
really ardent were "the Protestant zealots headed by Lord
Shaftesbury. If these people had their way England would
make a crusade against Austria."[31] No doubt, too, the
Protestant zealots would scarcely have scrupled to attack
Rome; but for Napoleon the Pope was a difficulty. "The
last conversations which I had with him and with his ministers," wrote Cavour, "were such as to prepare the way for
a warlike declaration. The only obstacle which I foresee is
the Pope. What is one to do with him in the event of an
Italian war?"[32]

What to do with him was decided at the famous Plombières interview between Cavour and Napoleon in July,
1858. Cavour's own account of this interview is surely one
of the most astonishing documents in the history of European diplomacy. But the letter to Victor Emmanuel in
which he relates what happened is long, and we must rest
content with what concerned the Pope.[33] The first part recounts how Cavour suggested various pretexts which the
Emperor might use as excuses for an intervention in Italy
against Austria; they were, however, very trivial—small commercial quarrels, and the like—and the Minister was told
he must think of something better.

"My position," recounts Cavour to his King, "became embarrassing, because I had no longer anything very definite
to propose. The Emperor came to my assistance, and we
put our heads together to run through all the states of
Italy to find there that cause for war which was so difficult to discover. After having travelled through the whole
peninsula without success we arrived, almost without expectation, at Massa and Carrara, and there we discovered
what we searched for so ardently. When I had given the
Emperor an exact description of that unhappy country,

of which, indeed, he already had a fairly clear idea, we agreed that an appeal from the inhabitants to Your Majesty should be provoked demanding protection and even asking for the annexation of those duchies to Sardinia. Your Majesty would not accept the proposed protection; but, taking up the cause of the oppressed peoples would address a haughty and threatening note to the Duke of Modena. The Duke, confident of the support of Austria, would reply to it in impertinent fashion. Thereupon Your Majesty would occupy Massa, and the war would begin . . .

"This first question being settled, the Emperor said to me: 'Before going further it is necessary to consider two serious difficulties which we shall encounter in Italy, the Pope and the King of Naples. I must be circumspect with them, with the first so as not to raise up against me the Catholics in France, with the second so as to preserve for us the sympathies of Russia which makes it a sort of point of honour to protect King Ferdinand.'

"I replied to the Emperor that, as far as the Pope was concerned, it would be easy for him to safeguard him in the quiet possession of Rome by means of the French garrison which is established there, while leaving the Romagnuols free to revolt; that, the Pope not having chosen to follow, in respect of the Romagnuols, the advice which he [the Emperor] had given him, he could not complain if those regions profited by the first favourable opportunity to free themselves from a detestable system of government which the Roman court persisted in not reforming; that, as for the King of Naples, there was no need to bother about him unless he chose to come to the assistance of Austria. . . ."

"This reply satisfied the Emperor, and we passed on to the great question: what should be the end of the war?

"The Emperor admitted, without difficulty, that it was necessary to chase the Austrians right out of Italy, and not to leave them any territory this side of the Alps and the Isonzo. But then, how should Italy be organised? . . . The valley of the Po, the Romagna, and the Legations would become the Kingdom of Upper Italy,

over which would rule the House of Savoy. Rome would
be left to the Pope, together with the surrounding territory. The rest of the States of the Pope would form with
Tuscany the Kingdom of Central Italy. There would be
no interference with the boundaries of the Kingdom of
Naples; the four Italian States would form a confederation along the lines of the Germanic Confederation, and
the presidency of it would be given to the Pope, to console
him for the loss of the greater part of his States.

"This arrangement seemed to me entirely acceptable,
since Your Majesty, being sovereign by right of the
richest and strongest half of Italy, would in fact be sovereign of the whole Peninsula. . . ."

The rest of the letter is concerned with Napoleon's request for Savoy and Nice, with military particulars, and
with the efforts of the Emperor to persuade Cavour that
his cousin, Prince Napoleon—the notorious "Plon-Plon"—
was not such a despicable fellow as people supposed and
had really treated his mistresses very well. (It was necessary
for the Emperor to stress this point because it was part of
the bargain that the Prince should marry Victor Emmanuel's daughter, the pious and much-beloved princess Clo-
thilde, who was only fifteen.)

Pio Nono and Antonelli had, of course, no knowledge of
these plans, but they knew what everybody else knew, that
Cavour and Napoleon were hatching war against Austria,
and that the outcome was likely to be a Kingdom of
Northern Italy which would include the Romagna. Sacconi, the Papal Nuncio in Paris, wrote in October, 1858:

". . . important people here are talking disparagingly of
the state of things in the States of the Holy See. I know,
too, that one of the imperial family has spoken words of
sympathy and has mentioned (only, indeed, in the course
of conversation) possibilities of a restriction of territory,
so that the Head of the Church might be less embarrassed . . ."[34]

The anxiety to relieve Pio Nono of the embarrassment of
his State increased rapidly amongst Napoleon's supporters

in France as the Emperor's secret plans were guessed at,
and in Italy as Cavour's agents and Minghetti's friends
undertook more seriously the "softening up" of the Romagna, preparatory to the proposed annexation. But it was the
publication in February, 1859, of a pamphlet known to be
inspired by the Emperor, though written by his friend La
Guéronnière, *Napoléon III et l'Italie* which set gossip
buzzing. The pamphlet was an embellishment of the crude
Plombières compact, decked out to try to seduce the
French Catholics. To the Pope, as President of a Federal
Italy, would accrue a great increase of moral influence: he
could well afford to forego some of his temporal power and
devolve his political functions upon others. He would
"stretch out his hand over all Italy to bless her and lead
her". Nobody at the Vatican, scarcely any Catholic political observer anywhere, certainly not Louis Veuillot—who
was still strongly supporting Napoleon in the *Univers*—was
deceived by this nonsense, which the historian of the
Second Empire has called "the purple robe thrown by the
Jews across the shoulders of the dying Christ".[35] It was
part of Napoleon's political technique to throw out pamphlets of this kind to test the public reaction, in conformity
with his claim to exercise a popular, as contrasted with a
constitutional sovereignty; and the measure of opposition
which La Guéronnière's pamphlet met made him adjust
his plans, with the result that when he went to war against
Austria, at the end of April, '59, he was at pains, before
leaving Paris, to write a personal letter to Pio Nono:

> "I want to declare frankly to Your Holiness that in my
> heart I do not separate the cause of religion and the
> temporal power of the Holy Father from the cause of
> the independence of Italy, because I must make it clear
> that they are equally dear to me. This declaration will
> prove to Your Holiness that the object of my endeavours
> will always be to reconcile these two great interests and
> that wherever my troops show themselves the authority
> of Your Holiness and the interests of religion will be
> safeguarded and protected."[36]

Meanwhile Napoleon's Foreign Minister, Walewski, was speaking in the same terms to the Papal Nuncio, Sacconi, in Paris, and was telling the Duc de Gramont, now French Ambassador at Rome, that he was free to give the Pope, and Antonelli:

"the most formal assurances of respect and devotion for the Pope and for the double authority with which he is vested. Our sentiments on that matter have not varied and will not vary . . . and whatever may be the outcome of the activities of which the North of Italy will be the theatre, our presence at Rome ought to be a guarantee of security for the Holy Father and for the august concerns which he represents . . ."[37]

Pio Nono therefore proclaimed his neutrality in the coming war, and exhorted the Church throughout the world to offer up prayers for the early restoration of peace. Antonelli asked de Gramont for an assurance that the neutrality of the Papal State would be respected, and Walewski instructed him to reply that the Emperor's government "considered neutrality to be the very essence of the Pontifical Government" and added that he was "determined, so far as he was concerned, to do nothing which could violate it".

All this seemed reassuring, but it did not dispel the doubts of Antonelli or the Pope; the essential point was missing. France had not *guaranteed* the Papal State. She had promised, herself, to respect its neutrality, and she had reminded the Pope of the presence of her troops at Rome; but she had not said anything which would bind her to prevent her ally, Piedmont, from violating the Papal frontiers. It was clear enough where the danger would come from; and it was not sufficient for France to point to the presence of her troops at Rome. The real question was whether those troops would be used to defend Bologna, and there was little reason to suppose they would be.

That summer, at Magenta and Solferino, the Imperial armies, with Piedmontese support, defeated the Austrians in the Lombard plain. Then (July) came the Armistice of Villafranca: the Emperors of Austria and France were to join in sponsoring an Italian Confederation under the

Presidency of the Pope. Austria was to relinquish Lombardy but not Venetia; and—Pio Nono was to be asked to introduce reforms! If he objected it would, of course, be easier to leave him in the lurch. These "reforms", no longer even specified, had their value as a bargaining counter.

But it was Cavour, and the projects of Plombières, that were sacrificed at Villafranca, sacrificed to Napoleon's urgent desire to pull out of the war. He had been disillusioned by the failure of the Italian populations to rise;[38] he was now very nervous of what other powers, particularly Prussia, were going to do.

Whichever way the curious and, on both sides, rather incompetently managed struggle in Lombardy had gone the Papal government had stood to lose. France and Austria were both the Pope's natural protectors, being the two strongest Catholic powers in the world. The defeat of either must make Rome unduly dependent upon the victor; thus the war, quite apart from the opening it gave for Piedmontese aggression, was wholly unwelcome to the Holy See. Austria had had high hopes of victory, and in late May was still informing the Papal Legate at Bologna that there was no question of an Austrian withdrawal from the Romagna. Yet actually her general, Gyulai, had lost his great chance at the outset when he failed to strike promptly from Parma and Modena against the Piedmontese before the French had arrived. As the French moved forward, further north, so the Austrians withdrew from those two duchies and then from the Romagna (they evacuated Bologna on June 11th).

The withdrawal of the Austrians from the Romagna, where they had provided the only police force, left a vacuum in authority of which revolutionaries, Piedmontese sympathisers, and Piedmontese "agents" naturally took advantage, so that the Junta which promptly seized power there forthwith demanded annexation to Piedmont. But this development, though allowed for in the Plombières plot, was far ahead of Napoleon's ideas at Villafranca; and although he allowed Cavour to send d'Azeglio to Bologna, to act as a sort of "Royal Commissioner", to "keep order and provide help for the war", he would not allow him to send, in addition, a couple of Piedmontese battalions.[39]

Cavour's anxiety as to whether the Romagna could be regarded as safely "hooked" was due to the fact that, although the uprising at Bologna had been followed by others at Ancona (whence the Austrians had also withdrawn), at Perugia, and at other cities of the Papal provinces of the Marches and Umbria, Antonelli had reacted to the crisis with vigour, sending a small force of 2,000 Swiss Guards, under General Schmidt, to put down the movement at Perugia (June 20th),[40] with the result that the disturbances throughout Umbria and the Marches had subsided, and Pio Nono remained in quiet possession of his territories outside the four Legations of the Romagna. It was not too clear to Cavour that the small Papal force would not also try to recover the Romagna; but, in fact, Pio Nono and Antonelli, while never for a moment relinquishing the legal right of Rome to sovereignty over that province too, were realist enough to recognise that the revolt in the Romagna had more depth and strength to it than had the ephemeral movements elsewhere and in any case was certain to be sustained by other interested parties.

One of these interested parties was now the neighbouring State of Tuscany. Her ruler, the benevolent Grand-Duke Leopold, although he had behind him thirty years of mild and liberal rule at Florence, was an early casualty of the new upheavals because he would not go to war against his relatives the Hapsburgs. There was thus a new revolutionary government of Tuscany, pledged to support Turin, and it was not part of its interest or policy to see the Papal power re-established in the Romagna, whose territories were contiguous. The Romagna was, in fact, hemmed in to the North and West by territories where the Piedmontese cause was triumphant, in as much as Modena and Parma, whence the Duke and Duchess (as allies of Austria) had fled, were now firmly controlled by agents from Turin. To attempt to recover the Romagna, even if it had not meant fighting Piedmontese troops, would certainly have meant fighting a revolutionary group reinforced by volunteers and arms from Tuscany and the Duchies, and this was beyond the powers of the tiny Papal force. Only the French could have done it and Napoleon, though disillusioned both with Piedmont and with the Italians generally, was unable to reverse, so abruptly, the previous course of his diplomacy.

3. De Mérode Creates a Volunteer Army

The period from the Armistice of Villafranca (July 9th, 1859) to March, 1860, was one in which the "Italian Question", and the future of the Papal State in particular, were in the melting-pot. The Romagna had been lost to Turin; would Pio Nono recover it, or lose the rest of his State? Nobody could foretell what would happen; Napoleon seemed to be the key figure in the situation, and Napoleon was looking to the emergence of a Federal Italy. But what sort of a Federal Italy would he sponsor?

Pio Nono, delighted that peace was restored between France and Austria, assumed that the nationalist revolt in the Legations of the Romagna would not be countenanced either by Napoleon or by the Austrians. This and the other revolts had been the natural consequence of Napoleon's famous appeal from Milan at the outset of his campaign:

"Italians! . . . take the opportunity that is offered you. Unite yourselves in a single purpose, to win the freedom of your country. Range yourselves as soldiers under the banner of the King Victor Emmanuel . . . tomorrow you will be citizens of a great country."

Not the Legations only, but Parma, Modena, Tuscany had thrown over their rulers in order to join forces with the French and Piedmontese. But in suppressing the similar movements at Ancona and Perugia, in protesting against what had happened in the Romagna, and in refusing to join in the war against Austria, Pio Nono had been acting strictly in accordance with his agreement with Napoleon that the Papal State should be neutral; and he had maintained that neutrality impartially, having protested, at the outset of the campaign, against an Austrian occupation of

Ferrara. For his part, Napoleon, despite his provocative appeal from Milan, which amounted to no less than an exhortation to revolution, proceeded to pursue a correct policy in refusing to allow Victor Emmanuel to take over territories outside Lombardy, although, not unnaturally, the provisional governments set up by the revolutionaries at Parma, Modena, Bologna, and Florence wanted to unite themselves to Turin, and so to safeguard their irregular position. The most Napoleon would allow was Cavour's despatch of d'Azeglio to act as "Commissary" at Bologna—a permission which did, in fact, go far to ensure that the Legations would ultimately be detached from the Papal State and annexed to Piedmont.

At Villafranca the only territorial changes proposed were the cession of Lombardy and Parma to France, to be handed on by her to Piedmont. The rulers were to return to Florence and Modena, and the Pope was to be confirmed in his rule over the whole of his State, including the Romagna; but he was to carry out (unspecified) reforms. There was to be an Italian Confederation, under the Presidency of the Pope, of which the Austrian-ruled province of Venetia was to form part—this is interesting evidence that an Italian Federation which yet embraced Austrian-ruled provinces (as envisaged by Pio Nono in 1848) seemed to others, besides the Pope, to be a practicable arrangement for Italy.

If the two Emperors were still thinking in terms of a Federal Italy there was also very strong support for the idea in Tuscany. It was all very well for Turin to think in terms of a Northern and Central Italy dominated by the House of Savoy and conforming to Piedmontese law, and to the Piedmontese civil service, but Florence, possessed of a cultural tradition unsurpassed in Europe, could hardly be expected to confine her thinking to those terms. Her great scholars and public servants, Vieusseux, of the *Antologia*, Gino Capponi, and Lambruschini looked to a Central Italian State, embracing the Duchies, and probably the Romagna, with Florence for her capital, which should take her place alongside Piedmont, and within an Italian Federation. There was a move, in which the Tuscan politician

Salvagnoli interested Napoleon in private interviews, both
before the war and during it, to give Prince Napoleon the
crown of this new Central Kingdom. When it is remembered that between July, '59, and January, '60, Cavour was
out of power, and the Turin government was resigned to
obeying Napoleon (who resolutely refused to allow Victor
Emmanuel to accept the various offers he received from
interested revolutionary régimes to take over new territories) it is understandable that many sage observers were
expecting the outcome to be some sort of Federal Italy
without an undue Piedmontese predominance.

But during this crucial period that strange, obstinate, and
high-minded "Puritan",[41] the Baron Bettino Ricasoli, provisional ruler of Tuscany, held the fort for Cavour's idea.
He resolutely resisted the pressure for a separate Central
Italian State, insisting, every few weeks, upon "offering"
Tuscany to Victor Emmanuel—who was not allowed by
Napoleon to accept it. Central Italy was in the hands of
three men: Ricasoli at Florence; our old friend Farini at
Modena (now capital of a new revolutionary state—Emilia)
and at Bologna, as successor to d'Azeglio, a determined and
ruthless ruler, Corsini (from Leghorn). These men ruled
their regions during the autumn of '59 with a fair measure
of mutual agreement and with their eyes fixed upon Turin.
A little in the background, but active between the three,
we find Minghetti and Pasolini, still the same type of liberals, believing in Piedmont, in parliamentary democracy
based upon a narrow franchise such as would admit their
own class to power, in science, and progress, and the wick-
edness of the Jesuits; hoping all things from Turin, sympathetic with the spoliation of the Church in Piedmont,
and really sorry that their old friend and chief, the kindly
Pope, was being so ill-advised.

Was he?

It certainly looked as though, in the matter of the Romagna, he was. Geographically distinct, looking—anyhow
since the days of the Cisalpine Republic and Napoleon I's
"Kingdom of Italy"—northwards towards the Po, and to the
commercial cities of Lombardy, rather than towards Rome,
peculiarly anti-Austrian (owing to the occupation) and

thus turning naturally to Piedmont, turbulent in tradition, the Romagna was so distinct a problem within the Papal dominions that it might have been the better part of wisdom for Pio Nono to recognise that his government was powerless for good in her regard. Certainly, by this time, the periodic refrain "Reform in the Papal State" repeated by the Duc de Gramont at Rome, or by Palmerston in London, had come—in so far as it was more than diplomatic music to soothe the ears of anti-clericals—to mean a separate lay government (under Papal suzerainty) for the Romagna.

This had become Napoleon's own idea of what would be most practicable for the Romagna and thus for the Legations as a whole. He had come to see that what he had agreed for Italy with Francis Joseph, at Villafranca, was quite impracticable because he was certainly not prepared to let the Austrians turn out the revolutionary governments from Bologna, Modena, and Florence, nor was he prepared to do it himself, nor was he prepared to let Piedmont take them over. Baffled, he agreed at the Treaty of Zürich (November, 1859) to refer the Italian Question to a new Congress. The Pope, readily agreeing to the idea of a Congress, prepared to send Antonelli, as Head of a distinguished delegation, to represent the Papal State—the abrupt termination of the war had pleased him and the general dispositions of Villafranca had seemed promising. He saw a new hope dawning of a peaceful settlement of the Italian Question, under international guarantee, along the lines of the federation of her existing states under his own Presidency.

He was to be sharply disabused. Antonelli was about to leave Rome, at the beginning of December, to attend the Congress, when there appeared from the pen of "La Guéronnière" a new inspired pamphlet entitled *Le Pape et le Congrès*. It proclaimed to the world the Emperor's acceptance of the *fait accompli* of the revolt of the Romagna. Only on the basis of the separation of the Romagna from the Papal State would a Federation of Italy now be discussed, and the Pope at once withdrew from any countenancing of a Congress on those terms.

To Pio Nono the whole of the Papal State was part of
the temporal patrimony of the Church, a patrimony with
which she was invested by God to enable her to perform
her spiritual function, a patrimony analogous to her religious buildings and all her other property, throughout the
world, which went to make up the outward, visible, material part of her existence. It was sacrilegious to lay hand
upon it in the same sense that it was sacrilegious to secu-
larise a cathedral or to seize a monastery. He did not distinguish as his critics—particularly his Protestant critics—
distinguished between one kind of Church property and another; nor, in reality, did he distinguish in the sense that
they distinguished between his spiritual subjects and his
temporal subjects. He always spoke of the "special character
of Our sovereignty", even when he was speaking of his
temporal power. He had never accepted Mamiani's theory
of the two distinct powers. His temporal subjects were, as
Newman had called them in the sermon already quoted, a
people "set apart" for a special service towards the Church;
they might be compared with the Levites of the Temple.
So it is that we find the Pope, at the height of this crisis,
taking a wholly religious view of what was happening in
the Romagna. In writing (July 26th, '59) to Queen Isabella of Spain, who had commiserated with him, he says:

"First of all let me say that, being Vicar of the Crucified
God it is a real comfort for Me to be able to share,
though in the smallest degree, in His glorious Passion.
For the rest, now that peace has been made, it may be
hoped that events will take a turn for the better . . ."[42]

And in writing to Victor Emmanuel, in September, after
the King had received sympathetically, at Monza, a delegation from the Romagna:

"I sympathise deeply with the difficult position in which
Your Majesty finds himself: but I cannot pretend to
understand how You, a Catholic Sovereign, belonging to
a Royal House which has always produced so many
Sovereigns eminently Catholic and devoted to this Holy
See can have failed to speak, at Monza, the language, in

regard to the Legations, which alone was fitting to Your Majesty . . ."43

A little later, on December 3rd, when it seemed that the Congress would be held, Pio Nono wrote again:

". . . The European Congress, as I understand, will be opening before long, and Your Majesty will send Your Representative to this Congress. Do I need to interest Your Majesty himself in assuming the sacred duty of protecting and sustaining the rights of this Holy See? Certain it is that when I reflect upon what is taking place in the Legations [Romagna], where they are making laws, governing, taking possession of a part of the goods of the Church, and committing many other arbitrary acts, all in the name of Your Majesty, I am bound to apply myself to interesting you in favour of the Patrimony of the Church, which is oppressed and despoiled under the protection of Your Name. And what might well lead me to abandon all hope of finding comfort and support is to see how Your Majesty says not a word to discountenance all the evil, the very grave evil, which is done in your name, as though you were satisfied, at least to all appearances, to allow your soul to become weighed down with the burden of such heavy and terrible responsibilities before God and before men. Nevertheless, bearing in mind the Christian principles which you have received, the examples of piety and of religion handed down to you by your August Ancestors, not to mention the more recent examples of your angelic Mother and Consort, whose letters I preserve, full of sorrow as they are for the sad events which overtook them while they were yet alive; I have believed that a royal soul thus blessed would assuredly embrace the first opportunity to repent of its errors and restore itself to the grace of God. The right opportunity is the Congress, and it is there that Your Majesty's voice should be brought to bear to declare openly that you will not confiscate the goods of others, and much less a part of the robe of Jesus Christ, which remained whole even on the hill of Calvary. Repudiate the praises of the impious, the unbelieving, and the foolish, and that courage of yours which has shown itself heroic on the battlefield—put it into action with much greater glory at a Congress which, it is said, is about to meet for peace. This kind of courage is immeasurably more admirable than that other and in the depth of my heart I nourish the hope that Your Majesty, offspring of the illustrious House of Savoy, through the prayers of Your August Forefathers and Household, will obtain the grace to give it effect. Finally, I ask nothing for Myself, but I seek only that justice be rendered Me, that there be restored to the Holy See what was unjustly taken from it, and which I feel it my bounden duty, in conscience, energetically to bestir myself to reclaim . . ."[44]

"The robe of Jesus Christ." To Pio Nono the Romagna was part of that robe. How, then, was he to argue about it with Cavour and Napoleon, with Ricasoli, with Palmerston? It is easy to dismiss the Pope's conception of his State as mystical nonsense; but it is wildly incorrect, historically, to suppose that the tenacity, the intransigence, were Antonelli's, and that Pio Nono was a kindly liberal who had fallen into the hands of evil counsellors. The truth was that the intransigence—where the Church was concerned—was all the Pope's. It was nothing to him, personally speaking, that he should suffer, in and through his patrimony; he was perfectly sincere in saying that he "rejoiced to share" in the passion of his Lord. But to compromise on the principle at stake, to condone the rending of the seamless robe, that was impossible for him.

Before the appearance of the new Guéronnière pamphlet sanctioning the cession of the Romagna the Pope's relations with Napoleon had seemed to be better. De Gramont had been instructed to dissociate the Emperor's government, formally, from Victor Emmanuel's behaviour about the Romagna. But the pamphlet shattered everything. It was followed by a long personal letter from Napoleon to Pio Nono, dated December 27th, 1859—a very frank letter. The Emperor explains that his goodwill towards the Pope is evidenced by the presence of his troops at Rome and likewise by his anxiety to check a general [Mazzinian] revolution in Italy—an anxiety which was one cause of his making a hasty peace with Austria. He reminds the Pope that, after Villafranca, he suggested a separate, lay administration for the Romagna, under Papal suzerainty, and he thinks that, if the Pope had taken his advice then, he would have retained his authority there. As it is, there is no way of removing the existing régime at Bologna without a foreign intervention and occupation, which is now unthinkable. In the circumstances he can only suggest that the Pope should sacrifice the provinces—after all, they have been turbulent for at least fifty years. If he does that he will be able to ask for the guarantee of the powers for the rest.[45]

A frank letter, and rather an abrupt letter. The fact was that Napoleon was by now tired of the whole business; he did not expect the Pope to accept, and he was about to change his own policy again.

The Pope replied with equal candour:

". . . A project of such a kind presents insuperable difficulties; to convince oneself of that it is enough to consider My position, My sacred character, and the consideration which I owe to the dignity and to the rights of this Holy See, which are not the rights of a dynasty, but rather the rights of all Catholics. The difficulties are insuperable, because I cannot concede what is not Mine; and because I see very clearly that the victory which it is suggested should be conceded to the revolutionaries of the Legations will serve as a pretext and an incentive to the native and foreign revolutionaries of the other Provinces to play the same game, seeing the good success of the former . . ."

Then comes an amusing thrust, put in, possibly, by Antonelli, who was fond of turning the tables on the French:

". . . Your Majesty looks for the repose of Europe by obliging the Pope to yield the Legations which for fifty years have been such a source of embarrassment to the Pontifical Government, but since you say at the beginning of your letter that you are speaking frankly it may be permitted to me to turn the argument. Who can count the number of revolutions which have followed each other in France for the last seventy years? Yet at the same time who would dare to propose to the Great French Nation that for the peace of Europe it is necessary to curtail the boundaries of the Empire? The argument proves too much, and for that reason you will allow me not to admit it. And further Your Majesty is not ignorant by what persons, by what money, by what protection the recent disturbances in Bologna, Ravenna, and in other cities have been achieved . . ."

After reminding the Emperor that it is very certain that we must all soon appear before the great Tribunal to give a strict account of our every act, word, and thought, he ends by explaining: "I say all these things in My quality as Father which gives Me the right to speak the truth, ungarnished, to my children however great may be their position in the world . . ."[46]

These letters marked the end of a phase in the drama. Napoleon changed his Foreign Minister, Walewski, who was sympathetic to the Pope, for Thouvenel, who was not (January 4th, '60). Cavour returned to power in Piedmont (January 17th, '60). An understanding was quietly reached between the Emperor and the Piedmontese Minister that Savoy and Nice should be handed over by Piedmont to France (as originally envisaged at Plombières), and in return the Emperor would turn a blind eye towards Cavour's intrigues in Italy, always provided that he left Rome itself alone. The French garrison would remain for the time being in that city. All this was going to lead to the Pope's loss of Umbria and the Marches, as well as the Legations, to Piedmont, before the year 1860 was out.

Catholic France was outraged by the way in which "La Guéronnière" had "written off" the Romagna as lost to the Pope. Dupanloup, the ardent Bishop of Orleans, already the acknowledged leader of the French episcopacy, dealt with the religious aspect of the temporal power in two open letters; Montalembert, whose journal, the Correspondant, had warned Catholics, since the opening of Napoleon's campaign in Italy, that real dangers threatened the Church, now produced his great polemic *Pie IX et la France en 1849 et en 1859*. As leader, still, of the "Liberal-Catholics" Montalembert argued that in 1849 the Will of France had sent a French army to Rome; now, in 1859, when the Will of France could no longer express itself, France's ruler had abitrarily pursued a policy that was opposed to French principle, and to religion. Still more striking was the action of Montalembert's opponent, Louis Veuillot, editor of the *Univers* and the most powerful of all influences upon French Catholic thinking. He had hitherto strongly supported the Emperor. This, even more than differences of religious viewpoint, had been the cause of the rift between Veuillot, leader of the majority party in the French Church, on the one hand, and Montalembert, and his gifted friends—de Falloux, Lacordaire, de Broglie, and Foisset, all associated with the *Correspondant*—on the other. Even when Napoleon invaded Italy the *Univers* was still enthusiastic for him; when Villafranca was announced it became rhapsodic. Napoleon was the new Saint Louis who understood both how to win victory and how to show moderation. But Veuillot was a true ultramontane. His enthusiasm for Napoleon rested upon the better treatment which the Church had been receiving under his rule in France, and upon the Emperor's support for the Papacy and the Temporal Power. Once La Guéronnière's second pamphlet had been published, and it was no longer possible to believe that Napoleon was a new Saint Louis, the *Univers* bravely admitted its mistake. First, though warned not to by the Government, it published the Pope's Allocution of January 1st, 1860, in which Pio Nono had denounced the pamphlet. Then, without even seeking permission, it published the full text of the Papal Encyclical *Nullis Certe*, of January 19th, 1860, in which Pio Nono explained his rejection of Napoleon's counsels and condemned the acts of sacrilege committed against the sovereignty of the Roman Church. For this effrontery the *Univers* was promptly suppressed, and Napoleon's régime thereby lost its most powerful advocate. It was a brave martyrdom, and it earned, even from Montalembert, the admission that Veuillot's paper had died "a beautiful death".

Evidently Pio Nono and Antonelli were now at bay, and they knew it. Garibaldi was roaming about in the Romagna. Mazzini was at Florence. La Farina, head of the revolutionary "National Society", now working closely with Cavour, was seeking to incite revolution in Umbria and in the Marches. Austrian influence in Central Italy was gone. Napoleon was planning the withdrawal of his troops from Rome. It was clear that the Papacy would have to fend for itself.

To many it seemed no bad thing that it should. It was a favourite jibe then, and one still repeated by historians, that it required three armies to maintain order in the Papal State—the French, the Austrian, and the Pope's own Guard. What is overlooked is that the two foreign armies were, in fact, keeping guard over each other.

The Pope's view was that he should not be expected to impose conscription in his State, which was always abhorrent to him, nor was it suitable that he should maintain a considerable professional army. It seemed to him perfectly natural that the great Catholic powers of Europe, which maintained large armies, and which purported to guarantee the treaty settlements of Europe, should also guarantee his State. On the other hand he objected strongly to the occupation of his territory—whether by the Austrians or by the French. His antipathy to the presence of the Austrians in the Legations dated from his days as Bishop of Imola. His dislike of having the French at Rome grew steadily during the 'fifties, especially when they came to be commanded by General Goyon, whose eccentricities and interferences were the laughing-stock of the Roman aristocracy and a source of much annoyance to the Cardinals.[47] From the time of the Paris Congress of 1856 the Pope was tireless in trying to get Paris and Vienna to reduce the number of troops and ultimately withdraw them altogether.[48] But so far from doing this, both the Austrian and the French governments proceeded to increase their armies of occupation. The reason was, of course, that they were suspicious of each other and were both building up with an eye on the likely outbreak of war. Every increase in the Austrian garrison at Bologna gave rise to a corresponding increase in the French garrison at Rome. But the increases were not due to any increased need on the part of the Pope, and were deplored by him.

With the changed situation at the beginning of 1860—Austria powerless, and Napoleon unwilling any longer to defend the Papal State from Piedmont—Pio Nono found himself suddenly deprived of the military guarantee of the great Catholic powers. It seemed to him a monstrous thing that the heir to the "Most Christian Kings", the "new Saint Louis", should have brought about such a state of affairs, but it was clearly a fact. And though there might be other Catholic powers—Spain, Portugal, Belgium, Bavaria—ready enough to intervene, the new doctrine of non-intervention, strongly supported by Palmerston, who was in a position to enforce it, prevented them from taking action. By isolating the Italian peninsula, the doctrine of non-intervention in fact left the way open to whatever state was militarily strongest in that peninsula to swallow up the others. Piedmont was thus given a free hand. She had a possible rival in Naples, and for a time, early in 1860, it looked as though Neapolitan support might be forthcoming for Pio Nono, especially as Napoleon was toying, now, with the idea of a division of the peninsula into two Kingdoms, the North under the House of Savoy and the South under the Neapolitan Bourbons. But Cavour made it perfectly clear that the entry of a Neapolitan army into the Papal State would immediately be met by the entry of a Piedmontese army from the North, and Napoleon, well-satisfied with Cavour's cession of Savoy and Nice to France, was little disposed to press the issue against him. In any case, by May the young King Francis II of Naples had his hands full at home, with Garibaldi's invasion of Sicily. By the time Cavour finally launched his invasion of the Papal State (September, 1860) the French ruling was that Neapolitans could only go to the Pope's assistance as volunteers enrolled in the Papal army.[49]

The events of 1859 had shown that the tiny Papal army,

of which the 2,000 Swiss Guards were the effective part,
was sufficient to maintain order in Umbria and the Marches
though not to operate in the Romagna. But the State was
now menaced by armed invasion, guerilla bands organised
by Mazzini or La Farina, and led by Garibaldi or his friend
Nicotera who was in Tuscany with several thousand men.
And behind these stood the regular army of Piedmont,
though it was expected that Napoleon would not allow this
to move. Invasion was something that the existing Papal
army had never been designed to meet; it was something
that Rome had assumed the guarantors of the treaties of
1815 would not allow.

How was Pio Nono to meet it? Even if he had been
willing to conscript his subjects his armies would have been
too little and too late. But he had one last resource. If the
Catholic governments and what was called "diplomacy" had
let him down he could yet appeal direct to Catholics, appeal to them to become, once more, crusaders, to volunteer
for his defence. And he was sure of the response that he
would get, if the governments did not interfere to stop recruitment, because the Church, both clergy and laity,
throughout Europe, was indignant about what was happening. In Austria and Germany there was the "Work of Saint
Michael", praying and raising funds, in Belgium they were
collecting Peter's Pence, and in all European countries petitions to the Powers, proclamations and letters of sympathy
signed by thousands were appearing.

Antonelli took the view that these signs of sympathy
might yet bring salvation, that the anger aroused by Piedmontese policy might induce the governments to intervene
to stop Cavour's aggression. It was a forlorn sort of hope,
as he was aware;[50] yet he preferred to trust to this Catholic
pressure on governments rather than to arouse the suspicion
of the powers by forming his own volunteer force. But at
this vital juncture Pio Nono listened to other advice than
Antonelli's, he listened to the advice of a younger man,
Mgr. Xavier de Mérode, a Belgian, son of the great Félix
de Mérode, who had won Belgian independence, and
brother-in-law of Montalembert.

Since 1850 de Mérode had been a Chamberlain at the

Papal court. He was a man whose natural ardour and chivalry were reinforced by something like sanctity. A soldier of the French Algerian wars, his piety had driven him to study for the priesthood, and these studies he pursued at Rome throughout the disturbances of '48 and '49. The Pope, who always had an eye for generosity and devotion, had persuaded him to stay on at Rome, where he had thrown himself into works of charity and reform, of education, and of economic progress. He had many enemies at Rome, some of them caused by his short shrift with vested interest and inefficiency. He could scarcely count Antonelli amongst his friends, their temperaments were too opposed for that; but though he was generous and impetuous, while the Cardinal calculated, he had, like the Secretary of State, a rare tenacity of purpose.

In January, 1860, de Mérode persuaded Pio Nono that he was right in his notion that the State might yet be saved by creating a volunteer army, recruited from Catholics all over Europe. He also persuaded him that the soldier to lead such an army was General Lamoricière, the "hero of Constantine", veteran of Louis Philippe's North African wars. Negotiations were secretly undertaken with Lamoricière through the sometime French ambassador at Rome, de Corcelles, and when they proved favourable de Mérode went to France to clinch the matter, bringing the General back with him in April, 1860.

Thus began one of the strangest adventures in modern history. "When a father calls his son to defend him, there is only one thing to do—to go", Lamoricière exclaimed, when de Mérode reached him. But Napoleon could hardly be expected to see the matter quite in that light; it was too widely regarded as a good diplomatic joke against him. For Lamoricière had been Minister of War in Cavaignac's provisional government of 1848; after the proclamation of the Empire he had retired to Belgium, and was known as an enemy of Napoleon. When he turned up in Rome in the spring of 1860 Ambassador de Gramont had to affect to be deeply shocked, especially when the Commander of the French garrison, General Goyon, delightfully indiscreet as ever, welcomed his brother soldier with open arms!

Napoleon threatened to withdraw his garrison altogether
from Rome, but the sailing of Garibaldi's thousand for
Sicily, in May, and especially the landing of a few of these
redshirts on the Tuscan coast, at Orbetello, not far north
of Civita Vecchia, decided him to let his troops stay, as a
precaution, at Rome. The tension over Lamoricière's appointment was only eased when formal permission had
been obtained from the Emperor for the crusader's new
employment. Even then Napoleon remained suspicious, for
the motley collection of crusaders comprised legitimists,
and other opponents of the imperial régime. There was the
young de Charette, grandson of the Duc de Berry, ardent
royalist, and darling of the Franco-Belgian *tirailleurs*; Pio
Nono was delighted with him, and would hear nothing of
Antonelli's fears that he would give offence to Napoleon.
There was de Cathelineau, from the Vendée, with his band
of crusaders, who actually bore the crusaders' cross on their
breasts until Lamoricière, to avoid quarrels, persuaded
them to take it off and merge themselves with the Franco-
Belgians, under Becdelièvre. There were some five thousand Austrians under the Austrian Colonel von Vogelsang;
there was the Irish brigade under Major O'Reilly; there
were Poles, and Spaniards, and Portuguese.[51] Chief of Staff
to Lamoricière was de Pimodan, a French legitimist noble
who had served most of his life as a colonel in the Austrian
army but had returned to France—only to leave his family
to go off again and fight for the Pope. Most of the officers
were French; as Mr. Berkeley has shown, almost every noble family of France sent a son to this army. And there
was a small group of French nobility, the *Escadron des
Guides*, who paid for their own horse, kit, and maintenance, and were attached to Lamoricière for staff work. As
for the pay of the ordinary rank and file, it was 1½d. a day
as against the shilling to be earned at that time in the
British army. Whether these men were the "scum of the
earth", as the Piedmontese and their friends avowed, or
saints and martyrs, they were certainly not mercenaries who
enlisted to earn good pay, and their living conditions were
appalling.

Against the wishes of Antonelli, Pio Nono had made de

Mérode Minister of War in February, 1860, and he and
Lamoricière applied themselves with desperate energy to
equipping and organising the force; the kind of thing they
found themselves having to do was to clear out the painters
and coach-makers who had taken possession of the principal
magazines, close to the Vatican, get the machinery up from
the cellars, set up the forges again, and put the armour-
ers to work. All this made an unaccustomed bustle of activity in Rome and Pio Nono found it rather fun—not least
because Antonelli disliked it so. The Pope's generous nature
was warmed by the arrival of so many volunteers at their
own cost; he made a point of meeting them all personally,
of enquiring about their families, and of blessing them.[52]

But to Antonelli it meant de Mérode, as War Minister,
assuming some of the functions traditionally belonging to
the Secretary of State, it meant giving unnecessary offence
to Napoleon and annoyance to Palmerston, it meant a general disturbance in the atmosphere at Rome, all in pursu-
ance of a policy which, he could perceive, was hardly likely
to succeed.

4. Castelfidardo (1860)

The primary purpose of the new army was to deal with
revolution, particularly with revolution incited from outside; to prevent a repetition elsewhere in the State of what
had just happened in the Legations of the Romagna; and
to recover the Legations. It was to fulfil the age-old purpose of Papal armies, namely the local and immediate defence of the Pope, and of the Patrimony considered needful to his independence.

The menace of a revolutionary stimulus, coming from
outside, grew more and more serious as the summer progressed, because Garibaldi had crossed from Sicily to Naples, and was advancing north. So there was now a revolutionary situation both to the south of Rome, in Naples,
and also, to the north, in Tuscany, and in the Romagna;

what remained of the Papal State was, in fact, surrounded by revolution. It was quite inevitable that bands of enthusiasts should penetrate the straggling frontiers of the State, even if they were not prompted to do so by interested parties. But with the French army still covering Rome, there was good reason to hope that Lamoricière could deal with any guerilla bands in the provinces as he had dealt with the Arabs in Algeria. With this in view, as fresh volunteers became available throughout the summer he hastily and rather sketchily armed and equipped them, as they arrived, at Rome, or at Ancona, and then concentrated them in the most strategically placed strongholds—Ancona, Perugia, Spoleto, Terni—whence they could move wherever danger threatened.

But there was a much more serious threat, with which Lamoricière and de Mérode had not reckoned. How were they to guess that Napoleon had secretly met Farini and Cialdini, who were acting on behalf of Cavour, and had tacitly agreed to wink at an invasion of Umbria and the Marches by the Piedmontese army? Had they guessed, they would certainly have done what, too late, they attempted to do when the Piedmontese invasion began—they would have concentrated their army in the stronghold of Ancona. With the French army covering Rome they might have had a chance; at least a Piedmontese advance down the centre would have had its dangers. As it was, Lamoricière was caught in the midst of trying to withdraw to Ancona, and the flower of his force was scattered by the Piedmontese at Castelfidardo (September 18th).

The Piedmontese invasion had been very carefully prepared. Cavour was posing, before Europe, as the champion of law and order in the peninsula; it was as such that he had secured and for the most retained the diplomatic support of France and England. Yet in this summer of 1860 he was working intimately with La Farina, the leader of the revolutionary National Association, and was in close touch with Garibaldi and the Mazzinians. He was playing a complicated game of double-bluff with singular skill. Thus a band of Mazzinians, who were longing to invade the Papal State from Genoa, were shipped off to Sicily in-

stead, lest they should interfere with the projected Piedmontese invasion; money and arms were used to assist an
independent movement at Naples, lest Garibaldi should
become omnipotent in the South; and small uprisings were
engineered in Umbria and the Marches to give an excuse
for a regular invasion by the Piedmontese army to "restore
order". It is true that the twentieth century has familiarised
us with such techniques; but these manoeuvres were being
planned in 1860, which was a date prior even to Bismarck's
pioneer accomplishments in this style of diplomacy—a point
which we need to remember before we dismiss Pio Nono,
Antonelli, and de Mérode as politically naïve for not anticipating what Cavour was going to do.

A study was made by Mr. Berkeley of the local records
in the *Archivio storico Risorgimento Umbro* belonging to
this year. His description of the state of affairs in Umbria
in 1860 may be quoted:

"Below the surface the whole country was covered by
a network of revolutionary committees, directed from
Florence or from other towns outside the state and ultimately in touch with Cavour himself. Everywhere there
were bodies of conspirators communicating with each
other by cypher, sending news, spending money, distributing arms, and, in fact, leaving no stone unturned in
their effort to thwart the government. The Pope, of
course, was not without his supporters; he was beloved
in the country districts, and the country districts contained about five-sixths of the population. But the Um-
brian peasant in 1860—as even to-day—was practically a
negligible quantity, more interested in his vines and
small field of maize than in politics.

"The work of the revolutionaries might be roughly
classified under three headings. They worked: (1) By
initiating risings assisted by raids from over the border;
(2) By impeding the military work of the government:
bribing contractors, organising and assisting desertion,
sending out reports on all points of interest; (3) Through
the Press, of which the chief organ was the *Nazione* in
Florence, a clever and important paper only recently

founded in order to assist the cause of United Italy. The
Press worked in conjunction with the Committees: in
every town there was a secret correspondent who sent in
his report about the soldiers quartered there, stating
their numbers and armament, and adding any stories or
slanders that he could collect or invent against them."[53]

The press campaign was hotted up just before the invasion, Lamoricière's foreign volunteers being its particular
objective. When the Piedmontese general, Cialdini, actually crossed the Papal frontier on September 11th, 1860,
he issued a proclamation which began: "Soldiers!—I am
leading you against a band of drunken foreigners whom
thirst for gold and a desire for plunder have brought into
our country . . ." Bands of irregulars had been launched
across the frontier early in September with the double objective of drawing out the Papal forces, in pursuit, from
strongholds such as Perugia and Ancona, and of raising insurrections which would give an excuse for intervention.[54]
There is no mystery or dispute over all this since Cavour
was superbly frank about it. An ultimatum was despatched
on September 7th to Antonelli, carried by della Minerva,
and it reached the Secretary of State on September 10th.
But the invasion was launched the next day, before there
was time for a reply, and this was why Lamoricière, though
he proceeded by forced marches, just failed to get his men
across from Terni and Spoleto to Ancona, and most of
them were caught, on the evening of the 17th, at Castelfidardo. Knowing what was likely to be in store for the 6,000
of them, confronted by the better equipped 17,000 commanded by Cialdini, many that night made their confes-
sions; Lamoricière, Pimodan, and those officers and men
who had arrived the day before were able to receive Communion at the Holy House of Loretto, close by. Next day
the Franco-Belgians, part of the Swiss, the Irish, and part
of the Austrians were in the forefront of the fighting; Pimodan, three times wounded, the recognised hero of the hour,
to whom the Piedmontese accorded full military honours,
died that night. But all were scattered.

Some, especially some of the Italians, whose allegiance

was naturally divided, had little stomach for the fight. Lamoricière, with a handful of followers, got through to join the garrison at Ancona, and for some days it seemed they might hold out there. But Admiral Persano's steam frigates of the Piedmontese navy, arriving on the scene, outgunned the fortified lighthouse at the end of the mole and finally demolished it together with all but 25 of its 150 defenders. On September 28th the white flag flew over the citadel of Ancona and the brief campaign was at an end.

The possibility of a full-scale invasion of Umbria and the Marches by the Piedmontese regular army had not entered into Lamoricière's calculations because Rome had assumed that, although Napoleon would not help the Pope to recover the Legations, he would not allow Cavour to make a new invasion. Even when Antonelli had received the Piedmontese ultimatum (Lamoricière received one simultaneously from General Fanti) he and de Mérode still did not expect that the volunteers would have to meet the full weight of the invasion because rumours were flying around that French help was on the way. There certainly seemed to be good grounds for these rumours. On September 11th a telegram had been sent by Thouvenel, Napoleon's new Foreign Minister, at Paris, to the French ambassador at Turin, Talleyrand, demanding an assurance that the Piedmontese ultimatum to Antonelli would not be followed by an attack upon the Papal army; it stated that, if that assurance were not given, France would break off diplomatic relations.[55] Napoleon was then at Marseilles. He telegraphed to Victor Emmanuel, deploring what was being done, and saying that if it was true that Piedmontese troops had violated the Papal territories without just reason then he would "have to oppose him". De Gramont, mightily embarrassed by his position as French Ambassador at Rome, where Goyon's army was still in occupation, hastened to give Antonelli this good news, which he clearly thought meant French intervention; and he also sent it to the French consul at Ancona. On the strength of it de Mérode telegraphed to Lamoricière that the French were going to oppose the Piedmontese "with force" (an extension, though a natural one, of what the French Ambassador had

actually said),[56] and Lamoricière, like everybody else, including the Pope, certainly for a time believed it. Whether
Lamoricière's dispositions would have been different if he
had known that the French would confine themselves to
protecting the city of Rome cannot be said for certain; it
has been argued that he would have withdrawn his gar-
risons from Perugia and Orvieto, and even that he might
have fallen back with his main force on Rome rather than
on Ancona. However this may be he was soon to learn from
the Piedmontese themselves that they were perfectly confident they had nothing to fear from Napoleon, because
they understood that everything had been agreed with him
beforehand.

The only action which the French government took was
to send four regiments to reinforce its garrison at Rome,
and to recall Talleyrand from Turin while leaving a chargé
d'Affaires there. The despatch of the regiments to Rome
was due as much to the danger threatening from Garibaldi
as the danger occasioned by the Piedmontese; while the
recall of Talleyrand was a gesture of small importance but
the very least that Thouvenel could do to meet the bitter
protests of Sacconi, the Papal Nuncio at Paris, and the indignation with which French Catholics had learnt of the
news.

The truth was that the whole matter, as is well known,
was agreed in advance at the secret meeting of the Piedmontese envoys Farini (the historian) and Cialdini with
Napoleon at Chambéry, on August 28th. *Bonne chance,
et faites vite!* Napoleon is supposed to have said; others
have it that the Emperor was careful to say little or
nothing. But it was certainly approval for the invasion that
the Piedmontese obtained at Chambéry, whether tacit or
otherwise; and the envoys did not conceal their delight
from Cavour, on their return, nor he his delight at their
report. The Emperor, he said with some reason, had "been
splendid".

Napoleon had gone on from Chambéry to Marseilles;
he had planned a fortnight's Mediterranean voyage, calling
at Algiers. He actually embarked on the 12th, having first
sent the warning telegram to Victor Emmanuel, already

quoted, which was not, in reality, an ultimatum, and was probably a "face-saver" perfectly understood by Cavour. For the next two weeks he could not be got at by anybody—and these were precisely the two weeks for which the war lasted. The timeliness of his absence would not have been so obvious had he left instructions with Thouvenel at Paris. But to Sacconi Thouvenel could only protest that he had no instructions, and that he could do nothing at all without them; and then, to the astonishment of the whole diplomatic corps, he too left—for a week's holiday in the country! To complete the evasion the general in command of the French army at Rome, Goyon, happened at this time to be on leave in Brittany. There was a fine bluster about sending him back to Rome, and he uttered brave words, on his way through Paris, about what he would do to the Piedmontese if they "tried any tricks" with him. But his return took time.

Faites vite!: whether or no Napoleon had really used those words at Chambéry he had made his dispositions in such a way as to ensure that, if the Piedmontese did do it quickly, they would certainly succeed because there would be nobody to stop them.[57]

Why did Napoleon thus deliberately allow the Papal State, which he was nominally defending, to be overrun? The reasons for his behaviour were really quite simple, although the method of it was tortuous and deceptive. He had been angered by Pio Nono's refusal to surrender the Romagna. He had been determined to have Savoy and Nice (an acquisition very popular in France) and this had obliged him to give scope to Cavour's ambitions to the extent of allowing him to incorporate Tuscany and the Romagna in the new Kingdom; without this permission Cavour could not have pushed the unpopular cession of Savoy and Nice through the Turin Parliament. It was over this bargain that Napoleon and Cavour became, once more, "accomplices". Then, in April, Napoleon had been seriously disquieted by the arrival of Lamoricière, and the French volunteers who followed him, in Rome. He knew well

enough that strong Catholic groups in France had legitimist sympathies and were hoping for a Bourbon restoration,
so he suspected a potential threat to his own régime behind
this general rally of the legitimist nobility to Lamoricière's
banner. And all the time, at the back of his mind, he was
haunted by his fear of Garibaldi and of the Mazzinian revolutionaries. Cavour played continually upon this fear; Orsini's bomb had been a reminder that their long arm
stretched to Paris. With all the hatred of an ex-revolutionary who had "made good" he hated and feared these men.
If the spread of Victor Emmanuel's rule in Italy would
check them he was prepared to favour it. If the Piedmontese could halt the northward march of Garibaldi by themselves marching down through Umbria and the Marches he
would let them go. And if in marching they destroyed
Lamoricière and his legitimist following well and good; it
was an embarrassment that these French volunteers should
be actively defending the Pope while his own army rested
passive at Rome. But, to satisfy the Catholics, he would
defend the traditional Patrimony of St. Peter—the coastal
territory around Rome which the Carolingians had defended. So Goyon's troops caused the Piedmontese to withdraw from Civita-Vecchia, Viterbo, Orte, and other smaller
places which they had occupied within the Patrimony; the
immediate threat to Rome itself was removed, and, after
some hesitation, Pio Nono, who had been advised by
Sacconi to depart from the city, and to secure support for
his cause by visiting his Catholic subjects in different European countries, chose to remain at Rome.

In an Allocution of September 28th the Pope denounced
not only the Piedmontese but also the French government
for their behaviour, a stricture which irritated Thouvenel to
the point of making him threaten the Church in France
with "la plus affreuse pérsécution". It was unguarded of the
French Foreign Minister to use such language, and it deserved Antonelli's rejoinder that the Church throve on persecution. But, in fact, Thouvenel soon grew cooler and even
allowed the publication of the Allocution in the French
press.

The months which immediately followed the overrunning and annexation of Umbria and the Marches were months of distress and great uncertainty at Rome, and they aged the Pope rapidly. More than once he fell ill (though not with the epilepsy which some have suggested recurred at this time) and the belief was widely held that he could not live much longer. This belief was a factor in the postponement of a final settlement since Napoleon, who took the view that Pio Nono was incorrigibly unreasonable, was hoping for a more amenable Pontiff following the next conclave and Cavour was in touch with him with a view to trying to influence the election.

Clearly the existing situation, with the French army guarding the city of Rome and its immediate environment, could be only temporary. Napoleon undertook no more than that he would protect the person of the Pope; General Goyon might be well disposed, and willing enough to keep the enemy at bay a few miles from the city, but who could say when Goyon would receive fresh instructions from Paris? And for a few weeks, during October, 1860, it was not at all certain whether the attack upon Rome would not come from Garibaldi and the republican revolutionaries from Naples rather than from the Piedmontese. That doubt was settled by the unexpected resistance put up by the Neapolitan army, which checked Garibaldi on the Volturno, and thus played the game of Cavour by giving the Piedmontese armies time to cover the approaches to Rome and to thwart the would-be liberator from once more marching at the head of his redshirts into the Eternal City. Rome, nevertheless, was filling up with revolutionaries again, because the Piedmontese advance meant that the Mazzinian and other revolutionary elements, which had infiltrated into Umbria and the Marches (largely through the connivance of Cavour) now often preferred to escape the Piedmontese by passing over the frontier into the Patrimony of St. Peter. The city thus became the refuge and seemed likely to become the prey of all those to whom the new Piedmontese order of things was scarcely more congenial than had been that of the Pope. The British government, interested in assuming patronage of the risorgimento, so as to enjoy the friendship of the new nation whose unity it now regarded as certain, counselled the Pope to leave Rome and to find refuge in Malta, or elsewhere in the British Dominions. The French government, on the other hand, counselled him to remain under French protection at Rome, and warned him that, if he withdrew, his return might not be easy to effect. The scandal amongst French Catholics if the Pope, ostensibly protected by a French army, were again compelled to flee from Rome, was more than Napoleon could contemplate with equanimity; further French intervention, with incalculable consequences, might then become a necessity; and it would involve the Emperor in the grave embarrassment of disavowing and even making war upon his Piedmontese ally, whose fortunes he had done so much to promote.

Pio Nono hesitated. His final decision to stay at Rome rested upon the fact that the Romans wanted him to stay. In 1848 the rule over the city itself had been taken out of his hands—he could serve nobody by staying. But now—as later, in 1870—the challenge came from interested powers, outside. Against them he would stand his ground amongst his own people.

Chapter Six

NAPOLEON AND ROME
(1860–1864)

1. *Cavour and Pio Nono*

With Napoleon openly unfriendly and roundly accusing the
Pope of harbouring the legitimist enemies of his régime at
Rome, with the British government wholly hostile to the
Temporal Power, with Austria defeated and powerless, and
with the enemy at the gates of Rome there seemed no direction in which the Pope could turn even though Spain undertook a diplomatic initiative on behalf of the lesser Catholic
powers and the leading French Catholic writers risked
everything in issuing polemical pamphlets which pilloried
the subterfuges of the Emperor's diplomacy. In these circumstances it is not surprising that there were three
months, during the winter of '60–'61, when Pio Nono,
though himself scorning to parley with the enemy, was prepared to allow unofficial negotiations to proceed between
on the one side Cardinal Santucci, who was sympathetic
with the idea of an accommodation, and on the other Fr.
Passaglia, the ex-Jesuit,[1] and his friend Diomede Pantaleoni, who were in touch with leading liberals like d'Azeglio
and Mamiani. It was Pantaleoni who drew up, in November, 1860, a Memorandum embodying the idea of the renunciation by the Papacy of the Temporal Power in return
for complete independence of the Church from interference by the State. Cavour accepted the idea that Pantaleoni's Memorandum should be the basis of discussion,
Passaglia agreed to show it to Cardinal Santucci, and the
Cardinal showed it to the Pope, who was sufficiently interested to call in Antonelli to talk it over.

The Memorandum offered the Church material advantages. In the civil sphere the Pope would preserve the pre-
rogatives of sovereignty, with his own diplomatic corps,
complete independence from any temporal sovereign even
in civil matters, ownership of the palaces, galleries and
monuments traditionally belonging to the Papacy, and a
regular agreed income for his court, for the Sacred College,
and for the episcopate and clergy as a whole. There would
be free access to Rome from the whole world. In the

spiritual sphere the State would withdraw from the nomination and presentation of bishops, from interference with
Papal legislation in spiritual matters—the *placet* or *exequatur* required to give state approval would thus disappear—
and from all forms of inspection, or caveat. The Church
would be free in the sphere of preaching, teaching, the
press, and association. In its legislative and judicial function the Papacy would be able to call upon the support of
the "secular arm"—e.g. in the enforcement of an interdict
—but this support would be confined to the service of the
Papacy; the bishops, though they would be free in their
exercise of legislative and judicial power in religious matters, would not be able to call upon the secular arm to
assist them.[2]

Though Antonelli never liked the proposals, Pantaleoni
succeeded in persuading Cavour that there were grounds to
hope for success. Passaglia, against the wishes of Pio Nono,
decided to go to Turin, where he was lodged secretly in
Cavour's own house, and in February an accredited representative, Molinari (a Rosminian) was sent from Turin to
negotiate at Rome on behalf of Victor Emmanuel's government. The news of Molinari's coming in this honoured
capacity, at a time when most of the Papal State was under
Piedmontese military occupation, and Victor Emmanuel
and his ministers under the ban of excommunication,
threw the Pope into one of his occasional explosions of
wrath, and he declared that the envoy might be free to
come to Rome but he would not be free to return. Warned
of Pius' attitude Molinari was diverted at Civita-Vecchia
from Rome to Naples, and soon after Pantaleoni, whose
arrogant attitude and secret contacts with the revolutionaries irritated both governments, was given his passports,
and the unofficial conversations were at an end.

While there had never really been much prospect of success the talks occupy an important position not merely in
the evolution of the Roman Question but in the wider problem of the relations between Church and State, and in the
process of "reconciling the Church with Modern Society",
or with "Modern Progress", two phrases which were then
becoming popular. There is no doubt that what Cavour was

offering to the Church was, by contemporary Piedmontese
or French standards, generous, and that he would have had
plenty of trouble at Turin in persuading the Left—the followers of Rattazzi—to accept it. But his prestige at this
point was such that, with the sure support of Victor Emmanuel (for whom the quarrel with Pio Nono was turning
much of the pleasure of his success to bitterness), it is
probable enough that he would have carried a measure of
this sort in the Chamber and Senate at Turin. The accord
given there to his famous speech on "a free Church in a
free State" (March 27th, 1861) proves as much. It is also
true that Cavour has been shown by subsequent history to
have been largely right when he claimed that in a hundred
years' time the relations between Church and State would
normally be very much what he was advocating, no longer
a régime of special privileges, whether of Church or of
State, guaranteed by Concordats or Establishments, but the
clearest possible distinction between the two powers. He
could claim, moreover, though "more than half a Protestant", to be in line in his theory with some of the best
Liberal-Catholic thought of his time, and notably with that
of Montalembert, whom he was fond of quoting, even
though the great French writer repudiated him with scorn;
—looking at Cavour's handiwork, Montalembert called his
"free Church in a free State" nothing better than a "despoiled Church is a spoliative State".

But where Cavour was most right, and Napoleon was
most wrong, was in seeing that there was just a chance that
Pio Nono would accept these proposals, because they were
based upon a principle, whereas there was never any chance
that any of the Emperor's solutions to the Roman Question, which all involved reductions in the size of the Temporal Power, and thus a mere yielding to force, would be
acceptable at Rome. Cavour understood that for the Pope
the issue was entirely one of principle, a matter of conscience, and that he would never yield his standpoint on
the inalienability of the Temporal Power unless he could
be convinced that superior spiritual advantages could be
won for the Church by sacrificing it. To agree to sacrifice
the Legations, or Umbria, or the Marches, would be, for the

Pope, a yielding on principle. He might be compelled to see those provinces torn from him, but he would never agree that it was right that they should be; he would never recognise such a separation *de jure*. But if Cavour could show that he was able to offer a greater spiritual independence to the Pope and to the Church than had been secured to them through the enjoyment of the Temporal Power, then there was, indeed, some prospect of success in the negotiation, because the Pope always claimed, as his predecessors had, that the Temporal Power was necessary precisely in order to give him independence.

Why, then, did the negotiations fail? Why, when he seemed, at first, to be sympathetic, did Pio Nono end by showing more than his usual acerbity?

The reason lies in the glaring contrast between Cavour's fair words and his government's ruthless actions. It lies in the fact that during those very winter months while the conversations were proceeding the Piedmontese pro-consuls, Pepoli in Umbria, and Valerio in the Marches, were putting into operation, in the occupied provinces, the anticlerical laws of Turin, and Mancini was extending them, in even more violent fashion, to Naples. Nobody has written with greater understanding and sympathy of Cavour's vision of a free Church in a free State than Professor Arturo Jemolo, in his recent important book *Chiesa e Stato in Italia negli ultimi cento anni*;[3] yet the professor, who certainly holds no brief for the policies of Pio Nono and Antonelli, has pointed out how unsound was Cavour's religious policy at this juncture:

"He could well have delayed the extension of the Piedmontese ecclesiastical legislation to the annexed provinces; there would have been no harm in the convents conserving their juridical personality for a few months longer; Pantaleoni, who is certainly not to be suspected of tenderness for the cause of the religious, gave warning, on the 13th March, how difficult it was to make it acceptable at Rome that no religious corporation should have a juridical personality. Nor can it be claimed that it was simply a matter of weakness on the part of the government in the face of the party of action [the Revolutionaries]: was it not Cavour himself who, in the late autumn of '60 wrote to Pepoli, the commissioner in Umbria: 'Put into force energetic measures against the friars. You have done well to occupy some of the convents to recover there emigrants from Viterbo. Go on like that so as to heal the leprosy of monachism which infects the territories remaining under the Roman domination'?"

And Professor Jemolo goes on to condemn, in particular, the arrest of Cardinal Corsi, Archbishop of Pisa, and Mgr. Ratta, of Bologna, who refused—in obedience to Rome—to allow their clergy to sing the Te Deum in honour of the anniversary of the Piedmontese constitution; arrests approved by Cavour, although recognised by him as "of little legality".[4]

Cavour was bent—desperately bent at this stage—upon securing friendship between his new Kingdom and the Church, recognising clearly enough that an accord would immeasurably improve the prospects of the precarious new state, both at home and abroad. Yet he allowed and encouraged practices which were bound to ruin the chances of this accord. It is surprising; but Cavour was liable to make mistakes when he was handling the internal affairs of other states (notably Naples), and when he was handling people very unlike himself. He was at his best with Napoleon because his adventurous and cynical opportunism was of the same quality as that of the French Emperor. But in encouraging attacks upon the Church in the Papal State at the same time as trying to make an agreement with Pio Nono he was certainly making a serious error.

There was no reason why the anti-clerical outlook of Cavour, his dislike of certain basic elements in Catholic piety, or even his personal unscrupulousness should, of themselves, have prevented Pio Nono from doing business with him. The Pope had a marked penchant for doing business with political "realists" whether they were of doubtful orthodoxy like Pellegrino Rossi, or rather materialistic, like Cardinal Antonelli, or openly Protestant, like the later

French premier Émile Ollivier. But, from the time of the Siccardi Laws to the time of the occupation of most of the Papal State, the policy of Turin had been so hostile, not merely to the Temporal Power but also to the spiritual interests of the Church, that it was quite essential for Cavour's government, if Rome was to take its advances seriously, to give some evidence of a change of heart. If it didn't, of what value could any new understanding be between Church and State? It was slightly absurd to expect the Pope to hand over what remained to him, and especially the Eternal City, to politicians who seemed bent upon attacking and despoiling the Church. Ten years later much of the principle and the content of the Pantaleoni Memorandum was to be embodied in the Law of Guarantees, which governed the position of the Church in Italy between 1871 and the Lateran treaty of 1929; but bitter antagonism on both sides was to make its application variable and to demonstrate clearly enough that "a free Church in a free State" was not a magic formula capable of itself of dissolving all the knotty perennial problems which beset the relations between the two powers, and it was none other than religious naïveté on the part of Cavour to suppose they would melt away, even in an enlightened twentieth century, under the influence of his infallible formula.

Like Napoleon, Cavour counted upon the early death of the Pope, and the election of a more liberal successor. He did so the more readily after the events of Holy Tuesday, '61, in the Sistine Chapel, when the Pope, rising from his throne for the gospel, fell back again, and remained senseless for some minutes. It was the ensuing illness which caused Cavour to say that within six months such big changes would have taken place as would finally open to him the road to Rome.

But it was not the Pope who was about to die; it was Cavour. Seized with an intestinal infection on May 29th, '61, he died on June 6th. On June 5th he received the last sacraments from a friendly Franciscan, Fra Giacomo, who incurred the personal censure of Pio Nono for not having first exacted from the minister the formal retraction re-

quired by the Bull of Excommunication issued a year previously. Principle and personal sympathy were strangely in-
termingled in the reactions to this dramatic tragedy. Fra
Giacomo lost his rectorship of the Church of the Madonna
degli Angeli, at Turin; but he was awarded a pension of a
thousand lire by a grateful government! Pio Nono, strict in
upholding the law of the Church, and censuring the lax
priest, had yet, on first hearing of Cavour's death, raised his
hands to the sky crying, "My God, be merciful with the
soul of this unhappy man!" and for the repose of that soul
he had duly, himself, said Mass.[5]

It was one of the most attractive of Pio Nono's qualities
that he never harboured personal animosity against any of
his opponents. He always loved the sinner, while hating the
sin, and he held for Cavour a personal liking, and even respect, just as he held for Victor Emmanuel a positive affection. His feeling for both men was bound up with the fact
that he was, himself, such a good Italian; his quarrel with
the leaders of the risorgimento was inevitable, but it did not
prevent him from remaining a patriot, and being proud of
it. He was proud of the fact that before any of them he had
shown the way, in 1847, standing up to the Austrians and
compelling them to withdraw from Ferrara; and he still
loved Italy as he had loved her when he called out, in 1848,
Benedite Gran Dio l'Italia! When Antonelli was reading
him an account of Victor Emmanuel's success at Palestro,
during the Austrian war of '59, he had cried, uncontroll-
ably, *Vittorio! Vittorio! figlio mio!*, and to the astounded
Cardinal he had turned and exclaimed *Per bacco! sono
Italiano!*[6] And the diarist d'Ideville recounts how, some
three years after Cavour's death, the name of the minister
arose during his conversation with the Pope, whereupon:

"suddenly, in a low bass voice, as though he were speaking to himself, without bothering about my presence, he
murmured these words: 'Ah! How he loved his country,
that Cavour, that Cavour. That man was truly Italian.
God will assuredly have pardoned him as we pardon
him . . .'."

And d'Ideville goes on to say how he told the story to de Mérode, who did not love the Italians, and how the war minister was annoyed, but not at all surprised by it.[7]

2. *Napoleon and Pio Nono* (1860–1861)

Not long before his death, Cavour had written to Napoleon that there would be no reaching an understanding with Pio Nono

"until he had become convinced that not only could he make an accord without sacrificing his conscience and the duties of his sacred ministry, but that his renunciation of the temporal power would be useful to the Church and would serve the true interests of religion".

But Cavour did not take an equally lofty view of the whole of the Sacred College. Some, indeed, of the Cardinals —the proud d'Andrea, Amat (Pio Nono's old friend), Santucci—might be expected to support a compromise, for reasons of honest conviction, because they held "advanced" views, and were in general unsympathetic to the régime of Antonelli. But others of the "big fish" (Cavour's own phrase), including Antonelli, the Piedmontese minister planned to win over by offers of compensation "calculated to satisfy their ambition and their personal interest". It is not necessary to suppose that Cavour was justified in imagining that he could achieve success in this way, still less that Antonelli was prepared to bargain. The Secretary of State, whatever his peasant's love of gold, was absolutely loyal and quite fearless and tireless in his devotion to the Pope. But the question of what would become of some of those dependent upon the Papal Government in the event of a total liquidation of the Papal State was, of course, a genuine one, while the distribution of small presents to subordinate agents, in which the Turin government indulged, was a normal practice in the politics of the time.

Napoleon encouraged it strongly, being very anxious to see an accord reached between Rome and Turin and being less able than Cavour to appreciate that more than a mere transaction was needed.

Napoleon, when he came to understand the lines along which Cavour sought agreement, became very unsympathetic to them because he saw that if they succeeded it would be difficult for him to maintain the basis of his own relations with the Church in France. This basis was still the Organic Articles imposed by his uncle, and retained by the Bourbons, which left the Church much at the mercy of interference from the State in such matters as the appointment of bishops or correspondence with Rome. True, he had not normally invoked his rights in these matters; he had, on the whole, been friendly and liberal towards the Church, and had consequently enjoyed her support and especially that of the strong "Neo-ultramontane"[8] party which followed the lead of the journalist Louis Veuillot. But his Italian policy had shattered these relations and had turned into his enemies the most influential French Catholics, whether bishops or laymen, Neo-ultramontanes or liberals. They might, like Veuillot, conceal their criticism of himself, personally, behind criticism of his more anti-clerical ministers, Thouvenel and Persigny, or of his pamphleteers, like La Guéronnière, but a new estrangement none the less now existed between Emperor and Church, and the Emperor was going to avail himself more widely of the powers which the Organic Articles gave him. His mind was, in fact, moving quite away from the idea of "a free Church in a free State". He meant to have far more control over the Church than Cavour's formula would have given him.

On Christmas Day, 1860, Pio Nono resumed his correspondence with Napoleon, after an interval of a year which had been only broken by a note of sympathy from the Pope in August, on the occasion of the death of the Emperor's uncle Jerome, the sometime King of Westphalia. It is noteworthy that the Pope does not plunge into any recriminations about the part played by the Emperor in abetting the overrunning of his territories during the autumn. But he does plunge, with singular abruptness, into the matter of episcopal appointments in France:

"Majesty,

"The choice of the Bishops destined by God to rule His Church is a choice of great importance for the Church itself and for this Holy See. I would like to believe that Your Majesty also is anxious to ensure that clergy who are to be raised to so high a dignity have all those qualifications that may fit them to meet the present serious needs of civil and religious society. In most deplorable combination Your Majesty's Government has presented two candidates whom I could not and cannot admit on account of the doubts to which both give rise in Me, the one in the matter of doctrine and the other in the matter of morals: I speak of the abbés Maret and Mounig . . . It seems to me it would be much better, and I would even say necessary, to do what was done previously in France with other governments which preceded that of Your Majesty, and also with You yourself, and that is for us to agree together first, avoiding thereby that rumour which naturally spreads amongst the public and gives rise, in unfortunate fashion, to those conjectures which are born from seeing published in the *Moniteur* the name of some priest, who is supposed destined to some Episcopal See, and whom afterwards the Pope does not approve . . .

"As yet I remain almost without Temporal Power, and that end may be achieved by men of bad will, at least for a time: but without spiritual dominion will I never be, for all men are powerless to take that from the hands of the Vicar of Jesus Christ—that Vicar who enjoys a promise which is infallible and omnipotent, whatever certain wretched books may say which today issue from France into the sight of Europe, and of which also Your Majesty must at least have heard speak . . .

"In renewing to Your Majesty my sentiments of respect I pray with all my heart that God may show you the way to follow, especially in the present difficult situation, granting you that docility of mind and heart not only to hear but also to put into practice whatever His divine voice is ready to instruct you.

"From the Vatican on the solemn day of the Nativity of Our Lord Jesus Christ, to whom be honour and glory through all eternity.

Pius PP. IX.

"Churches to which provision will be made at the first Concistory:

Soissons, Troyes, Annecy, Nevers."

The firmness of Pio Nono's letter arises from his anger at a notion which found expression in the "wretched books" published in France, and which was also voiced in other parts of Europe, the notion that the collapse of the Temporal Power would lead to something like a collapse in the whole institution of the Papacy. If Napoleon thought that the time had come when he could encroach with impunity upon the Spiritual Power it seemed to the Pope that it was time to disabuse him.

Napoleon replied on January 28th:

"Most Holy Father,

"Your Holiness' letter dated December 25th gives me the opportunity to express my thought to him fully. I have always regarded an understanding between a sovereign and the religious authority as indispensable to the welfare of Catholic peoples because so long as that understanding exists all is smooth and questions of *amour propre* and standing out for rights give place to friendly relations and mutual concessions: but as soon as unhappy circumstances have given birth to mistrust and something like hostility between the powers created by God to live in harmony everything becomes difficult. The slightest differences of view degenerate into serious embarrassment and into ceaseless causes of antagonism. What has happened in the last eighteen months is the palpable proof.

"Ever since events, exploited by the parties, have thrown doubt upon my sentiments towards Your Holiness the spirit of mistrust has replaced the ancient harmony. At Rome as at Paris all that comes from the one country is suspect in the other. Yet, in the midst of embarrassments created by serious complications my conduct has always been straightforward in its acts, pure in its intentions. When nearly two years ago I set out for the war of Italy I declared to Your Holiness that I undertook that war with two sentiments firmly rooted in my heart, the independence of Italy and the maintenance of the temporal authority of the Holy Father; that I was under no illusion as to the difficulty of reconciling these two causes; that I would make every effort to achieve it. I have remained faithful to that promise in so far as the interests of France allowed me. The facts speak for themselves. At the peace of Villafranca I sought that the Pope should be at the head of the Italian confederation so as to increase his power and his moral influence. When the revolution developed against my wishes I proposed to the Catholic powers, in order to check its progress, that they should guarantee to the Holy Father the rest of his state. Although Rome had become the meeting place for all the enemies of my government I none the less maintained my troops at Rome. Your Holiness' safety was menaced; I increased the strength of my army of occupation. Yet how has my conduct been appreciated? I was stigmatised as an enemy of the Holy See. The leaders amongst the clergy of France were stirred up against me, matters were taken to the length of persuading the Archbishop of Paris to resign his position of Grand Almoner, an attempt was made to make of the bishops and their subordinates a foreign administration recruiting men and money in defiance of the laws of the country. In short, Rome was made the centre of a conspiracy against my government, and yet I authorised the man who had most openly acted as partisan of the republic to become the chief of the Holy Father's army.

"All these marks of hostility have changed nothing in my line of conduct. I have done all that was my responsibility to maintain the authority of the Pope without compromising the interests of France. It is considered, none the less, that I have not done enough. Well and good, but I reply that, despite my proper veneration for the head of the church, never will my troops, unless the honour of France is engaged, become a means of oppression between foreign peoples; and further, that having made war alongside Piedmont for the deliverance of Italy, it was absolutely impossible for me on the morrow to throw my arms against her, however severe a blame may elsewhere be placed upon my decisions."

But the sting of Napoleon's letter came in the tail. The Pope, in his own letter, had explained that he had done all he could to persuade the Archbishop of Paris (Francesco Morlot) to remain at his post, and still hoped he would do so. If, however, he insisted upon resigning, the Pope wished Napoleon to suggest:

"what candidate, or, much better, what choice of candidates, the Emperor has made up his mind to propose as occupant of the difficult See of Paris. My demand is not only deferential but also just, and I believe that Your Majesty likewise will recognise it as such".

Napoleon concludes his own letter with a reply on this matter:

"In the present state of things I regret deeply that our relations are not more informed by that conciliatory spirit which would permit me to accept Your Holiness' proposals. If you require the Archbishop of Paris to continue his functions I do not doubt that that prelate, who has many qualities which recommend him for the position, will conform himself to your wishes; if none the less he insists upon retiring, I shall find amongst the bishops whomsoever seems to me best to fulfil the religious requirements and to be politically convenient. I sincerely hope that the ill-will and uncertainty in which we find ourselves may soon cease and that I shall find once more Your Holiness' full confidence and friendship. It is with these sentiments of respect that I am

of Your Holiness

the devoted son

Napoleon.

"Palace of the Tuileries. January 28th, 1861."

The kernel of Napoleon's argument is clearly to be found in his sentence: "having made war alongside Piedmont for the deliverance of Italy, it was absolutely impossible for me on the morrow to turn my arms against her". The simple truth was that he had had to choose between Piedmont and the Pope, and he had chosen the former. That was a choice which conformed to his personal sentiments, as well as to the wishes of a certain proportion of French liberals. It was a choice which, however, seemed lamentable to a much larger proportion of his subjects,[9] so that the secrecy of the meeting at Chambéry, the bluff about opposing the Piedmontese if they invaded the Marches, the toleration of Lamoricière and the Legitimists, the strengthening of the garrison at Rome, and the protracted negotiations of the years 1861, 1862, and 1863 became necessary to the Emperor in order for him to "save face" with the French Catholics.

Implicit in Napoleon's interpretation of the events of 1860 is the view that it would be wrong for the French army to intervene in the Italian peninsula in order to impose a solution between different Italian parties. Still more strongly did the British government urge the doctrine of non-intervention, by which that government now meant that the Italians should be left to work out their own salvation.[10] The Papal argument, on the other hand, was that the issue was not one between rival groups within one country, but rather the invasion of a numerically small and lightly armed state by one which was numerically larger and strongly armed.

Against the Papal argument could be urged, with some show of reason, that the recovery of the Romagna, in the face of the results of the plebiscites (which had been overwhelmingly in favour of the change of rule) was manifestly impossible; and that the plebiscites in Umbria and the Marches pointed to a similar situation. The Papal reply was that the plebiscites (in which the voting made little pretence of being secret) and the whole revolutionary movement in the Papal State was what we should now call a "put-up job", stimulated from Piedmont and from abroad. And as for the recovery of these domains, this could be managed well enough without any help *if* the great powers kept the ring; that is, if the treaty boundaries of 1815 were respected, and their violation by interested parties—including Piedmont—were not tolerated. If non-intervention were worked, as the Pope and Antonelli saw it, honestly, by prohibiting the Piedmontese from occupying the Romagna, then the Papal army would suffice.

To the jibe that it had required the Austrian army to overawe the Romagna between 1815 and 1859 the Pope could reply that he had merely pursued the traditional custom of the Italian princes, who had been in the habit of letting the big powers look after security for them; but this policy had grown increasingly distasteful to him, as well as to the Romagnuols, and he had repeatedly tried to secure the reduction—leading to the withdrawal—of the Austrian garrison at Bologna as well as the French garrison at Rome, without success. Since the war of '59 he had been building up his own army and this had been held against him by the French and the Piedmontese. Now, indeed, he was dependent upon the French to protect Rome, because the bulk of his territory was occupied by a hostile and foreign army. In short, if that army, and the French, and the Austrians would *all* clear out (true non-intervention) he was satisfied that all would be well.

If we regard Italy as morally a nation—which is anachronistic for the middle of the nineteenth century—then the Papal argument will seem specious. But if we accept the facts as they appeared at the time, then the accusations of Montalembert, attacking Cavour in 1861, will appear cogent:

> "You have conspired for twelve years, and you boast of it, to make all government impossible in the Roman States. When the Pope has ecclesiastical ministers, lay ministers are demanded of him. When he appoints a layman, his throat is cut on the steps of the Parliament; when he has no army he is reproached for not being able to defend himself; when he forms one it is denounced as a peril to his neighbours . . ."[11]

Pio Nono replied in some detail, on February 14th, 1861, to Napoleon's letter.

The Emperor had linked the matter of the appointment of bishops in France with a settlement of the political dispute in Italy. This the Pope could not admit and he would deal with it first:

"Jesus Christ said directly to Saint Peter and to the Apostles: *Lo I send you,* etc., and He said equally: *Go forth and teach all peoples.* Now, Your Majesty, it is certain that this mission comes from God, and His Vicar on earth is he to whom it is reserved to entrust it to whomsoever, nor could he without violating his conscience entrust it to anybody whom He considers to be unsuitable to exercise it. Once this principle is recognised, that the spiritual power given by Jesus Christ to His Vicar is an independent power, all conflict disappears . . ."

The Pope then gives his own opinion of the unfolding of events:

". . . Now Your Majesty will permit me to speak openly. I assure Your Majesty that if ever there has issued any expression from my pen which has seemed harsh, I wrote it with a calm spirit with an absolutely calm peace within me. I will say more: while I feel the gratitude which I owe you for the help which You have given in support of the Church, what has happened since does not arouse in me any anger towards you, indeed if I had the opportunity to see You, I would embrace You as an affectionate Father, still seeing in You an exceptional Person, of whom God might avail Himself to restore order and peace to a harassed world, and to Religion her liberty and and independence. One may *hope* that this desire may yet be realised.

"After saying which I may be allowed to ask of Your Majesty whether he appreciates that the words addressed by Him to the Italians at the time that he set foot in the Peninsula were liable to influence and to excite the first disturbances amongst the people. Assuredly that invitation to arm themselves that they might be free, issuing from the mouth of a powerful Prince, at the head of a numerous and strong army, produced the effect which could be expected, contrary it may be to Your Majesty's intentions. It was at that time that the gates were opened to the wild beasts which came to dominate the field, while the timid cattle, though greatly more numerous, hid themselves frightened in their pens. In these conditions a Man who is a fanatic, and I would say almost beside himself with fury, first went forth in Bologna to cry in the piazzas to make the people tear down the arms of the Pontifical Government . . . Certainly these first moves were not calculated to inspire confidence and to strengthen the Temporal Dominion of the Holy See. It is very true that after the peace of Villa-franca Your Majesty was good enough to write to Me and to propose to Me the presidency of the Italian Confederation. But the offer was accompanied by the firm and express desire for the cession of a great part of the States of the Church. So, after showing myself grateful for Your Majesty's eagerness, I did not refuse the proffered Presidency, but I took the opportunity to point out the difficulties which would be involved, especially as it would be necessary to treat with an Italian Government which was and is obliged, so as not to fall foul of men of ill will, to hold the Church to ransom and thus to satisfy the unbounded appetites of those fierce wolves which it fears; and all this at the expense of honest men, of ministers of the Sanctuary, and of persons consecrated to God. None the less I accepted the offer, but indicated also that this would be under certain conditions, since it did not seem to me possible that in a matter of such great importance an immediate reply could be expected of me. What happened after that is well known to Your Majesty.

"You suppose that Rome has become a meeting place for your enemies. No, Your Majesty, the meeting place of your enemies is not here, and nobody has ever agitated or even thought of conspiring to the detriment of your government . . . It is quite true that I called from France a man who held a great reputation in the profession of arms and was able to create a small army, which was intended to have no other purpose than to maintain peace at home and to repel certain freebooters who had attempted to attack the State from without . . . This army was not only sufficient to achieve that end but was in conformity with the wishes of Your Majesty's government which had suggested more than once that we should create it. And I take this opportunity of thanking Your Majesty for having agreed that this French General might come to me in this capacity. But unfortunately a third enemy was added, unforeseen, against the States of the Church, the regular army of Piedmont which, strong in numbers and provided with all the means for attacking a small army not yet in fighting condition, committed a violent spoliation, and did not hesitate, by the aid of its guns to penetrate even to the walls of Rome. By an even greater misfortune, either advantage was taken of the good faith of Your Majesty by two Italians in Savoy, or else these men used Your name without warrant, but certainly the Piedmontese army claimed to be invading the Marches and Umbria with Your consent. I cannot hide the fact that these events caused My heart deep sorrow."

After referring to the matter of the Archbishop of Paris, which had been settled by the Pope's persuading him to stay at his post, Pio Nono ends his letter:

"And now, to conclude, let me say that Your Majesty having declared in His last speech that He would not hesitate to condemn whatever violates justice or the right of nations I am confident that he will condemn the invasion of the Marches and Umbria by the Piedmontese troops because this is clearly contrary to the right of nations and of justice. Nor can the invaders claim that the vote of the populations has justified the unjust occupation, because, apart from the fact that it cannot be admitted that the principle of universal suffrage can remove a Sovereign from a Throne which he already legitimately and justly occupies, there are abundant proofs to show

that the different votes were a tissue of deceptions and
frauds. If to this is added the usurpation of the property
of the Church, the expulsion ordered of the Religious
and the Monks from their Cloisters, the refusal to admit
the new Bishops to vacant Sees even in the State of the
Church, the impossibility of writing to or receiving letters from the overrun Provinces, even those of a purely
ecclesiastical nature, the policy pursued, in varying de-
grees, of maligning the Clergy and destroying everything
which, coming from the Clergy, could influence the morality of the people, Your Majesty will be convinced
that the right of nations has been violated and justice
destroyed . . .

"May it please the Lord to put an end to such great
evils, restoring us to peace and tranquillity, making clear
to all the true causes of the mistrust engendered by human malice, and thus may be settled so many matters
that are neglected, so many rights that are thwarted, but
especially those of the Church of Jesus Christ in whose
favour I will never cease to claim that liberty and independence which are necessary to her, praying God with
the very words of the Church: 'We beseech thee, Lord,
favourably to receive the prayers of Thy Church, that,
all errors and adversities being destroyed, she may serve
Thee in freedom and safety.'

"I pray to the Lord from the bottom of my heart that
He may keep Your Majesty in His holy grace and give
you all the assistance of which You may stand in greatest
need . . ."[12]

To this letter of the Pope's there was no reply from the
Emperor. But the day after it was written (February 15th,
1861) there appeared in Paris a third pamphlet over the
ominous signature of La Guéronnière, entitled *La France,
Rome, et l'Italie*. That it represented the latest pronouncement on official French policy nobody doubted; according
to Vimercati, Cavour's envoy at Paris, it was written by the
Minister of the Interior, the anti-clerical Persigny, in close
co-operation with Napoleon himself.

The pamphlet was an expansion of Napoleon's letter to

the Pope, and very probably the letter had been intended to pave the way for it. It runs over the main events and arguments of the previous eighteen months, and, after placing the blame for the failure to reach a settlement upon the intransigence of the Pope's advisers, and after criticising his government for not introducing reforms, it ridicules the Holy See for the position of political impotence to which it has been reduced in Italy and points out that what little territory remains to the Pope would disappear tomorrow if it were not protected by the Emperor's generosity in the form of the French army. No doubt all this was intended for the education of French public opinion, as was Persigny's printing of several thousand copies of Prince Napoleon's cynical speech, in the same strain, to the Senate, on March 2nd, and the posting up of a copy in each commune in France.

But the pamphlet did not go unanswered. Dupanloup wrote an open letter to La Guéronnière; Louis Veuillot undertook a lengthy review of the situation in his pamphlet *Le Pape et la diplomatie*. Sometimes Veuillot hit the nail well on the head, as in this comment on the matter of the reforms:

> "M. de la Guéronnière tells us again that Diplomacy demands 'the cessation of numerous abuses'. The only abuse which the enemies of the pontifical government wanted to correct in it was its existence . . ."

It was salutary, too, for his readers to be reminded:

"The Italian Question has been created by the Revolution"—by the Principles of '89.

But Veuillot's most interesting, though contentious paragraph ran:

> "The Pope holds that which humanity has desired, honoured, believed for sixteen centuries. The Christian world feels and affirms it; the revolutionary world feels and denies it. The Christian world wants to maintain the Pope at Rome, because God has placed him there to stand at the head of humanity. The revolutionary world wants to drive the Pope from Rome because the Revolu-

tion, which is satanic, as Joseph de Maistre said, and
consequently the enemy of humanity, aims at decapitat-
ing humanity. The Revolution wants to replace Christ
and Peter at Rome, as Christ and Peter, eighteen centuries ago, replaced Satan and Nero there. Such is the
Roman Question. M. de la Guéronnière doesn't seem
to suspect it, M. de Cavour has some idea of it; M. Mazzini understands it perfectly."[13]

It was the role of Antonelli, obstinate, persistent, and
thorough, to go systematically through the La Guéronnière
pamphlet, sentence by sentence, and to instruct the Papal
Nuncios in the different capitals what were the facts and
what arguments they might well use in combating Napoleon's apologia. For ten more years the tenacious Cardinal
was going to hold the French government to its task at
Rome, by the skill with which, through the Nuncios, he
placed before Catholic Europe the facts and arguments in
support of the Papal position; and he thereby made it impossible for Victor Emmanuel's army or for Garibaldi to
enter the Eternal City. It would be tedious to reproduce
much of the 50,000-word circular letter which he sent out
on this occasion,[14] which is concerned with the facts and
arguments already considered in some detail; but its concluding lines are interesting in the way in which they raise
the matter of the role of France, in defence of Rome, onto
a lofty plane, and counter the view, widely accepted in that
country, that de Mérode and Lamoricière, under guise of
defending Rome, were really building up a force to unseat
Napoleon in the interests of the Comte de Chambord, legitimist claimant of the French throne:

". . . The religious movement in France on behalf of the
Holy See did not constitute something very different
from that which showed itself in Spain, in Belgium, in
Germany, in Ireland and elsewhere. A universal effect
presupposes a cause equally universal. . . . If from
France there came some hundreds of brave men to fight
beneath the Papal banner, from other countries they
came in much more effective numbers. Will it then be
said that it was dynastic opposition to the present Em-

peror of the French that moved the generous sons of the various other nations mentioned to perform the magnanimous deed? It is a waste of time to argue with anyone who reasons in that way.

"It is true that in France the religious movement for the defence of the threatened Pontiff was expressed with more excitement and ardour; but the reason for that is much more noble than the pamphlet thinks. The reason is the natural fear which came upon Catholic France that she would see snatched from her brow the precious halo that encircles it, that she ran the risk that the work of Charles the Great would be undone. Charles the Great it was who rescued and extended the dominion of the Holy See which was attacked and invaded by a Lombard King who aimed, as is being done at present, at the possession of the whole of Italy. He it was who established it upon a firmer basis and gave it public recognition in Europe. And it was not now to be thought of that such an achievement, which constitutes, in the eyes of the Catholic world, the most envied and the most unsullied glory of the eldest daughter of the Church, should now be frustrated, thus bringing dishonour, as has been shown, upon the repeated assurances, both public and private, in which the Emperor of the French and his ministers have declared that the said temporal power would not be destroyed but strengthened. And if anybody wants to find further causes for these fears he might, for example, find them in the notorious proclamation directed by the Emperor to the Italians at Milan, in the interpretation put upon the conversation at Chambéry between the Emperor of the French and one of the Piedmontese generals, in the introduction of the principle of non-intervention in such a form as to favour the revolution and to prevent the Catholic powers from coming to the defence of the Sovereign Pontiff, in the refusal of steps which would have effectively stopped the sacrilegious spoliation which was taking place in the States of the Church, in the putting forward of impossible proposals; these things, to mention no others, may be considered in conjunction with the memory of what happened at the Congress of Paris, in 1856."

The responsibility for causing the Piedmontese spoliation was thus placed squarely by the Pope and Antonelli,
with the full agreement of Catholic Europe, upon Napoleon; and their verdict has been endorsed by history. Confronted by the hard choice between supporting Rome or
supporting Turin, striving, always, to avoid the unpalatable
commitment, the Emperor, confronted by the crisis, had
yielded to Turin. He might later give effective support, in
the last decade of its existence, to what remained of Papal
Rome; but at the critical time he had proved that he was
certainly not what Louis Veuillot had so fervently hoped
and prayed that he would be—a true successor of Charlemagne and Saint Louis.

3. The Defence of the Patrimony of St. Peter
(1862–1864)

It has been necessary to linger over the events of the winter
of '60–'61 because it was then that Pio Nono had to make
the great decision, whether or no to treat with the Revolution; and upon the answer to that question hung more than
the Temporal Power, there hung the attitude Rome would
adopt in her dealings with nineteenth-century liberalism,
both within the Church and without. There was a time,
around Christmas, 1860, when, if the Piedmontese had
shown respect for the property and the laws of the Church,
in the overrun provinces, if they had shown similar respect
for the persons of Archbishops and Bishops, and if Cavour
had restrained the more offensive impieties of the anti-
Catholic press, an agreement along the lines of his "free
Church in a free State" was not impossible. Antonelli
would have negotiated it if the Pope had told him to. The
most powerful of the personal influences acting against
agreement was not Antonelli but de Mérode, whose generous soldierly pride, combined with a contempt for the
Piedmontese, and for Italians generally, led him resolutely
to oppose an understanding. But de Mérode, though the

Pope loved him, was never for long a paramount influence upon policy, because he never carried with him a strong group in the Sacred College, most of whom regarded him as an eccentric; and this, indeed, in his social behaviour, but also in his organising zeal he certainly was. Probably as persuasive an influence as any was the Englishman, Mgr. Talbot. Talbot was very close to the Pope, as he was, too, to Manning, who was later on to exercise an equally strong anti-liberal influence at Rome. Strange, indeed, it is, that at this juncture an Englishman should have played so large a part in maintaining the Pope's hostility to the Piedmontese, and that later another Englishman should have led the more determined Neo-ultramontanes at the Vatican Council!

When the Syllabus of Errors was issued, in 1864, it condemned, in its most famous clause, those who taught that "the Roman Pontiff can and should reconcile himself with and accommodate himself to progress, liberalism, and modern civilisation". This condemnation was lifted direct from the Encyclical *Jamdudum Cernimus*, in which, on March 18th, 1861, the Pope finally denounced the Piedmontese aggression, and put an end to all idea that he would treat with Cavour and his government about the Temporal Power. This is the direct link between the events of the winter of '60–'61 in Italy and the great battle, on the ideological plane, which resounded round the world in the days of the Syllabus of Errors, the Vatican Council, and the *Kulturkampf*. To pretend that the Pope's attitude towards the irreligious tendencies of his times was not coloured by these happenings on his own doorstep is clearly almost as absurd as the opposite error, that which pretends that he "created Catholic dogmas" to spite his enemies! The argument between Rome and Turin has a significance not merely local and temporary because basic questions of principle, and particularly the right relations between Church and State, are raised in it; and some of the theory (which was spoilt by the practice) on the Piedmontese side contained seeds of truth which have since borne fruit. By comparison the argument between Rome and Napoleon, which was similarly concluded by the decisive publication

of *Jamdudum Cernimus* on March 18th, was of smaller
consequence. Neither the arguments of Napoleon, nor those
of his henchman La Guéronnière touched upon questions
of basic principle. The Imperial Government was merely
saying that it was impracticable or inconvenient to interfere effectively with the Piedmontese aggression, which had
been rendered possible by the French victories over Austria,
and that if the Pope were only reasonable he would reconcile himself to the loss of most, or even all of the Temporal
Power. This attitude was intelligible enough, as a matter of
political expediency; but it was hard to reconcile with the
Emperor's declared championship of the Temporal Power,
and it was galling for the Pope to be expected to accept
the resulting acts as "all done for his own good".[15]

The arguments which ran to and fro between Rome and
Paris and Rome and Turin and Paris and Turin from the
time of *Jamdudum Cernimus* until the next important development, the "September Convention" of 1864, are not
of great interest to-day because they do no more than play
variations upon the themes which each party to the dispute
had adopted as its own. In the Encyclical Rome had made
it clear that, to her, the overrunning of the Papal State was
an act of unjustifiable aggression which she could in no wise
regard as legally valid; and that the anti-religious behaviour
of the new régime in the occupied territories was wholly
reprehensible. Napoleon's attitude was that Rome should
at all costs reach agreement with Turin because he had no
intention of leaving an army in the Eternal City indefi-
nitely, and if the Pope were not careful he would find himself without any defence against the Piedmontese.

The situation was extremely uncertain and dangerous for
the Pope and his court. At any moment either the democrats might "rush" Rome, in the wake of the exasperated
Garibaldi, or the Piedmontese army might appear in force,
especially after Cavour's formal insistence, in the Turin
Parliament in March '61, that Italy must have Rome for
her capital. The French might, perhaps, be relied upon to
deal with Garibaldi, for whom they had little love, but
would they fight the Piedmontese? And how could Pio
Nono and Antonelli feel any confidence, after the events of

autumn, 1860, that Napoleon had not got some new secret understanding with Cavour or his successor—that they were not, still, "accomplices"? And if they were not, who could say that they would not be next month, or the month after?

But Antonelli was not wholly without resources in playing the difficult hand of persuading Napoleon effectively to defend the Patrimony of St. Peter. The strongest card he held was the mounting indignation in France at the treatment the Pope had received, indignation which Napoleon, for all his harsh words to Pio Nono, could not afford to ignore. This popular pressure upon the Emperor was reinforced by the rather tentative diplomatic efforts of Austria and Spain, directed towards securing some guarantee for what remained to the Pope of his State. The leading spirit in these efforts was the Spanish Ambassador at Paris, Mon, supported at Madrid by the Bourbon queen, Isabella II, who was devoted to the Pope. Their weakness consisted in the strength of the liberal and revolutionary opposition at Madrid, and in the powerlessness of Austria; but they were not wholly ineffective. In reaching his final determination to maintain the Pope at Rome, Napoleon was certainly influenced by the knowledge that Vienna and Madrid favoured such a policy; in face of the now strongly pro-Turin policy of England it was necessary that he should have at least that measure of diplomatic support. The excesses of Prince Napoleon and his democratic friends of the Palais-Royal, which included the nomination of the Prince as Grand Master of the French Freemasons, had deprived that group of much of the influence which it had formerly held at the Tuileries; with Persigny also out of favour the influence of the Empress Eugénie, Pio Nono's best ally, was correspondingly increased.

In one important respect the Pope and the Emperor were coming to think in the same terms about the state of affairs in Italy; they were both sceptical about the viability of the new Piedmontese order of things, and especially about Victor Emmanuel's assumption of sovereignty over the ancient Kingdom of the Two Sicilies. It had never been part of the Napoleonic idea—it had not even been part of Cavour's master-plan—that Naples should be incorporated in the Piedmontese Kingdom; it was only Garibaldi's adventure which created the diplomatic problem of what to do with the "Southern Kingdom". So long as the young King Francis II and his heroic queen held out at Gaeta, against Victor Emmanuel, in the last months of 1860, Napoleon and Antonelli were at one in supporting him; the Emperor went so far as to use his fleet to safeguard the fortress-port from being attacked and destroyed by the Piedmontese navy, as the port of Ancona had been destroyed in the previous September, after Castelfidardo. In January, however, partly under pressure from London, Napoleon withdrew his fleet, and Francis and his Queen were soon compelled to evacuate, by sea, to Rome. Thus by January, 1861, the whole peninsula, apart from Venetia and the Patrimony of St. Peter, had fallen to Victor Emmanuel, to whom Garibaldi had surrendered Naples; but Napoleon's policy remained, for a time, the establishment of two Italian kingdoms, with a Papal State of indeterminate size between the two; and, so far as Naples was concerned, this remained also the policy of Antonelli.

With the death of Cavour, in June, '61, a further estrangement between Paris and Turin was soon occasioned by the character and policy of his successor, the proud Baron Bettino de Ricasoli. The Baron was quite as pressing at Paris as his predecessor—perhaps he had to be—and far less tactful. He offended Napoleon deeply by warning France publicly that she could expect no more territorial gains at the expense of Italy. He sent a special envoy, Arese, to Napoleon, to press his demands for Rome, until the Emperor declared "Italy, with her unlimited pretensions, has ended by tiring even her friends". Meanwhile he sent letters to the Pope and to Antonelli, together with proposals for a settlement along lines similar to those previously put forward by Passaglia and Pantaleoni. The great defect of these despatches from Turin was that they showed too much of the intentions of the Baron for reforming the Church. Whereas Cavour had urged that his "free Church in a free State" would give the Church greater freedom, Ricasoli underlined the notion, which Cavour had been too tactful to stress, that changes of the kind proposed were needed for the reform of Catholicism. Coming from one who was only nominally a Catholic these proposals were felt to be out of place. Moreover the new premier's idea that Italy should swallow up the revenues of the Papal State, while the Catholic powers of the world made provision for the Pope, while possessing a certain logic, was not calculated to make a wide appeal outside Italy.

There were influences, then, at work, estranging Napoleon from his friendship with Victor Emmanuel; indeed his recognition of the new Kingdom of Italy in June, '61 (a severe blow to Antonelli, but almost necessitated by the previous recognition granted by England), was the last important favour bestowed by the Emperor upon the protégé for whom he had done so much, but who was destined to be rather the ally of England, and later of Germany. Increasingly irritated, especially by England, who seemed to have reaped all the advantages while contributing nothing to the sacrifices of the risorgimento, Napoleon determined —despite England's cry of "non-intervention"—to maintain the Pope at Rome, not merely to satisfy Catholic sentiment, but to give France effective influence in the peninsula.

But the difficulties remained baffling. It was essential for the Emperor to secure some settlement between Rome and Turin because it was intolerable, as well as dangerous, to have to maintain an army at Rome and at the same time to incur the hostility both of the new Italian State and of the Catholic world. It is difficult to withhold sympathy from the Emperor in his dilemma, though it is equally difficult not to wonder at the want of realism and of resolution which he displayed, especially in a remarkable talk he had with the Papal Nuncio, Chigi, on February 3rd, 1862. He had held a dinner in Chigi's honour, and after dinner he took the Nuncio aside and unburdened himself of his difficulties. Chigi reports his words:

". . . 'Indeed I could wish that the Holy Father could obtain a true picture of the state of the Italian question and of my position. Everything goes round and round in a vicious circle. I say to Piedmont: you cannot succeed either in uniting or in governing Italy. And she replies to me: Give me Rome, and likewise stop the agitation which is going on in the two Sicilies, and I will restore order in Italy. For my part I hold that even if she had Rome she would not ever be able to effect that unity, which is a chimera . . .'

". . . 'The King of Naples belongs to a family which is at enmity with me, yet I cannot be estranged from him and would like to see him back on his throne, but I can do nothing for him. The leaders of the Legitimist party are all the time in intimate relations with him; how could I associate my action with theirs? . . .'

"He then went on to protest his firm intention of finding a means of coming to the help of the Holy Father, but having obliged himself to exclude any project which required the use of force, he found he was surrounded by the very greatest difficulties. He, the elect of the people, could not fight against a country which had been established by the will of the people. And at this point I was lucky enough to be able to call His Majesty's attention to something which he could not deny, that is, I was able to remind him by what means the annexations had been carried out, and what tyrannies the people of Italy suffered. At this the Emperor smiled and showed that he fully agreed with me. Then he concluded: 'Italy has need to suffer for her own good. It is no bad thing that the Italians should have experience of their pretended greatness. I am sorry that they are unhappy, but I hope it will be salutary. To me this has always seemed the best way of undeceiving them and of finishing with the revolution. Let us wait a little longer and events will justify me. The great thing is to take away from Piedmont every pretext which may serve to excuse her incapacity to achieve what she has promised. I won't deny to you that if the Holy Father, following my idea, could bring himself to agree to allow the King of Piedmont to come right to Rome, so that he saw that, even in the capital he has dreamed of, he could not hold together a United Italy, nor govern her, then all my difficulties would disappear, and everything could be arranged.' "[16]

Napoleon did not press this remarkable suggestion upon the Nuncio, nor does he seem to have supposed very seriously that it could be entertained. Yet the practical scheme which he did press upon Victor Emmanuel and upon the Pope, namely that the former should rule as the viceroy of the latter, in the Papal State, was not dissimilar in its lack of realism, being absolutely unacceptable both at Turin and at Rome. Possibly the Emperor merely wanted to trick the Pope into opening the gates of Rome to the King; yet he must have known that Chigi would report the conversation not to Pio Nono but to Antonelli, and it was scarcely worth while to try to trap Antonelli with a plot of that kind.

Antonelli at this time was attempting to establish a policy upon a quicksand, the quicksand of Napoleon's irresolution, which had lost two-thirds of the Papal State eighteen months earlier and which was a poor guarantee for the remaining third, if Chigi's reports from Paris indicated the way the Emperor's mind was working. Yet there was no other direction in which he could turn; and so long as the people of France were staunchly behind the Temporal Power[17] there was hope. But some nasty shocks were in store during this year—1862—for the Pope in the form of a courtesy visit by the French navy to Naples, the recall of General Goyon from Rome, and a visit by Prince Napoleon to Turin. On the whole, however, the situation seemed to be clearing. A new, and at first very acceptable, successor to General Goyon was sent from Paris to Rome at the end of May in the person of the Comte de Montebello. It was part of Napoleon's policy, in trying to mollify Pio Nono at this time, to send him more personally congenial Frenchmen—he wisely took the advice of the Empress in selecting them. Thus he sent him, as Ambassador, in October of the same year, the sympathetic Prince de la Tour d'Auvergne. But much more important to the Pope and Antonelli was the contemporaneous replacement of Thouvenel, the Foreign Minister, by Drouyn de Lhuys. This replacement had been a real victory for the party of the Empress, and Walewski, over that of the Prince Napoleon, and the Palais-Royal. The disappearance of the frigid Thouvenel, who had played his part in the deceptions of the autumn of '60, and his replacement by a minister who was actively sympathetic with Pio Nono was indeed a break in the clouds for the hard-pressed Antonelli. So was the recall of the hostile Benedetti from the French Embassy at Turin, and his replacement by the Comte de Sartiges. It seemed that these changes, taken together with the repeated assurance that the French would guarantee the Pope in the frontiers of the Patrimony, afforded some temporary security. Napoleon did not yield his standpoint that an accommodation must be worked out between Rome and Turin. Pio Nono did not yield his standpoint that the whole of his State was inalienable, either by himself, or by the Sacred College, or even by a General Council. Yet a temporary halt had been called to the Piedmontese advance, and the most embarrassing event of that year, the publication by Prince Napoleon of Louis Napoleon's letter to Pope Gregory XVI, in 1831, calling upon the Pope to renounce his temporal power, merely served to reduce still further the effective influence of the Palais-Royal upon the Tuileries. The new outlook prevailing at Paris was, perhaps, best illustrated by the versatile La Guéronnière. That imperial pamphleteer now went back on the arguments of his last pamphlet, *La France, Rome, et l'Italie,* and produced, instead, in the periodical *La France,* a series of letters based upon the notion that the Italian peninsula should be divided between two great autonomous states, with the Patrimony of St. Peter, in between, preserved to the Pope.

The new orientation of French policy had been partly due to an attempt on the part of Garibaldi to "rush Rome", in August, 1862, an attempt which the government of Rattazzi (who had succeeded Ricasoli) had felt obliged to thwart, so as to maintain its position in the eyes of Napoleon and to retain the support of monarchical and conservative elements. The escapade had been a bad business from the standpoint of the progressive elements at Turin, resulting, as it did, in Piedmontese regulars opening fire upon Garibaldi's followers (something Cavour had been able to avoid) and wounding the hero himself in the foot, in the engagement at Aspromonte. In France, supporters of Turin praised Victor Emmanuel's government for having successfully thwarted revolutionary action; but Napoleon made it clear to Chigi that, in his view, Garibaldi's attempt showed the strength of the revolutionary organisation and made it doubtful whether a government which had previously availed itself of Garibaldi's services would be able now to keep down the revolutionary element.[18]

If it was a relief to the Pope to find himself, by the opening of '63, apparently protected in his possession of "Rome with a garden", it was not so pleasant to have the French once more raising the question of reforms, particularly as any practical steps of an economic, administrative or constitutional character which he might take must necessarily tend to harden the existing situation, with its separation of the Patrimony of St. Peter from the rest of the State, and so cut off the city of Rome from its economic support in the provinces.[19]

However, the new French initiative on this subject had been entrusted to Pio Nono's old friend de Corcelles, for whom he had conceived a great liking at Gaeta, at the time of the fall of the Roman Republic; had it been entrusted to anybody less acceptable it is hardly likely that Pio Nono would have taken the surprising step of writing a long personal letter explaining in some detail what he felt about the renewed request for reforms. De Corcelles, co-operating closely with Drouyn de Lhuys (who was anxious to prove to the French liberals that, if the Pope was to be preserved in the Patrimony, his subjects were yet going to enjoy the latest advantages of modern civilisation) had made four main suggestions: (1) that the membership of the Council of State and the Council of Finance should be broadened and enlarged, (2) that the Council of Finance should have deliberative, not merely advisory powers, (3) that there should be a new legal code, (4) that municipal counsellors should be elected by popular vote.

In his reply Pio Nono says:

". . . It is not the reforms that matter to anybody, but something quite other; to these people (his critics) reforms may be irritating, they will not be satisfying . . . but now, most dear Signor Corcelle . . . replying to (1) let me say that the Pontifical State, having lost four-fifths of its subjects, it would be ridiculous to increase the number of councillors in the existing state; besides which we need to economise and not to increase expense. And I reply to (2) that the actual revenues of this State do not supply a half of its needs; the rest of the revenue comes in great part from the generosity of Catholics, and it is not right that the Council of Finance should deliberate upon this generosity. . . . I reply to (3) that our laws are very much superior to those of Piedmont; proof of this are the declarations made in the Parliament of Turin by the deputies from the Legations, the Marches, and Umbria, who have deplored the legislation of the Subalpine Kingdom and praised that of the Pontifical Government; for this reason it is better to await the restoration before publishing the Code. I reply to (4) that, having the Piedmontese five leagues from Rome, I do not think it prudent to put into operation the machinery of popular elections, in as much as the excitement would be likely, when helped by the subtle means that would be employed, to introduce confusion and disorder amongst the many voters. . . ."[20]

De Corcelles and Drouyn de Lhuys seem to have been favourably impressed by these arguments; the proposals were reduced to a mere matter of certain economic reforms concerning customs dues, fishing rights, irrigation, and the like, together with administrative reforms in the postal system and the judicial procedure. Moreover de Corcelles had a great deal to say about the need for less vexatious treatment by the imperial government of the Church in France and for better behaviour by the French army authorities in Rome towards the pontifical government and the pontifical army. Finally, around the negotiations, floated the question, very important for the hard-pressed State, of a French loan, and of securing that responsibility for a proportionate share of the public debt of the Papal State should fall upon that power which had recently taken over four-fifths of its territory.

By the summer of 1863 the new turn of events was giving rise to something approaching optimism at Rome. If, as La Guéronnière's latest output suggested, Napoleon were now reconciled to defending the Patrimony, might he not soon be prepared to insist that the Piedmontese withdraw from Umbria and the Marches? It was common knowledge in France that matters were going badly for Turin in the new kingdom, with the Mazzinians everywhere defying the government.

But those who thought in this way (and they did not include the Pope or Antonelli) mistook the position at Paris. Napoleon was, indeed, reconciled by now to the idea that the defence of the Patrimony was the least he would have to pay for the support of Catholic opinion at home, but it was also the most he would pay; and he had come to believe that he might pay it without having to keep an army at Rome. The maintenance of that army had become, in the eyes of Turin, an affront to the new nation. The government there was, after all, in the hands of men who passed as "moderates"; they were, indeed, the moderates of the old days of 1848, for first Farini, then Minghetti attained to the premiership in 1863, while Pio Nono's old friend Pasolini reached the exalted rank of foreign minister. These were men of the sort that Napoleon felt he understood, as he understood Nigra, their ambassador at Paris. With Nigra repeating, at regular intervals, that the French army at Rome was the sole obstacle to Italo-French friendship the Emperor naturally came increasingly to feel that it was intolerable that he should have to allow Italy's friendship to be transferred to England, when it was he who had risked his throne, on the battlefield, in a war which had made the new position of Turin possible. He felt he had a right to a friendly Italy, under his patronage, especially as the colour of Turin's "modernism" at this time was rather the colour of his own. The Pope, he felt, should recognise this, should recognise in himself the heir to Charlemagne and Saint Louis, not so much in the sense of the soldier with the sword, defending the Papacy, as that of the enlightened ruler, reconciling the Faith with contemporary civilisation.

"The interest of the Holy See," he had told Thouvenel the year before, "and that of religion require that the Pope be reconciled with Italy, which amounts to the same thing as reconciling itself with modern ideas, safeguarding within the orbit of the Church 200 million Catholics and raising religion to a new splendour by showing that the Faith promotes the progress of humanity."[21]

There is no reason to suppose that Napoleon was insincere in these opinions, even though he may have been subject to some self-deception. But they led him into undertaking secret negotiations with Turin in which he most definitely deceived the Pope, and in due course he appeared once more at Rome in the light of a traitor to the Church. In June, 1863, Pio Nono was ill for some time, with a serious fever, which gave rise to the idea in Napoleon's mind that he might plan a gradual withdrawal of his troops which would not be completed until a new conclave had elected a more amenable pontiff. Pio Nono recovered, but the Emperor's ideas went on maturing. Insistently he assured Nigra that, if only he could produce some visible guarantee that neither the Italian army nor Mazzini and Garibaldi would occupy the Eternal City when the French troops were gone, he would be only too happy that they should go. Thus came to birth the idea of the transfer by the Italians of their capital from Turin to another city— probably Florence—which the Emperor, either naïvely or cunningly, affected to suppose would ensure that they would not want to move it again to Rome. This was the essential basis for the September Convention (September 15th, 1864), agreed between the two governments, in which Napoleon undertook to effect the complete withdrawal of the French army from Rome within two years and Turin undertook (1) not to attack the Papal territory, and to prevent any revolutionary attack upon it, (2) to allow the Pope to form his own army, which might include foreigners, but which must not be large enough to be a threat to Victor Emmanuel (!), (3) to bear her just proportion of the debt of the old Papal State, (4) to remove the capital of

Italy, within six months, from Turin to any other city of the government's choice.

On both sides, in Italy, it was taken for granted that by the September Convention Napoleon had once again sold the pass; it was assumed that as soon as France was occupied elsewhere the Italian army would march in—whether to "restore order" or in answer to some request put out by the leaders of an uprising could be left to depend upon the circumstances. In these opinions those at Turin and at Rome were neither quite fair to Napoleon, as the events of three years later, at Mentana, were going to prove. But essentially, they correctly anticipated what did occur in 1870.

The new French ambassador at Rome, Sartiges (moved from Turin), had to break the news of the September Convention to Antonelli. This was a delicate matter, especially as he carried a letter from Drouyn de Lhuys containing some choice phrases of Napoleon's about the two governments being ordered upon different principles, in as much as the Curia maintained itself by special laws irreconcilable with the ideas of the times.

This was too much, even for the proved patience of the Secretary of State. Some say that Antonelli broke off the interview and refused to receive the letter.[22] But the more usual account is that he let fly, telling Sartiges that France was free to do as she liked, that the Pope would provide, himself, for his own defence, that the French occupation had been a source of expense and humiliation, that the Romans had disliked having the French at Rome and endured with impatience the pretensions of their soldiers in maintaining public order over the head of the local police, that the various generals had never made themselves popular and had not seemed to care to do so, that for these reasons the departure of the army would not be an event calculated to displease the majority of the inhabitants of Rome.[23]

If, with Antonelli, the Neapolitan *contadino's* elemental fury had, for once, broken through the perfect manners

and discretion of the trained diplomat, Pio Nono's reactions
were more characteristic:

> "Poor France! . . . You tell me to have confidence in
> the Emperor; but I repeat to you that I trust only in
> God, and that He is my one support. Ah! in my sadness
> I think not so much of myself as of those who are hostile
> to the Church . . ."

and a little later:

> "I have placed all my trust in God; if He chooses to
> preserve me in peace, I will praise Him; if He chooses to
> prove me with tribulations I will not cease to extol Him."

But he was riled by further suggestions that the Emperor
hoped he would reach an understanding with the Italian
government: "My God! when I want to I can do that for
myself, without the intervention of foreigners. When all is
said and done, We are Italian!"[24]

And then there was all this talk about "modern civilisation". His reply to that was to issue, within less than three
months of the September Convention, the Syllabus of
Errors.

Chapter Seven

PIO NONO VERSUS LIBERALISM
(1863–1870)

1. *The Syllabus of Errors* (1864)

The Syllabus of Errors and the Encyclical *Quanta Cura* which accompanied it[1] are formidable documents, sweeping in their denunciations, and harsh in tone; they were profoundly upsetting to many within the Church and to others outside who were friendly disposed to her. They gave most satisfaction to the more authoritarian party within and to the more ardently hostile without. To the former they seemed to give official justification; to the latter they seemed so completely unreasonable and absurd as to spell the doom of the Papacy.

They were therefore documents of some consequence, in one sense of even greater consequence than the two dogmas defined in Pio Nono's pontificate, the Immaculate Conception and Papal Infallibility, because those definitions only made dogmatic what the Church as a whole believed, whereas the Encyclical and the Syllabus plunged—though not with dogmatic force—into the most controversial problems of thought and politics. So wide were their implications and repercussions that it is wise, before considering them, to recollect within what limits and having what immediate purposes Rome issued them. The immediate purpose of the Encyclical was to announce a Jubilee, during the following year, 1865, when a plenary indulgence might be gained. It is not long, and, while it runs over much the same ground as the Syllabus, and condemns most of the same ideas and teaching, it does so in terms which, though indignant, are measured and conventional in form; had it been issued by itself it would probably have attracted little more attention than that small measure which it is usual for Encyclicals to meet, and would have taken its place along with others issued by Pio Nono or with Gregory XVI's *Mirari vos*, which had condemned, in 1832, the principles of Lamennais' *Avenir*.

But the Syllabus was another matter. It was sent out together with the Encyclical, though it was not signed by the Pope, and the only clue to his personal responsibility for its issue is that given by Antonelli in his short introduction:

> "Our Holy Father, Pius IX, Sovereign Pontiff, being profoundly anxious for the salvation of souls and of sound doctrine, has never ceased from the commencement of his pontificate to proscribe and condemn the chief errors and false doctrines of our most unhappy age, by his published Encyclicals, and Consistorial Allocutions and other Apostolic Letters. But as it may happen that all the Pontifical acts do not reach each one of the ordinaries, the same Sovereign Pontiff has willed that a Syllabus of the same errors should be compiled, to be sent to all the Bishops of the Catholic world, in order that these Bishops may have before their eyes all the errors and pernicious doctrines which he has reprobated and condemned.
>
> "He has consequently charged me to take care that this Syllabus, having been printed, should be sent to your [Eminence] on this occasion. . . ."[2]

The Syllabus is headed: "A Syllabus, containing the principle Errors of our times, which are noted in the Consistorial Allocutions, in the Encyclicals, and in other Apostolic Letters of our most Holy Lord, Pope Pius IX." It is, in fact, as Newman called it, an *index raisonné*, drawn up by the Pope's orders and conveyed to the Bishops, through his Minister of State; and its real value lies in its references, i.e. in the Allocutions, etc., to which, in each case, the reader is referred. Read straight through, as though it were an independent document in its own right, it is as irritating and as indigestible as any summarised index of condemnations read consecutively must necessarily be.

Strictly speaking neither the press, nor the public, nor governments were concerned with it, because it was a technical document, requiring theological knowledge for its interpretation, addressed to Bishops, with a view to giving them guidance upon certain matters, for use at their discretion in teaching the faithful. But Antonelli was realist enough to know very well that it would be publicised, and would raise a storm. He had been told as much by those in a position to know, and notably by Dupanloup. He may not have foreseen that in France and in Italy the governments would go so far as to allow the press to publish and to comment (with inevitable ignorance) upon the text, while not allowing the Bishops equal freedom to expound and explain the propositions, which they alone could do authoritatively; but he knew it would not be ignored, if only because for at least four years there had been much talk of the Pope's intention of issuing a document which would condemn the errors of the century. Europe was, in fact, waiting for it.

The responsibility for publication rests with Pio Nono, even though he seems to have concerned himself very little with the precise form in which the condemnation was issued. He had considered various drafts, similarly concerned with condemning "errors of the times". There was one by Veuillot, which he liked, and which later formed the basis of the journalist's pamphlet *l'Illusion Libérale*. There was another by Mgr. Gerbet, the Bishop of Perpignan. He seems to have been dissuaded by Dupanloup from publishing either of these. He eventually decided in favour of a collection to be made from his own pronouncements, but publication was delayed because Antonelli was very anxious not to offend Napoleon, who believed in, and whose government rested upon, several of the censured propositions, and whose attitude and behaviour were, indeed, one of the objects of the Pope's attack. But the Convention of September, between Paris and Turin, ended in 1864 the long doubt about Napoleon's intentions finally convincing Rome that the "new Saint Louis" had merely served to eliminate the power of Austria in her defence and then to hand her over to the tender mercies of the anticlerical forces of the risorgimento. In these circumstances, persuasion at Paris having become useless, Antonelli's objections to the issue of a condemnation lost their force.

The Syllabus catalogues 80 propositions which were being taught in one place or another, in Pio Nono's lifetime, and which had been adjudged by him to be erroneous. The first 7 concern Pantheism, Naturalism, and absolute Rationalism. 8 to 14 concern "Moderate Rationalism". 15 to 18

concern Indifferentism and Latitudinarianism, and it is immediately following these that a paragraph is included
condemning Socialism, Communism, Secret Societies, Bi-
ble Societies, Clerical-Liberal Societies. 19 to 38 concern
the Church and her Rights. 39 to 55 concern Civil Society,
considered in itself and in its relations to the Church. 56
to 64 concern Natural and Christian ethics. 65 to 74 concern Christian Matrimony. 75 and 76 concern "the Roman
Pontiff's civil princedom". 77 to 80 are "errors which have
reference to the Liberalism of the day".

Of all the condemned propositions, it was number 80
which caused the most stir. It reads as follows: "The Roman
Pontiff can and should reconcile and harmonise himself
with progress, with liberalism, and with recent civilisation."[3] Like all the other propositions it is stigmatised as
an error, and the Allocution from which the condemnation
is drawn is that *Jamdudum Cernimus* of March 18th, 1861,
with which, as we have seen, the Pope concluded all idea
that he would treat with Cavour about the Temporal
Power, or about the setting up of a new relationship between Church and State. Coming at the end of the series,
and seeming, in some sort, to sum up the whole, it appeared, in England, or Belgium, or France, to be an
anathema hurled at the most cherished ideals of the nineteenth century. Actually, as reference to the Encyclical
from which it is drawn shows, it was the Piedmontese government's idea of what constituted progress and civilisation
with which the Pope was declining to come to terms. Similarly, the Clerical-Liberal societies which are condemned
under proposition 18 are found to be those groups of dis-
sident clergy, in Piedmont, who were opposed to the attitude of Rome about the Siccardi Laws, or the closure of the
monasteries, or the Temporal Power, and which were fostered and supported by the government at Turin—they are
not, as was widely supposed, Montalembert and his distinguished friends in France. Error number 45, which asserts
that entire control of schools, including the appointment of
teachers, belongs as of right to the Civil Authority, is condemned in accordance with an Allocution of November 1st,

1850, which stigmatised the Piedmontese education law. Error number 60, which declared that "Authority is none other than the sum of the material forces", is condemned in accordance with an Allocution of June 9th, 1862, which, while it is a lofty exaltation of the spiritual over the material, and of Right over Force, has obvious reference to the Piedmontese seizure of territory in Italy and to the subsequent justification of that seizure by the holding of plebiscites; it does not condemn plebiscites, but it does imply that plebiscites are not to be regarded as the sole source of legitimate authority. Error number 62, the assertion that "It is necessary to proclaim and observe the principle of non-intervention", is condemned in accordance with an Allocution of September 28th, 1860, which was wholly concerned with the situation created by the invasion of Umbria and the Marches. Errors 75 and 76 specifically concern the Temporal Power.

These are examples of errors denounced in the Syllabus which had specific reference to Italy. But in a wider sense most of the Syllabus was prompted by the Italian situation. Pio Nono was witnessing, in Italy, the practical results, as he saw it, of atheist, rationalist, pantheist, or protestant propaganda, of secret societies, of indifferentism, of a wrong view of the relations between the Church and the State. In a sense it was almost all a cri-de-cœur against the Turin government and its religious and political works; but it was a cri-de-cœur, too, against Mazzini. Mazzini at Rome was not forgotten; and Mazzini, in the wake of Garibaldi, was still, behind the Piedmontese, a likely enough heir to the leadership of that United Italy which he had been the first to preach. Nobody had taught about progress, or liberalism, or recent civilisation, with greater eloquence or sincerity, or interpreted those concepts in a less Catholic sense than the sometime Triumvir and prophet of the new religion of God and the People.

Piedmont, and Mazzini. When to these are added the fanatical extravagances of Garibaldi, who was now talking of the Papacy as the "Cancer of Italy", and all the other iconoclastic elements in the risorgimento, together with the not negligible progress of protestantism, especially in Piedmont and Tuscany, and the increased prestige and influence of Italian Freemasonry,[4] it will be recognised how naturally the publication of the Syllabus followed upon the Pope's view of the state of affairs amongst Italians.

But it is equally natural that Europeans as a whole did not interpret the Syllabus as though they were Italians. Every Italian knew that "Progress, Liberalism, and Recent Civilisation" meant the closure of the convents and monasteries, and the imposition of secular education. It meant railways, too, of course, and street-lighting by gas, and all those improvements which so interested men like Pasolini, Minghetti, or Cavour; but Italians were not likely to put such matters in the forefront of their thinking; in their context in controversy the terms stood for secularism and anti-clericalism. In England, however, Progress and Recent Civilisation meant primarily the Great Exhibition of 1851, while Liberalism meant conservatives like Peel or Mr. Gladstone who had very few counterparts in Italy. The French interpretation of the phrases was more analogous to the Italian, meaning, to most men, the "Principles of 1789", or just "the Revolution". But in America the words stood, of course, for all that was held most sacred. The question inevitably poses itself whether words capable of such various interpretation, and drawn from an encyclical specifically reprimanding the overrunning of Umbria and the Marches, should have been used as the conclusion to a Syllabus sent to Bishops at Birmingham and New York.

The hierarchies of most western countries found themselves embarrassed in their relations with their governments and with public opinion as a consequence of the Syllabus. That might well be a small matter; but to meet a situation in which "the majority of Catholics were stupified"[5] was a big one, and particularly big in December, 1864, because some of the greatest leaders of Catholic thought in Europe, and notably Montalembert, had recently been engaged in urging politico-religious concepts of a kind that were specifically reprobated in the Syllabus.

With much of the Syllabus, of course, there was no quarrel
on the part of Catholics or of other Christians. Thus it
condemned propositions such as the denial of the Divinity
of Christ, or the validity of Atheism, which any Christian
teacher would condemn. But it also condemned certain
propositions which were not only generally held outside the
Catholic Church but were also widely held within it, and
the most controversial of these related to the concept
of Toleration. Thus the Syllabus condemned the propositions that: "in our age it is no longer expedient that the
Catholic Religion should be regarded as the sole religion
of the State to the exclusion of all others" (No. 77); that
"The Church has not the power to employ force nor any
temporal power direct or indirect" (No. 24); and that
everybody should be free "to give public utterance, in every
possible shape, by every possible channel, to all his notions
whatsoever", an attitude which was held to lead to "corruption of manners and minds" and to the "pest of indifferentism" (No. 79). These condemnations were generally taken to mean that religious toleration and freedom of
speech were condemned.

The answer of the Church to those who criticised the
Pope's teaching on toleration and the explanation given to
the bewildered faithful were supplied by Dupanloup in his
pamphlet *The September Convention and the Encyclical
of December* 8. The indefatigable Bishop of Orleans received the thanks of no less than 630 Bishops for this
pamphlet, as well as the approval of the Pope.[6] Dupanloup's line of argument at once brought to light the background against which any series of pontifical statements of
principle must be seen, namely that the Pope was talking
in terms of absolute and eternal principle, or of "the perfect society", not of what at a given time in any given country might be either expedient or even just. Her enemies
were laying down principles which they conceived and
claimed were of universal and eternal validity; the Church
was denying that they had such validity. Thus, in condemning the claims of the Rationalists, she was denying the
absolute supremacy of Reason, without Faith, not the valid-

ity of Reason as such, or as the ally of Faith; and in condemning the claim to absolute freedom of belief, worship, speech, and press, she was saying that she could not contemplate, as the ultimate ideal, a society which held false beliefs, or tolerated propaganda against the sacraments or other essentials of Catholic practice, or which taught such errors in speech or print. The "true society" would not do these things, and it was therefore erroneous to teach their acceptance as an ultimate ideal. Further, she was saying that in some Catholic countries it would be wrong, even at that day, to disestablish Catholicism and to permit other Churches (this condemnation comes from an Encyclical concerned with Spain); while in others it might be wrong to try to hold on to the privileges of establishment. Throughout Dupanloup's pamphlet runs the distinction between the *thèse* (the ideal of the true society) and the *antithèse*[7] (what is possible or just in the existing state of society). Her opponents were talking in terms of absolutes; so the Church had to make clear what were the true absolutes, or at least must deny those that were false. The great mistake was to suppose that when she condemned a proposition on the absolute plane there might not, yet, be much relative good in it, and that some measure of its practice might not often be healthy and beneficial. And when the absolute claims of a proposition were denied it by no means followed that the contrary proposition was always valid—thus it was erroneous to say that the Catholic Church should everywhere be disestablished, but it was not true to say that she should always be an Established Church.

This relativism was valid argument, even if to those who looked upon the Church only as one amongst competing "interests" it seemed like opportunism. Nor was the criticism that Dupanloup was "watering down the Syllabus" a fair one; he was arguing in strict accord with the implied thought of the Church; and if the lay press considered him specious he was entitled to reply that the Syllabus had not been addressed to them but presupposed an audience familiar with the terms of theological argument.

2. *The Eclipse of Liberal-Catholicism: Mont-alembert, Döllinger, Acton, and Pio Nono* (1863–1865)

More serious than the hostility which the Syllabus aroused amongst governments, or in anti-Catholic circles, was the embittering effect which it had upon the Liberal-Catholics, and notably upon Montalembert, Döllinger, and Acton. It ended the hope of these men that Rome would embrace liberal principles, at least in Pio Nono's lifetime.

It is incorrect to call Liberal-Catholicism a movement, because it was never organised as such, and because the term is used to embrace too many divergent principles and personalities. Thus Newman had much in common with Döllinger's intellectual attitude, but nothing in common with Montalembert's or Lacordaire's political liberalism; while Acton's obsession about Absolute Freedom was very much *sui generis*. But on the Continent, at least, many of the Liberal-Catholics' ideas derived from Lamennais and it is to his *Avenir*, of 1831, that we must first, for a moment, return. The political, social, and religious freedom invoked by that paper had been condemned in the following year by Gregory XVI in *Mirari vos*; but Gregory had tried to avoid making a pronouncement and it had really been very unwise of Lamennais, in view of the novelty of his ideas, to go to Rome and press for a verdict forthwith because the Church could not adopt as her programme that of the *Avenir*, when, throughout the world, she was, in fact, organised on the basis of concordats with governments, and had to be so organised because her very existence was threatened by the leaders of the revolutionary liberal societies. Yet the ultramontane side of Lamennais' teaching, his hatred of Gallicanism and Josephism, was very congenial to Rome, and, during the first two years of the pontificate of Pio Nono, Rome seemed also ready to support his liberal ideas; for those were the days of the religious ascendancy of Fr. Ventura, and of his sermons, attended and approved by the Pope, at *S. Maria degli Angeli* at Rome—sermons about liberty that might have been preached by Lacordaire at Notre Dame.

We have seen what turned Pio Nono away from liberal visions. But in France the Liberal-Catholics had flourished. After watching Lamennais drift into apostasy Montalembert and his friends of the *Correspondant* had made good progress in winning liberties for the Church in France, and most notably in winning wider freedom for Church schools by the Falloux Education Law of 1849. This victory had been very welcome to Pio Nono, but he had grown cool towards their faith in political liberty, in freedom of expression, and in toleration, which made them enemies of Napoleon III, and enemies, too, of the larger and more powerful stream of Catholic opinion in France, that which followed Louis Veuillot and which (till 1860 and Castelfidardo) supported Napoleon III. During the 'fifties, deprived of effective political influence, Montalembert's band of brilliant friends, Dupanloup and Lacordaire (their spiritual guides), de Falloux, de Broglie, and Augustin Cochin made common cause, as best they could, in advocating liberal institutions, using either the Academy, of which the first three were members, or the pages of the *Correspondant*. Twice his criticism of the government brought Montalembert into the Courts; it also brought him into contact with the Legitimists, and their candidate for the throne, the Comte de Chambord, from whose succession men like Montalembert hoped at least for those political liberties that had existed in the time of Louis Philippe.

The hostility between the "Veuillotists" (heirs to Lamennais' Ultramontanism) and Montalembert's friends (heirs to Lamennais' Liberalism) was temporarily obscured by their common denunciation of the Piedmontese aggression, and of Napoleon's part in it—Lacordaire and Cochin were the only French Liberal-Catholic leaders who allowed their principles about political liberty to cool their ardour for the Temporal Power. But the two French groups were thrown into still worse conflict in the early 'sixties by the determined and often violently expressed support given

by men of Veuillot's way of thinking to absolutist principles
in politics, in religious history, and in the realm of thought.
Both schools of opinion were staunchly Papal when there
was any question of conflict between Church and State,
such as occurred over the independence of the Church
schools, or the nomination of Bishops. But on the issue of
liberty, both inside and outside the Church, they differed
irreconcilably.

Pio Nono, from the time of his return from Gaeta, in
1850, had acquired the absolutist viewpoint, a viewpoint
closely analogous to Veuillot's, in matters political and intellectual, as well as in the government of the Church. This
absolutism, like Napoleon III's, should be distinguished
from mere reaction. It took account of the positive achievement even of the Revolution; to the end Pio Nono would
not hear the "principles of '89" condemned wholesale:
"there was yet some good in them", he insisted, "equality
of all before the law, for instance". He was a convert to
absolutism primarily on account of the murder of Rossi
and the Roman Revolution of 1848–49; ("Your Holiness
will remember how they treated Rossi," Antonelli would
murmur when he contemplated again extending liberties)
and secondarily on account of the religious and political
aggression of Piedmont. He was guided in his thinking
partly by the able group of Jesuits who edited the *Civiltà
Cattolica* at Rome, and partly by Louis Veuillot himself,
to whom he might on occasion recommend moderation, but
who was welcomed for months at a time at Rome, and
whose *Illusion Libérale* (1865) the Pope regarded as fully
expressing his own views. Particularly Pio Nono's was the
belief, born of his own experience, that you could not afford
to give power to the moderate liberals, to the Pasolinis and
the Minghettis for instance, because behind them lurked
the Mazzinis and the Garibaldis. So he linked the cause of
the other dispossessed Italian princes with his own, and
deplored Victor Emmanuel's weakness in always bowing
before the votes of the Chamber; and he thus seemed to
give the Church's preference to absolutist rulers. Finally, he
signed a whole series of Concordats—with Tuscany, the
Italian Duchies, Spain, and, most important, in 1856 with

the young Francis Joseph of Austria. This last Concordat, so long considered, while concerned mainly with removing Josephist State control over the Church, yet retained, to her advantage, many of the privileges and protections of State establishment.

Pio Nono, then, though he accepted conditions in these same years for the restored hierarchies of England and Holland which put the Church very much on the footing of a "tolerated" rather than a "privileged" institution, was nevertheless protecting the Church where he could, in Catholic countries, by securing the special protection of the State on terms as advantageous as he could get. And in France, where the Concordat was very favourable to the State, he was making no attempt to denounce it, but was trying, as we have seen in his correspondence with the Emperor, to persuade Napoleon to interpret it and carry it out in a spirit of friendship and forbearance, and not to have resource to those "Organic Articles", introduced by his uncle, which could be used to put the Church almost at the mercy of the Civil Power.

So it was that the condemnations of the Syllabus concerned with Church and State and those concerned with freedom of expression were the natural reflection of the Pope's policy since 1850, being designed to safeguard Catholicism and to protect the faithful in countries predominantly Catholic. They did not rule out toleration, a free press, and disestablishment; but they did say that it was erroneous to assert that such concepts were the ideal universal prescription.

But, unfortunately, that was exactly what the French Liberal-Catholics had decided that they were. Montalembert had reached the conclusion that toleration, a free press, and disestablishment were *absolutely* desirable in the modern world, and that the Church had *everywhere* everything to gain from them; and, carrying over his enthusiasm for liberty into the political sphere, he was condemning Napoleon III, praising Belgian liberties, and extolling the British Constitution—though he was scornful enough of British politicians for censuring the Papal Government while supporting the Sultan and for themselves tyrannising in Ireland and India. The greatest orator in France, he was the critic whom Napoleon found most embarrassing; but he was beginning to be something of an embarrassment, too, to the Pope.

Pio Nono, however little he might like some of Montalembert's views, was profoundly aware that the orator had done more than any other man to win back a position for the faith in France, so he was prodigal in his congratulations and thanks and was even ready to support him, on occasion, against Veuillot. He recognised that the Count's pamphlet, *Pie IX et Lord Palmerston* (1856), and his *Pie IX et la France en 1849 et en 1859* were political advocacy as timely and as powerful as his Temporal Power ever received. But the advocacy of toleration and freedom, which Montalembert crystallised in 1860 into the phrase Cavour borrowed, "a free Church in a free State", ran counter to the Pope's policy; while the French orator's enormous enthusiasm for the constitutions of Belgium and England contrasted somewhat with Pio Nono's dislike of the constitutions that had come his way at Rome and Turin.

Matters came to a head when Montalembert was invited to address a big Catholic Congress at Malines in the summer of 1863. The invitation was very natural, because, although he never enjoyed a following numerically comparable to that of Veuillot (the *Correspondant* [a monthly] sold about three thousand copies), he had the profound respect of the greatest French and Belgian political and religious thinkers of his time whether Bishops, like Dupanloup or Sterckx, or politicians like Thiers or Guizot. Since the aim of the Congress was to reconcile the Church with civilisation in north-western Europe he was the obvious man to invite.

Yet he hesitated for long. It was very painful to him to think that what he would say would be likely enough to cause further pain to a long-suffering Pope. But he could hardly refuse the invitation of Archbishop Démoulins of Namur. Leading figures in the Church, archbishops, bishops, regulars, laymen would be present. They were to confer together, the Archbishop explained, on the means to be adopted to defend the common faith in this hour of danger. . . . "It is of the very highest importance that the result should be liberal and that the programme which emerges should be yours: Catholicism and liberty . . ." So he promised to go, and to express his whole mind on "the future of modern society and of the Church".

His first speech (August 20th) was about: "a formula already famous: *a free Church in a free State*, which, though snatched from us and put into circulation by a very guilty man remains none the less the symbol of our convictions and our hopes . . ." The ancient régime of absolute monarchies and privileges guaranteed by concordats "had its great and beautiful side: I do not pretend to judge it here, still less to condemn it. It suffices for me to recognise in it one defect, but that a capital one: it is dead . . ." The theocratic régime of Charles X in France had been entirely disastrous for the Church, whereas, divorced from the political power, under Louis Philippe, she had been reborn: "In 1830 all the priests, the abbé Lacordaire amongst others, were reduced to not going out into the street except in the disguise of a layman. . . . In 1848 that same Lacordaire appeared in a Dominican habit in the Assembly."

But he is just as bitter about Democracy, which, to him, as to any serious continental thinker, then meant Jacobinism, centralisation, bureaucracy, and a state monopoly of education. "The more one is a democrat the more it is necessary to be Christian; because the fervent and practical cult of God made man is the indispensable counter-weight of that perpetual tendency of democracy to establish the cult of man believing himself God."

And he ends his speech, which was received with tumultuous enthusiasm, by invoking Liberty of Education, of Association, and of the Press; and by quoting Dupanloup: "We accept, we invoke the principles and the liberties proclaimed in '89. . . . You made the revolution of 1789 without us and against us, but *for us*, God wishing it so in spite of you."

His second address, the following day, he devoted to religious toleration. He denies absolutely that the principle

of toleration is non-Catholic in origin and bases it firmly
upon St. Peter: "We cannot be silent concerning those
things which we have seen and heard." He points out, with
Dupanloup, that Protestant countries have often been more
guilty than Catholic of using the power of the State to
suppress religious liberty, but he quotes Louis XIV's revo-
cation of the Edict of Nantes, and the more recent policy
of Spain, Naples, and Charles-Albert's Piedmont: "those
Paradises of religious absolutism have become the scandal
and the despair of all Catholic hearts". He protests against
Veuillot's *Univers* for demanding liberty for all in March,
1848, and liberty only for the Church in March, 1853. Yet
he does not mean *absolute* separation of Church from State,
which is impossible, or hostility between the two. Thus
Cavour, for example, was offering merely "a despoiled
Church in a spoliative State". And there was always one—
and only one—exception to his general rule: the Papal State.
The identity of Church and State in that unique case was
the guarantee of freedom everywhere.[8]

Montalembert was careful to make it clear that he did
not regard a society in which religious beliefs were in conflict as an ideal society; on that point he was at one with
the "thèse" of the Syllabus of Errors, which appeared in
the following year. But he was very clear indeed that intolerance, and in particular reliance upon the strong arm of
the State, were immensely prejudicial to the health of Catholicism and were rooted in false principle, whereas the
Syllabus implied, at the very least, that in some circumstances they were proper. Cardinal Wiseman, who was at
Malines, and the Papal Nuncio, who was also present, were
well aware, not only that Montalembert's thesis ran counter
to Pio Nono's practice, but that the Pope was planning a
Syllabus which would put modern liberties into a very
different light. Though Dupanloup tried hard at Rome to
prevent it,[9] a condemnation of Montalembert was really
inevitable, and it duly arrived, courteous, confidential, and
friendly, in February, 1864, pointing out that in 1791 Pius
VI had condemned the Edict of Nantes, and reminding the
orator of Gregory XVI's *Mirari vos*. Dupanloup had done
all he could for his friend; but Mgr. Pie, Bishop of Poitiers,

and a host of others had used their influence in the opposite sense. The *Univers* had not printed the speeches, but it had denounced the principles.

At the Malines Congress Montalembert's friend, Augustin Cochin, had spoken about free intellectual enquiry, and especially of scientific investigation, in relation to the Church. But this was more particularly the theme of an equally significant Congress which met at Munich in September, '63. The same purpose prevailed as at Malines, namely, the harmonising of Catholic thought, the drawing together of leading Catholics the better to co-ordinate their power to meet the advance of unbelief. But whereas Malines was mainly preoccupied, under the influence of Montalembert, with the relations of Church and State, Munich, under the influence of Ignaz Döllinger, was mainly concerned with the independent intellectual rights of history, reason, and science, and their relations both with theology and with religious authority. It was a gathering mainly of Germans, but of Germans living under very different conditions. Some came from Catholic states, such as Austria or Bavaria; some from mixed states in the Rhineland; some from Protestant states like Prussia pursuing tolerant policies, or like Baden, pursuing intolerant policies. The dominant figure was Döllinger; and Döllinger, despite his immense prestige as an historian, and the favour with which his exposure of the realities of the Lutheran revolution were regarded at Rome, had, two years previously, given some offence by criticising, shortly after the disaster of Castelfidardo, the character of the Pope's government in his state.[10]

At the Munich Congress Döllinger gave offence to Rome by claiming that true theology depended upon a proper understanding of history and of philosophy, and that Germany possessed a monopoly of both; and he had a good deal to say about the inadequacy of Italian scholarship. Coming on top of the audacities of Malines, this was altogether too much for Pio Nono. At the end of January, '64, and after full consultation with Reisach, Archbishop of Munich, he sent a Brief expressing his hope for good results from the Congress, but deploring the absence of any permission from

the hierarchy for the holding of such an assembly of
theologians, and maintaining that Catholic thought was not
only bounded by dogmatic definitions but should also be
guided by the ordinary magistracy of the Church, by the
decisions of Roman Congregations, and by the teaching of
theologians.[11]

The intention of making the Munich Congress an annual
affair was abandoned on account of the Pope's attitude.
Malines was repeated in the following year, when Dupanloup achieved something of the personal success of Montalembert, though only in the less controversial field of
Catholic education. To Englishmen the point of special
interest in these contretemps is that the Pope's rebuke to
the leaders of the Munich Congress altered the course of
the life-work of the most liberal English Catholic scholar,
Sir John Acton. A pupil of Döllinger, and editor in 1864
of the periodical the *Home and Foreign Review* (successor
to the *Rambler*), Acton felt bound to discontinue his
paper's publication. He had welcomed the Munich Congress because he saw in it the most serious attempt of the
age to begin the work of defining the relations of thought
with authority and tradition, and he considered that the
transactions of the first meeting showed that it would take
its stand firmly on the twin principles of submission to the
dogma of the Church and respect for the independent
rights of science.[12] But the Pope's Brief meant that the
scientific pursuit of truth was obliged to have respect not
merely to the small area covered by dogma, which any
Catholic would naturally respect, but also to the Roman
Congregations, and in particular to the Congregation of the
Index, and to the theological opinions currently acceptable
to the hierarchy, even though none of these carried dogmatic force. So Acton announced the discontinuance of the
Home and Foreign Review, explaining that:

"one of the essential principles of this *Review* consists in
a clear recognition, first of the infinite gulf which in
theology separates what is of faith from what is not of
faith . . . and next, of the practical difference which
exists in ecclesiastical discipline between the acts of in-

fallible authority and those which possess no higher
sanction than that of canonical legality".[13]

In short ". . . the conductors of this *Review* are unable to
yield their assent to the opinions put forward in the
Brief."[14]

The way for the publication of the Syllabus was thus
paved by the rebuke to Montalembert, the Brief about
Munich, and the indirect condemnation of the *Home and
Foreign Review*. All these events belonged to the fateful
year 1864, at the end of which the Syllabus itself was issued.
The leaders of Liberal-Catholicism were thus more than
half prepared for what was coming. Even so it was a shock;
nor was the able editing done by Dupanloup so calculated
to soften it as Veuillot's commentary, in his *Illusion
Libérale*, was calculated to sharpen it. The Syllabus might
add nothing new to Roman teaching, but it maintained the
reserves of Gregory XVI about liberalism and quite clearly
discountenanced what Malines, Munich, and the *Home and
Foreign* had been attempting, namely the erection of new
liberal ideas, in politics and thought, into principles of universal validity. The Syllabus embittered Montalembert, and
so frightened his friends of the *Correspondant* that they
eschewed their previous line of Liberal-Catholic propaganda;[15] it diverted Acton from reconciling the ways of
God to man into pursuing, instead, the paths of secular
history; and it drove Döllinger far along that road which
was eventually to lead to his apostasy.

These were serious results, and their cost to the Church
would be hard to count. Was it necessary to checkmate in
this way these Liberal-Catholic initiatives?

Pio Nono thought that it was, and we have already seen
why he thought so; it was because of his experience of Mazzini at Rome and of Cavour at Turin. In his experience, the
claim for liberties, not necessarily in themselves harmful,
led in fact to Mazzini's Religion of Humanity and to the
persecutions of Turin. "Liberty, Progress, and Recent
Civilisation", in their Italian guise—the guise in which the
Pope had met them—meant something which the Church
could not tolerate. And on this he was in agreement with

the leading Liberal-Catholics themselves. Montalembert's views on Turin have already been quoted; Acton was scarcely less severe. He welcomed a draft drawn up for the use of the Bishops assembled at Rome in 1862, in which they were to denounce:

> "the perfidious and oppressive policy of the Court of Turin in terms which we certainly should not think either exaggerated or undeserved. We have neither right nor inclination to complain . . . of the indignation which the system prevailing at Turin must excite in every man who in his heart loves the Church, or whose intelligence can appreciate the first principles of government. Whatever may have been the censure proposed, it certainly did not surpass the measure of the offence."[16]

And Döllinger, while critical of the régime in the Papal State, considered no effort too great to be expended in trying to save it from Turin.

When Pio Nono found the formula which Cavour had made so odious to him being repeated, as indeed it had first been publicised, by Montalembert; when he saw around him in Italy the assault upon the Church levelled by men who never ceased to speak of Progress and Liberty; when the spread of indifference, pantheism, or agnosticism, in all western Europe, was so much more conspicuous than the Catholic revival, and seemed so closely related to free thought and to free expressions of opinion; and when the vast majority of the episcopate and of the Curia, as well as of lay opinion, was advising him that a state of siege existed for the Church, which necessitated a stricter obedience to authority and an uncompromising assertion of her rights, can we wonder that he followed the line of policy marked out for him by the Jesuits of the *Civiltà Cattolica?* And, leaving aside Veuillot (whose following was yet so much more numerous than Montalembert's), can we be sure that men of the quality of Wiseman and Manning in England, of Pie in France, or Ketteler in Germany, were not right in supporting Pio Nono in the line he adopted? It can seldom be the role of the Papacy to lead the way into new and untried fields; the Pope is shepherd of the whole flock; if he had supported the liberals of Malines and Munich he would have discountenanced, at a time of acute crisis, the vast majority, in every land, of the most ardent of the Church's sons.

It has often been found necessary to curtail liberty in time of crisis, and the Pope had reason to consider this was a time of crisis for the Church. But it is equally important, in such circumstances, not to add fuel to the fire of hostility, and this he unfortunately did by the form in which he allowed the Syllabus to be issued. It is not sufficient to say that the document was technical, and intended only for the Bishops (although this explains much) because the rumour of its issue had reached too far, in advance. And for the same reason it is not sufficient to say that he was thinking mainly of Italy, or that he may have personally concerned himself little with the form it took. It shocked the world, unnecessarily, and Pio Nono, who was always reluctant to shock those whose intentions he recognised as good, was himself distressed by this outcome though he retracted nothing. According to de Falloux he admitted that the Syllabus was "raw meat, needing to be cooked and seasoned".[17] But was it wise to provide raw meat for an enemy, especially an enemy with such an appetite? Why did he leave it to be cooked and seasoned at Orleans, when there were chefs at Rome as skilful?

Darboy, the Archbishop of Paris, appealed to him: "You have distinguished and condemned the principal errors of our epoch. Turn your eyes now towards what she may hold that is honourable and good and sustain her in her generous efforts . . ."[18] But as blow succeeded blow, as Rome was occupied, as the government of Victor Emmanuel continued its anti-clerical campaign, and as Bismarck launched the *Kulturkampf*, the aged Pope—small wonder!—could only see that a storm was raging over Europe, and that the threatened flock must huddle closer under the shelter of the saving truth. So it was left to his successor to provide, in the great Encyclicals *Immortale Dei* (1885) and *Libertas praestantissimum bonum* (1888) the positive teaching that was complementary to the negative Syllabus, while perfectly in harmony with it; to assert, alongside the pest of unrestricted liberty, the benefits of freedom when governed by acknowledgement of the primacy of truth. With Leo XIII the "Principles of 1789" at last received baptism at Rome—an adult baptism, received after due confession!

3. *From the Syllabus to the Vatican Council* (1864–1869)

The Syllabus was widely regarded as a gesture of defiance hurled by an outraged Pope against the nineteenth century. The summoning of the Vatican Council was suspected of being intended to reinforce the Syllabus, and when it defined the dogma of Papal Infallibility it was taken as having done so. Such was the broad interpretation placed upon these events, notably by Gladstone and by Bismarck.

What was the reality?

The Syllabus, though issued to the whole Episcopate and intended for the Church's general guidance, had been prompted, as we have seen, by events in Italy. Does this, then, mean that we are to escape from saying that the Pope was condemning his age as a whole by saying that he was only condemning the risorgimento? Clearly not; the importance of the risorgimento, religiously speaking, was that it was the mirror through which the Pope saw and judged the nostrums of his age;—if there was talk of "a free Church in a free State" his mind naturally leapt to Cavour or to Ricasoli rather than to Montalembert. But on the whole the risorgimento was a faithful mirror of the age because it reflected most of the varied thought and activity and the overweening self-confidence of the European nineteenth century.

What Pio Nono saw reflected in the risorgimento, and what he condemned in the Syllabus, was none other than a mighty wave that threatened, perhaps more dangerously than any previous wave, to submerge the barque of Peter altogether; he saw reflected no less than the rationalism, pantheism, and naturalism of the eighteenth century, the "principles of '89", the new notions of popular sovereignty and human self-sufficiency which sprang from Rousseau and Voltaire. But he would not have seen the danger so clearly if he had not had to suffer from it, personally, at Rome. He would not have reacted so vigorously but for Rossi, Gaeta, and Castelfidardo. There was this great difference between his position and that of his predecessors who had had to meet the earlier storms—he experienced and suffered the impact in his person. When Urban II preached the first crusade he did so because he had been told of the fall of Jerusalem; he had not, himself, met the Mohammedans. When Innocent III met the menace of the Albigensians and sponsored the new Orders, Dominican and Franciscan, and the courts of the Inquisition, for the reconversion of the territories affected, he was acting to meet a peril of which he had heard tell—the actual conflict took place beyond the Alps. When the Popes of the sixteenth century, at Trent, and through the Society of Jesus, met the onrush of Protestantism, they had scarcely experienced Protestantism in Italy. But Pius IX, and his predecessors Pius VII and Pius VI, had suffered the impact of the French revolution, and its offspring, the new nationalism, in their persons and on their doorstep. Exiled, imprisoned, losing their states and Rome itself, the sacrilege they suffered was the backwash of the turbulent tide which, at its height, in France, had totally submerged the Church, in revolutionary Paris, for a decade.

Seen in its wider aspect, then, the Syllabus was a reply—an interim reply—to the eighteenth-century "enlightenment" incarnate in the French revolution and the risorgimento; what people like Prince Napoleon boasted of as "Modern Civilisation". But what greatly excited and perturbed friend as well as foe, between 1864 and 1870, was how much of the Syllabus was to be given precise, positive and dogmatic significance. The difficulty was that it embodied such a wide range of condemnations, denouncing, in surprising juxtaposition, obvious heresies such as atheism and more ambiguous notions such as the assertion that the Church could manage very well without the Temporal

Power. Once it was known, in 1867, that a General Council of the Church was, indeed, to meet at the end of 1869, it became a source of dread for some—though an aspiration for others—that all the condemnations of the Syllabus, including the more ambiguous ones of a political nature, would be given positive dogmatic precision. There seemed, for example, a likelihood that the Church was not to rest content with teaching, negatively, as in the Syllabus, that it was an error to say that a free press should be introduced universally, but was about to teach, positively, that to allow a free press was always wrong.

There were those who hoped that a wholesale dogmatising of the Syllabus was precisely what the Vatican Council would do, that it would even make belief in the necessity of the Temporal Power dogmatic. It did, however, nothing of the kind. In the Constitution *Dei Filius* it gave dogmatic precision to matters of traditionally accepted faith, concerning the nature of God, and of Revelation, which had been denied, for example, by the Deists and the Pantheists; in this strictly theological field it did "dogmatise" some of the denunciations of the Syllabus. And it defined the dogma of Papal Infallibility, which was another traditionally accepted belief of the Church. But the relations of Church and State, though down for discussion, were never in fact discussed; nor were the problems surrounding political liberty, religious liberty, and freedom of expression; nor were the "principles of '89", nor was the Temporal Power. Those parts of the Syllabus which Gladstone and Bismarck, as first ministers of crowns, regarded with anger, were left as the Syllabus had left them; that is, the universalist claims of European liberalism remained reprobated, but the policies and principles of London and Berlin continued (until Bismarck launched the *Kulturkampf*) to give no offence at Rome, but rather to commend themselves there. As for infallibility, it had no relation to the Syllabus, for the Syllabus was not an infallible pronouncement. It remained rash for Catholics to deny the condemnations of the Syllabus, as it was for them to deny any other Papal pronouncements on miscellaneous matters. But the Syllabus had not fulfilled the conditions of an ex-cathedra pronouncement, on a mat-

ter of faith and morals, it had not condemned the stigmatised propositions as heretical, it had not been couched in
such a form as could make it a part of the infallibly pronounced *depositum fidei.*

If the political world perturbed itself about the forthcoming Council because it feared to see the Syllabus reinforced in its teaching on Church and State the Church itself was more exercised on the matter of Papal Infallibility.
Some, like Veuillot or Manning, wanted a Council because
they wanted to see the Papacy strengthened in its authority
by the definition of this dogma. Others, like Dupanloup,
wanted a Council for the opposite reason—they hoped to see
Infallibility defined in such a restricted way as would end
the extravagances of Veuillot. The Sacred College, including Antonelli, disliked the idea of a Council because it
would bring German or French theologians to Rome, who
might dispute the authority of the Roman Congregations;
but also because it might make trouble with Napoleon, who
was still protecting the Patrimony of St. Peter.

The large majority of the Bishops, consulted from 1865
onwards, favoured the summoning of the Council because,
like the Pope, they were profoundly aware of the onslaught
upon the Christian faith which had resulted from eighteenth-century "enlightenment" and from the revolutions.
To them, as to him, it seemed that, just as the onslaught
of Protestantism had been met by the definitions of the
faith drawn up at the Council of Trent, so the new attacks must be met by a new Council, and the truth, where
it was challenged, must be authoritatively defined. Very
much in their minds, for example, were the popular success
of Strauss' *Leben Jesu* in Germany and Renan's *Vie de
Jésus* in France, books which represented the peculiarly
dangerous tendency, characteristic of the times, to discredit
the unique, supernatural and miraculous element in Christianity, while professing respect for the principles and human values emerging from the gospel story. It is easy to
lose sight of this essential purpose, in which Pio Nono was
at one with the Bishops of the world in invoking the aid
of a Council. The argument over the nature and working

of the Infallibility was so acrimonious, and so public, that although it was settled by the Council in a way which no Bishops, and only a very few others, whose hearts were already estranged, found finally unacceptable, yet it raised a dust which has much obscured the Council's real objective.

The Council was to be the climax of the Pontificate of Pio Nono, a climax for which, to some extent consciously, the way was carefully prepared.

First, in 1862, he had invited the whole episcopate to attend, at Pentecost, the canonisation of the twenty-six missionaries martyred in 1597 in Japan. Despite the prohibitions imposed by Napoleon and by Victor Emmanuel, which prevented some of the French and all the Italian Bishops from attending, there were yet united at Rome 323 Cardinals, Patriarchs, Archbishops or Bishops; more than 4,000 priests; and some 100,000 of the faithful.[19] Not far away, Garibaldi was sailing from Caprera, with his message "Rome or Death". In the Sistine Chapel a priest entoned: *Oremus pro Pontifice nostro Pio*, and three times the Bishops replied: *Dominns conservet eum et vivificet eum, et beatum faciat eum in terra et non tradat eum in animam inimicorum ejus.*

In 1866, on December 8th (date of the Feast of the Immaculate Conception, chosen by Pio Nono for the major acts of his reign, and notably for the opening of the Vatican Council), the Bishops were again invited to Rome. This time they were invited for the eighteenth centenary of the martyrdom of Saints Peter and Paul—to be celebrated on the feast of those saints, June 29th, 1867. Once more there was danger abroad; when the invitation was issued the last of the French troops were about to leave Rome (Christmas, 1866), and when the Bishops assembled Garibaldi, peculiarly incensed by the solemn reunion, planned another invasion, which he launched without success in October, and which ended in his defeat at Mentana. More than 500 Bishops attended this time, with 20,000 priests and 130,000 other pilgrims. The solemnities and ceremonies of this reunion exceeded even those of five years earlier, and the vitality and tirelessness of the Pope contrasted with the frequent rumours, in the interval, of his illness and approaching death. It was at this reunion that some supposed the dogma of Papal Infallibility might be pronounced, as that of the Immaculate Conception had been at a comparable gathering in 1854. Actually, however, Pio Nono took the opportunity, on this occasion, of announcing to the Bishops his intention of convoking a General Council.

In April, 1869, the Pope celebrated his sacerdotal jubilee —the fiftieth anniversary of his ordination on April 11th, 1819, and of his first Mass, at *Sant' Anna dei Falegnami*, in Rome. It was a more intimate occasion than the huge episcopal gatherings of 1862 and 1867; it was characterised by prayers for peace, and for the Church, all over the world, and by letters and presents ranging from the 25,000 golden Napoleons sent by the Empress Eugénie from Paris, or the enormous porcelain vase deemed suitable by the King of Prussia, to the touching gifts of the orphan children of the *Tata Giovanni* Institute at Rome, which Mastai Ferretti had once directed.

These occasions saw Pio Nono witty, courteous and serene. His stream of visitors found in him none of the bitter complaint with which he often thought it his duty, in his letters and encyclicals, to upbraid the Church's opponents. He would gently tease those outside her Communion, telling two Puseyites, for instance, that their master was like the Church clock which rang for Mass but didn't itself go in, and blessing some Anglican clergy with words taken from the blessing of the incense, in the Mass: *Ab illo benedicaris in cujus honore cremaberis.*[20] He had a brisk, humorous manner with the ceaseless stream of deputations; characteristic was the greeting he gave to a delegation of 1,500 French pilgrims: "*Vous êtes venu ici pour deux choses: voir le Pape et recevoir sa bénédiction. Le Pape, le voici; quant à la bénédiction, vous la recevrez après que je vous aurai addressé quelques mots . . .*"[21]

As the material prospect grew worse and worse Pio Nono became more and more cheerful. No doubt a Pope, trusting as he trusted in the words of Christ to Peter: "I have prayed for thee, that thy faith fail not", is unlikely, even when afflicted as Pio Nono was afflicted, to feel that he and the Church are deserted. He was very fond of quoting these words; but the channel through which his faith seems most particularly to have come was his trust in the protection of the Blessed Virgin; and it was made manifest to others in his serenity, but even more in the gaiety of his manner, especially in the worst crises.

The most recent and authoritative historian of the Church in this pontificate states that:

> "the decisive element in the rapid and conclusive triumph of ultramontanism was the personality itself of Pius IX and the immense prestige, surpassing by far that of any of his predecessors over centuries, which the Pontiff enjoyed with the great mass of Catholics and of the clergy during more than a quarter of a century".[22]

But how was this prestige acquired? Occasions at Rome, like those just described, no doubt had their influence, but necessarily a limited influence. His sufferings pleaded for him—but he was not the first Pope who had suffered. He was charming, intelligent, and good; but nobody has pretended that he was a statesman, nor has the Church yet beatified him, as she has already beatified one of his successors.

The answer is to be found in the sensitive quality of his sympathy. He was more sympathetic than many Popes have been towards the temporal and spiritual aspirations of those under his care. In temporal matters this quality led him on too fast and too far, in the promiscuous period of his reforms before the murder of Rossi. In spiritual matters it led him to perceive, and so enabled him to lead the Catholic revival which was looking to Rome for leadership. He was far more sensitive to the Ultramontane movement than his three predecessors had been, and the Ultramontanes were now determined upon a new assertion of the *privilegium Petri* as the antidote to the errors and oppressions of the era. He could see what the Church wanted from him, and he was neither too recluse nor too cautious to give it.

It is easy, though inaccurate, to confuse this attitude with

one of personal vanity. No serious critic—not even Döllinger
—accused him of vanity; they could see that he was working
for the greater glory of the Church through the exaltation
of the Papacy, that he was genuinely convinced that he
must respond to the call which was being made upon him
to gather the reins more firmly into his own hands. It was
to this end that he was ready to summon Bishops more
frequently to Rome *ad limina*, to distribute Roman titles
—and particularly that of Monsignor—more widely, to encourage the general adoption in the Church of Roman rites,
liturgy, and clerical costume, to intervene in disputes between priests and their own Bishops, to respond, after only
informal consultations, to the demand that he should proclaim the dogma of the Immaculate Conception. But when
the Church demanded of him that the traditional belief
in Papal Infallibility, in matters of faith and morals, be
dogmatically defined, then, though he might have adopted
the same procedure as he had chosen in the previous definition, he declined to do so; he saw that the matter involved
him, personally, too closely. He left it to the General
Council, which he had summoned for quite other purposes,
to introduce the proposal if it chose to; and not until a late
stage did he interest himself in the progress of the discussions, being fully persuaded by then that the Church demanded it of him.

An important source of Pio Nono's influence consisted
simply in the length of his reign, which was the longest in
Papal history, exceeding by more than six years the traditional twenty-five assigned to Saint Peter, which had never
previously been exceeded and, it had been widely supposed, never would be exceeded. In the course of this reign
he was able to renew almost the whole episcopate. He was
also able to create a large number of new Cardinals, preferring to confer the hat upon non-Italians, and thus to
emphasise the universal character of the Church. But if in
these ways he was himself tending indirectly to strengthen
Ultramontanism it has to be remembered that it was from
the parish priests, and from the laity, who seldom saw
Rome, or her influence, that the force of the movement
issued. Amongst these people it was the Catholic journalists

and pamphleteers who rekindled devotion to the Church, in her discipline and her practices, and the desire to see her assume a position in modern society such as she had held in earlier days. Easily the most widely influential was Veuillot; but the position acquired by his friend Donoso Cortès in Spain, or by W. G. Ward, with the *Dublin Review*, amongst English Catholics, bore some analogy. The large majority of these literary men were not merely Ultramontanes in the sense that they wished to see the Pope and the Church freed from secular control, they were also Ultramontanes in the newer (Neo-ultramontane) sense that they believed in the centralisation of authority within the Church in the hands of Rome, and often—certainly in the case of Veuillot—in an authoritarian state which, while submissive to the Church, would restrict the free exercise of the "principles of '89". In both these latter standpoints they were, of course, at issue with most of the Liberal-Catholics.

It was by responding to the aspirations of the Neo-ultramontanes that Pio Nono exercised his most powerful influence, and gave to the Papacy its enhanced status in the Church. He might, after all, have supported the Liberal-Catholics instead. Had he done so there can be no doubt at all that the relations between the Papacy and the Church, and between the Church and society, would, at least for a time, have developed differently. Some have seen the Pope's policy as tragic, others have seen it as providential. What is certain is that it was crucial, and that it might have been different.[23] And if it is difficult even to imagine the Pio Nono of the 'sixties decentralising the Church or encouraging a free field in society for the pursuit and expression of any and every opinion it is salutary to recall the first two years of his pontificate. It was not in itself impossible that Pio Nono should hearken in the 'sixties to Montalembert, as he had hearkened in the 'forties to Fr. Ventura. It was only impossible that he should do so after he had experienced Mazzini and Cavour.

Pio Nono admired and liked Veuillot, just as he admired and liked Manning, and both men urged him forward in his centralising policy. His relations with Manning are too well known to require repetition;[24] Veuillot was constantly

in Rome, and was almost always supported by the Pope—
to the distress of Dupanloup and Montalembert. But if the
Pope made it very clear that he favoured the Neo-ultramontanes, he never forgot his duty of promoting peace between the Church's different champions. Within the new
English hierarchy division between the authoritarians and
the anti-authoritarians was sharp, and a real concern to
Pius, as also to Wiseman. When the English Bishops were
in Rome for the canonisation of the Japanese Martyrs in
'62 the Pope summoned them on one notable occasion to
the Vatican, and told them they must take the highest and
largest mountain in the Alps and put it over all past questions and dissensions without any tunnel through to get at
them. He so abashed his visitors that they left without having once spoken—even to ask for a blessing on their return
journey to England, or a message for their flocks! Later they
were found sitting dazed and dejected in St. Peters.[25] He
could be equally firm with Veuillot, urging upon him the
duty of taking more thought before chastising his opponents. But except in the quarrel over the teaching of the
secular classics to future priests, in the French seminaries,
in which he decided against Veuillot and the Abbé Gaume
(who had been crusading to stop such teaching), the Pope
was not inclined to censure Veuillot's opinions. Nor was he
at all inclined to favour the attitude of Dupanloup, who
felt it intolerable that lay journalists should interpret the
pronouncements of Rome without awaiting the views of
their own episcopal superiors; but then he liked Veuillot's
interpretations of his pronouncements better than he liked
the Bishop of Orleans' interpretations!

The decisive date in the quarrel over Veuillot had been
as far back as the year 1853. The Archbishop of Paris and
Dupanloup had both just condemned Veuillot's *Univers*,
and Veuillot had appealed to the Pope. The upshot was
the Encyclical *Inter Multiplices* in which he exhorted the
Bishops to be:

"generous in their encouragements, and to show their
goodwill and their love towards those men who . . . de-
vote the watches of the night to writing books and papers

so that Catholic doctrine may be propagated and defended, so that the ancient rights of this Holy See and its acts may enjoy their full force, so that opinions and sentiments contrary to this Holy See may disappear, so that the darkness of error may be dissipated and the minds of men flooded with the blessed light of the truth".

So the Bishops had to withdraw their condemnations with the best grace possible. They had also to accept the strong approval given, in the same Encyclical, to the movement for the adoption of the Roman liturgy throughout France. That purpose, too, had divided Catholic opinion; the victory which the Pope's Encyclical represented for the Benedictine Abbot of Solesmes, Dom. Guéranger, who had made the cause of uniformity in the strict Roman liturgical tradition his own, was also a victory for the Ultramontanes and for Rome.

By the time of the Vatican Council a more important paper than the *Univers* had gained a paramount position as the focus of Neo-ultramontane opinion, and the semi-official voice of the Vatican: the Jesuit *Civiltà Cattolica* at Rome.

Pio Nono had not always been noted for any close association with the Jesuits. He had valued their work for souls, and had deplored the attacks upon them at Rome, in 1848. All the same, in the first years of his pontificate he had his reserves about them,[26] and it was not until some little time after his return from Gaeta that their influence became preponderant. But with the development of the Neo-ultramontane movement, and of his own policy of centralisation, it was really inevitable that he should turn to the Society whose very *raison d'être* was the defence of the authority of the Holy See. With the Church once again in a state of siege, from whom, indeed, should he have sought assistance if not from that same body which had so successfully defended her, in the hour of her peril, against the onslaughts of the Lutherans and Calvinists?

Its influence, strong in the Roman Congregations, was exerted chiefly through the *Civiltà Cattolica*. Pio Nono was personally responsible for the launching of this journal. The idea had originated with Fr. Carlo Curci, of the Society, who felt, in 1849, the need for an exposition, at the highest intellectual level, of the point of view of the Papacy in matters religious and political. His own general, Roothan, thought the enterprise too hazardous; so did the "Red Triumvirate" of Cardinals then ruling at Rome on behalf of the Pope. It was the Pope himself who insisted that Curci was right that the flood of anti-Papal propaganda could only be met by a reasoned statement of the Papal case; and, while still in exile, he put up the necessary money to enable the fortnightly to be launched.[27] It was not an official organ of the Papal government, indeed the Pope often expressed the keenest displeasure with what it said. Curci was independent-minded; so were his collaborators, the ablest of whom was Massimo d'Azeglio's brother Luigi who, Massimo admitted, had more brains than himself. They refused to come down in favour of absolute governments, or against democracies, maintaining the correct Catholic line that the Church was not concerned with forms of government. For this the journal was banned, for a time, in the Kingdom of Naples. But in October, 1863, Curci enunciated in the Civiltà the famous notion of the thèse and the antithèse which Dupanloup adopted in the following year in explaining that the Syllabus was only denouncing the thèse, and that the antithèse (e.g. "toleration is often desirable in actual circumstances") was equally valid. Pio Nono was affronted, and relieved Curci of his position. From this time the Civiltà became more evidently "inspired", which was why an article that appeared in the number of February 6th, 1869, Matters Relating to the Future Council: Correspondence from France, attracted so much attention. Up to that date the Liberal-Catholics had regarded the forthcoming Council with some optimism, in as much as the resolutions of a Council of Bishops were likely to be more conservative and less "Neo-ultramontane" than the preachings of the Univers, and might be expected to reduce what were regarded as the "extravagances" of Veuillot and his friends to more reasonable proportions. But this "inspired" article of the Civiltà[28] put quite a different complexion on the matter. The Liberals read, to their astonishment and consternation, that: "nobody is unaware that the Catholics of France are unfortunately divided into two parties: one, simply *Catholics*; the other those who call themselves *Liberal-Catholics*." The latter, the article points out, are patronised by the French government, with whom they share a fear that the Council will proclaim Papal Infallibility and will give to the Syllabus dogmatic effect. Whereas:

> "the Catholics properly so called, that is the great majority of the faithful, entertain, for their part, quite opposite hopes . . . they hope that the Council will be very short . . . they hope that it will proclaim the doctrines of the *Syllabus* by announcing, by means of affirmative formulae, together with any necessary developments, the propositions which are there stated negatively. They will receive with joy the proclamation of the dogmatic infallibility of the Sovereign Pontiff . . . It is hoped that the unanimous manifestation of the Holy Spirit through the mouth of the Fathers at this future Oecumenical Council will define it by acclamation".[29]

This article was, quite simply, a disaster. It is certainly true that the Liberal-Catholics had been writing and speaking as though the Council would put an end to the "extravagances" of Neo-ultramontanism; but no bishops had yet publicly expressed themselves against the desirability of defining Papal Infallibility, nor had the governments—though they were generally suspicious of the Council—as yet made any moves to interfere with its freedom. If the article had been concerned with the elucidation of necessary truths no doubt the risk of offending governments and even of disquieting some parts of the Church would have been rightly run, as many felt that it had been rightly run when the Syllabus was issued. But how was it right, in a semi-official paper, to imply that Liberal-Catholics were not true Catholics? And was the Council really to make the Syllabus affirmative and dogmatic? And could it be wise to prejudge the outcome of the Council by saying that "Catholics" hoped that Papal Infallibility would be "defined by acclamation" and that the Syllabus would be "dogmatised"? And finally, what sort of a definition was a "definition by acclamation" likely to be? The whole difficulty about the infallibility was exactly in what terms it should be defined. Its acclamation, without analysis, debate, and precise definition, seemed hardly likely to be helpful. The *Civiltà*, however, was supported by Veuillot, who argued that the Holy Spirit had no need of time, and debate, to formulate an opinion; but he, and others, were thereby giving a strange interpretation of the way in which the Church had always arrived at truth, a process which had always involved thought, argument, and the study of history; the divine guarantee against ultimate error had never dispensed her from the duty of using the human means available to avoid it.

The reactions to this *Civiltà* article, in the spring and summer of 1869, were sharp. There was concern amongst the governments at the prospect of seeing the Syllabus affirmed positively, and much talk of Gregory VII and Boniface VIII. But, in the previous year they had accepted the view that governments should not themselves participate in the deliberations of the Council (as they had done at Trent); and, despite the efforts of the Archbishop of Paris, Darboy, to persuade Napoleon to intervene, and Döllinger's more successful efforts, to the same end, with the Bavarian President, no governmental action was, in fact, taken to gain control by the Powers over the Council.

Even more unfortunate was the effect of the article within the Church. Döllinger, indeed, had already reached a position irreconcilable with the Catholic faith, and the *Civiltà* article merely led him, (as "Janus") to give extravagant expression, in articles in the *Allgemeine Zeitung* (collected and translated under the title *The Pope and the Council*) to his hatred of the Papacy, behind which lurked his Germanic contempt for all things Roman or Italian. But of deeper concern to Pio Nono was a meeting of German Bishops, in September, 1869, at Fulda. The majority considered the time inopportune for the proposed definition; and fourteen wrote a secret letter to the Pope, expressing their fears.[30] In France, Dupanloup was soon in the field, anonymously at first, in *Le Français*, where, in March, he declared the proposed definition inopportune. But he was soon at work more openly. He visited Germany in the summer of 1869 primarily, no doubt, to go into retreat at Einsielden; but he saw Döllinger, whom he certainly wanted to persuade to present himself at Rome during the Council; he went to Cologne, and Coblentz, and down as far as Vienna. He wrote a short note for presentation to the German Bishops assembled at the Fulda conference. Some day it may be possible to speak with certainty as to whether, as was believed by Veuillot's friends, the Bishop of Orleans was deeply involved in Germany in preparing the opposition to the Ultramontanes at the Vatican Council.[31] His journey there was blamed by the Pope; his letter to the Fulda conference was translated into English and Spanish and was given an enormous circulation. But, more significant, he used a strongly worded pamphlet, *Observations on the question: Is it opportune to define the infallibility of the Pope?*, published at Munich by Brentano, a disciple and friend of Döllinger, as the textual basis for a pamphlet of his own, *Observations sur la controverse soulevée relativement à la définition de l'infaillibilité au prochain concile*, which he finally published boldly, over his own signature, in November, 1869, and caused to be issued to the entire episcopate.

If the February article of the *Civiltà* had been a grave mistake on the Ultramontane side, the publication of Dupanloup's pamphlet, only a month before the Council was due to assemble, and when many of the Bishops were already at Rome, was an equally grave error on the Liberal side. It was the first time that a Bishop had openly pronounced himself against the known views of the Pope and of the majority of the Church, and in expressing his opinion in advance upon the most controversial topic likely to be discussed at the Council he was prejudicing both his own position and the Council's. His pamphlet did not confine itself to the usual argument that it was inopportune to define Papal Infallibility because of the susceptibilities of governments, or because of the danger of alienating still further the Protestants; it went further in that it suggested that the

dogma might be incapable of accurate definition: could it,
he asked, be said what precisely constituted an ex-cathedra
pronouncement? Could it be demonstrated when the Pope
spoke only as "doctor" and when as "Universal Father"?
Might not this digging under the roots of the tree, to find
the "original gland", kill the tree itself? To the Ultramontanes the pamphlet seemed to throw doubt upon fundamentals of the faith. Veuillot was not slow to attack it, and
the Bishop replied to the journalist in so bitter a pamphlet,
his *Avertissement à M. Veuillot*, that he only made matters
worse. It was a real misfortune, admitted by his friend de
Broglie, that Dupanloup, who could, and possibly should
have been the dominant figure at the Council, so spoilt his
position by publicly taking up his standpoint in advance.
Inevitably, and with no need of the constant promptings of
Veuillot, Pio Nono was affronted; the more so because
Dupanloup had had an interview with Napoleon, at St.
Cloud, on October 3rd, 1869. This interview resulted in
the Emperor having a letter sent to the French Ambassador
at Rome instructing him that, while there was no intention
of interfering with the liberty of the Council, the French
government's reaction to the issue of the Syllabus might be
taken as an indication of what would happen if the Council
issued any similar pronouncements. Napoleon, in fact,
prompted by Dupanloup, had sent a blunt warning to
Rome not to use the Council to make the Syllabus
dogmatic.

If it was difficult for Pio Nono to acquit Dupanloup from
suspicion of collusion with Napoleon it was much harder
for him to regard the Archbishop of Paris, Darboy, as other
than "the Emperor's man". The quarrel between the Pope
and Darboy dated from the Archbishop's investiture in
1863; he had resisted the centralising tendencies of Pio
Nono by delaying the introduction of the Roman liturgy,
and by endeavouring to assert his own authority over the
Jesuits in Paris. But his Gallicanism, and that of his friend
Mgr. Maret, had been made manifest in the crisis over the
Syllabus, when both had urged Napoleon's minister, Ba-
roche, to negotiate with Rome for modifications and expla-
nations, and had meanwhile recommended the French gov-

ernment to stop publication of the Syllabus by the Bishops. Darboy was now seeking Napoleon's intervention at the Council.

Not unnaturally, Pio Nono had, for a long time, steadily refused Napoleon's demands that Darboy should be created a Cardinal—a dignity normally to be expected for the Archbishop of Paris. Darboy, in his turn, had been extremely blunt in what he said to Pio Nono. He had told him that, contrary to Roman opinion, the Imperial Government was, in fact, favourable to the Holy See; "but those who know have not your confidence, and those who have it do not know".[32] This was an attack upon the Papal Nuncios at Paris, Sacconi, and then Chigi. But it is difficult to harmonise Darboy's picture of the Emperor with the Napoleon of the collusion with Cavour, or of the September Convention; and it is not surprising that Rome came to associate French Liberal-Catholicism with Gallicanism, so that the famous *Civiltà* article of February, 1869, concerned itself quite as much with denouncing the French Organic Articles, of 1802 (still in force), or the Gallican Charter of 1682 (still appealed to), as with casting aspersions upon the Liberal-Catholics. Liberalism and Gallicanism were both seen at Rome as French divergences from Ultramontane orthodoxy.

But the most dangerous opponent, at Paris, of the Papal view was not Darboy but Maret, who, at the crucial moment, two months before the opening of the Council, published his compendious *Du concile général et de la paix religieuse* in which he argued that Infallibility only rested in the Papacy acting in co-operation with the episcopate, and that the Papacy was not an absolute but a constitutional monarchy. He thus formally resurrected the Gallican decrees of 1682, with their acceptance of the teaching of the later (invalid) sessions of the Council of Constance on the superiority of General Councils to the Pope. By openly claiming that Gallican theology was a valid part of the tradition of truth he put back the clock to the days of Louis XIV and resurrected all those claims of the State to control the Church which had made for the weakness of Catholicism in the eighteenth century and which de Maistre,

Lamennais, Montalembert and their friends had successfully fought in the earlier days of the Ultramontane revival.

Napoleon paid for the publication of Maret's book;[33] it
was widely distributed in the diocese of Orleans.[34] Thus
did the "Neo-Liberal-Catholics" show themselves to be
Gallicans, Döllinger invoking the State against the Church
in Bavaria; Darboy, Maret, and even Dupanloup doing the
same in France.

What a spectacle was thus opened up before the eyes of
the dying Montalembert! For the best years of his fighting
life he had identified the cause of Ultramontanism with
the cause of freedom. A free Church in a free State. But,
since the rise of the star of Veuillot, and the *Civiltà*, it had
seemed to him that the menace to the freedom of the
Church came less from the State, without, than from the
Papal absolutists within. Passionately liberal, both politically and religiously, extolling freedom into an Absolute, he
could not, like Darboy, invoke Napoleon to redress the
balance within the Church, nor, like his level-headed friend
de Falloux, could he see that there was nothing to worry
about because the Council would be unable to define Infallibility without thereby automatically limiting it to its
proper proportions. He was urging Döllinger to go to Rome,
he was pushing his friends to maintain the campaign of the
Correspondant, he was extolling the courage of Dupanloup.
Then, furious at his own impotence, after the Council had
already been sitting for more than two months, he wrote
his most unguarded letter, and published it, on March 7th,
1870, in the *Gazzette de France*:

". . . But who could have led us to suspect, in 1847, that
the *liberal* pontificate of Pius IX, acclaimed by all the
liberals of the two worlds, would become the pontificate
represented and personified by the *Univers* and the
Civiltà?"

Who could have foreseen:

". . . the permanent triumph of those lay theologians of
absolutism who have begun by making a sacrifice of all
our liberties, of all our principles, of all our earlier ideas,

before Napoleon III, in order, in due course, to offer up justice and truth, reason and history, as a holocaust to the idol which they are erecting at the Vatican?"[35]

Within a week of writing this letter Montalembert was dead. In the last week of his life, the greatest champion of the Church in the long pontificate of Pio Nono had bitterly offended the Pope, who characterised his attitude as full of rashness, folly, unreasonableness, imprudence, hatred, and violence. And such, as his own friends have admitted, it was; but then he was a deeply suffering and a dying man.

Pio Nono has been criticised for stopping de Mérode's plans for a solemn Requiem Mass at the Aracoeli, in Rome, in honour of his illustrious brother-in-law. But such an occasion must have been made into a Liberal-Catholic demonstration, in the midst of the Council. He preferred to do honour to his great servant by attending, quietly, a Mass for him at *Santa Maria in Traspontina*. He praised his devotion; but he alluded to his pride.

The Pope, so often, it had been thought, at the door of death, seemed destined to outlive them all. The next year it would be Darboy who would die, shot in cold blood by the communists at Paris. Bitterly Pio Nono was to grieve for his old enemy; warmly he would admire and envy his martyrdom. Pio Nono had the religious faculty for separating his disagreements about principle from his feelings about people so that seldom was the one allowed to interfere with the other.

Contrary to popular, and especially to Protestant estimation, there was, actually, an atmosphere of peace and calm about the Pope's relations with the Bishops during, and still more after the Council, which contrasts pleasantly with the vehement tones of the controversy during the months before it assembled. But then, as Pio Nono put it, "A Council always passes through three phases. First there is that of the devil; then comes that of men, finally that of God."[36]

Chapter Eight

TRIUMPH, DEFEAT, AND DEATH
(1870–1878)

1. The Vatican Council

It is easy to mistake the significance of the conflicts discussed in the last chapter, all those animated arguments which preceded the Vatican Council. They gave at the time, and they have given since, a false impression amongst those hostile to the Church that a fearful plot was on foot, on the part of a clique of Jesuits and Cardinals at Rome, to slip through a dogma about Papal Infallibility which would impose a stifling despotism. Failing to realise that the process which has normally preceded the definition of Catholic truths has been animated argument both within Councils and without them; that, from the very outset of the Apostolic ministry, argument, division, and even quarrel—never more evident than at Nicea—has only marked the outward appearance of the spiritual ferment working within, observers have assumed that so much dust could only have been kicked up if somebody was illegitimately trying to get away with something, and that in this case it was Pio Nono trying to get away with the dogma of Papal Infallibility.

That, from first to last, the Council was "rigged", that free discussion was prevented, that the opposition was brow-beaten, that the abler Bishops (and especially those representing the more populous areas of northern Europe) were almost all hostile, that the outcome "divided the Church", consummated the intellectual and moral suicide of Rome, and finally cut off Catholicism from all that was best in modern civilisation became the commonplaces even of historical scholarship. To-day, a fair consideration of what did, in fact, take place at Rome in 1870, of what were the actual decisions of the Council, of what was the unanimous reaction to those decisions of even the Bishops most hostile to the Ultramontanes, compel, when considered in conjunction with the expansion and life of the Church since that date, a very different interpretation. But the source of the earlier mistake should not be attributed only to a want of understanding, by the historians concerned, of the nature and working of Catholic institutions because it is also attributable to the character of the evidence they were handling. Most of this came from the opposition. The Liberal-Catholic polemicists, both before and during the Council, were much more prolific, and much more intelligible outside Catholic circles, than were the wiser amongst their more orthodox opponents. Moreover, after the Council, when the Church was in harmony again, she allowed—with a singular want of worldly wisdom—her avowed opponents to be the only informants of the world at large as to what had occurred. As Dom. Cuthbert Butler pointed out in 1931, in his *Vatican Council* (still the only balanced account of the Council that has appeared in English), the writings of those hostile to the Council, of "Quirinus", of Pomponio Leto (pseud. for the Marquis Vitelleschi) and of the German historian, Friedrich, remained unanswered from the other side for thirty years—until, that is, the Vatican made the full papers available to Theodore Granderath, thus enabling him to write his lengthy history of the Council. In England opinion was formed entirely upon Döllinger (whose writings were quickly translated), upon Acton's essay in the *North British Review*, upon Leto (translated), upon the hostile gossip picked up by Gregorovius (translated) and that picked up by the *Times* correspondent Mozley who knew neither French nor Italian, and had therefore to depend upon hearsay, but who knew that his readers expected to be given ridicule of what was going on.[1]

Surprisingly, the Council assembled at Rome in an atmosphere of tranquillity and security; tranquillity because it had become clear from the work of the preparatory commissions that there was going to be no attempt to rush matters—there would be full debate; and security because the Powers, despite the Liberal pressure, had decided against intervention and because the remnant of the Papal State had become free since the victory of Mentana over Garibaldi, in 1867, from the daily expectation of a revolutionary or a Piedmontese incursion.

This last was, indeed, a providential matter for the

Church. There were many who told Pio Nono that it was
foolhardy to summon this huge gathering of more than 700
Bishops to Rome, and to embark upon so colossal an undertaking as the holding of a General Council there, when the
city itself was virtually in a state of siege. But the September Convention, by which Napoleon had undertaken, in
1864, to withdraw his troops from Rome within two years,
had not proved, in practice, to be the sell-out for the Papal
State that had been generally expected. For as soon as the
last of the French had been withdrawn (December, '66)
another incursion from Garibaldi (this time bent upon asserting the Revolution, as against both the Pope and Piedmont) had brought them tumbling back again to fight in
support of the Papal army outside Rome at Mentana
(November, 1867). The brunt of the fighting was borne by
the Papal army, and particularly by the Zouaves and by the
new Legion of Antibes which Napoleon had allowed to be
recruited on French soil, following the September Convention. De Mérode was no longer War Minister, General
Kanzler had replaced both him and Lamoricière and was
in entire charge of the Papal army. But the same families
of France and Spain, which had fought at Castelfidardo,
were represented once more—the Charettes, the Quatre-
barbes, and the many names with a Bourbon prefix—fighting alongside the Irish, the Belgians, the Swiss, and the
Austrians; indeed the sad memories of Castelfidardo were
now eclipsed for this strange little army, so soon to be dissolved. Contrary to expectation it had achieved, at last,
some positive success; for though the French chassepots
gave the coup-de-grâce to the Garibaldians at Mentana they
only appeared on the scene at the end of the battle. And if
it was only a three-year respite that Kanzler's army thus won
for their sovereign it yet materially helped to instil confidence, and to lessen the sense (though perhaps not the
reality) of dependence upon France; and this was a factor
in enabling a General Council to meet with a sense of freedom from external pressure.

For some time after Mentana the Italian government,
under the wise guidance of Menabrea and others of the
Right, maintained an ostentatiously correct attitude to-

wards Rome. In the face of French troops back in the city, and of the famous *Jamais!* pronounced by Napoleon's minister Rouher, there was, indeed, little else that the new Italian government (now at Florence) could do. It was compelled to follow the policy of not antagonising Napoleon; and Napoleon had now embarked upon the experiment of the "Liberal Empire", which meant that he was obliged to take closer account of public opinion. Since public opinion was now, as it always had been, emphatically sympathetic with Pio Nono, the Emperor had to be sympathetic too. So the Florentine government had to abandon the notion of underground collusion with Mazzini, Garibaldi, and the revolutionaries—the policy of Rattazzi and of a part of the Left—and Menabrea made it clear that he would put no difficulties in the way of the summoning of the Council. When Lanza and Sella followed him, in December, with a coalition government, just after the Council had opened, they adopted the same correct behaviour, even though the anti-clerical party was again becoming very vocal in the Chamber.

But though they found it wise to behave correctly the political leaders of the New Italy generally feared the Council because they expected it would give dogmatic validity to the articles of the Syllabus denouncing the opponents of the Temporal Power. And this fear was natural enough because the *Civiltà* and the *Univers* had both supported the idea that the assembled Fathers should make the Syllabus affirmative and dogmatic; and if that happened might it not become the duty of Catholics, not only in Italy but everywhere, to fight for the recovery of the Temporal Power?

Free, then, from political pressure, but not free from ill-will and suspicion, the Fathers gradually assembled from all over the world, during October and November, 1869. In some respects it was a unique occasion. Never before had the Bishops assembled at Rome from every continent, because at the time of the Council of Trent not every continent had been settled; the presence of no less than 120 English-speaking Bishops bore witness to the most important of world changes since the last General Council. There were reckoned to be about 700 at the opening ceremony. All Bishops, including those without Sees, all Generals of Orders, the greater Abbots, and all Superiors of Congregations had been invited. Only the Russian government refused to allow the Catholic Bishops under its jurisdiction to attend; as a gesture of friendship towards the persecuted Polish Church, thus deprived of a voice, Pio Nono allowed a simple Polish priest, Sosnowski, from Lublin, who had escaped through the "iron curtain", to sit with the Fathers.[2] The decision not to invite the Heads of Catholic States to participate directly—as they had at Trent—recognised the *de facto* separation of Church and State which had been effected during the century.

Invitations were sent to the Greek Orthodox Bishops, without result, and a general appeal was made to all Protestants to make this the occasion for reconsidering the multiplication of sects and the dilution of doctrines and to take the opportunity afforded of reunion with the See of Peter; but again nothing practical was accomplished. Nevertheless, there were not wanting many, outside the Church, in England, in France, and in Germany, who agreed with the verdict of the Protestant Guizot:

"Pius IX has given proof of admirable wisdom in convoking this great assembly, whence will issue perhaps the saving of the world; for our societies are gravely sick, and for great evils great remedies are needed."

On December 8th, 1869, the Feast of the Immaculate Conception, Pio Nono formally opened the Vatican Council. Early in the morning it was pouring with rain, which did not prevent a vast crowd from reaching the *piazza San Pietro* and some eighty thousand from squeezing themselves into the cathedral. By 8.30 a.m. the Fathers had assembled above the portico of St. Peter's, and thence, intoning the *Veni Creator*, they processed into the cathedral, past the specially berobed seated figure of St. Peter, past the Blessed Sacrament exposed beneath Bernini's *baldachino* above the High Altar, where the Pope intoned prayers; then round, to the right, into the South Transept, which had been specially prepared as the Council Chamber. The prayers, litanies, Mass of the Feast, Synodal Gospel from St. Luke (the sending forth of the Seventy-two), Sermon, Papal Allocution, and voting of the formal decrees inaugurating the Council took until 3.30 p.m. During the whole time the crowd remained in the cathedral, and though doors to the huge screen, specially constructed to separate off the transept, should have been closed once the Council was inaugurated, on Pio Nono's instructions they were left open, so that the crowd could still hear the intoning, and catch glimpses of the ceremonies, and with characteristic Italian informality they proceeded to join in the responses and litanies. When, finally, the Pope had retired, and the Fathers poured out, "You saw," said Ullathorne, Bishop of Birmingham, "continental prelates meeting their old school companions come from remote and strange countries and all sorts of joys, tendernesses, and congratulations."

Altogether, a very Roman occasion!

By universal consent, Pio Nono was at his best. He was very well at this time, and he insisted upon receiving many of the Bishops personally, as well as in audiences by nations. The poorer ones, especially the missionary Vicars Apostolic from distant territories, were lodged at his own expense, and this constituted a large part of that financial burden upon the Pope which gave rise to one of his better-known witty remarks. It depends upon the Italian: "*Non so se il Papa uscirà di questo Concilio fallibile od infallibile; ma questo è certo che sarà fallito.*"[3]

The situation during the first four months of the Council was that both the "Special Congregations" (Committees of Bishops elected to consider any suggested amendments to the *schemata* drawn up by the theologians) and the "General Congregation" (the whole Council, sitting in committee on the *schemata*) were busily at work considering two principal drafts (*schemata*), one concerning Faith, the other concerning "The Church". The one concerning Faith, after much debate, was unanimously agreed on April 24th, and duly confirmed by the Pope, in the formal Constitution *Dei Filius*. It is concerned with rejecting

rationalism, pantheism, and naturalism, and with affirming
the nature of God, of Revelation, of Faith, and of the relations of Faith and Reason. Whereas the Council of Trent
had been mainly concerned with defining propositions
denied by the Protestants, the Vatican Council, in this
Constitution, was concerned with reaffirming and with defining the very foundations of the Christian faith itself,
which had been assailed by the post-Protestant rationalists
and pantheists of the eighteenth and nineteenth centuries.
This Constitution was the larger part of the work of the
Council, and although there was a vast amount of argument, and still more of oratory, before it was settled, there
was no deep cleavage of opinion.

The really controversial issues were all contained in the
schema put forward on January 21st for the other Constitution, the one on the Church, *de Ecclesia*. In this it was
proposed to define, amongst other things, the nature of the
Church as a "perfect", "spiritual" and "supernatural" society, with a visible unity, the juridical authority of the Pope
within the Church, the nature of the Temporal Dominion,
the rights and duties of the Civil Power, and the relations
between Church and State. On all these topics there was
great variety of opinion amongst the assembled Fathers—
not, generally, as to the principle, but certainly as to what
they thought it practicable or prudent to say by way of
formal definition. Thus about half the Council sent in
memoranda of observations and amendments, even though
these had to be confined to the less controversial first ten
chapters of the *schema*, no comments yet being invited on
the chapters about the Papacy, or about the Temporal
Power, or about Church and State, all of which came in
later chapters. This last was the really thorny question, and
opinion amongst the Fathers ranged from that of Bishops
who would have liked to see the Syllabus of Errors made
affirmative and dogmatic, to that of liberals like Dupanloup
who clung to the distinction between thesis and antithesis,
and certainly did not want to see the thesis defined.

During these early months, the argument over the Infallibility was going on between the formal sessions, and the
Majority, which wanted a definition of the Infallibility, was

getting more and more impatient as it became clear that, if matters took their normal course, the great subject would not be brought on before the heat of the summer months made an adjournment necessary. Yet the Pope would not move; it was not, he said, his business; the affairs of the Council were in the hands of its five Presidents, and they were not disposed to alter the programme. This meant that even when the Council came to debate the circulated *schema de Ecclesia*, they would have, first, to consider the ten chapters on the nature of the Church, and its powers, before they reached the Papacy. It was in these circumstances that Manning and his friends were finally induced to approach the Pope to secure that the Infallibility Question be brought on out of its turn.

Certainly, they were encouraged by an obvious, though quite unofficial change in the Pope's attitude and behaviour. "The Pope," wrote Ullathorne on April 1st, "takes every opportunity of expressing his views on the infallibility, both in audiences and in letters that at once get into the papers. He has quite changed his old policy on our arrival, when he professed neutrality before the Council."[4] Irritation with the attitude of some of the Minority opposition leaders, outside the Council as well as within, was growing in Pio Nono. He read, at the end of February, that unguarded letter of Montalembert's, quoted at the end of the last chapter, in which the orator had spoken of Veuillot's friends "setting up their idol in the Vatican", and under its influence he had sent, on March 12th, a letter to the Benedictine Abbot of Solesmes, Guéranger, to congratulate him on a pamphlet he had written in support of the Infallibility. In this letter the Pope used exceptionally unguarded language concerning the Liberal Minority:

". . . they do not believe, as do the other Catholics, that the Council is governed by the Holy Spirit; full of daring, folly, irrationality, imprudence, hatred, violence, they employ, in order to excite those of their faction, the means by the aid of which it is customary to catch votes in popular assemblies: they undertake to remake the

divine Constitution of the Church and to adapt it to the
modern forms of civil governments."

The cause of the Pope's peculiar bitterness on this occasion must be sought, first, no doubt, in Montalembert's outburst, but also in the efforts which he had good reason to
believe were being made, in letters from Rome, by Maret
to Paris, by Acton to London, by Friedrich and others to
the German Courts, with a view to securing governmental
interference to prevent the Vatican Council from pronounc-
ing either on Infallibility or on Church and State. And
again, as the same letter to Dom. Guéranger shows, he was
indignant at their having pushed impudence to the point
of "giving the name *ultramontane party* to the generality
of the Catholic family which does not think as they do".[5]

By the end of March, then, the Pope had become profoundly irritated by the tactics of the "inopportunist" or
Minority group, and was saying so much more freely, so
that when the Presidents of the Council, in April, turned
down the request of some two hundred Bishops that the
"Question" be brought on out of its turn Manning and his
friends (April 19th) appealed directly to Pio Nono, with
some hope of success. And they were rewarded, for the
Pope, convinced by now that the temperature of the argument had so risen that it would be unwise to postpone a
decision for a year or more (as was inevitable if the logical
order of the *schema de Ecclesia* were followed) gave instructions that the draft chapters on the Papacy be considered forthwith. After many revisions, arising from the
bishops' comments upon the circulated draft, the chapters
on the Papacy were therefore introduced into the General
Congregation on May 13th.

During this April crisis an "inopportunist" group had not
been slow to follow Manning's example, and to plan an
appeal of its own, urging that consideration of the Question
be postponed till the following year. And Dupanloup had
written the Pope a moving letter:

"Most Holy Father:
    "My name is not pleasing to you; I know it, and it is
my sorrow. But for all that, I feel myself authorised and

obliged, in the profound and inviolable devotion of which I have given so many proofs to Your Holiness, to open my heart to you at this moment.

"The report is confirmed that many are soliciting Your Holiness to suspend suddenly our important works and invert the order of the discussions, in order to bring before the Council on the spot, abruptly, before its time and out of its place, the question of the Infallibility. Allow me, Most Holy Father, to say to Your Holiness: Nothing could be more dangerous.

"This question has already set Europe on fire: the fire will become a conflagration, if by a violent haste it seems that, at all costs and by a change in the natural order of things forestalling the hour of Providence, the thing is being carried by assault . . ."

Ten days later Pio Nono replied:

"Venerable Brother:

"Your name is no less pleasing to us now than in the past, nor do we love you less, or esteem less than formerly the gifts that God has bestowed upon you. But our paternal affection for you compels us, when you are stiffly dissenting from most of your venerable brothers and from the greatest part of the clergy and Catholic people of the whole world, to warn you not to wish to be wise in your own eyes, or to rely on your own prudence; for you know that all errors and heresies have arisen from the fact that their authors thought they were wiser than others, and would not acquiesce in the common opinion of the Church. It is right for the Fathers at the Council to put forward clearly difficulties they think stand in the way of any definition; but it is not right to strive by all means to bring all over to one's way of thinking: especially as we know the Council is under the guidance of the Holy Ghost, and that nothing can be defined that is not true and revealed, or that is not for the good of the Church. We say this to you with all the more confidence, in that for many years we have known you to follow the simplicity of faith of believers, and to be quite differently minded than you are now. Return, brother, I pray you to that golden simplicity of little ones. . . ."[6]

When we remember the prodigious efforts of Dupanloup, throughout Europe, to build up the Minority opposition before the Council, and the "bales of baneful literature" which he "despatched to every centre of intrigue in Europe—notably to Paris and to Munich",[7] it is difficult not to be impressed both by the calm tone of the Pope's letter and by his reminder that the proper place for a decision to be sought was in the Council Chamber. Manning ("Chief Whip" of the "Majority", as Dupanloup was of the "Minority") was equally energetic; but his energies were directed towards the legitimate end of organising and strengthening, at Rome, his party in the Council, which was a necessary activity in a gathering of 700 which could never have achieved anything except by party organisation.

Dupanloup was indefatigable in his efforts to build up opposition in Europe; and this had its effect, whether directly or only indirectly, in helping to bring about certain political attempts to interfere with the free discussions of the Council. There was a French governmental intervention in February in the form of a cautionary memorandum to Antonelli. It was prompted by the appearance of the *schema de Ecclesia* in January with its draft chapters on Church and State. But it was not followed up because Antonelli made a firm reply, and although a new French memorandum was sent personally to the Pope the French Foreign Minister, Daru, resigned soon afterwards and his successor, the premier, Ollivier, though a Protestant, was sympathetic to the Council, and a warm admirer of Pio Nono.[8] This French attempt at intervention was the most serious political move that was made, but the Bavarian government, inflamed by the letters of Acton and Friedrich (published by Döllinger) contemplated action; so did England, where Gladstone (also played upon by Acton) was disposed to intervene when the *schema* appeared. A united démarche by the governments was the dream of the Protestant premier of Austria, Beust, but his movement came to nothing largely because Manning presented the British Agent at Rome, Odo Russell, with a full account of the position, pointing out that the appearance of the *schema de Ecclesia* was no indication that anything comparable, on the subject of Church and State, would be finally approved. Russell agreed, and persuaded Clarendon, who carried the cabinet against Gladstone.[9] In the event, as it happened, only the chapters of the *schema de Ecclesia* on the Primacy of the Pope, with a new chapter added on his Infallibility, were ever even debated.

The importance to our subject of these rather nervous attempts at governmental intervention consists in the effect which they inevitably had in embittering Pio Nono against the Minority Bishops. Some of these were, indeed, playing with fire, because the key position occupied by France, in defending the Pope at Rome, made it easy for her government at any moment to torpedo the Council by letting in Garibaldi or Victor Emmanuel. French intervention was regarded at Rome as only too likely; and, indeed, it is really rather surprising, especially when one remembers the traditional practice of Catholic governments, that Napoleon did not at least insist upon being represented at the Council. The reason must be sought in the pro-Papal attitude of French public opinion and in the perception of the premier, Ollivier. But even with these advantages, if the Council had come to debate the chapters of the *schema* on Church and State—an even more dangerous topic than the Primacy or the Infallibility—there might well have been trouble, despite the fact that the *schema* was framed in moderate and measured terms, well contrasted with the harsh abruptness of the Syllabus. It was the memory of the Syllabus that made the *schema* suspect.

The original *schema de Ecclesia* had contained two chapters on the Pope's Primacy and none on his Infallibility. On March 6th had been circulated a short new draft in place of these two chapters. It contained three chapters on the Primacy and one on the Infallibility. Comments had been invited, and 140 commentaries, many of them jointly signed, had been sent in; these had been summarised by the theologians and circulated to the Fathers on April 29th and 30th.[10] There was still no reason why these chapters should be debated before the main body of the *de Ecclesia*.

The logical order of events would have been to proceed (after the completion of the Constitution on Faith, *Dei Filius,* April 24th) to take the first ten chapters of the *de Ecclesia,* which were not specially controversial, and on which the Bishops had already had the opportunity to send in comments. Antonelli was very nervous about having the new chapters debated, foreseeing further foreign opposition. He begged Pio Nono to withdraw them. But the Pope, as we have seen, not only declined to withdraw them, but acceded, at the end of April, to the Majority request that they should be introduced for debate forthwith, and out of their turn. And so it was that on May 13th the discussion on the Papal Primacy and Infallibility was opened in the General Congregation by the Majority leader, Mgr. Pie, Bishop of Poitiers.[11]

It has been necessary to recount these events in some detail because of the frequent accusation that Pio Nono bullied the Council into defining the dogma of Papal Infallibility. The truth is that he showed that, "as private doctor", he believed that such a definition should be made, and, as Pope, he yielded to the pressure of the Majority, and agreed—gladly enough—that the Question be brought on out of its turn.

Had he in any other way exerted pressure upon the Council tending towards the securing of the definition?

There are accusations levelled by Acton, Quirinus, and the other numerous critics which need brief mention here, even though they have been exhaustively examined, in English, by Butler in the two volumes of his *Vatican Council.* First there is the matter of the selection of the theologians who were invited to Rome, before the Council met, in order to draw up the *schemata.* Why were not leading theologians who were unsympathetic to the Neo-ultramontanes brought to Rome such as Newman or Döllinger, or, in particular, Hefele, the great historian of the Councils? The answer is that Pio Nono, personally, was always in favour of bringing in opponents in this way; but the various Nuncios, to whom the matter was left, were usually more cautious. Newman was invited, but he declined on grounds of health; Döllinger was vetoed by Cardinal Reisach, one of the first Presidents of the Council; Hefele was, in due course, invited and attended.

Again, why were all five Presidents of the Council, and a disproportionate number of the Bishops Italians? The first question implies a fair criticism; but actually, the first of the five was Reisach of Munich, who died on December 29th. That he was replaced by a leading Italian Cardinal, de Angelis, does appear unfortunate.[12] The large proportion of Italian Fathers (some 200 out of a total of 700) was mainly due to the traditional small size of Italian bishoprics.

Much more important: why did the Special Congregation *de Fide*, which dealt with proposed amendments to the *schemata*, include no members of the Minority, or Opposition? The answer is that Manning secured that a block vote was taken for or against a complete list of 24 names, carefully drawn up by himself and his sympathisers.[13] Pio Nono was disturbed about this; he wanted Minority Bishops, and Dupanloup in particular, to be members. Manning was clearly guilty of high-handed behaviour in this matter, and it probably did his cause more harm than good.

Why did Pio Nono control the choice of topics to be introduced into the Council, and the procedure of its deliberations? It was hardly possible that matters should be arranged otherwise. If the Council was to be held at the Vatican it was quite impossible that anybody but the Pope should be the ultimate court of appeal. Was he to be the only Bishop without a say in the Council? Somebody had to regulate the consideration of the enormous number of suggestions to be expected from a body of 700; actually, Pio Nono, following Hefele's advice, created a Special Congregation *de Postulatis*, to deal with suggestions, and, avoiding Manning's mistake, he chose three of the Minority Bishops (Vienna, Turin and Antioch) to sit on it, as well as others who belonged to neither party.

Later on there was a complaint from some because a "guillotine" was introduced to meet the problem of the interminable speeches in the General Congregation, repeating one another and holding up business. Some such device was certainly required; the really remarkable thing is that it was only applied by the Presidents once, on June 3rd, when the general debate on the Primacy and Infallibility *schema* had been going on since May 13th and the speeches had become mere repetitions of what had been said, and often said several times. On this occasion the guillotine was invoked by more than 150 Bishops and was greeted with relief and enthusiasm by the large majority.[14]

The Pope having ignored the mutterings of governments, the fears of Antonelli, and the passionate appeal of Dupanloup, the three chapters on the Primacy and the one on the Infallibility had been duly introduced for debate. It soon became clear that the main objection to the three chapters on the Primacy was that they asserted the Pope's primacy of universal jurisdiction, without making it equally clear that Bishops, too, in their own dioceses, exercised "ordinary" jurisdiction, which they did not derive from the Pope, but from God. Certainly, the true proportions of the matter would have been clearer if the chapters on the nature of the Church had been taken, as provided in the *de Ecclesia*, before these chapters on the Papacy; and further, Pio Nono laid himself open to criticism by causing certain words to be inserted late into the draft condemning not only those who asserted that the Pope possessed "only the principal part" of this power (sharing it with the Bishops) but those who denied that he held "the full plenitude of this supreme power". What was objected to in this addition was not the doctrine, which was agreeable at least to the very large majority, but its introduction, at the last moment, as an "amendment to an amendment"—which, in fact, it was not. There is, however, no reason to suppose that the Pope was personally aware of the rather curious way in which it was introduced.[15]

Objections to the fourth chapter, the one on the Infallibility, were more important. There were some—the "Minority"—probably at no time more than about 140,[16] and in the final vote in the General Congregation only 88, who were definitely opposed to any dogmatic definition of this subject. This does not mean they did not believe the generally accepted tradition of the Infallibility of the Pope when, as supreme teacher, he defined with authority what in matters of faith and morals was to be held by the universal Church. With very few exceptions (perhaps Maret in France, Hefele in Germany, Strossmayer at Prague) they did believe this. It means that they considered it was very unwise, and inopportune, to attempt the definition (in itself a very difficult task) because it was bound to antagonise governments (particularly Napoleon) and, more important, it would create a serious obstacle to the return of Protestants to the fold. This latter was the objection of some two-thirds of the influential American Bishops, and notably of Kenrick of St. Louis; of Dupanloup and some twenty French Bishops; of Strossmayer of Prague, together with all the Hungarian Bishops; of some dozen of the German Bishops, and of a similar number of the Austrians, and half-a-dozen of the Orientals. So it was broadly speaking true that those who were in closest contact with Protestants or with the Greek Orthodox were the apprehensive ones. But, as against this, it has to be noted that in each of the countries mentioned, except Hungary and America, as many or more of the Bishops were in favour of a definition, while of the English Bishops only Clifford, of Clifton, was a convinced "inopportunist". Manning, in his long speech in the General Congregation,[17] urged the view that the definition would attract Protestants to enter the Church, and there were certainly some who shared this view with him. It is also interesting to find that there were Irish and Italian Bishops—four even from Southern Italy—in the Minority. There, too, de Mérode found himself, though in daily attendance upon the Pope, and enjoying, always, his close confidence and affection.

This, then, became the main issue at the Council: was it wise to define the Infallibility, and, especially, was it opportune? But the speeches in the great debate are also much taken up with the other principal problem: in what terms should they define this Infallibility, in which there existed so general a belief?

Concerning this latter question there were two main

issues. First, it had to be made abundantly clear that the
Infallibility did not attach, as some of the more ardent
"Veuillotists" conceived, to any or every of the Pope's ut-
terances, or to his letters and speeches as "private doctor",
but only to his solemn definitions, of universal application,
on matters of faith and morals. There was, actually, very
general agreement about this amongst the Fathers, most of
whom were by no means Veuillotists, and the form of words
which they finally hammered out safeguarded their view in
the published definition. The Roman Pontiff was declared
to be infallible only when he spoke "*ex cathedra*, that is
when, exercising the office of pastor and teacher of all
Christians, he defines with his supreme apostolic authority
a doctrine concerning faith or morals to be held by the
universal Church . . ." Thus was a stop put to the wilder
theological extravagances of some of the Neo-ultramontanes
—perhaps the greatest achievement of the Vatican Council.

The other major problem of drafting was one which
exercised the minds of some of the Majority, who supported
a definition, as well as of the Minority, who opposed; it was
the effort of some to secure a form of words which would
show that before making an *ex cathedra* pronouncement
the Pope must consult the Church. But the Special Congregation, *de Fide*, in revising the *schema*, would never
concede this, partly because it was impossible to define how,
or to what extent the Pope should consult the Church
(obviously he could not consult all the Bishops, on every
question) and still more because many were frankly determined that the great Gallican controversy over the allocation of sovereignty within the Church should be settled
once and for all in favour of the Pope. It was, of course,
assumed that before making dogmatic definitions the Pope
would make proper enquiries, as Pio Nono had done in the
years preceding his definition of the Immaculate Conception in 1854. It was, indeed, unthinkable that he should do
otherwise. But no wording to this effect was put into the
definition; indeed in the last few days a modification was
introduced in the opposite sense, to make the definition
still clearer on this score, so that it finally read (following
consecutively upon the quotation given above):

". . . through the divine assistance promised to him in St. Peter, is possessed of that infallibility with which the divine Redeemer willed his Church to be endowed in defining doctrine concerning faith and morals: and therefore such definitions of the Roman Pontiff are irreformable of themselves and not from the consent of the Church".

The last eight words were added on July 16th; the final vote and enactment was on July 18th. The events of the last few days, though confused, were extremely dramatic. Darboy, Archbishop of Paris, had led a deputation to the Pope on July 15th; and the next day, at the Pope's request, he produced a written statement to the effect that, if a clause such as "the Bishops not being excluded" were introduced after "when exercising the office of pastor and teacher of all nations", and if the clause added at the last moment to the third chapter on the Primacy (the one which claimed for the Pope "the full plenitude of this supreme power") were removed, and one other small excision made in the same sense, then the Minority would vote with the Majority for the whole Constitution on the Papacy.[18] Ketteler, of Mayence, who had gone with Darboy to the Pope, had fallen on his knees to implore him. It is reported that Pio Nono was moved, but was subsequently won over by Manning and Senestrey; anyhow, he said, it was a matter for the Council, not for him.[19] After mutual consultations the Minority was persuaded by Dupanloup to withdraw rather than to appear at the final Public Session and there vote *non-placet* in front of the Pope. So July 18th saw Dupanloup and his friends already en route from Rome[20] and 533 Fathers voting *placet*, amidst the rumblings of a thunderstorm (variously interpreted according to the viewpoint of the witnesses) and only two Fathers, the Bishops of Little Rock, U.S.A., and of Cajazzo, in Southern Italy, voting *non-placet*. The *Times* reported the scene:

"The storm was at its height when the result of the voting was taken up to the Pope, and the darkness was so thick that a huge taper was necessarily brought and placed by his side as he read the words *Nosque, sacro approbante*

Concilio, illa, ut lecta sunt, definimus et apostolica auctoritate confirmamus. And again the lightning flickered around the hall, and the thunder pealed. The "Te Deum" and the Benediction followed; the entire crowd fell on their knees, and the Pope blessed them in those clear sweet tones distinguishable among a thousand."

As soon as the Pope had finished speaking the two Bishops who had voted *non-placet* fell at his knees and consented. During the course of the next few months the consent of all those who had withdrawn before the final vote was received at Rome; they had, indeed, made it clear in advance that whatever the Council decreed they would necessarily accept, and believe, with Catholic obedience and full faith, since the Holy Spirit would necessarily have guided the Council into the truth. No Bishop withheld his assent. Such delays as occurred were mainly due either to the Franco-Prussian war, which broke out on July 15th, or to the belief, which existed in some quarters for a time, that, since the Council was only adjourned, the matter was not finally settled. Antonelli quickly dispelled any idea that acceptance was not already obligatory, and the occupation of Rome by Victor Emmanuel's troops on September 20th led to the prorogation *sine die* of the Council and so to the disappearance of the notion that further amendments might yet be introduced. Haynald, of Kalocsa (Hungary), who yielded in October, 1871, and Strossmayer, who withheld his consent until the end of 1872, were exceptions; before the end of 1870 almost all the other members of the Minority had adhered, mostly expressing the joy with which they had always promised they would accept whatever might be the verdict of the Council.[21]

That the debates in the Council were free, that the voting was free, and that no improper pressure was brought to bear upon the Fathers to influence them are now accepted; the journal kept by M. Icard of Saint-Sulpice, at Paris,[22] and the letters of Bishop Ullathorne have put this beyond question, should any doubt linger after a perusal of the verbatim record of the speeches in Congregation and in committee, the reports, the minutes, and the petitions, all

of which are contained in the six thousand folio columns of
Mansi. The commentaries of Döllinger and Acton, and of a
host of lesser critics who suffered, with them, the disadvan-
tage of not being members of the Council, have lost their
importance as evidence, and the charge of irregularity in
the conduct of the Council has broken down. Nor can much
be said in support of the remaining criticism of substance,
namely that "moral unanimity", rather than a mere majority, was required when Councils were defining matters of
faith. There were, indeed, grounds, based upon the tradition of General Councils, for demanding moral unanimity;
the question is whether it was obtained in respect of the
Constitution *Pastor Aeternus* in which the Pope's Primacy
and Infallibility were defined at the Vatican Council. At
the last of the votes in the General Congregation, on July
13th, there were 451 who voted *placet*, and 88 who voted
non-placet. But there were also 62 who voted *placet juxta
modum*, meaning that they were in general agreement but
still wanted certain amendments. A number in this category
wanted the definition to be more "intransigent", that it
should assert more strongly the Pope's independent authority; others wanted to see his authority more controlled.
So we may fairly leave out the "juxta modums", which
makes the majority slightly better than five to one. At the
final vote, after most of the Minority had withdrawn, there
were only the two dissentients previously mentioned. But
what, in the minds of many, provided the moral unanimity
needed was the adhesion so soon afterwards of the Minority
Bishops who were absent.

The Council was certainly both free and oecumenical,
and it performed a highly useful service in defining fundamentals of faith in the Constitution *Dei Filius*, and in
quietening both Gallicans and Ultramontanes by its definition of the Pope's jurisdiction and infallibility in *Pastor
Aeternus*. The vast majority of Bishops were edified, and
Pio Nono himself won, as never before—not even at the
great assemblies of 1862, 1867, and 1869—the devotion of
the Fathers of the Church.

Yet it is still permissible to regret that even the semblance of pressure was brought to bear upon those at the

Council who thought differently from the Pope on the main matters at issue. It was certain, from the start, that the Infallibilists were in the large majority; if the opposition had not been irritated by Manning's tactics, and by the insertion of clauses at the last moment, it is likely that the majority would have been larger still, and fewer opportunities would have been given to hostile critics.

More important, it would have been better if Pio Nono had not made his personal standpoint so clear. In view of the enormous respect and the warm devotion felt for him by the Bishops it was a pity that he threw his personal prestige into the scale, where it was bound to have such considerable effect, and that he gave way to occasional outbursts of irritation, such as he showed in his letter to Dom. Guéranger. His angers were, however, the outbursts of a quick-tempered, warm-hearted, and essentially direct and generous nature; they were certainly, in no sense, part of any deliberate plot to introduce coercion over the Council. The idea that he was privy to some such plot is as absurd as the idea that he held out inducements, in the form of promises of preferment, to those who would vote as he wished. A glance at the names of those who received the Red Hat after the Council is sufficient to show that the leaders of the Majority worked for no reward. There were no recipients at all for three years, then, in roughly equal proportions, members of the majority and of the minority were honoured in this way. Manning, to whom the Pope was most indebted, and who had succeeded Cardinal Wiseman in 1865 as Archbishop of Westminster, was not elevated to the purple until 1875.

De Mérode, closest of all the Bishops to the Pope, on account of his duties as Chamberlain, was one of the Minority. He deliberately absented himself from the final vote, and there is an interesting account of his conversation with Pio Nono the evening after that crucial occasion:

". . . when the hour came for me to retire, and I knelt, as usual, to take leave, Pius IX said to me, 'Monsieur has nothing particular to say?' I answered, 'Most Holy Father, If I have been wanting in my duty in anything, I beg your Holiness to tell it to me and I will hasten to do whatever I may have omitted.'

" 'But, no, no!' replied the Pope, smiling, 'I only asked you if you had anything you wanted to say to me. You may retire.'

"I went away full of admiration for the Holy Father, saying to myself: 'The Holy Ghost is there and not among the prophets of his supposed indignation against me. I saw that he wished, from a motive of natural and human curiosity, to know what I thought, and the motives of my attitude; but he would not go beyond that first feeling. He has respected my inner faith, my honest convictions, my position as a Bishop; he understood that I had acted simply according to my conscience. In consequence, not a word of blame or displeasure fell from his lips'."[23]

2. *The Prisoner in the Vatican*

On July 12th, 1870, the day before the General Congregation voted the Constitution *Pastor Aeternus*, the Duc de Gramont (now Napoleon's Foreign Minister) sent to Ems that telegram which has become notorious in history. The next day, the one when the Primacy and the Infallibility were actually voted, Bismarck, by editing the Ems telegram, made the Franco-Prussian war inevitable. On the 15th Napoleon declared war. On the 18th Papal Infallibility received Pio Nono's assent, and became an Article of Faith. To anybody looking back from the middle of the following century, the century of the military challenge issued by Bismarck's offspring, the new Germany, but the century, too, of the Catholic revival manifested by Pio Nono's rejuvenated Church, it must appear that that July week was a fateful one.

In his sore need Napoleon had tried, at the last moment, to secure the alliance of Victor Emmanuel, at Florence. But since he was not prepared to abandon the defence of Pio Nono, at Rome, he did not secure the alliance—an impressive victory, this, for Veuillot and the French Catholics, but a barren one, because once war was declared Napoleon needed every soldier he could find, so the French garrison at Rome was recalled as a matter of military necessity and started to embark from Civita-Vecchia on August 4th.

Thus had come about the situation anticipated by Antonelli at the time of the September Convention in 1864 —France preoccupied and unable to intervene in Italy, and the Pope at the mercy of the Piedmontese. With the 13,000 troops, including the Zouaves, now at their disposal, Antonelli and Kanzler took such steps as were possible to fortify Rome, Viterbo, Frosinone, Civita-Catellana, and Civita-Vecchia, and as a last despairing gesture the Empress Eugénie, now regent at Paris, on her own responsibility sent the French cruiser *Orénoque* to Civita-Vecchia to evacuate the Pope, if he wished, to France.

On September 2nd came the disaster of Sedan, on the 4th the end of Napoleon's Empire. Pio Nono was deeply affected by the news of these cataclysmic events, yet, characteristically, this did not prevent him from producing a little verbal pun (one of his worst), "La France a perdu ses dents."

Forthwith Victor Emmanuel sent an envoy, San Martino, to the Pope, bearing a letter couched in language that had become familiar.

"Most Holy Father,
    "I address myself, as before, to Your Holiness' heart, with the affection of a son, the faith of a Catholic, the spirit of an Italian . . ."

On account of the Franco-Prussian war, the King continues, he feels responsible for keeping order in the Italian Peninsula. The danger of revolutionary disturbances has become greater. His envoy is therefore instructed to arrange with the Holy Father for the occupation by the royal troops of places of key importance within the Patrimony.

Pio Nono brushed aside the excuses. Since he now had 13,000 men, including the Zouaves, at his disposal, and the

Florentine government had detained Mazzini at Gaeta and Garibaldi on Caprera, he was, indeed, in no danger at all at Rome. So he told San Martino that his masters were "whited sepulchres and vipers" and added that, though he was neither prophet nor son of the prophet, he could assure him he and his friends would not enter Rome. It was a stormy scene; but it was effectively lightened when the Pope called back the retreating Ambassador and added with a smile: "but that assurance is not infallible!"

On the 16th the Pope went up to the Church of the *Aracoeli*, on the Capitol, to pray before the Holy *Bambino*, protector of Rome. And on the 19th he made his last journey through the city. It was to St. John Lateran, where de Charette had his troops assembled. Here it was that he had once escaped from Rome by night, in disguise; here, too, that he had been given his great welcome on his return. Now, his hair snow white, within view of his army drawn up in front of the Lateran, he left his carriage and, supported on the arm of a companion, very slowly made the long ascent of the *Scala Santa* on his knees. When he had reached the top, and had prayed in a loud voice there, he turned and blessed the troops. This was the last act of a Pope in Papal Rome. As he drove back to the Vatican the crowd cried to him not to leave them—it was supposed that he was going on board the *Orénoque*. But he had made up his mind not to leave. He would remain in the Vatican unless they dragged him out.

At 5.30 a.m. on the 20th the observer at *Santa Maria Maggiore* reported that the enemy had begun the bombardment of three of the city gates; soon after, from the Vatican, artillery fire against the other side of the city was reported. The Pope had given instructions that there should only be a token resistance, enough to show that he was yielding to force, and that when the bombardment started the ambassadors should repair to the Vatican to receive his protest for transmission to their governments. So between 7.0 and 8.0 in the morning the ambassadors arrived, only to be invited to attend the Pope's Mass in his private chapel. His voice was clear and firm, but the windows were shaking with the cannonade. The Protestant Ambassador of Prussia, von

Arnim, spent the time scouring the Janiculum through the
window with his telescope, watching the troops of Nino
Bixio, who had fought on the same site under Garibaldi in
1849. After Mass Pio Nono received the ambassadors and
made his protest. By 9.30 he became perturbed because he
saw no sign of the white flag and Bixio was visibly directing
an onslaught upon the Villa Pamphily centre of Garibaldi's
last stand against the French in June, '49. To leave no
excuse for doubt Pio Nono had the white flag hoisted upon
the cupola of St. Peter's. Even then Bixio pretended not to
see and St. Peter's itself was in some danger; but soon the
cannonade ceased, the ambassadors departed, and the Pope
occupied himself by composing a riddle on the verb *tremare*
—to tremble.[24]

General Cadorna, directing the attack, had been puzzled
by the failure of the population of the Patrimony to rise as
he advanced. He was now puzzled and rather disconcerted
by the quiet within the city when he arrived before the
walls. He had the strictest instructions to appear as the
champion of law and order—but there was no insurrection
to suppress. It was not going to prove possible for Victor
Emmanuel's government to deny, what Antonelli lost no
time in pointing out to the world, that a deliberate invasion and assault had, indeed, taken place.

An armistice was concluded between Cadorna and Kanzler on the afternoon of the 20th.

At first the Leonine city—the region immediately around
the Vatican, St. Peter's, and the Trastevere, with the Sant'
Angelo on the other side of the river—was exempted from
the occupation, and the Zouaves spent the night of the 20th
sleeping under the great Bernini colonnade outside St.
Peter's. The next day they were to be disbanded. Early in
the morning they were drawn up for the last time, and
perceiving the Pope through a window of the Vatican they
cried out "long live Pius IX, Pontiff and King". Quite overcome, the Pope had to be supported while he gave them
his blessing for the last time; later he was found by General
Kanzler and his wife pacing up and down the corridor of
the Raphael loggia.

The inrush of democrats of all sorts created disturbances on the 21st within the Leonine city, including Mazzinian demonstrations against Victor Emmanuel as well as against the Pope; so Antonelli requested that the occupation should be extended to the whole city. Only the Vatican, St. John Lateran and Castel Gandolfo remained in Papal hands. The loss of the Quirinal was the bitterest pill. Requested to hand over the keys Pio Nono flatly refused, and, remembering the events of October, '48, he remarked that if they were determined to enter they could no doubt force their way in; which, in fact, they did.

The occupation of Rome produced a chorus of protest from the whole Catholic world but very little action by the governments. Little, of course, was to be expected from the provisional government in France, now headed by Jules Favre; but Favre did declare that his government would exert itself to protect the Pope's spiritual position. Strong pressure was brought to bear by Austrians upon their government, but Beust refused to make a protest. Bismarck, concerned to earn the goodwill of Bavarian and Rhineland Catholics, and to mollify the militant fury of the French Ultramontanes, declared it to be his business to see that the dignity and independence of the Head of the Church were maintained. Gladstone, against some opposition in his own party, declared: "the government believe that the liberty of the head of the religion of many millions of our fellow-subjects—his liberty and personal independence—is a legitimate matter for the notice of this government."[25] However, the purport of all this was only to impress upon Victor Emmanuel's government that it could not treat the Pope with impunity, that he was an object of world concern; there was no question of an expedition to restore the Patrimony to him, let alone the whole State. Its practical influence was that it strengthened the hands of the moderates at Florence, and particularly of the Foreign Minister, Visconti-Venosta, in insisting, against the Italian anticlericals, that a proper provision be made for the Papacy.

Pursuing precisely the line they had adopted since the loss of the Romagna in 1859 the Pope and Antonelli refused to consider a settlement until what had been seized

from them was restored. The plebiscite held on October
2nd, by which 133,681 from the Patrimony voted for annexation to the kingdom as against 1,507 who were opposed, made as little impression upon them as had the previous plebiscites—and for the same reason. Pio Nono withdrew into the Vatican, not under constraint, but as a protest, a voluntary prisoner, because, as he made clear, he
could not move about Rome as a subject while insisting
that he was her Prince.

Meanwhile, at Florence, the government of Lanza and
Visconti-Venosta—a government of the Right—despairing of
an agreement with the Pope, settled down to produce a
modus vivendi, rightly interpreting the attitude of the
Powers to be one of waiting for Florence to produce a
settlement, while reserving to themselves the right to criti-
cise it when made. So in November, 1870, appeared the
Law of Guarantees which regulated the relations of Italy
with the Papacy until the Lateran Treaty of 1929. The law
was not a treaty because the Pope would have no hand in
it; it was a parliamentary law, like any other law, resulting
from a bill for which Visconti-Venosta was mainly responsible. In its first part it invested the Pope, though deprived of
territory, with the full attributes of a sovereign. His person
was declared sacred and inviolable, immune from arrest
and protected by the treason laws protecting the King. His
diplomatic relations with other governments were to be protected in the same way as those of the King. He was allowed
to keep his personal Guard. He was to have his own postal
and telegraph services and the exclusive use—though not
the ownership—of the Vatican, Lateran, and Castel Gandolfo. In compensation for his lost territories he was to
receive an annual sum of 3,225,000 *lire*. So much for the
Papacy. As regards the Church, the principle adopted,
though not fully implemented, was the Cavourian separation of Church and State. The State abandoned the claim
to nominate Bishops. The civil courts were no longer to
entertain any spiritual cases. The *exequatur* and *placet* of
the State were abolished except—and this exception was
fundamental—in the allocation of benefices to the clergy.

Pio Nono and Antonelli ignored the law.[26] When the

first instalment of his new allowance was produced the Pope rejected it. "I need money badly," he admitted, "but you, what do you bring me . . . ? A part of what you stole from me? Never will I accept it from you by way of reimbursement and you will obtain no signature which might seem to imply an acquiescence in or a resignation to the Spoliation." But to the anti-clericals the law seemed fantastically generous and calculated to confer "an odious privilege".

In considerable measure the Law of Guarantees embodied the principles contained in Cavour's earlier proposals, and those proposals the Pope had at one time been prepared, unofficially, to consider. What had prevented his considering them more seriously at that time had been the behaviour of Cavour's government in the occupied territories, behaviour inconsistent with any sincere desire to reach an understanding with the Church. The same behaviour, Pio Nono believed, would soon be indulged in by the authors of the Law of Guarantees; it seemed, therefore, useless to abandon his traditional rights, which a new turn of the whirligig of European politics might well restore to him, for the sake of a law which the new government could amend at will and could interpret as it chose. There was substance in this argument, as the behaviour of the Italian government, when the Left won power in 1876, was soon to show. But it is necessary to take account of an alternative line of argument, which embodied the views of the moderate leaders of the Right, Sella, Visconti-Venosta, and Minghetti, and of many enthusiasts for the risorgimento who were also good Catholics. These men urged that the Church should abandon its boycott of the State, now embodied in the formula that Catholics should be "neither electors nor elected", and should enter the parliamentary arena to support the Right and so defeat the dangerous anti-clerical plans of the Left. It was not a point of view that appealed to Pio Nono, who preferred to take his stand on his principle, and who received much encouragement from abroad—notably from Veuillot—in doing so.

To the Pope the Right were hypocrites, in some ways more dangerous than the Church's open enemies of the Left. But there were sincere Catholics in Minghetti's party

who felt very keenly the danger from the anti-clerical Left,
and, most notably, Minghetti himself made a firm stand
in support of the Church when Bismarck tried to interfere
to secure that the Italian Prime Minister should amend the
Law of Guarantees to the prejudice of the Pope's position.

This interference of Bismarck's in Italy arose out of that
campaign, commonly and correctly called the *Kulturkampf*
(although the prudent Chancellor preferred to treat it as a
purely political dispute), which was directed towards the
complete subjection of Church to State in Germany; it was
a campaign that soon took on a cosmopolitan flavour on
account of the support given by the Church everywhere to
the exiled German priests and on account of the peculiar
ascendancy in Europe of the successful German Chancellor.
The chief weapons in his attack were the May laws of May,
1873, which subjected not merely the ordinary schools in
Germany but the training for the priesthood itself to the
closest state supervision. Candidates for the priesthood had
to be approved by the State, they had to study for three
years at a university, they could not be appointed to par-
ishes without the approval of the Oberpräsident of the
province. Led by Bishop Ketteler of Mayence, the German
Bishops, as a body, preferred imprisonment or exile. On
February 5th, 1875, Pio Nono issued an Encyclical declar-
ing the laws null and void, thereby enraging Bismarck who
vented his wrath not only on the Pope but on the Italian
government, taking the line that Minghetti should have
followed his own example and have waged a *Kulturkampf*
in Italy, and in particular that the Law of Guarantees, under whose protection the Encyclical had been issued, gave
the Pope far too great a freedom. That law, Bismarck urged,
must be modified.

With considerable courage Minghetti stuck to his guns,
insisting that his government understood very much better
than a German government could how to deal with the
Papacy, and that Catholic opinion in Italy would never
tolerate interference in the matter. Thanks to Minghetti's
courage there was a possibility, in 1875 and 1876, when
Italian conversations were going on both with Austria and
with the pro-Papal government of MacMahon in France,

that the Italian Right might, with some support from the Vatican, effect a Catholic grouping strong enough to induce Bismarck—as later he was induced—to call off his persecution in Germany; at all events Bismarck feared as much.

The episode suggests that, in view of the newly emerging anti-clericalism everywhere in Europe, Pio Nono might have done well to ally his policy with moderate Catholic opinion everywhere, and especially in the new Italy. But in view of the extension of the Piedmontese religious laws to the rest of the Kingdom he inevitably saw Victor Emmanuel's ministers, of whatever complexion, as the spoliators, for a generation, of the Church; spoliators of her monasteries, of her convents, and of her Temporal Power. The Right seemed to have little advantage over the Left; both were anathema. And there even seemed some advantage in the rule of the Left in that it was more likely to incite foreign indignation and intervention. Certainly, regarded as a group, the politicians of the Right were hardly likely to inspire the Pope's confidence. Lanza, by whose government the occupation of Rome was effected, might be a moderate and cautious statesman, but Sella, his finance minister, who opposed the Law of Guarantees as too generous to the Pope, was a determined opponent of the Church. Anti-clericalism was, indeed, by no means confined to the Left.

With the Left, however, anti-clericalism was a main plank of policy. Their leader, who came into power in 1876 and held it for eleven years, the veteran Freemason and professional politician Agostino Depretis, was a shrewd man, and rightly convinced that he could secure his position by giving support to policies restrictive of the Church's influence. Those more immediately responsible for what was done were his Minister of Justice, Mancini, of Education, Professor Coppino, and of the Interior, Nicotera—once one of Garibaldi's legionaries. They soon showed their metal. When Pio Nono wrote to Dupanloup to congratulate him on his protest against the conscripting of the Italian clergy for the army the *Osservatore romano*, which published his letter, was confiscated—in defiance of the Law of Guarantees. Nicotera forbade outdoor religious processions, a well-established feature of Italian Catholic life but now denounced as reminiscent of pagan celebrations and as something which had long since been abandoned by the enlightened countries of the north! Bismarck's policy was openly spoken of as the right model for Italy. Secret attempts to live under monastic rule, despite the closure of most of the convents, were hunted out more assiduously, and prohibited. Catholic congresses, notably the great congress assembled at Bologna in September, 1876, were summarily dissolved.

Depretis' policy was popular with a majority of the electorate, that is, with the "enlightened" bourgeoisie which formed the bulk of the quarter-million (on a national population of 24 million) who voted at the elections. He was returned with an improved majority in November, 1876. A more serious attack was immediately launched upon the Church, notably in the notorious "Clerical Abuses Bill" which proposed to subject the clergy to special penalties for criticism of the State. Despite the indignation of many of the Right the bill was voted in the Chamber in January, '77. Pio Nono greeted it with an Allocution on March 12th which was the most unrestrained that he ever issued against the new régime—perhaps Antonelli, who had died in the previous November, would have prevailed upon him to moderate it. The existence of the new Italy he now roundly declared to be incompatible with the independence of the Holy See. Catholics everywhere were urged to induce their governments to intervene to restore to the Pope his rights, which were essential to his spiritual independence.[27]

The bill, even in the view of some of its supporters—such as Sella—was injudicious. In attempting to muzzle the clergy it was also muzzling the Pope. It made nonsense of the most important provisions of the Law of Guarantees, but that law was already openly spoken of by Depretis himself as only "a transition or a transaction . . . between the past and the future". Catholic reaction abroad was so sharp that, in spite of Bismarck, governmental intervention in Italy once more seemed possible, and this strengthened the Pope's language. In truth, the Left had over-reached itself and the Senate, in throwing out the bill, was certainly representing the feeling of the country. On the other hand, neither the Papal Allocution nor the denunciations and threats from abroad were helpful to the Italian moderates who were trying to defeat the bill. And on an issue of equal importance the Pope had been obliged to give way, in January of this same year (1877). This was over the *Exequatur* in respect of episcopal appointments. The Minister Mancini was insisting that if a Bishop refused to obtain the approval of the State to his investiture with his temporalities he should lose his spiritual as well as his temporal rights. Rather than see the whole structure of the Church destroyed in Italy Pio Nono allowed the Bishops to comply and accept investiture with their temporalities from the State; but it was hardly possible for the Left even to pretend any longer that they were implementing that separation of Church and State which was supposed to be the basis for the Law of Guarantees. And Pio Nono was justified in his contention that so long as the position of the Papacy was wholly subject to the whims of the Italian Parliament it was neither independent nor free.

The closing years of Pio Nono's pontificate appeared to the Church, and to him, as a period, in Europe, of gathering darkness, a darkness that seemed unillumined by the ray of brilliant light which he could see shining through it. The ray was growing brighter, and wider, but the darkness seemed also to be growing darker. Living in the light of the ray Pio Nono could exult in it, in the terrific fervour of the Ultramontane faithful, in a world-wide devotion such as no modern Pope had enjoyed, in the growth of the Church in distant, Protestant lands, very notably in the United States, in Holland, and in Britain;—almost his last act was to prepare for the restoration of the hierarchy in Scotland, brought about in March, 1878, one month after his own death. And he could look to the missionary expansion in Africa and Asia and Australasia. But on the European mainland the bright promise of his liberal days, of the eighteen-forties, when he was a critic of Gregory XVI, the days of the Amnesty, the days when Montalembert and Lacordaire were in their prime, when in Belgium, and in Germany, indeed, in every European country Liberal-Ca-

tholicism seemed to be bearing the hope of a wider reconciliation of all men within the bosom of the Church—that
promise had faded, and disappeared, leaving behind something different, leaving this ray, indeed, of ardent Ultramontane Catholicism, but outside its light hostility and
persecution on every hand such as had not been suffered
since the French revolution, governments hostile to the
Church as never since 1815, governments that looked with
indifference upon the occupation of Rome.

The situation was most serious in Germany. Partly this
was because of the personal ascendancy of Döllinger, at
Munich, his refusal to recognise the validity of the Vatican
Council, the sympathy which he received from university
circles, and the political support given to him by Prince
Hohenlohe of Bavaria. In itself, the resulting "Old Catholic" movement, which Döllinger disliked, and which soon
lost the theological traditionalism that had marked its
master's teaching, was of small importance. None of the
Bishops who had opposed the definition of Papal Infallibility supported it; the claim that a new Lutheran movement
was at hand was belied when it resulted in but a little band
of rebels numbering, at their fullest extent, only some hundred and fifty thousand. But it had this importance that it
suggested, for a time, to Bismarck, that he would seriously
weaken the Church if he lent his great influence to the
support of these Old Catholics. And to gain control over
the Church rapidly became, for political reasons, one of his
major purposes. It was clear to him that the French Ultramontanes were the Frenchmen most determined upon the
recovery for their country of her previous influence in
Europe and thus the greatest menace to his new German
Empire. He saw that the priests in Alsace-Lorraine were
generally unsympathetic to the annexation of those provinces to Berlin, and that the same was often true of the
Church in the South German states. In the Prussian province of Posen he found the priests sympathetic to Polish
aspirations. He knew that Pio Nono's sympathies rested
with France, and that he still hoped for the recovery of the
Temporal Power through the assistance of that country.
But, most important, he was determined to educate Ger-

mans into a new attitude of respect for and obedience to the State, and he knew that he could count upon the support of a strong body of opinion which gloried in the scientific and philosophical achievements of Germans, and still more in their military triumphs; which looked down with contempt upon other "effete" peoples, and especially upon Italians; which identified the Church with the Roman Curia; in short whose attitude was well summed up by Gregorovius at Rome:

"Once more before the German intellect will be placed the task of delivering the world from the Roman deception . . ."

". . . enthusiasm for an exalted idea, consciousness of a great future, good fortune in arms, practical intelligence and control of the will by the categorical imperative of Kant—all continue to make Germany irresistible".[28]

The *Kulturkampf* which began, like all such movements, with the expulsion of the Jesuits and an attack upon the other Religious Orders ended, as we have seen, by subjecting the very training of priests themselves to the will of the State. It was a notable offensive on the part of the State in its perennial struggle with the Church, and, although in the end it failed, it yet gave rise, on account of the prestige of Berlin, to comparable movements in Austria and Switzerland, in Belgium, and, as we have seen, in Italy. A little later—Pio Nono did not live to see it—a similar ruthless anti-clerical campaign was launched by the French government which drove the Religious Orders from France; many of them settled and started schools in more tolerant England. The Pope has been accused of promoting all this strife by throwing down the gage to civil society with the decrees of the Vatican Council. But, as Newman and Manning had no difficulty in pointing out to Gladstone, who, in these same years, was accusing the Pope of dividing men's allegiance, the Council did no more than define more clearly where, within the Church, the seat of authority ultimately lay.[29] Certainly, the Council may be said to have buried Gallicanism, but Gallicanism was already quite discredited; Ultramontanism, whether of the liberal or the intransigent variety, whether Montalembert's or Veuillot's, had already killed it. What the Council did was to kill Conciliarism. It settled that a Council was not necessary for the final settlement of problems of dogma. But whether a Council or the Pope were the final arbiter of dogma made no difference whatsoever in respect of civil allegiance. Both Council and Pope—like conscience—were extra-national; no new principle of authority, of an extra-national kind, was set up by the Council. Many men, many very intelligent men, as intelligent as Lord Acton, had thought that some new arbitrary power would emerge, as a result of the Council; that a despotic Pope, reviving the claims of Boniface VIII in the much quoted *Unam Sanctam*, would be interfering in every department of civil life and, as Gladstone put it, in every act of three-quarters of a man's day. All that can now be said of these fears is that some of the wilder dreams of some of the least balanced intransigents before, or even during the Council, may have justified them; but the Vatican Decrees themselves—to quote Manning—"in no jot or tittle changed either the obligations or the conditions of civil allegiance".

Bismarck's onslaught upon the Church was, in fact, in no sense provoked by the Vatican Council, but was the natural consequence of the achievement of national unification and of imperial success by a masterful political leader, a leader who was as little inclined as Henry VIII had been to tolerate an *imperium in imperio*. Yet, as Newman pointed out in his *Letter*, an *imperium* there always must be in the State's *imperio* so long as man retains a conscience and free will; and there is no difference in this respect between the Protestant and the Catholic, both, alike, refusing to acknowledge the sovereignty of the State in matters spiritual. And the position in Italy was essentially similar to that in Germany, though complicated, of course, by the existence of the Temporal Power. The new spirit of nationalism, nurtured in Italy by Mazzini, as it had been nurtured in Germany by Fichte and Herder and a host of others, achieved in both countries its political triumph in 1870, and the anti-clerical legislation of the next decade, which was common to both, was the natural result. Nor was the

new nationalism confined to Germany and Italy; nationalism founded upon the new notion of the omnipotent "will
of the people" was an integral part of European development in the nineteenth century, and was the real cause of
the renewed hostility to the Church in the 'seventies and
'eighties, in Austria, in France, and in Switzerland.

In the pontificate of Pio Nono the Church, vis-à-vis
Society, was on the defensive. In their various ways Rationalists, Nationalists, Liberals and the rest were laying claims
to men's allegiance that were new and the Pope—most notably in the Syllabus of Errors—was condemning these claims
in the sense that he was rejecting the notion that their
doctrines offered an alternative means of salvation to that
offered by the Church. Within the framework of the
Church's teaching the new ideas might have validity; on
the political plane they might be useful; but in antithesis
to the Church's teaching, and offered as a philosophical
alternative, they were anathema. In so far as men like Mazzini, or Proudhon, or Bakunin (operating on a wide front
in Italy), or Marx, or Treitschke, or, on the political plane,
Napoleon, Cavour, or Bismarck represented "modern society"—and in the accepted sense they did—the Pope was
prepared to say that he would not be reconciled with modern society; nor would he be reconciled with Progress
or Liberalism as those ideas were manifesting themselves
around him, whether in the risorgimento, or in Germany,
or in the anti-clericalism of the republicans in France. So,
in an important sense, he did throw down the gage to modern civilisation; but he threw it down in the Syllabus of
Errors, not at the Vatican Council which was irrelevant to
the issue; and he threw it down against movements and
tendencies which may have had good in them, but which
were showing themselves in so hostile and arrogant a light
during the last years of his life, after 1870, that he felt no
occasion, in his closing years, to withdraw, but rather to
emphasise afresh his strictures.

So, as the end approached, it seemed to Pio Nono that
the darkness was dark, indeed, and was growing darker and
spreading more widely. But he had lit a bright light in the

Church. He had recalled men to a truer vision of her universality, and of her unity, he had reasserted, in contradiction to the current emphasis upon the "autonomous man" or the "autonomous state" the existence of the divine law and the role of the Church as its interpreter. He had imparted a new emphasis to prayer, to devotion, to sacrifice, to personal purity; and he had recalled Catholics to the traditional faith of the Church in the merits, as intercessor, of the Blessed Virgin Mary. At the end of his life he stimulated the devotion to the Sacred Heart, contributing 50,000 francs, in the penury of his last years, to the new cathedral dedicated to that name which Parisians, in expiation of the crimes of the Commune, were beginning to raise high on the hill of Montmartre.

"When the history of the Pontificate of Pius IX shall be written," said Manning, "it will be found to have been one of the most resplendent, majestic, and powerful—one that has reached over the whole extent of the Church with greater power than that of any other Pope in the whole succession".[30] Now that Professor Aubert, of Malines, has written a balanced and authoritative history of the Church under Pio Nono considered scholarship has, in an important sense, endorsed Manning's bold prediction. No achievement of mere administrative centralisation was Pio Nono's; nor was it just an excitement of the human emotions of affection and devotion towards the Papacy. He made the Church, as Professor Aubert puts it, *sensiblement plus "Réligieuse"*.

What more can be asked of a Pope?

This, perhaps, that he should have a profound understanding (or at least that his entourage should) of the intellectual tendencies of his times; that he should understand, too, social and economic trends and tendencies and how they must affect society and the Church. Pio Nono cannot be acquitted of a certain ignorance and indifference towards the great writers and thinkers of his age; he was far from being a scholar, with the result that the Curia was below that level of intellectual eminence that was desirable. And he cannot be acquitted of some responsibility for what

was the greatest tragedy of his pontificate; namely the failure of the Church, as a whole, to win the affection and
respect of the new proletariat in the rapidly growing towns.
Some of her leaders—and notably Manning—saw the problem and strove heroically to meet it; but it was more obvious in London than in Rome, and Pio Nono and his
Curia, though prodigal in private charity, scarcely perceived
that firm teaching was needed, especially by employers, in
the principles of social justice. It was left to Leo XIII to
provide the necessary guidance, in his Encyclical *Rerum
Novarum*. But by the time this was issued Marx and
Bakunin had had a long start.

By the end of the year 1877 hardly any of those in whom
Pio Nono had been most interested were still alive. His
brothers and sisters, at Sinigaglia, were all dead. Antonelli's
end had come on November 6th of the previous year. "Tell
him to make a good confession," said the Pope, when he
heard he was dying. And when he heard that the Cardinal
was dead he added "let us speak of him no more". Clearly
Pio Nono, towards the end, became increasingly perturbed
by some of the stories he was told about the Cardinal, and
he was deeply shocked when Antonelli left all his money to
his relatives. Even so, this dismissal of so faithful a servant
was curt. De Mérode had died in July, 1874, just before
he was to have received his Cardinal's hat; and the same
year saw the death of Cardinal Barnabò, very closely associated with the development of the new hierarchy in
England. But strangest of all, Victor Emmanuel, whose
rude health was a byword, succumbed to a fever at the
beginning of the year 1878 and died on January 9th at the
age of only 58. The Pope's interest in the King who had
supplanted him at the Quirinal had never abated, and he
had, of late, been corresponding with him secretly, using
that great Piedmontese saint, Don Bosco, as his intermedi-
ary. On hearing that the King was *in extremis* he sent a
priest, armed with powers to lift the censures of the
Church, so enabling him to receive the last sacraments.
Victor Emmanuel was duly given Christian burial in
Agrippa's Pantheon, on the understanding that he was not

called King of Italy in the liturgical prayers! When his son
Humbert was proclaimed King of Italy Antonelli's successor, Cardinal Simeoni, sent a protest against this claim to
sovereignty over Rome and the States of the Church.

The political protagonists in the drama of Pio Nono's
life were now all gone: Napoleon had died at Chislehurst
in 1873; Mazzini at Pisa in 1872 protesting vehemently,
with his last breath, his faith in God; and conscientious
Pasolini, appropriately President of the Senate, at Ravenna,
in 1876, after enjoining his son: "I should wish you never to
think of your father, alive or dead, without remembering
the word 'duty'."[31]

Some of the protagonists in the religious struggle, however, were still very much alive. Not Montalembert, of
course, or Lacordaire, or Lamennais; but Dupanloup and
Veuillot were still arguing vehemently over the old issues
in France while Manning, indifferent to opposition, was
pursuing, single-minded, with much success, but terribly
alone, the cause of the Church at Westminster. And Pio
Nono, from his "prison" in the Vatican, was helping him,
notably over the abortive Catholic University of Kensing-
ton, which had the Pope's strong sympathy and support.
In March, 1875, Manning had been elevated to the Car-
dinalate. The occasion was noteworthy partly, as Newman
pointed out to him, because "it is striking to observe the
contrast between the circumstances under which you return invested with this special dignity, and the feelings
which were excited in England twenty-five years ago on
occasion of the elevation of your predecessor, Cardinal
Wiseman . . .";[32] partly, also, because he became titular
of the Church of St. Gregory the Great, on the Caelian Hill
at Rome, and, as he noted, "From this very Caelian Hill
went forth in holy mission, in days long past, the first Archbishop of Canterbury. The names of the first Bishop of
Rochester, that of the first Bishop of London, and that of
the first Archbishop of York, are inscribed on the walls of
these cloisters."[33]

Manning and the Pope. The two most intransigent of
them all were left, now, from the struggles of the past. And
fate willed that it was this Archbishop, whom Pio Nono

had first seen kneeling in the *piazza di Spagna*, kneeling—still an Anglican Dean—to receive his blessing, who should console the last weeks of his life. He arrived in Rome on December 22nd, 1877, and was constantly with the Pope till he died on February 7th, 1878.

"I had the happiness of sitting by the side of his sick-bed to console his last days. No subject of his manifold and great anxieties was ever spoken of; no business, however slight, was ever introduced. I felt that the sick-bed of Pius IX was sacred . . . that I had the happiness of conversing with him only on such thoughts and things as were consoling and cheerful and free from all anxious thought. More than once in those five weeks I was able, as I hope, to bring before him some momentary solace; and I thank God that my lot was so ordered that I stood beside the Pontiff, whom we have so revered and loved, in the last days and in the last moments of his great and glorious life."[34]

What did they talk about?

We don't know, and it is not very easy to guess. But it is sobering to remember that Manning had not got Pio Nono's sense of humour. We cannot be sure that, in his anxiety to avoid topics of high policy, he could readily relax and joke about their common memories of the Vatican Council; about Bishop Verot of Savannah, who used to interrupt to plead that clerics should be prevented from hunting with guns, or Martin of Paderborn who wanted them all to be made to grow beards. The Pope's humour often turned upon biblical phrases. But can we be sure that Manning would have quite appreciated his scrawling at the bottom of a bad photograph of himself, bought by a nun, and brought to him to be autographed, the words of Our Lord, as He walked upon the waves: "Fear not, it is I"?

But if the Pope, in those last days, was seeking reassurance; if Manning told him that his faithful stand against error and spoliation and his refusal to accept at their face value the overweening pretensions of the "enlightenment" or the "revolution" had been a thousandfold worth while;

that he had been right to reject the role of best-loved Prince in Europe and to embrace that of best-hated; that despite apparent failure he had really won victory for the Church in the future; if this was what the Pope wanted then the Archbishop was probably the most suitable death-bed companion that, in his last agony, he could have found.

On the morning of February 8th Cardinal Pecci tapped the forehead of Pio Nono three times with the little silver hammer, calling upon him by his baptismal name, Johannes-Maria. There was no reply, and he turned to the cardinals present with the ritual words: "The Pope is truly dead." By February 20th Pecci had been elected Pope Leo XIII.

It remained for the Roman crowd, so adept throughout history at alternating the cries of "hosanna!" and "crucify!", to play its self-appointed role in the last phase of the drama. On February 10th the penitentiaries of St. Peter had clothed the body in full pontifical robes, and it reposed in the Chapel of the Blessed Sacrament, with the feet touching a grill. Outside, past this grill, the crowd filed ceaselessly for three days, to kiss the feet of the dead pontiff, and to touch them with some religious token. Then, on the 13th, Manning reports:

> "We went down into the chapel of the Blessed Sacrament and kissed the feet. I laid my pectoral cross on the left foot as a pledge of fidelity and a prayer for perseverance in all I have learned from Pius IX. We then went across St. Peter's to the Chapel of the Choir. The procession then went to the Confession of St. Peter, and the bier was lowered to the ground before it, as if to receive the blessing of St. Peter on his successor . . ."

After the body had been placed in the coffin the Sacred College retired:

> ". . . and the coffin was carried and deposited in the *loculus* over the side door of the choir. This was our last function, and our last assistance rendered to Pius IX."[35]

But it was not the last adventure of that worn-out body. Three years later, as had been planned, it was to be carried for final burial to the Church of *San Lorenzo Fuore le Mure*. The anti-clerical campaign, under Depretis, was raging, so it was thought wiser to move the coffin by night. Even so there were ugly demonstrations, and mud was hurled at it by the Roman crowd. The journey, however, was at last safely made, and a worthy tomb was erected in the Church with offerings sent from all over the world. Yet even then it was not destined to lie quite undisturbed, for this Church, by a curious chance, was to be the one building in Rome to receive, in the Second World War, the latest products of "Progress" in the shape of a "direct hit".

Macaulay, in his essay on Ranke's *History of the Popes*, designated the Enlightenment and the Revolution as the fourth and most dangerous onslaught launched, in all its long history, upon the Catholic Church. It was Pio Nono's fate, after travelling, with sympathy, in his earlier years, more than half way to meet the Revolution, to be compelled, though not naturally a fighter, to turn and withstand its pretensions. It was his glory that "he confronted the tempest without flinching, and was faithful to the end." He died a hero to his followers; to the world, apparently, a failure. Few thoughtful men, in 1900, thought he had been right. It was necessary to find excuses for the Syllabus —better, even, to forget it. But we, today, who have met the children and the grandchildren of European Liberalism and the Revolution, who have seen Mazzini turn into Mussolini, Herder into Hitler, and the idealistic early socialists into the intransigent communists are able from a new vantage ground to consider once more whether Pio Nono, or the optimistic believers in an infallible progress, like his cultured friend Pasolini, will have, in the eyes of eternity, the better of the argument.

Footnotes to Text

PREFACE

1. Paris, Bloud et Gay, 1952. This is Volume 21 of the *Histoire de l'Église* edited by Fliche et Martin.
2. *Miscellanea Historiae Pontificiae*, Vols. VIII (1944), XVI (1951) and XVII (1951).
3. Oxford, 1932–40.
4. Longmans, 1930.

CHAPTER ONE

THE LIBERAL POPE AND HIS INHERITANCE

1. Such is the traditional story, graphically recounted by Pelczar, and accepted by the Italian historians Bianchi, Monti, and Vercesi. But for a different version, emanating from Cardinal Fieschi, which suggests that Lambruschini was more overcome by the occasion than was his successful rival, see A. M. Ghisalberti, *Nuove ricerche sugli inizi del Pontificato di Pio IX e sulla Consulta di Stato*, Rome, 1939. The Dutch representative at Rome, de Liedekerke, a shrewd observer to whom Professor Ghisalberti pays close attention, saw the struggle, at the time of the conclave, rather as one between *statisti* and *stranieri*, meaning by the former cardinals belonging to the Papal State who were anxious to assert the spiritual and temporal independence of Rome against the great Catholic governments, and notably against that of Vienna. Amongst these *statisti* must be reckoned Mastai; even at that date he should, rightly, be seen as authoritarian in his concept of the Papal position while liberal, and Italian, in his dislike of Vienna.
2. The latest biography of Pius IX, that by Fernand Hayward, *Pie IX et son temps*, Paris, Plon, 1948, inclines to accept the story. But the considerations put forward by G. F. H. Berkeley (*Italy in the Making*, Vol. 2, p. 34) strongly suggest that Vienna intended not to present one against either Gizzi or Mastai. Such is the sense of a despatch from the Austrian ambassador at Rome, Lützow, to Metternich, as well as the implication of Metternich's own *mémoires*, Vol. VII, p. 248. Cf. also Aubert, *Le Pontificat de Pie IX*, p. 14, and Ghisalberti, *op. cit.*, pp. 10–18.
3. Ghisalberti, *op. cit.*, p. 10.
4. *Pio IX Da Vescovo a Pontefice, Lettere al Card. Luigi Amat.*

(*Agosto 1839–Luglio 1848*). *Introduzione e note di Giovanni Maioli*. Modena, 1949.

5. The relevance of this last ambition to the first two years of Pio Nono's reign will be easily appreciated. There were not lacking, amongst the conservatives at Rome, those who believed that the Pope had, unwittingly, allowed himself to be seduced by notions which originated with the Carbonari.

An account of the rise and development of the Carbonari and other sects in Italy in this period may be found in Albert Falconielli: *Les Societes Secretes Italiennes*, Payot, Paris, 1936. The disguised skill of the Carbonari attack upon the Church is described in Pelczar: *Pio IX e il suo pontificato*, Vol. I, Chap. IV. Bishop Pelczar draws upon a wide range of sources, but largely upon Crétineau-Joly, *L'église romaine en face de la revolution* (3rd edition 1861). Crétineau-Joly published in this book, by permission of Pius IX, the secret instructions and correspondence of the *"High Lodge"* of the Carbonari which were captured in 1846, and are now in the Vatican archives.

6. L. C. Farini, *Lo Stato Romano*, Turin, 1850, Vol. I, p. 62.

7. Rayneval's report of 1856 on the Condition of the Papal States is considered on p. 162, etc.

8. Almost the only ecclesiastic for whom he has a good word is Bishop Mastai Ferretti.

9. Maioli, *op. cit.*, p. 24.

10. Maioli, *op. cit.*, p. 30.

11. Maioli, *op. cit.*, p. 45.

12. Pier Desiderio Pasolini in 1880 collected his father's memoirs into two volumes under the title *Giuseppe Pasolini, Memorie raccolte dal suo figlio, 1815–76*. References here are to the fourth edition, Turin, 1915. (There is an abridged English translation in one volume, Longmans, 1885.)

13. Maioli, *op. cit.*, p. 47.

14. Officially King of Sardinia; Savoy, Piedmont, Genoa and Sardinia became one kingdom by the treaties of 1815.

15. These articles (1) denied the right of the Church to interfere in civil and political affairs in France; (2) asserted the validity of the decrees of the Council of Constance and the authority of General Councils over the Pope; (3) insisted that the exercise of the apostolic power in France had to be in conformity with the laws and customs of the Gallican Church; (4) maintained that even in questions of faith the ruling of the Pope was not infallible unless the consent of the Church had been given to it.

16. The movement of State control over the Church initiated by the Emperor Joseph II.

17. Lacordaire, so passionately liberal, always regarded absolute religious orthodoxy as the first essential. In 1835, while still suspect as a friend of Lamennais, he appealed to the Arch-

bishop of Paris: "Monseigneur, I ask for justice at your hands: I claim the one possession, the one honour of a priest,—the right to preach Jesus Christ, until at least I fail in orthodoxy, which is the first of all things, the thing which, with God's help, I will never fail in, never at least wilfully."

18. K. O'Meara, *Frederic Ozanam*, Kegan Paul, 1878, p. 124.
19. K. O'Meara, *Frederic Ozanam*, Kegan Paul, 1878, p. 273.
20. *ibid.*, p. 269.
21. An interesting account of these matters is given in Berkeley, *op. cit.*, Vol. 2, Chap. II.

CHAPTER TWO

THE REFORMING POPE (1846–1848)

1. Metternich's arguments against the amnesty were interesting: "Amnesty is, in effect, none other than a declaration of *forgetting*; it is not the fault but the consequences of the fault which it annuls. . . . *All power comes from God.* The Sovereign, as the apostle Saint Paul says, is *minister Dei in bonum* . . . God never grants amnesties; for the very idea of such an act, in as much as an amnesty ignores the existence of the crime, would be in contradiction to the idea of divine justice which necessarily holds the moral evil in horror so long as it exists. The mercy of God is only extended by way of pardon, and repentance is the condition necessarily required for pardon . . ." (*Mémoires*, Paris, Plon, 1883, Vol. 7, p. 255.)
2. Giuseppe Spada, *Storia della Rivoluzione di Roma dal I Giugno 1846 al 15 Luglio 1849*, Florence, 1868, Vol. I, p. 395.
3. Giuseppe Spada, *Storia della Rivoluzione di Roma dal I Giugno 1846 al 15 Luglio 1849*, Florence, 1868, Vol. I, p. 234.
4. He was at school at Volterra, in Tuscany.
5. *Mémoires*, p. 256.
6. The story of the quarrel between Pio Nono and Metternich over the occupation of Ferrara is told by Farini (I. 230–280). But see also the evidence, particularly from the Vienna Staats-Archiv, given in Berkeley, II. 218, etc.
7. G. Mazzini, *Scritti editi ed inediti*, E.N., Vol. 36, p. 225.
8. *Mémoires*, Vol. 7, p. 341.
9. Metternich, *op. cit.*, p. 443.
10. Letter to Lützow at Rome, *ibid.*, pp. 570–572.
11. Farini, I, 347.
12. They are printed in Farini, I, 361–376. Farini himself took office as Under-Secretary for the interior, i.e. under the new premier, Recchi, also a layman. Pasolini was Minister of Commerce and Fine Arts, and his friend, Marco Minghetti, of Public Works (the letters and memoirs of these two men give, with Farini's history, the most authentic picture of the

events of the next few months). The majority of the cabinet were laymen, and the Minister of Police was Mazzini's friend, the amnestied Giuseppe Galletti. But it is in this Ministry that we first meet Cardinal Antonelli in office as Secretary of State. He had previously been President of the *Consulta*.

13. Farini, II, 63–65. M. Minghetti, *Ricordi*, I, 365, 366. Minghetti regarded the proclamation as unnecessary and unwise. Farini called it a "gross error".

14. Farini, II, 65.

15. Letter of April 18th, 1848, printed in A. M. Ghisalberti, *Rapporti delle cose di Roma* (1848–49), Rome, 1949, p. 33.

16. The report was found by the Berkeleys in the Florentine archives and published as an Appendix to Volume III of their work.

17. It may be read in Farini, II, 105–112.

18. Farini, II, 137.

19. For the evidence about Lord Minto's mission see Berkeley, II, Appendix B. His own reports on his mission are in the *Record Office* (F.O. 44. 2). He encouraged some of the most dangerous revolutionaries in Rome, being evidently under the impression that they were good liberals of the English variety. He seems to have supposed Ciceruacchio was such. (G. Spada, *Storia della rivoluzione di Roma*, Florence, I, 382.) Minto's advice was a determining factor with Palmerston, whom we find, after the Revolution and the Pope's flight, insisting that the key points in re-establishing the Pope on a sound basis at Rome are (1) his maintenance of the Constitution of March, 1848; (2) his separation of the spiritual and temporal powers; and (3) his carrying out the recommendations of the Memorandum of 1832 (*Correspondence Respecting the Affairs of Rome*, 1846–49, Blue Book, Part I, p. 14). Yet, in the event, his carrying out of (1) and (2) had led straight to the disasters of November '48!

20. See Rosmini's letter to Gioberti of October 30th in Farini, II, 374–376. Rosmini had been clear enough that the Papacy could not launch a crusade against the Austrians, and he regarded the Allocution of April 29th as most honourable. Yet he had held the interesting opinion that, the cause of Italian nationality being essentially just, the Pope should support it, and should similarly support other nations "struggling to be born", and notably Germany. Austria should seek her compensation by heading the Germanic national movement. If, in pursuing this policy, the Holy See became involved in war it would be honourable war, whereas the kind of war in which Napoleon had tried to involve Pius VII, and which that Pope had so honourably refused, would have been a sinful war for mere personal aggrandisement. (See Rosmini's letters to Cardinal Castracane of May '48, quoted in E. Vercesi, *Pio IX*, Milan, 1930, pp. 102–106.) Thus Rosmini

thought that the Pope might baptise the new principle of nationality as well as the "principles of '89"; he viewed the Italian question in much the same way as Gioberti did. But whereas Gioberti became increasingly Piedmontese in outlook, until in the following year he was openly hostile to Rome (laying the blame for the disasters at the door of the Jesuits), Rosmini blamed Turin, and remained by the side of the Pope in his exile at Gaeta.

21. See Berkeley, III, 403, etc., for an analysis of the Rossi-Rosmini negotiations based upon the despatches of Bargagli, the Florentine envoy to Rome. Rossi published an article on the negotiations in the *Gazzetta di Roma* for November 4th, which Farini reproduces (II. 378). Farini, despite his ardent Piedmontese enthusiasms, shows strong sympathy with Rossi, Rosmini, and the Pope in this matter.

22. So called because the medieval Guelf party in Italy looked to Rome, while the Ghibellines looked to the Holy Roman Emperor; to many Turin seemed to stand for the "secular power" in the same sense that, e.g., Frederick Barbarossa had.

The issue as to whether the neo-Guelf programme provided a real alternative to the Mazzi-Cavour risorgimento which actually occurred is one much argued by Italian historians—see the article by R. Palmarocchi, *Alcuni aspetti della politica di Pio IX nei primi due anni del governo* (*Rassegnia Storica del Risorgimento*, June, 1936, Vol. XXIII, p. 695, etc.), and the reply of Adolfo Omodeo in his *Difesa del Risorgimento* (Einaudi, 1951, p. 551).

23. It was not proved, at the trial which lasted from 1849 to 1852, that Sterbini actually planned the murder, but it seems extremely probable. It was proved that it was carried out by Ciceruacchio's son. The evidence, including the *procès-verbal* of the trial, is in twenty volumes at the State Archives at Rome; it is analysed in Berkeley, III, XXII.

24. In his *Memorie Autobiografiche* (Florence, 1888, pp. 213, 214) Garibaldi wrote: ". . . Our affairs were thus in a deplorable condition, as we have previously described, when a Roman spear gave us the chance of being no longer proscripts but of belonging to the army of Rome.

"The ancient capital of the world worthy, on that day, of her ancient glory, freed herself from a most dangerous satellite of Tyranny, and bathed the marble steps of the Campidoglio in his blood. A young Roman had found once more the blade of Marcus Brutus! . . ."

25. The historian of the dramatic events of the autumn of 1848 at Rome must always be much indebted to the analysis of the evidence made by the Berkeleys, especially *op. cit.*, Vol. III, Chaps. XVIII and XX-XXIV. But there are several contemporary accounts of the ghastly events of October; Farini's is in II, 403–413, and that of the Dutch ambassador at Rome,

A. de Liedekerke, is in his letters, published by A. M. Ghisalberti, *Rapporti delle cose di Roma (1848–49)*, Rome, 1949,
p. 117. Liedekerke was the Protestant representative of a
Protestant power who was held in high regard at Rome. A
constant critic of the Papal government, he was a warm admirer of Pio Nono. "I think," he wrote on November 24th,
"that never has a Sovereign, so worthy of the love and devotion of his subjects of all classes, found himself so basely
and so completely abandoned as at the present time." (Ghisalberti, p. 115.)

My account of the events of the next few days is drawn
from the memoirs of Pasolini and Minghetti, Farini's history
(Vol. II, Chap. XVIII, and Vol. III, Chap. I), R. Ballerini,
Premières pages du pontificat de Pie IX, Rome, 1909, Ghisalberti, *op. cit.*, and Spada, II, Chap. XIX, and III, Chap. I.
See also *Rivista storica del Risorgimento italiano*, Vol. XIX,
1932, p. 252, for article by L. Simeoni giving Count Spaur's
account of the Pope's flight to Gaeta.

26. Farini, III, 109.
27. According to Commander Key (on shore off a small British
warship, the *Bulldog*, then in Roman waters) there existed "a
nearly universal desire for the Pope's return". The clamour
for the Constituent came, he asserts, only from the Clubs
in Rome and from some of the provincial towns. "The feeling now existing against the Constituent, though but little
expressed in the provinces from want of union, and in Rome
from fear of the troops, is not the less general, and is very
evident from the sullenness with which it has been received,
and the refusal to join in any rejoicings for its adoption."
Letter of January 3rd, '49, in *Correspondence Respecting the
Affairs of Rome, 1846–49*, Part IV, p. 25.
28. Farini, III, 118–122.
29. These are the figures given by Pelczar (Vol. I, p. 426). Accounts of the circumstances of the election may be found in
Farini, III, and Spada, *Storia della rivoluzione di Roma*, III,
109–113. See also Mollat, *La Question Romaine*, 251. What
specially laid open the elections to every sort of fraud and
illegality was the general resignation of the municipal authorities on account of the prohibition placed by the Pope
upon the voting. On the other hand, the democrats claimed
that the elections were orderly, and often joyful occasions,
and in many places the number of voters numerous. It is difficult to feel any confidence about the figures of the returns,
which are variously reported; but it is likely enough that the
accounts of joyful scenes at the voting printed in the extreme-
democrat paper, the *Pallade*, which was violently anti-clerical,
give a true picture of what went on in many places. The *Pallade's* picture of the elections forms the basis of an interesting article, from the anti-clerical standpoint, by Bruno Gatta,

Le elezioni del 1849 in *Archivio della Societa romana di Storia patria*, Vol. LXXII (1949).

CHAPTER THREE

THE REVOLUTION (1848–1849)

1. Letter of M. to Michelangelo Accursi, December 5th, '48. E.N. 37, 184.
2. E.N. 41, 8.
3. Farini, III, 313.
4. *Acta Pii IX*, 1, 167.
5. E.N. 41, 35.
6. *ibid.*, 90.
7. Mazzini, *Life and Writings* (Smith, Elder, 1891), V, 296–302.
8. See A. C. Jemolo's analysis in *Il giansenismo in Italia*, Bari, Laterza, 1928. Jansenism was even more anti-Papal in Italy than it was in France; the support which it often gave to princes had the end in view of opposition to Rome. Jemolo traces the revolutionary ancestry through which the Carbonari movement in Italy derived from the parent movements, Freemasonry and Jansenism, in the eighteenth century. In this lineage Mazzini, as the son of a Jansenist, as a member of the Carbonari, and as sole parent of *Young Italy*, occupies a significant position. The same subject is also explored in F. Landogna, *Giuseppe Mazzini e il pensiero giansenistico* (Zanichelli, 1920; Chap. 4). Perhaps the most important inheritance from Jansenism, which entered the blood of Mazzini, was its Calvinistic belief in the unity of politics and religion, the concept of Prophet-Leaders of Republics, in short—Calvin at Geneva.
9. Letter. E.N. 9, 277.
10. Transl. from *Adam Mickiewicz the National Poet of Poland* by Monica M. Gardner (Dent, 1911), p. 143.
11. Letter. E.N. 9, 420.
12. E.N., Vol. III.
13. E.N., Vol. VI.
14. Letter. E.N. 10, 143.
15. E.N. 15, 92.
16. E.N. 14, 206.
17. Leroux, like Mazzini, was much influenced by the Saint-Simonians, to whom he had once belonged. He was an intimate friend, as all these men were, of Georges Sand (it was Georges Sand who introduced Mazzini to Lamennais). He was a Pantheist, with a strong belief in Progress, which led him, logically enough, to the transmigration of souls and

reincarnation. Mazzini disliked this, clinging to the idea of God *outside* Humanity, and to a distinct Heaven, after death. This may have been the last surviving remnant of the Jansenist Catholicism taught him by his mother.

18. Gioberti's letter is published in E. Solmi, *Mazzini e Gioberti, Biblioteca Storica del Risorgimento Italiano*, 1913, pp. 97, 98.
19. E.N. 24, 160.
20. See below, Chapter V. And for a recent analysis of the diplomatic relations between Turin and Rome from July, 1848, to July, 1849 (the efforts first of Rosmini and Rossi, then of Gioberti, and finally of Balbo at Gaeta to reach an understanding), see Guido Quazza, *La Questione romana nel 1848–49*, Modena, 1947.
21. *Acta*, I, 167.
22. Pelczar, I, 445.
23. They were misled by the French agent, M. de Forbin-Janson (cf. G. Mollat, *La Question Romaine*, p. 256, note). Forbin-Janson may well have been correct in interpreting the general Roman temper as in favour of conciliation, but he did not allow for that of Mazzini, Garibaldi, and their followers. See also Farini, 4; 13, 14.
24. Pelczar, I, 469, 470.
25. Della Genga had a reputation for reactionary tendencies. Altieri was one of the greatest and most saintly figures of the time. In the summer of 1867 he died of cholera as a result of insisting upon himself nursing those afflicted in his diocese of Albano.
26. Pasolini (Letter to Minghetti of July 29th, in the *Carteggio tra Marco Minghetti e Giuseppe Pasolini*) says that Farini has told him of burials alive and "unrepeatable horrors" at Rome.
27. There is an interesting, though violently Mazzinian account of this episode by J. Foster Palmer, entitled *Spola—Easter Day in Rome, 1849*, in the Transactions of the Royal Historical Society, New Series, Vol. V. After the Restoration, Spola fled to England, and settled at Liverpool, where he taught English at the Queens University. He gave the facts to J. C. Redish, who told Gladstone that "It was, in fact, a matter of the highest, nay, of vital importance, to have the sacred functions performed on that Easter Sunday, in the normal way, or the Republic would have fallen."

The sentence imposed upon the Canons of St. Peter's for refusing to say Mass at the Papal altar was imposed because they "had grievously offended the dignity of Religion, and exerted scandal, and it was the duty of the Government to defend Religion from contamination"!

As regards Daily Mass, an interesting account of the state of affairs is given by the Jesuit Raffaelle Ballerini who remained at Rome (*Les Premières Pages du Pontificat de Pie IX*,

Rome, 1909—posthumous publication—pp. 205, 206). There were not normally any Masses at all in most of the Churches, even on Feast days. He used, himself, to say Mass secretly, on a cupboard, where people came to him to Communion. There was one Canon, Pergoli, who used to say Mass at Saint John Lateran. There was a Canon at the Vatican who used to say Mass, secretly, very early in the morning. This persecution was, of course, conducted by ardent anti-clericals, as well as by hooligans—it was not official policy.

28. One of his few religious acts was to send an officer of the state to each convent, to announce publicly to the monks that they would be protected if they chose to abandon their religious vows, and also to encourage monks and secular priests to join the army.

29. De Lesseps, *Ma Mission à Rome* (Paris, 1849, p. 39).

30. Farini, III, 321–323.

31. In Vols. XLI and XLIII of the national edition of his writings.

32. *Garibaldi's Defence of the Roman Republic* (1919, Ed. Longmans), pp. 123, 124 and appendix I (i) and appendix K. Dr. Trevelyan was satisfied that the Ligurians, the Lombards, and those from the Romagna were the "soul of the defence".

33. Farini, III, 83, 84.

34. An important article dealing with the problem of the will of the Roman people at this time has recently been published by Professor A. M. Ghisalberti (*Mazzini e la repubblica dei Romani*, in *Il Risorgimento*, Anno IV, N.1, February, 1952). He stresses the extra-Roman leadership, moral, political, and military, of the Republic, and especially Mazzini's religious vision of a "Third Rome"; but he rejects the idea of "a glorious little band of foreigners self-constituted as political and military guide of an inert and passive if not positively hostile city . . ." (p. 14). "Undeniable the inspiration and support from without, effective the incitement and the example of Mazzini, but such a seed could not have yielded fruit without a prepared soil, a material condition, a moral preparation, a conscious will on the part of the Romans" (p. 10). He draws attention to republican enthusiasts in the Assembly before Mazzini's arrival, but he accepts that it was Mazzini who made the Republic a "creative ideal".

Another careful Italian scholar, belonging, like Professor Ghisalberti, to the *Istituto per la storia del Risorgimento*, at Rome, Dr. Emilia Morelli, in publishing in 1949 the minutes of the Executive Committee of the Roman Republic in the period immediately before Mazzini's Triumvirate (*Archivio della Società romana di Storia patria*, Vol. LXXII, p. 29), has demonstrated that the Roman Constituent Assembly was a reality until it yielded its effective power to Mazzini at the end of March; and that it became a reality, again, when it withdrew that power from him on June 30th. Her arguments support the view that there was a strong republican anti-clerical group at Rome, which created the Constituent Assembly and which was always suspicious of the "foreign element". But they do not, of course, demonstrate that the Assembly represented the will of the Roman People; and her revelations scarcely serve to enhance the reputation of the Roman republicans for political wisdom or vision.

35. Farini, IV, 140–142. Mazzini similarly ignored the advice of Lord Napier, who visited Rome in May.

36. The exiles from Rome, after the fall of the Republic, went to Switzerland, France and America, as well as to England. But the fact that the British Consul at Rome, Mr. Freeborn, issued, on his own initiative (he was subsequently rebuked by Palmerston), some hundreds of passes to revolutionaries who were trying to escape was a reason why England received more than her fair share.

37. F. A. Simpson, *The Rise of Louis Napoleon*, Longmans, 1922, p. 50, etc.

38. Mazzini was counting heavily upon Ledru Rollin to raise a revolution in Paris in June, '49, which would create a government that would call off the intervention. Ledru Rollin did try, but he failed completely.

39. See E. Bourgeois et E. Clermont, *Rome et Napoléon III*, Paris, 1907, p. 339, for a succinct statement of what French Catholics demanded in return for their support of Napoleon.

CHAPTER FOUR

PEACE AND RECONSTRUCTION (1850–1859)

1. *Three Studies in European Conservatism*, Constable, 1929, p. 321. To Professor Sir Llewellyn Woodward, the Pope's encyclical *Quanta Cura* and the Syllabus (1864) were "a final throw to keep that rule over a few square miles of land which seemed of more importance than the peace of mind of thousands of Catholics". This suggestion that the Encyclical and Syllabus (which were a summary of the Pope's teaching over fourteen years) were issued to the world in order to safeguard the Papal State implies that, for Pio Nono, the Church, and indeed truth itself, existed only to maintain him in his Principality; in such a view cause and effect seem to have become oddly inverted. Clearly the principal reason for the denunciations of liberalism is to be found in the fact that revolutionary Jacobinism, to which it seemed generally to lead, had everywhere and always sought to assail the Church and to disperse the Religious Orders. What Pio Nono suffered at Rome disabused him of the idea that the principles of '89 could be

"baptised", and hardened him in the view of his predecessors that liberalism leads to revolution, anti-clericalism, iconoclasm, and the persecution of the Church. So far as the nineteenth century was concerned (and in many countries the first half of the twentieth century as well) his view proved to be generally correct. Belgian and English liberalism, however, showed themselves to be, on the whole, exceptions. The Syllabus is discussed in Chapter VII.

2. "*Adesso sono tranquillo*", Pelczar, II, 47.

3. See the article by P. H. Catcheside, *Father Gentili and the Restoration of the Hierarchy*, in the *Tablet* for September 23rd, 1950 (the Hierarchy Centenary Number). In the same number Fr. Philip Hughes gives a useful sketch of the careers and capabilities of "the bishops of 1850" extracted from his essay in *The English Catholics; 1850–1950*, Burns Oates, 1950. English affairs were handled by the Congregation of Propaganda, because England was regarded as a missionary country. This remained the position until the year 1908.

4. Pelczar, II, 50.

5. The miscalculation at Rome was clearly described by Mgr. Talbot in March, 1851, to Nassau William Senior: "If we had had the slightest suspicion of the storm which we were about to excite it would have been easy to avoid it. The Bull was signed three years ago, and has been acted on ever since. If instead of formally, perhaps I may say ostentatiously, promulgating it, we had merely continued to act on it quietly and silently, the fact that there was a Roman Catholic Archbishop of Westminster would have gradually oozed out, and at length have become notorious without alarming anybody." (N. W. Senior, *Journals Kept in France and Italy*, Vol. 2, p. 96.)

    Antonelli, in his conversations with Lyons, the British Agent at Rome, made no secret of his concurrence in the view that Wiseman had been unwisely provocative in his attitude in England (cf. Lyons' letter of March 28th, 1854, Record Office, F.O. 43. 58). Rome was full of rumours that the Cardinal would be withdrawn and given a position within the Holy City and a Coadjutor put in charge at Westminster; but Pio Nono—surely with reason—retained his confidence in Wiseman.

6. E. F. Richards, *Mazzini's Letters to an English Family* (Bodley Head, 1920), I, 193.

7. Aubert, *op. cit.*, p. 62.

8. E.g. in the *Dictionnaire Encyclopédique de la Théologie Catholique* or the *Catholic Encyclopedia*.

9. Aubert, p. 279.

10. According to an article in the *Dictionnaire Encyclopédique de la Théologie Catholique* (edition of 1871, article *Vierge*) it

was officially stated, in reply to this suggestion, that "if the sovereign Pontiff, alone, pronounced the definition, to which all the faithful spontaneously adhered, his ruling would furnish a practical demonstration of the sovereign authority of the Church in the matter of doctrine, and of the infallibility with which Jesus Christ has invested His vicar on earth". (Cf. Aubert, pp. 279, 280.)

11. See below, p. 296.

12. See *History To-day* for November, 1951, *Italy: the Papal Victory 1848–1948* by Elizabeth Wiskermann.

13. Amongst the opinions expressed by those in a position to know that of the French premier, Ollivier, is particularly interesting and convincing. See his *L'Église et l'État au Concile du Vatican*, Vol. I, p. 309, for the Pope's independence of the Jesuits, and pp. 502–507 for his independence of Antonelli.

14. Some of the English descriptions of Antonelli have been rather highly coloured. Thus Professor Sir Llewellyn Woodward says he came from a "robber family" of Sonnino. He also quotes the gossipy Gregorovius, who remarked upon Antonelli's jaw: "A jaw that is thousands of years old and belonged to the creatures of the mud who devoured, devoured, devoured"; and he endows him with a pointed nose, which does not appear in his portraits. (*Three Studies in European Conservatism*, Constable, 1929, p. 296.) Disinclination to speak ill of Pio Nono has led those most hostile to his policies to give short shrift to his very loyal Secretary of State.

15. Yet it excluded too many, so that it was widely regarded less as an amnesty than as a proscription. Those specifically excluded were the members of the Provisional Government, the members of the Constituent Assembly who had actually taken their seat there, the members of the Triumvirate and of the Government of the Republic, the chiefs of the military corps, and all those previously granted an amnesty who had yet joined in the revolutionary movement.

Dalla Torre (*L'Opera Riformatrice ed Amministrativa di Pio IX fra il 1850 e il 1870*, p. 17) gives the number who were excluded from the amnesty, and mostly imprisoned, as 262, and the number who were encouraged to leave the country as 644. By the year 1857 these numbers were reduced to 203 and 492. Out of the large number of soldiers and government employees who had entered the service of Mazzini, and who were examined by the restored Papal government, 38 were sentenced, and all of these were allowed to go into exile, being furnished, like the other exiles, with passports and some travelling money.

The tribunals were, of course, largely concerned with bringing to light and imposing punishment for crimes of common violence.

16. On this debate see Montalembert's pamphlet, *Pie IX et la France en 1849 et en 1859* (Paris, 1859).

17. Such as the revision of the currency and the punishment of those revolutionary leaders who had not escaped. The Dutch ambassador, Liedekerke, had anticipated that efforts would be made to delay the Pope's return to Rome: "Sachant combien (le Pape) est peu fait, par la bonté de son cœur, pour ordonner des mesures de rigeur, et combien ce même cœur est accessible à toutes les infortunes, quelle qu'en soit l'origine, on voudrait, une fois Rome occupée par les forces étrangères, l'en tenir longtemps éloigné pour n'être pas contrarié par sa présence dans le développement du plan réactionnaire que la camarilla s'est proposé de poursuivre et dont on ne lui a probablement laissé entrevoir que les dispositions les moins acerbes, afin qu'il ne se refusât pas à le sanctionner. (*Rapporti delle cose di Roma*, p. 158.)

18. It is still commonly asserted, in the English histories, that the Pope never carried out, after his return, what he had promised at Portici. There is no justification for this assertion, which seems to rest upon the idea that he had promised to restore the Constitution, and to grant a General Amnesty, for both of which Napoleon, and the Moderates in Italy, had been pressing, but neither of which the Pope had, in fact, promised. On the other hand, there were many who felt, as did Liedekerke, or Nassau William Senior, that a great opportunity was lost, with the Restoration, for establishing a government fully acceptable to the moderate liberals; cf. A. M. Ghisalberti's article, *Una restaurazione "reazionaria e imperita"* in *Archivio della Società romana di Storia patria*, Vol. LXXII, Rome, 1949. Professor Ghisalberti follows Liedekerke, who was very critical of what was done in 1850. But the question remains, was there a moderate party in the Papal State strong enough to form the foundation for a constitutional régime?

19. Dalla Torre, p. 20. The proportions given by the French ambassador Rayneval, in his report of 1856 to Walewski, discussed below, are similar.

20. See the account of these events in A. J. Whyte's *Political Life and Letters of Cavour*, p. 207. Palmerston, at London, was out of Cavour's reach, but the Piedmontese ambassador, Emanuele d'Azeglio, received his instructions: *Echauffez Palmerston!* (Whyte, p. 199.)

21. Lyons, the British "Agent", was subordinate to the British Minister at Florence, to whom he sent his dispatches.

22. He was removed in the following year to St. Petersburg and replaced at Rome by the Duc de Gramont. His report was sent by Walewski to Clarendon; it was also published in Eng-

land and in Belgium, thus causing some embarrassment to the British and French governments.

23. Rayneval's report was published in Paris in 1861. An English translation is printed as an appendix to J. F. Maguire's book, *Rome, its ruler, and its institutions*, Longmans, 1859. After Rayneval's Report, and the unpublished letters of the British Agent at Rome, Lyons (see Appendix), the most useful general account of the condition of the Papal State at this time is given in the correspondence of Louis Doubet with Eugène Rendu published in *Un Siècle d'Histoire Italienne* by J. Gay, Paris, 1931. Doubet was in Rome in 1853 looking at infant schools on behalf of the French government.

24. See the *Carteggio tra Marco Minghetti e Giuseppe Pasolini*, Turin, Fratelli Bocca, 1924, Vol. I. The letters quoted in this paragraph come from the period 1849–53.

25. Pasolini, I, 267–269.

26. Pasolini, I, 256, 257.

27. A. Monti, *Pio IX nel risorgimento Italiano*, Bari Laterza, 1928, p. 257. Pio Nono's letters to his brother Gabriele, covering the period 1830–67, together with some other letters of interest, are printed as an appendix to this volume.

28. *Pio IX e la rivoluzione romana del 1848, Saggio di storia economico-sociale*. Società tipografica modenese, 1947.

29. Dalla Torre, p. 25. It is interesting to note that Pio Nono's personal expenditure is computed by Dalla Torre to have been as low as 4,260 scudi a year, and that a large part of the gifts of the Catholic world went, in fact, through his charities, to the benefit of the people of his state.

30. The story comes from more than one source, and is recounted by Dalla Torre, *op. cit.*, pp. 68, 69.

31. R. de Cesare, *Roma e lo Stato del Papa dal Ritorno di Pio IX al XX Settembre*, Rome, 1907, Vol. I, p. 182.

32. Newman, *The Pope and the Revolution*. Sermon preached in the Church of the Oratory, Birmingham, October 7th, 1866. From *Sermons preached on various occasions*, Burns Oates, 1874. Newman was in Rome (as an Anglican) early in 1833, and, as a Catholic priest for a year, 1846–47, when Pio Nono was helpful to him about his plans for the Birmingham Oratory. His lack of French and Italian limited his conversations with Pio Nono; his great friend was that Bishop Palma who was shot through a window, at the Quirinal, the day after Rossi's murder, October 16th, '48.

33. The famous Plombières pact of 1858 between Napoleon III and Cavour envisaged a Confederation under the Presidency of the Pope; but Cavour pointed out to Victor Emmanuel that "being sovereign by right of the richest and strongest half of Italy [he] would in fact be sovereign of the whole Peninsula". See below, pp. 195–96, 197.

1. P. Pietro Pirri, S.J., *Pio IX e Vittorio Emanuele II Dal Loro Carteggio Privato*, Vol. I, p. 7, note. The three volumes of this correspondence so far edited and published by Fr. Pirri at Rome in 1944 (Vol. 1) and in 1951 (Vols. II, Part 1, and II, Part 2) are the chief source upon which I have drawn in this chapter, and in Chapter 6.

    A succinct statement of the purposes and behaviour of Cavour and his friends at Turin is given by A. J. Whyte in his *Political Life and Letters of Cavour*, Oxford, 1930. It is strongly anti-clerical.

2. Letter from Charles Albert to Pius IX, September 10th, '48. Pirri, I, 18, 19.

3. Described by the Nuncio, Antonucci, in a letter to Antonelli. Pirri, I, 42. Grignaschi acquired a considerable following. He claimed he was a reincarnation of Jesus Christ, and gave Communion with the words "Corpus *Meum* custodiat te . . ."

4. Pirri, I, 48.

5. Pirri, I, 32.

6. N. Bianchi, *Storia Documentata Della Diplomazia Europea in Italia Dall' Anno 1814 all' Anno 1861*, Vol. VI, p. 355, etc.

7. Pirri, I, 38.

8. Pirri, I, 57, etc.

9. See also *ibid.*, 66, 67, note, for further evidence that it was no part of the policy of Pio Nono or Antonelli to undermine the Piedmontese Constitution. Sir James Hudson, who became British Ambassador at Turin at the end of 1852, seems to have assumed that this was always the Papal purpose. Yet the Holy See repeatedly reaffirmed itself unconcerned about the constitutional issue, and no evidence is given by Whyte for his assertion (*op. cit.*, p. 100) that "Piedmont was faced with a deliberate conspiracy between these latter powers [Austria and Rome] directed, not merely against her legislation or her policy, but against her Constitution". The clearest statement of the Papal attitude is to be found in the letter addressed to Victor Emmanuel by Pio Nono on March 23rd, 1852. The King had been maintaining, in a letter of the previous month, that if he only had a free hand, and were not fettered by the form of his government, he would be behaving very differently. To which the Pope replied, "I wish, also, that Your Majesty would be assured that the form of government adopted in Piedmont cannot constitute, on Our side, the slightest obstacle to an understanding, in as much as ne-

gotiations are conducted often enough with governments having republican forms and these forms, though much more extreme than the constitutional form, do not delay or vitiate the possibility of settling the matters which are the object of examination and discussion. I beg you, again, to assure yourself that the difficulty does not come from that side . . ." (Pirri, I, 97).

10. Pirri, I, 41.

11. 334 Congregations, comprising some 5,500 persons, were suppressed. Those expelled represented about two-thirds of those living in Religious Communities in the kingdom.

12. Pirri, I, 177–179. Mr. Lyons, British "Agent" at Rome, had a number of conversations with Antonelli with a view to urging him to reach an agreement with Turin, and even left with him a paper summarising the pro-Piedmontese arguments of the British Ambassador, Hudson, at Turin. But he was clearly much impressed by Antonelli's counter-arguments. The Secretary of State insisted (1) that the million lire was a payment for Papal property in Piedmont taken over by the House of Savoy on its restoration in 1814 and guaranteed by treaty, (2) that the Turin government had stated (June 24th, 1850) that it did not regard itself as bound by agreements made before the Constitution of 1848, (3) that the Piedmontese Chargé d'Affaires, Count Pralormo, showed no desire to negotiate, (4) that Rome could not condone Turin's treatment of Archbishop Fransoni.

To Hudson's charge that Rome "disliked" the Piedmontese Constitution and that her policy was governed by this dislike Antonelli did not feel called upon to reply. (See Lyons' interesting despatches of March 10th and June 20th, 1854, Record Office, F.O. 43, Vol. 58.)

13. Letter of the Bishops to Antonelli, May 4th, 1855. Pirri, I, 207.

14. Speech of February 16th, 1855, A. Brofferio, Storia Del Parlamento Subalpino (Milan, 1869), Vol. VI, pp. 819–826.

15. Five thousand in a population of five million.

16. Acta, II, 5.

17. Pirri, I, 141.

18. A proposal to introduce civil matrimony.

19. The allocution.

20. Chiala, Lettere Ed. e Ined. di C. Cavour, Turin, 1883, Vol. II, p. 114.

21. The King, it is fair to note, was very enthusiastic for this war.

22. Pirri, I, 145.

23. Whyte, op. cit., 185.

24. Chiala, op. cit., II, 134.

25. A little later, during the Paris Conference, Cavour produced the suggestion, really astonishing for a champion of the Will of the People, that a sort of general post should be played,

by which the Duke of Modena should be made King of Moldavia and Wallachia in the Balkans, the Duchess of Parma should be given Modena, and the King of Piedmont should acquire Parma!

26. Chiala, *op. cit.*, II, 175.

27. Pirri, II, Part 2, 38.

28. Montalembert, *Pie IX et la France en 1849 et en 1859*. The orator makes no pretence that all is perfect in the government of the Papal State, but he claims that Pio Nono is the most irreproachable sovereign of the century: "Quel serment a-t-il violé? Quelle constitution a-t-il abolie? Quel sang a-t-il versé? Quelle propriété a-t-il confisquée? Quel piège a-t-il tendu? Quel mensonge a-t-il proféré? Qui au monde a-t-il trompé ou persécuté? Il avait amnistié, sans exception, tous les anciens adversaires du Saint-Siège: ils l'en ont récompensé en le détrônant une première fois. Quelle liberté a-t-il détruite? Il les avait toutes données à son peuple avec une générosité qu'il ne faut pas cesser de bénir, quoiqu'elle ait paru imprudente à beaucoup: on s'en est servi pour assassiner son ministre, pour l'assiéger dans son palais, pour le contraindre à la fuite, pour le déclarer déchu de son trône. Enfin quelle bassesse a-t-il commise? Il est le seul souverain de l'Europe qui ait vu sa capitale occupée depuis dix ans par des troupes amies, mais étrangères: or, je le demande aux plus délicats et aux plus dédaigneux, quel prince a eu, pendant ces dix ans, une attitude plus noble, plus calme et plus digne?"

29. De Barral, *Les Zouaves pontificaux*, Paris, 1932, p. 27.

30. "Si vous êtes dans l'embarras vous pouvez compter sur nous" —Bianchi, *Storia Documentata Della Diplomazia Europea in Italia Dall' Anno 1814 all' Anno 1861*, Vol. VII, p. 625.

31. *ibid*, 631.

32. Letter of April 11th, '56. *ibid*, 626.

33. *Il Carteggio Cavour-Nigra dal 1858 al 1863* (Bologna, 1926), Vol. I, p. 103.

34. Pirri, II, Part 2, 43.

35. La Gorce, *Histoire du second Empire*, II, 358.

36. Pirri, II, Part 2, 54.

37. *ibid*, 61.

38. Cavour had completely misled him on this point. The failure of the Italians to rise, as expected, against their "oppressors", is a consistent feature of the risorgimento. It checkmated Mazzini's many ventures and was the chief cause of failure in 1848. In the Papal State it was to be a source of astonishment to Garibaldi in 1862 and 1867, and to the Piedmontese armies marching on Rome in 1870. It compels the question what was this "cri de douleur" which the "generous hearts" of Napoleon and Victor Emmanuel felt compelled to answer?

39. Cavour's instructions to d'Azeglio are given in Bianchi, VIII, 529.

40. Most historians have followed Italian revolutionary propagandists in denouncing the "atrocities" of the Papal recovery of Perugia. But there has always been contradictory evidence (noted by Bolton King, *History of Italian Unity*, Vol. 2, p. 88, note), and the stories are quite discountenanced by the letter of an eye-witness published in *Archivio Storico Italiano*, V, 25, 301.

41. Puritan in spirit, and, on the whole, theologically. Like Cavour, however, he preferred to remain nominally a Catholic, apparently because he took "Catholic" and "Italian" to be synonymous.

42. Pirri, II, Part 2, 124.

43. *ibid.*, 129. Victor Emmanuel had written, on the 18th, in humble vein to the Pope: ". . . I have need of much indulgence on the part of Your Holiness, yet I think perhaps I am not so very guilty, which emboldens me to beg, again, that Your Holiness may grant me His Paternal Blessing . . ." But he didn't get it. The Pope ended his letter: "God safeguard Your Majesty and grant You in Your difficult position the many graces of which you have need, and by their help and their efficacy may He render you worthy of his heavenly Benedictions . . ."—which was a little different. Victor Emmanuel pretended that at Monza, as on other occasions, he was only doing what Napoleon required of him, though this was hotly denied by the Emperor. The Pope's frequent reminder, in his letters to the King, that he was heir to illustrious Catholic ancestors, was partly intended to strengthen his independence and self-esteem and wean him from the tutelage of Napoleon. (See Pirri, II, Part 1, pp. 170–172, for an account of the strange mission of the Abbé Stellardi to Rome, on behalf of Victor Emmanuel, when he tried to throw all the blame on Cavour [then out of power] and on Napoleon.)

44. Pirri, II, Part 2, 135.

45. Pirri, II, Part 2, 146.

46. Pirri, II, Part 2, 149.

47. The Pope himself was always fair and good-tempered towards the general. But his opinion of him peeps through a letter he wrote to Napoleon: ". . . The general whom Your Majesty has sent to command the Imperial Troops in Rome is very gentlemanly and full of fine qualities. All the same, as he is, perhaps, a little lively in his imagination, and ready to lend his ear to rumours, which always abound in Rome, I think that he does not always or in every case form an exact opinion of some circumstances . . ." (Letter of March 29th, '57. Pirri, II, Part 2, 19.)

One of the Pope's chief complaints was that the parades of the French troops did not leave them free to attend Mass on Sunday. Napoleon had to intervene personally to secure that they were able to attend. (Letter of Napoleon, February 14th, '55. *ibid.*, 2.)

48. See, e.g., the Pope's letter to Napoleon of July 29th, '57 (Pirri, II, Part 2, 38), and his formal protest to the French ambassador of February 22nd, '59 (*ibid.*, 55).

49. For the diplomacy centering on Naples, January–April, 1860, see Bianchi, Vol. VIII, and particularly pp. 274–285. The French attitude towards Neapolitan help for the Pope, in the crisis of September, 1860, was made clear by Thouvenel to the Papal Nuncio, Sacconi, at Paris—see Pirri, II, Part 2, 167, note.

It is interesting that Cavour's diplomacy, in the summer of '60, which was to try to raise a revolution at Naples, was unsuccessful. The populace, like the army, and navy, remained uninterested. But this did not prevent them, when Garibaldi's troops arrived, from greeting their "deliverers".

50. Particularly so on account of the attitude of Russell and Palmerston. Napoleon, indeed, had cooled in his support of Cavour, but he had had his pound of flesh, in the shape of Savoy and Nice, and he could hardly go to war against Piedmont. England, on the other hand, was becoming increasingly sympathetic with Cavour. As the formation of a United Italy became a real possibility it was inevitable that Napoleon should see a danger to French hegemony, whereas Palmerston saw a possible counterpoise to France.

51. A fascinating account of this army is to be found in Chapter III of G. F. H. Berkeley's book, *The Irish Battalion in the Papal Army of 1860*, Talbot Press, Dublin, 1929. Mr. Berkeley rejects the nominal total of 27,000; Lamoricière only admitted to having 10,000 fighting effectives. The numbers of the different nationals are given as: Italians 6,500, Austrians 5,000, Swiss 3,500, Irish 1,040, Belgians 610, French 530, besides other nationalities whose numbers are not known. Governmental interference soon stopped or interfered with recruitment in most countries, and notably in France. The Austrian contingent was the most effective, and the Austrian government the most friendly—another reason for Napoleon's suspicion.

52. Cf. the anonymous *Dix ans au Service du Roi Pie IX*, Fribourg, 1880.

53. G. F. H. Berkeley, *The Irish Battalion in the Papal Army of 1860*, Talbot Press, 1929, p. 41.

54. The attempt to raise insurrections was, in fact, as at Naples, almost wholly unsuccessful. The main practical value to Cavour of these incursions was the colour they lent to the assertion that Umbria was in revolt, and the dispersal of units of Lamoricière's force which pursued them around the countryside. One of the leaders of these bands was Masi, who had been a revolutionary leader at Rome, at the time of Rossi's

assassination, and later a follower of Garibaldi. His band of
800 claimed to be revolutionaries from the Papal State, but
actually about half were from Tuscany and elsewhere. (Berkeley, p. 95.)

55. The account which follows of the diplomatic proceedings in
this critical autumn of the year 1860 is based upon the traditional sources, together with Chap. XXV of Vol. II, Part 1,
of Pirri's book and the relevant documents printed in Vol. II,
Part 2. For the documents concerning the part played by
Cavour, see, in particular, *La Questione Romana negli anni
1860–61 Carteggio del Conte di Cavour con D. Pantaleoni,
C. Passaglia e O. Vimercati* (Bologna, 1929), Vol. I.

56. But Cavour's confidant at Rome, Pantaleoni, certainly feared
the worst, and wrote that the ambassador said Napoleon "ne
saurait jamais tolérer une occupation des troupes piémontaises
dans les États romains, et que dans tous les cas il était pret
à s'y opposer avec ses forces . . ." (*La Questione Romana*,
I, 38).

57. Even after Napoleon's return—he landed at Marseilles again
on September 24th—it was impossible for anybody to catch
him. Gramont sent Cadore for this purpose, who failed to
see the Emperor either at Marseilles or at Paris. Sacconi could
not see him; yet Napoleon frowned upon the Nuncio's request that he might visit Rome, telling him, rather, to take
some leave in the country. The Emperor's policy of evasion
was eminently successful; there were protests from many of
the Catholic countries, but with Napoleon holding his hand,
and England frankly sympathetic with the Piedmontese,
there was nothing any power could do.

CHAPTER SIX

NAPOLEON AND ROME (1860–1864)

1. Fr. Passaglia left the Society of Jesus in 1858, but his reputation for learning was such that he was given a Chair at the
Sapienza and his advice was sought by the congregations.

2. Pirri, II, Part 1, 333, 334. Cavour elucidated his conception,
which was that of the Memorandum, and Napoleon pointed
out the difficulties, from the standpoint of his own government, in correspondence published in *La Questione Romana*,
I, 134–185.

3. Einaudi, 1952, pp. 134–146.

4. Jemolo, *op. cit.*, pp. 230, 231. The verdict of another Italian
historian of importance may be compared: Pio Nono's "genuine affection for Italy might well have caused him to reverse
his non-possumus . . . but the religious policy of Piedmont

wounded him in the very core of his being, for he was before everything else a priest." (S. F. Jacini, *La Politica Ecclesiastica Italiana da Villafranca a Porta Pia*, Bari, 1938, p. 22.)

5. Pelczar, II, pp. 278–280.
6. A. Monti, *Pio IX nel risorgimento Italiano*, Bari, Laterza, 1928, p. 9.
7. H. d'Ideville, *Pie IX, sa vie, sa mort. Souvenirs Personnels*, Paris, 1878, pp. 55–56.
8. A term used to distinguish the followers of Veuillot, in the 'fifties and 'sixties, who were anti-liberal, both religiously and politically, from the old ultramontane group of Montalembert, Lacordaire, and their friends, who were liberals in the 'thirties and 'forties, basing their liberalism (after Lamennais) upon the support of the Papacy. Montalembert and his friends remained liberals—religiously and politically—in the 'fifties and 'sixties, opposing Napoleon, and opposing Veuillot's group. Their paper was the *Correspondant*; that of Veuillot was the *Univers* until its suppression in February, 1860, when it was replaced by the *Monde*.
9. The strength of the Catholic opposition in France surprised everybody, especially the Piedmontese. Vimercati, Cavour's agent, wrote: "I would never have believed that the clergy and the Pope had such power in France! This blessed Roman Question has so excited opinion that the position of the political societies is becoming impossible. I could wish that our enthusiasts [at Turin] could come and see how things are; I assure you it would cool their ardour." (Pirri, II, Part 1, 354.)
10. Mazzini, in particular, had by now accustomed the English to think in terms of a unitary Italy. But few Italians, outside the ranks of the Mazzinians, were yet thinking in this way.
11. Quoted Lecanuet, *Montalembert*, III, p. 226.
12. Pirri, II, Part 2, 196.
13. Louis Veuillot, *Le Pape et la diplomatie*, Paris, 1861, p. 46.
14. February 25th, 1861. It is printed in Pirri, II, Part 2, 205.
15. Pio Nono complained in a letter of thanks to Don Pedros, King of Portugal, who had sent his sympathy: "A spirit of hypocrisy and deceit governs the course of the present events, and while the principles of justice are violated, and Religion and her ministers are insulted, it is perfectly seriously said that all this is done for the good of Society and of Religion." (October 22nd, 1860. Pirri, II, Part 2, 185.)

That a case existed, on the religious plane, for freeing the Church from the embarrassment of the Temporal Power is certainly true. It had been admirably argued in a memorandum written by the Marquis de la Tour du Pin (a Legitimist living in Italy) and sent by him in October, 1849, to the then French Foreign Minister, de Tocqueville. (See the interesting article, *Il Problema del potere temporale*, by A. M. Ghisalberti, in *Ricerche Religiose*, Vol. XX, 1–4, Rome, 1949.) But Pio Nono's Italian critics and enemies were not primarily concerned with the welfare of the Church.

16. Pirri, II, Part 1, 461, etc.

17. Important minorities, represented, e.g., in literature by Georges Sand, in politics by Jules Favre, in the Church by Lacordaire, were either hostile to or critical of the Papal State. Yet Neo-ultramontanes and Liberal-Catholics were agreed, in overwhelming majority, in supporting Pio Nono's attitude, and so, whenever it came to a vote, were the Legislative Assembly and the Senate, where even anti-clericals voted in favour of keeping the Piedmontese out of Rome, because they regarded the honour of France as involved in the maintaining of the Pope there.

18. Pirri, II, Part 1, 527.

19. Antonelli pointed out that it was odd that Rome, which was regarded as "the one city worthy to be the capital of 25 million people, should remain instead the capital of only about 700,000 subjects, so that there appeared the monstrosity of a gigantic head with an infantile body". He told Chigi: "the revenues of the State, in the restricted limits to which it is reduced, bring in only 5 million (francs); the offering of Saint Peter (Peter's Pence), as you will have read in our journal, in the space of three years, has amounted to 5,150,000, so that the annual deficit is more than 3 millions."

20. Pirri, II, Part 1, 556.

21. Pirri, II, Part 1, 501.

22. Cf. Pelczar, II, 304.

23. Cf. Hayward, p. 302. Antonelli's actual words are not recorded.

24. Pelczar, II, 305.

CHAPTER SEVEN

PIO NINO VERSUS LIBERALISM (1863–1870)

1. *Acta*, III, 701, etc.

2. In his *Letter to the Duke of Norfolk* Newman plays amusingly around the question of Antonelli's responsibility for the drawing-up and issue of the Syllabus. ". . . intrinsically, . . . it is nothing more than a digest of certain Errors made by an anonymous writer . . . Who is its author? Some select theologian or high official doubtless; can it be Cardinal Antonelli himself? No surely: anyhow it is not the Pope . . ." Later in the same chapter (Chapter 7), he saddles Antonelli with responsibility for the unfortunate planning and wording of

the Syllabus—cf. p. 102 of 4th edition of his *Letter*. However, whatever share Antonelli may have had in selecting or supervising the selection of the specific condemnations, he had never encouraged the idea of the publication, foreseeing the storm it would cause. This responsibility rests rather, so far as the Pope's entourage is concerned, with de Mérode. (cf. Aubert, p. 254.) But the responsibility for the decision to issue some such omnibus condemnation belongs, without doubt, personally to the Pope, who had been rendered intransigent by the events of 1859–64 in Italy.

3. Romanus Pontifex potest ac debet cum progressu, cum liberalismo et cum recenti civilitate sese reconciliare et componere.

4. In 1859 the *Ausonia* was founded at Milan. In the following year Turin became a central Lodge for the new Grand Orient of Italian Freemasonry, which had hitherto been regulated from the Lodge at Paris. Nigra was Grand Master until 1861. He was succeeded by the general Cordova.

5. Aubert, p. 255.

6. The Pope's Brief of approval was, however, extremely guarded. Its emphasis is upon the courage of the Bishops, with whom Dupanloup has now associated himself, and who, already, had "reproved these errors in the sense in which we reproved them ourself". It congratulates Dupanloup upon having joined his voice with these others—which was not quite what he had done. And it ended by hoping that he would as effectively show forth the true thought of the Encyclical as he had confounded its critics. It is possible that had Dupanloup not ingeniously combined his conciliatory exposition of the Syllabus with a denunciation of the September Convention and of the behaviour of Napoleon in forbidding the Bishops to expound the Syllabus in Church he might have received no mark of approval from Rome, even though he was certainly the man who calmed the storm. By this date the Neo-ultramontane party were profoundly suspicious of the tendencies and activities of Dupanloup, whom they regarded as the effective leader of the Liberal-Catholics, and the Pope, while conscious of his own and the Church's debt to the Bishop of Orleans, shared more closely the viewpoint of his critics. See *Monseigneur Dupanloup et M. Lagrange* by U. Maynard (Paris, 1884) which may usefully be compared with the standard biography of the Bishop by Lagrange.

7. These terms had been introduced into the argument by the *Civiltà Cattolica*. Pio Nono in his Allocution *Acerbissimum*, of September, '52, had outlined the ideal harmony of Church and State.

8. Montalembert, *L'Église Libre dans L'État Libre*, Paris, Didier, 1863.

9. Lecanuet, III, p. 371, etc. Pio Nono received Dupanloup

fourteen times during the winter of '63–'64, and the Bishop attended almost daily upon Antonelli. Werner de Mérode (Xavier's brother), writing to Montalembert at the end of November, reports a conversation he had with the Pope: "I did my best to defend you. I maintained that you only intended to speak of civil liberty, of political tolerance, and in no sense of dogmatic and theological indifference. . . . He replied 'Oh! There is nothing to be said about that; but, my dear friend, it is a sin not to believe that there is no assurance of salvation outside the Church' . . . You see around what a misunderstanding the conversation always turns, dogmatic indifference confused with civil tolerance . . ." (Lecanuet, III, p. 365). Pio Nono's viewpoint was, however, clearly expressed in October, 1863, to a visitor: "The Church will never admit it as a benefit and a principle that error and heresy should be preached to Catholic peoples" (Mgr. Baunard, *Histoire du Cardinal Pie*, Paris, 1883, II, 215).

10. In his *The Church and the Churches: the Papacy and the Temporal Power*. Döllinger's standpoint was that the Temporal Power was extremely important to the Church, but that it was both unhistorical to regard it as inextricably part of the Papacy and unwise to do so in view of its probable collapse.

11. *Acta*, III, 638. The case of Dr. Frohschammer, who had asserted that the Church could not condemn philosophical or scientific opinions, even where they ran counter to the essentials of faith (e.g. to the dogma of transubstantiation) was much in the mind of Rome at this time.

12. His article on the Munich Congress has been published in *Lord Acton, Essays on Church and State*, Ed. Douglas Woodruff, Hollis and Carter, 1952.

13. Acton, *Conflicts with Rome*, in *History of Freedom and Other Essays*, Macmillan Ed., 1922, p. 484.

14. *ibid.*, 487.

15. In 1868 Montalembert wrote a long article on the revolution of that year in Spain. In it he blamed the close association of the Church in that country with absolute monarchy, but he blamed equally the revolutionaries who, in their turn, had shown their intolerance by expelling the Jesuits. His friends of the *Correspondant*, however, unanimously refused to publish the article, on the grounds that he was "reviving the programme of Malines". (Lecanuet, III, 349, etc.)

16. Article on Cardinal Wiseman in the *Home and Foreign Review*, *History of Freedom and Other Essays*, p. 445.

17. Lecanuet, III, 438.

18. Aubert, 261.

19. Pelczar, II, Chap. XIX, gives a vivid description of the occasion, and Veuillot describes it in his *Parfum de Rome*.

20. "Mayest thou be blessed by Him in whose honour thou shalt be burnt."

21. *Acta et Decreta sacrorum conciliorum recentiorum, collectio lacensis,* Column, 1540. His address on this occasion, as well as many of his addresses on similar occasions, may be found here.

22. Aubert, 289.

23. It is, of course, Pio Nono's disciplinary policy, not the validity of his dogmatic decisions which is discussed here.

24. Vol. 2 of E. S. Purcell's rather double-edged life of the Archbishop is useful for its quotations from his letters and journals bearing upon his life in Rome.

25. Letter of Wiseman to Manning, June 17th, 1862, *Dublin Review* for October, 1921 (Vol. 169).

26. Cf. Aubert, p. 286.

27. See the article *La Civiltà Cattolica Nei suoi inize e nelle prime prove* on p. 19 of Vol. 2 for the year 1924 of the periodical.

28. According to the *Civiltà* for December 15th, 1934 (review on p. 262 of volume for 1934), the article was contributed by the Papal Nuncio at Paris, Chigi, and was published in accordance with the wishes of the Holy See.

29. *Civiltà Cattolica,* Series VII, Vol. V, pp. 349–352.

30. Aubert, p. 318.

31. See Maynard, pp. 184–207, for a hostile account of Dupanloup's activities at this time. Maynard's view is endorsed by Granderath, *Histoire du Concile du Vatican* (French translation, Brussels, 1908), Vol. I, pp. 331–349.

32. Letter of February 12th, 1865. Maurain, *La Politique Ecclésiastique du second empire de 1852 à 1869,* p. 728, note.

33. Maurain, p. 883.

34. Maynard, *op. cit.,* p. 192. Lagrange, however, claims that the Bishop had advised Maret against publication.

35. Lecanuet, III, 467.

36. F. Mourret, *Le Concile du Vatican,* Paris, 1919, p. 129.

CHAPTER EIGHT

TRIUMPH, DEFEAT, AND DEATH (1870–1878)

1. The verbatim report of the proceedings of the General Congregation of the Council, together with the relevant letters, petitions, reports, etc., was printed at Paris, 1923–27, as Vols. 49–53 (folio) of Mansi's *Amplissima Collectio Conciliorum,* hereafter referred to as Mansi.

2. Pelczar, II, 495.

3. "I don't know whether the Pope will emerge from this Coun-

cil fallible or infallible; but it is certain that he will be bank-rupt."

4. Butler, II, 35. Pio Nono still preserved the attitude that he would not say or do anything, *as Pope*, to influence the decision of the Council. He expressed his opinions only "as private doctor". "I, Giovanni Maria Mastai, believe in and accept the infallibility, but as Pope I ask nothing of the Council. The Holy Spirit will illuminate it." (Pelczar, II, 525.)

5. ". . . Ecclesiam inclinare conentur ad sententiam suam, seque solum sapere arbitrati, reliquam omnem Catholicorum familiam aliter sentientem *ultramontanae partis* nomine designare non erubescant . . ." This direct attack by Pio Nono upon the Liberal-Catholics was published in the *Civiltà Cattolica* (Series VII, Vol. X, p. 222, etc.) and is also to be found in the *Acta et Decreta Sacrorum Conciliorum Recentiorum, Collectio Lacensis*, Column 1537. Columns 1525–40 of Vol. 7 of this important collection are devoted to letters of a similar kind, sent out by Pio Nono during the Council, to enthusiasts for the definition, such as W. G. Ward, of the *Dublin Review*, Herbert Vaughan, of the *Tablet*, and Louis Veuillot. The editor of the *Univers* has the distinction (denied even to Guéranger, or to Ward) of being addressed as *Dilecte fili*. Such letters were published at the time in the *Civiltà Cattolica*, or in the *Unità Cattolica*, or, abroad, in the *Univers* and similar papers, and they provide the most authentic information on the Pope's personal attitude.

   See, also, Ollivier, *L'Église et l'État au Concile du Vatican*, II, Chap. VII and p. 170, etc.; Aubert, 345; Butler, II, 201, 202.

6. Butler, II, 40–42. For the petitions and counter-petitions concerning the introduction out of its turn of the Infallibility Question, see Mansi, 51, columns 722–732.

7. Manning's words (see Purcell's *Manning*, II, 429).

8. See Ollivier's own account of the matter in Vol. 2, Chap. VII, of his *L'Église et L'État au Concile du Vatican*.

9. Butler, II, 9–14. For Acton's share in these strange events see *Selections from the Correspondence of the First Lord Acton* (Longmans, 1917), Vol. I, pp. 84–119. Acton firmly believed in State intervention at the Council to secure the ends he desired: "I live almost entirely with the opposition, and seeing and hearing what I do, and knowing the bishops as I have learned to know them before and since coming here, I am bound to say that I do not believe that the means of preventing the worst excess exist within the Council. . . . It is to give these men strength and courage that the help of the State is needed" (p. 96). This was written to Gladstone on January 2, in a letter which Acton concluded with the words: "If you do not altogether reject the idea even of in-

direct action, the time has unmistakably arrived when it is most likely to take effect." On February 16th he wrote even more urgently, and as the approved agent of minority bishops, to the British Prime Minister: "The opinion which I expressed to you many weeks ago, that the opposition would prevail with aid from the European Powers, and would fail without it, has been adopted by the leading bishops of the party. I am writing now not only with their knowledge, but at their express and most urgent request, renewed several times during the last week . . ." (p. 102).

10. The thelogians' summary of the commentaries is printed in Mansi 51, Cols. 929–1070. From these columns can be ascertained the views of a large proportion of the bishops on the Infallibility Question.

11. Mansi, 52, Col. 722.

12. But the moderation and good sense of the Presidents, and their fair treatment of the Minority, is constantly attested by Ullathorne and other observers. And we have just seen that they were far from enthusiastic about bringing on the debate on the Infallibility. They were certainly not "sycophants".

13. See the Bishop of Ratisbon's account given in Mansi, 53, Cols. 158, 159.

14. Mansi, 52, Cols. 442, 443. The names of those Bishops who protested against the closure are given in Cols. 444–446.

15. Butler, II, 86–89.

16. This was the number who, in January, had signed a counter-petition against a Majority petition which requested that the subject be discussed in the course of the Council. (It was not in either of the original circulated *schemata*.)

17. May 25th. It can be read in Mansi, 52, Cols. 249–261.

18. Darboy's letter is printed in Mansi, 52, Col. 1322. Two last-minute appeals by Dupanloup to Pio Nono to postpone confirmation of the Council's decisions, on account of the outbreak of the Franco-Prussian war and the need for calm and reflection are printed in Cols. 1321 and 1323 of the same volume.

19. Butler, II, 157, discusses the evidence.

20. Their letter of July 17th to Pio Nono, explaining their departure as due to their inability "palam et in facie patris dicere *non-placet*" and to the needs of their long-neglected flocks, now faced with war, is printed in Mansi, 52, Cols. 1325 and 1326.

21. These letters of the Minority Bishops, adhering to the decisions of the Council, are to be found in Mansi, 53, Cols. 935–1062.

22. The basis of F. Mourret's book, *Le Concile du Vatican, d'après des documents inédits*, Paris, 1919.

23. *Frederick Francis Xavier de Mérode,* by Mgr. Besson, transl. Lady Herbert, W. H. Allen, 1887, p. 344. (The story is given as a translator's personal note.)

24. *Il tre non oltrepassa il mio primiere. E l'altro molte volte è molto infido. Che spesso spesso fa provar l'intero.* (Tre (three) is no more than my first. And the remainder [mare—sea] very often proves treacherous. Which frequently, frequently, gives rise to the whole.)

25. For the reaction of the Powers see Halperin, *Italy and the Vatican at War,* Chicago, 1939, p. 80, and for Gladstone's statement, Hansard, CCIV, p. 649.

26. Later, in the Encyclical *Ubi Nos* of May 15th, 1871, which defined his position, he formally condemned the Law and the whole behaviour of the "Subalpine Government". (*Acta Sanctae Sedis,* Vol. 6, p. 257.)

27. *Acta Sanctae Sedis,* Vol. 10, p. 49.

28. *The Roman Journals of Ferdinand Gregorovius, 1852–74.* Transl. Mrs. Hamilton, 1907, pp. 364 and 375. Gregorovius was in Rome during the Council. He portrays Pio Nono, alternately, as "weak, trembling, cowardly and visionary" and as "imposing his will upon the Council", two views not uncommonly expressed by hostile critics but difficult to reconcile. Antonelli he rather admired.

29. Gladstone, *The Vatican Decrees in their Bearing on Civil Allegiance* (1874). Manning, *ibid.* (1875). Newman, *Letter Addressed to His Grace the Duke of Norfolk* (1875).

30. Purcell, *Manning,* II, 553.

31. Pasolini, *Memorie,* II, 322.

32. Purcell, p. 540.

33. Purcell, p. 534.

34. *ibid.,* 553.

35. Purcell, 549, 550.

Select Bibliography

(On religious questions the detailed bibliographies given in *Histoire de l'Église* (Ed. Fliche et Martin), Vol. 21, *Le pontificat de Pie IX*, by R. Aubert, Paris, Bloud et Gay; 1952, should be consulted; and on political questions relating to the Italian Risorgimento the bibliographies published in the Roman review, *Rassegna storica del Risorgimento Italiano*.)

1. GENERAL

The most useful books covering the whole period of the pontificate of Pio Nono are:

R. AUBERT, *op. cit.*

F. HAYWARD, *Pie IX et son temps* (Paris, Plon, 1948). This is the most detailed recent biography, but it gives no references.

A. MONTI, *Pio IX nel risorgimento italiano* (Bari, 1928). Contains a number of the Pope's letters to his brother the Conte Gabriele Mastai.

E. VERCESI, *Pio IX* (Milan, 1929).

G. S. PELCZAR, *Pio IX e il suo pontificato* (Italian translation in 3 vols. from the Polish, Turin, 1911). By a Polish Bishop. The most useful of the older clerical histories.

G. MOLLAT, *La question romaine de Pie VI à Pie IX* (Paris, 1932). Still very useful.

A. C. JEMOLO, *Chiesa e Stato in Italia negli ultimi cento anni* (Einaudi, 1952). A critical study of Italian thought in the field of Church and State.

A. OMODEO, *Difesa del Risorgimento* (Einaudi, 1951). An anti-clerical reinterpretation of the risorgimento.

The Pope's Encyclicals, Allocutions, etc., are contained in the *Pii Pontificis Maximi Acta* (quoted as *Acta*) and his political *motu proprio, chirografi*, etc., for the Papal State in the *Atti del Sommo Pontefice Pio IX* (*Atti*). (Rome, 1857, etc.) The more important Papal pronouncements after the year 1865 can be found in the *Acta Sanctae Sedis*, a collection started in that year. For his speeches to pilgrims after 1870 see P. Don Pasquale de Franciscis, *Discorsi del Sommo Pontefice Pio IX* (Rome, 1872, etc.).

The articles in the *Dictionnaire Encyclopédique de la Théologie Catholique* are useful for the whole period.

In English, the original unpublished sources available (at the Record Office) are the accounts of the British Agents at Rome: Petre (1844–52), Lyons (1853–58) and Odo Russell (from 1858)—see Appendix for consideration of the Lyons letters, which have received little attention hitherto.

Amongst secondary sources in English, Bolton King's *A History of Italian Unity* (Nisbet, 1899) remains the fullest survey of the whole period of the Italian Risorgimento. It is strongly anti-clerical. The briefer, and more recent *Evolution of Modern Italy* by A. J. Whyte (Blackwell, 1944) also belongs to the liberal tradition of English scholarship in the field of the Risorgimento. The essay by Sir Llewellyn Woodward on *The Catholic Church* in his *Three Studies in Conservative Statesmanship* (Constable, 1929) approaches the religious history of the pontificate from the same standpoint, as does J. B. Bury, *History of the Catholic Church in the Nineteenth Century* (1864–78) (Macmillan, 1930). From the Catholic standpoint there is much that is relevant to the whole period in three big works by Wilfrid Ward: *William George Ward and the Catholic Revival* (Longmans, 1912), *The Life and Times of Cardinal Wiseman* (Longmans, 1897), and *The Life of John Henry Cardinal Newman* (Longmans, 1912). See also *The Life and Times of Bishop Ullathorne* by Cuthbert Butler (Burns Oates, 1926) and the earlier chapters of D. A. Binchy's *Church and State in Fascist Italy* (Oxford, 1941).

2. CONDITIONS AND IDEAS
IN THE PAPAL STATE BEFORE 1846

The following list should be supplemented by reference to the bibliography given in G. F. H. and Mrs. Berkeley,

Italy in the Making: 1815 to 1846 (Cambridge, 1936).

Contemporary accounts:

M. D'AZEGLIO, *Degli ultimi casi di Romagna* ("Italia", 1846).

V. GIOBERTI, *Del Primato morale e civile degli Italiani* (Brussels, 1843).

N. TOMMASEO, *Delle nuove speranze d'Italia* (Paris, 1836).

METTERNICH, *Mémoires* (Paris, 1883), Vol. VII.

Later studies:

A. MONTI, *op. cit.*

G. MAIOLI, *Pio IX Da Vescovo a Pontefice. Lettere al Card. Luigi Amat* (Modena, 1949). The best picture of the life of the future Pope when he was still Bishop of Imola.

A. C. JEMOLO, *Il giansenismo in Italia* (Bari, 1928).

A. LUZIO, *La Massoneria e il Risorgimento Italiano* (Bologna, 1925).

A. FALCONIELLI, *Les Sociétés Secrètes Italiennes* (Paris, 1936).

In English, by far the fullest and most useful and impartial study is that of G. F.-H. Berkeley, *Italy in the Making, 1815 to 1846* (Cambridge, 1936). But translations have been made of certain contemporary Italian writings, and notably of the *Memorie* of G. Pasolini (*Memoir of Count Guiseppe Pasolini*, Longmans, 1885—abridged) and of F. Orsini (*Memoirs*, Edinburgh, 1857) and of Farini's important history (L. C. Farini, *The Roman State from 1815 to 1850*, transl. by W. E. Gladstone).

3. LIBERAL-CATHOLICISM AND ULTRAMONTANISM IN EUROPE BEFORE 1860

Primarily, of course, the works of the leading Catholic writers of the time, and notably de Maistre, Lamennais, Montalembert, Lacordaire and Veuillot in France, Gioberti and Rosmini in Italy, Döllinger in Germany.

R. P. LECANUET, *Montalembert* (Paris, 1909), Vols. II and III.

J. T. FOISSET, *Vie du R. P. Lacordaire* (Paris, 1870).

K. O'MEARA, *Frederic Ozanam, his life and works* (Keagan Paul, 1878).

DE FALLOUX, *Mémoires d'un Royaliste* (Paris, 1888).

E. VEUILLOT, *Louis Veuillot* (Paris, 3rd. Ed. 1901), Vols. I and II.

G. WEILL, *Histoire du catholicisme libéral en France* (1828–1908) (Paris, 1909).

J. FRIEDRICH, *Ignaz von Doellinger* (Munich, 1899), Vols. I and II.

G. GOYAU, *L'Allemagne réligieuse, Le Catholicisme* (Paris, 1905–1909).

K. PRUSZYNSKI, *Adam Miczkiewicz* (Fore pub., London, 1950).

U. PADOVANI, *Vincenzo Gioberti ed il cattolicismo* (Milan, 1927).

W. WARD, *William George Ward and the Catholic Revival* (Longmans, 1912).

4. 1846–1849 AT ROME

A. M. GHISALBERTI, *Rapporti delle cose di Roma, 1848–49.* (*Istituto per la storia del Risorgimento Italiano*, Rome 1949.) Professor Ghisalberti, President of the *Istituto per la Storia del Risorgimento Italiano* has edited, in this volume, the important letters of the Dutch Ambassador at Rome during these years, A. de Liedekerke. See also the Professor's *Nuove ricerche sugli inizi del pontificato di Pio IX e sulla Consulta di Stato* (Rome, 1940).

D. DEMARCO, *Pio IX e la rivoluzione romana del 1848.* (*Collezione Storica del Risorgimento Italiano*, 1947, Vol. XXXVI, Series II), and his *Una Rivoluzione Sociale. La Republica Romana di 1849* (Naples, 1944). These should be consulted for the economic interpretation of the upheavals of these years.

R. PALMAROCCHI, *Alcuni aspetti della politica di Pio IX nei primi due anni del governo.* (*Rassegna Storica del Risorgimento Italiano*, June, 1936, Vol. XXIII.)

G. PASOLINI, *Carteggio tra Marco Minghetti e Giuseppe Pasolini* (Turin, 1924), Vol. I.

M. MINGHETTI, *Miei Ricordi* (Turin, 1888).

G. SPADA, *Storia della rivoluzione di Roma dal 1 Giugno 1846 al 15 Luglio 1849* (Florence, 1868). An anti-revolutionary but balanced and fair-minded history, and well documented.

G. GABUSSI, *Memorie della rivoluzione degli stati romani* (Genoa, 1852). The events told by one of the revolutionaries.

P. S. BALLERINI, *Les premières pages du pontificat de Pie IX.* (Posthumous publication, Rome, 1909.) Ballerini was a Jesuit who was commissioned to write a "semi-official" life of the Pope. Owing to the disturbances and the dispersal of the Jesuits it was never completed but these first chapters are a useful source of information provided that the auspices under which they were written are borne in mind.

G. MAZZINI. The volumes of the *Edizione Nazionale* of Mazzini's writings which are mainly concerned with the year 1849 are XXXIX–XLIII. His *Open Letter to the Pope* is on p. 225 of Vol. XXXVI.

On the French intervention:

F. DE LESSEPS, *Ma mission à Rome* (Paris, 1849). The apologia of one of the participants in the drama.

L. DE GAILLARD, *L'Expédition de Rome en 1849* (documents) (Paris, 1861).

P. DE LA GORCE, *Histoire de la Seconde République Française* (Paris, 1887), Vol. I.

E. BOURGEOIS et E. CLERMONT, *Rome et Napoléon III* (Paris, 1907).

There exist, in English, in addition to the translations from Farini, Pasolini, Orsini, already mentioned, and Bolton King's History, the two fundamental volumes by G. F.-H. and J. Berkeley, *Italy in the Making, June 1846 to 1 January 1848* (Cambridge, 1936) and *Italy in the Making, January 1 1848 to November 16 1848* (Cambridge, 1940). The bibliographies included in these volumes should certainly be consulted. There are also G. M. Trevelyan's classic but quite openly anti-clerical and anti-French *Garibaldi's Defence of the Roman Republic* (3rd. Ed., Longmans, 1908) and G. O. Griffith's warmly Mazzinian *Mazzini, Prophet of Modern Europe* (Hodder and Stoughton, 1932). A large proportion of Mazzini's articles and letters first appeared in English and are reprinted in that language in the compendious *Edizione Nazionale* (Imola, 1905, etc.) of his works. Others are to be found in English in *Life and Writings of Joseph Mazzini* (6 vols., Smith, Elder, 1890) and *Mazzini's Letters* (Dent, 1930).

In the Foreign Office publication, *Correspondence respecting the affairs of Italy, 1846–49* (4 vols., 1849), are to be found letters written by official English agents in Italy in this period.

Arthur Clough (see *Prose Remains*, 1888) and Margaret Fuller (see M. F. Ossoli, *Memoirs*, Vol. 3) were in Mazzini's Rome.

5. THE RESTORATION OF 1850 AND LIFE IN THE PAPAL STATE, 1850–1870

In addition to the contemporary accounts of Pasolini and Minghetti:

In Italian:

P. DALLA TORRE, *L'Opera reformatrice ed amministrativa di Pio IX fra il 1850 e il 1870* (Rome, 1945). Clerical in outlook, but scholarly and balanced and including a valuable bibliography.

S. NEGRO, *Seconda Roma, 1850–70* (Milan, 1943). Extensive bibliography.

A. VENTRONE, *L'amministrazione dello Stato Pontificio dal 1814 al 1870* (Rome, 1942).

A. M. GHISALBERTI, *Una restaurazione "reazionaria e imperita"* in *Archivio della Societa romana di Storia patria*, Vol. LXXII (Rome, 1949). A critical estimate.

R. DE CESARE, *Roma e lo stato del papa dal ritorno di Pio IX al 20 settembre* (Rome, 1907). (Abridged English transl., *The Last Days of Papal Rome*, Constable, 1909.)

In other languages:

F. GREGOROVIUS, *The Roman Journals of Ferdinand Gregorovius, 1852–74*. (Transl. from the German, 1907.) Anti-clerical, complacent, very Germanic, but often amusing.

J. F. MAGUIRE, *Rome, its Ruler, and its Institutions*. (2nd

Ed., Longmans, 1859.) Clerical, but contains a lot of useful information and publishes, in an appendix, the important report of the French Ambassador at Rome, de Rayneval, of May, 1856.

J. GAY, *Un siècle d'Histoire Italienne* (Paris, 1931). Chapter II reproduces much of the important correspondence of Louis Doubet and his brother-in-law Eugène Rendu, travellers in Italy, in which the condition of the Papal State is discussed.

H. A. D'IDEVILLE, *Journal d'un diplomate en Italie* (Paris, 1872).

N. W. SENIOR, *Journals kept in France and Italy*, Vol. 2, pp. 93–152 (Henry King, 1871).

See Appendix for consideration of the unpublished letters of Mr. Lyons, British Agent at Rome, 1853–58.

6. NAPOLEON, VICTOR EMMANUEL, CAVOUR, AND THE POPE

Much the most important source for the diplomacy and war which resulted in the liquidation of the Papal State is to be found in the three volumes so far published by the Gregorian University at Rome in their series *Miscellanea Historiae Pontificiae*, entitled *Pio IX a Vittorio Emmanuele II dal loro carteggio privato*, edited by P. Pietro Pirri, S.J. The first volume covers text and letters for the period 1848–56, the second (numbered II, Part 1) text for the period 1856–64, and the third (numbered II, Part 2) the letters for the period 1856–64. The first was published in 1944 and the others in 1951. The Vatican made available to Fr. Pirri the Pope's correspondence with Napoleon as well as with Victor Emmanuel, Antonelli's correspondence with the Papal Nuncios, and other documents of importance: he has also drawn extensively upon other sources.

In Italian:

N. BIANCHI, *Storia documentata della diplomazia europea in Italia dall' anno 1814 all' anno 1861*, Vols. VI, VII and VIII (Turin, 1865, etc.).

C. CAVOUR, *Lettere* (Chiala, Turin, 1883).

C. CAVOUR, *La questione romana negli anni 1860–61*, carteggio del Conte di Cavour con D. Pantaleoni, C. Passaglia, e O. Vimercati (Bologna, 1929). For Cavour's overrunning of Umbria and the Marches and his attempt to settle the relations of Church and State.

S. F. JACINI, *Il tramonto del potere temporale nelle relazioni degli amabasciatori austriaci a Roma* (Bari, 1931).

S. F. JACINI, *La politica ecclesiastica italiana da Villafranca a Porta Pia* (Bari, 1938).

A. C. JEMOLO, *La questione romana* (Milan, 1938).

In French:

ANON., *Dix ans au service du roi Pie IX* (Fribourg, 1880).

DE BARRAL, *Les Zouaves Pontificaux* (Paris, 1932).

E. BOURGEOIS et E. CLERMONT, *Rome et Napoléon III* (Paris, 1907).

P. DE LA GORCE, *Histoire du Second Empire* (Paris, 1894–96). Still the standard work.

A. DE HÜBNER, *Neuf ans de souvenirs d'un ambassadeur d'Autriche à Paris, 1851–1859* (Paris, 1904).

J. MAURAIN, *La Politique Ecclésiastique du Second Empire de 1852 à 1869* (Paris, 1930). This book is indispensable to an understanding of Catholic and anti-Catholic opinion in France and of the Emperor's policy. It is, in general, critical of the Pope's policies.

C. DE MONTALEMBERT, *Pie IX et Lord Palmerston* (Paris, June, 1856; transl. London, 1856) and *Pie IX et la France en 1849 et en 1859*. (In the *Correspondant* for October 25th, 1859.)

L. THOUVENEL, *Le secret de l'Empereur* (Paris, 1889). For de Gramont's correspondence with M. Thouvenel.

L. VEUILLOT, *Le Pape et la diplomatie* (Paris, 1861).

In English:

G. F.-H. BERKELEY, *The Irish Battalion in the Papal Army of 1860* (Dublin, 1929). Valuable information about the Papal army and the events leading up to Castelfidardo.

MGR. BESSON, *Frederick Francis Xavier de Mérode* (Eng. transl. by Lady Herbert, with important addition in Note, W. H. Allen, 1887).

G. M. TREVELYAN, *Garibaldi and the Making of Italy* (Long-

mans, 1911). Chapters X and XI give a vivid picture of
the campaign of Castelfidardo. Despite his strong Piedmontese sympathies the writer is not impervious to the
idealism in the Roman defence.

A. J. WHYTE, *Political Life and Letters of Cavour*, Oxford,
1930. The story of the Piedmontese aggression from
Cavour's standpoint.

7 · THE SYLLABUS OF ERRORS AND THE VATICAN COUNCIL (1864–1870)

(A) *The Syllabus, and the argument before the Council*
The bibliographies given by R. Aubert, in *Le pontificat
de Pie IX*, should be consulted. Chapters VIII, IX and X
of his book give quite the most useful general account of
the controversy between Neo-ultramontanes and Liberal-
Catholics in the eighteen-sixties. It can best be pursued further in the files of the leading journals and papers concerned, and notably in the *Civiltà Cattolica* (especially
Series VII, Vol. V) and the *Univers, Correspondant, Français, Tablet*, and *Dublin Review*, more particularly for the
last few months of the year 1869.

To these may be added the more important pamphlets
which were issued, especially Mgr. Dupanloup: *La Convention du 15 Septembre et l'Encyclique du 8 Décembre* (his
defence of the Syllabus, Paris, 1865) and *Observations sur
la controverse soulevée relativement à la définition de l'infaillibilité au futur concile* (Paris 1869); L. Veuillot, *L'Illusion libérale* (Paris, 1866); C. de Montalembert, *L'Église
libre dans l'État libre* (Paris, 1863); Janus (Döllinger),
Der Papst und das Konzil (Leipzig, 1869; transl. *The Pope
and the Council*, London, 1869); and Lord Acton's essays,
Conflicts with Rome (1864, pub. in *History of Freedom
and other essays*, Macmillan, 1922) and *The Munich Congress* (1864, pub. in Acton, *Essays on Church and State*,
Hollis and Carter, 1952).

Amongst the many secondary authorities the following
should not be missed:

F. LAGRANGE, *Vie de Mgr. Dupanloup* (Paris, 1883–84).
(Eng. transl.—abridged—by Lady Herbert in two vols.,

Chapman and Hall, 1885.) This work is useful for the
whole period of Pio Nono's pontificate.

F. LAGRANGE, *Lettres choisies de Mgr. Dupanloup* (Paris,
1888).

U. MAYNARD, *Mgr. Dupanloup et M. Lagrange son historien*
(2nd Ed., Paris, 1884). The reply to Lagrange from the
camp of Veuillot.

E. LECANUET, *Montalembert* (Paris, 1905), Vol. III.

E. VEUILLOT, *Louis Veuillot*, Vols. III and IV (Paris, 1905
and 1913).

E. S. PURCELL, *Life of Cardinal Manning* (Macmillan,
1896), Vol. II.

DOUGLAS WOODRUFF, Introduction to Lord Acton's *Essays
on Church and State* (Hollis and Carter, 1952).

(B) *The Vatican Council*
The bibliographies given in R. Aubert, *op. cit.*, and in
Cuthbert Butler, *The Vatican Council* (Longmans, 1930),
should be consulted.

The speeches in the General Congregations and all offi-
cial documents such as proposed amendments during the
Council and the letters received after the Council from
Bishops who had abstained from voting are published in
the five folio volumes of Mansi, *Amplissima Collectio
Conciliorum*, Vols. 49–53 (Paris, 1923–27). Unofficial
documents, such as commentary of all sorts outside the
Council, including Pio Nono's own letters and speeches
on sundry occasions, are in the *Collectio Lacensis: Acta et
Decreta Sacrorum Conciliorum Recentiorum*, Vol. VII
(Fribourg, 1890).

Secondary sources:
These divide themselves clearly between those that are
favourable to the Council and those that are hostile.

Favourable:
CUTHBERT BUTLER, *The Vatican Council* (Longmans,
1930). A clear and scholarly analysis of the development
of the Council, based largely upon the diary kept by
Bishop Ullathorne of Birmingham, but also upon all
available sources. Concerned to refute the attacks of

Quirinus (Döllinger) and the other hostile critics outside the Council upon whom English scholars (e.g. J. B. Bury, *History of the Papacy in the Nineteenth Century, 1864–78* (Macmillan, 1930), or G. Salmon, *The Infallibility of the Church* (1st Ed., John Murray, 1888) have drawn. Easily the most important book in English on the subject.

T. GRANDERATH, S.J., *Geschichte des vatikanischen Konzils* (Fribourg, 1903–6). (French transl., *Histoire du Concile du Vatican*, 5 vols., Brussels, 1908.) Pius X made all the papers at the Vatican available to Fr. Granderath, and told him to consider nothing but the truth. This is the fullest work on the Council.

F. MOURRET, *Le Concile du Vatican d'après des documents inédits* (Paris, 1919). By a professor at Saint-Sulpice, Paris, and based largely upon the papers there and in particular upon the journal of M. Icard who was director of that seminary at the time of the Council and was in Rome throughout its sessions as theological adviser to the Archbishop of Sens.

E. OLLIVIER, *L'Église et l'État au Concile du Vatican* (Paris, 1877). A very interesting commentary upon the Syllabus as well as the Council by Napoleon's Premier in 1870. Ollivier was a Protestant, but the portraits which he presents of the Pope, of Antonelli, and of many of the Bishops are balanced and vivid.

L. VEUILLOT, *Rome pendant le concile* (Paris, 1872). Veuillot was in Rome during the Council.

Hostile:

LORD ACTON, *The Vatican Council* (1870, *North British Review*, reprinted in Acton: *History of Freedom and other Essays*, Macmillan, 1922). He was in Rome during the Council, but in view of the vow of secrecy imposed upon the participants he could only pick up the outside gossip. For his letters to Gladstone during the Council see *Selections from the Correspondence of the First Lord Acton* (Longmans, 1917), Vol. I.

ANON., *Ce qui se passe au Concile*. A pamphlet published in Paris in May, 1870, which shows inside knowledge

of the affairs of the Council. It was formally denounced
by the Council itself in July.

J. FRIEDRICH, *Tagebuch wahrend des vatikanischen Concils*
(2nd Ed., Nordlingen, 1873). Based mainly upon Döllinger's articles in the *Allgemeine Zeitung* and written
in defence of the Old Catholic position.

"POMPONIO LETO", *Otto mesi a Roma durante il Concilio*.
(Eng. transl., *Rome during the Vatican Council*, John
Murray, 1876.) A curious book, probably by a brother
of Cardinal Vitelleschi, a good deal concerned with the
author's own philosophical opinions.

T. MOZLEY, *Letters from Rome* (London, 1891). The collected letters of the *Times* correspondent in Rome at
the time of the Council. Of small value since he knew
no Italian and was quite out of touch. His articles in the
Times provided the Bishops with humorous relief between sessions.

"QUIRINUS" (DÖLLINGER). Letters published in the *Allgemeine Zeitung* at the time of the Council and subsequently collected and translated as *Letters from Rome
on the Council* (Rivingtons, 1870). The original letters
were sent by Acton and others at Rome to Döllinger who
reproduced and edited them. They provide the most
important of the hostile criticisms of the Council and the
foundation for most of the subsequent attacks.

8. THE LAST YEARS (1870–1878)

Events in Italy:

In addition to the biographies by Pelczar and Hayward
already quoted, and de Cesare's *Roma e lo Stato del Papa*,
see, in particular, the fundamental work by the American
scholar, S. W. Halperin, *Italy and the Vatican at War: a
Study of Their Relations from the Outbreak of the Franco-
Prussian War to the Death of Pius IX* (University of Chicago Press, 1939). Dr. Halperin made an extensive examination of the contemporary journals as well as the diplomatic
archives and gives full references. His work achieves a considerable degree of objectivity.

Events outside Italy:

In addition to Aubert's *Pontificat*, E. Veuillot's *Louis Veuillot*, Lagrange's *Dupanloup*, Purcell's *Manning*, and Ward's *Newman*, see:

H. E. MANNING, *The Vatican Decrees in their Bearing on Civil Allegiance* (Longmans, 1875). A reply to Gladstone's pamphlet under the same title.

J. H. NEWMAN, *A Letter addressed to His Grace the Duke of Norfolk on occasion of Mr. Gladstone's recent Expostulation* (Pickering, 1875).

E. LECANUET, *L'Église de France sous la Troisième République*, Vol. I, *Les dernières années du pontificat de Pie IX* (Paris, 1907).

G. GOYAU, *Bismarck et l'Église* (Paris, 1911).

J. B. KISSLING, *Geschichte der Kulturkampf im Deutschen Reiche* (Fribourg, 1911–16).

J. F. VON SCHULTE, *Der Altkathalicismus* (Geissen, 1887).

Appendix: The Lyons Letters

On July 9th, 1860 (two days after the Piedmontese ultimatum had been sent to Rome, and when interest in the
"Roman Question" was at its highest), Acton wrote to
Simpson, his fellow editor of the *Rambler*: "I send you
notes, which may help for a Roman article for this week,
on Lyons' papers. I got them and read them today. They
are a running commentary on some of my articles, con-
firming, thank God, all I said. Monsell, Maguire, etc., are
greatly disturbed by them. I think Lyons honest. Monsell
doubts it. . . ."[1]

The papers referred to by Acton were the despatches
sent by Mr. (later Lord) Lyons from Rome to his superior,
the British Minister at Florence (first Campbell Scarlett,
then Lord Normanby), during the years 1853 to 1858
when Lyons was British Attaché at Rome.[2] They can be
read at the Record Office (F.O. 43, vols. 58, 59, 60, 63,
66 and 69), and they provide evidence of some value as to
the character of life and institutions in the Papal States,
evidence which, though often reflecting adversely upon
the Roman administration, is very far from lending colour
to the lurid picture of liberal tradition. The reason why
they disturbed "Monsell, Maguire, etc.", was that these
men, with their ardent, Irish, Roman sympathies, looked
for a warmer appreciation than they found in them of the
qualities of life at Rome. Monsell and Maguire both had
much to do with the translation and dissemination in England and Ireland of the report of the French Ambassador at
Rome, Rayneval, on the same topic, and Rayneval was a
good deal more enthusiastic about the Roman government
than was Lyons.

Acton found the Lyons despatches congenial and con-

[1] Printed in *Lord Acton and His Circle*, Ed. Gasquet, Burns
Oates, 1906, p. 140.
[2] "Attaché to Her Majesty's Legation at the Court of Tuscany
to reside at Rome."

vincing because they reflected his own viewpoint in which misgivings about the Roman government were blended with a profounder mistrust of the revolutionaries. Lyons had a warm admiration for Pio Nono and a respect for Antonelli, whom he found accessible, courteous, and reasonable. He clearly had grave doubts about the efficiency of the financial administration, but he believed that the charge of corruption was "somewhat exaggerated" and he writes that "far greater blame than is just is attributed to Cardinal Antonelli" (January 23rd, 1854). He implies, in several of his despatches, that secularisation is needed in the administration, but one is left wondering how far this attitude was forced upon him by the policy of Clarendon and Palmerston. Certainly, the villain of the piece, in Lyons' letters, is the pro-Minister of Finance, Galli, who was a layman, and who was relieved of his office in November, 1854, and replaced by an ecclesiastic, Mgr. Ferrari, apparently with beneficial results. After the Congress of Paris, in 1856, it became Lyons' duty, under instruction from Clarendon, to urge upon the Pope "Reforms in the Papal State", and particularly secularisation; and he was obliged to put arguments in this sense to Antonelli. But it is quite evident (e.g. from his despatch of May 29th, 1856) that he found much substance in the views of Rayneval, and of Colloredo, the Austrian Ambassador, who considered it out of place to advise the Pope on his choice of ministers and who conceived that it was a matter of the first consequence to support the authority of the Papal government which had been prejudicially affected by the publicity given to the proceedings of the Congress—and no doubt particularly, though they were too polite to say so, to Clarendon's unguarded outburst there.

Rayneval told Lyons that most of the political prisoners imprisoned as a result of the revolution had, in fact, been amnestied. He had also had a return made for him from which he had found that the total number of prisoners in the Papal State was smaller, proportionally, than in France. Lyons checked up on this and found, from the police reports (made at that time to the French Embassy on account of the occupation), that arrests for political offences in Rome were in fact very rare, that there were only about seven or eight arrests daily for all crimes, many being for prostitution.

The general implication of the Lyons letters is that improvements could be made in the Roman administration if it would draw upon the wisdom of intelligent liberal laymen of the type of the Marchese Bevilacqua of Bologna, whereas Acton (who was in Rome in 1857) believed, and was at one with both Veuillot and Montalembert in believing, that the heart of the opposition to the Papal government was a determination to exclude the Pope wholly from temporal power, and perhaps ultimately from spiritual power, and that concessions on his part were as futile as were Austrian concessions at Milan or at Venice. The revolutionaries, in the name of their new ideas, had decided upon "No Pope" and upon "No Austria" and they would make the government of either unworkable.

Index

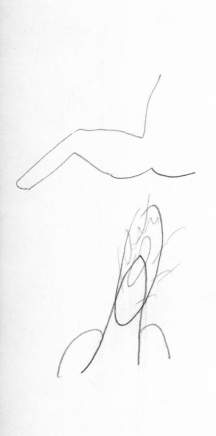